LAW BEYOND BORDERS

LAW BEYOND BORDERS

Extraterritorial Jurisdiction in an Age of Globalization

Steve Coughlan
SCHULICH SCHOOL OF LAW, DALHOUSIE UNIVERSITY

Robert J. Currie
SCHULICH SCHOOL OF LAW, DALHOUSIE UNIVERSITY

Hugh M. Kindred
SCHULICH SCHOOL OF LAW, DALHOUSIE UNIVERSITY

Teresa Scassa
FACULTY OF LAW, UNIVERSITY OF OTTAWA

IRWIN LAW

Law Beyond Borders: Extraterritorial Jurisdiction in an Age of Globalization

Published in 2014 by
Irwin Law Inc
Suite 206, 14 Duncan Street
Toronto, ON
M5H 3G8
www.irwinlaw.com

ISBN: 978-1-55221-370-4 e-book ISBN: 978-1-55221-371-1

Library and Archives Canada Cataloguing in Publication

Coughlan, Stephen Gerard, 1957–, author
Law beyond borders : extraterritorial jurisdiction in an age of globalization / Steve Coughlan, Robert J. Currie, Hugh M. Kindred, Teresa Scassa.

Includes bibliographical references and index.
Issued in print and electronic formats.
ISBN 978-1-55221-370-4 (pbk.). — ISBN 978-1-55221-371-1 (pdf)

1. International law — Canada. 2. Law and globalization — Canada. 3. Exterritoriality. 4. Jurisdiction (International law). I. Kindred, Hugh M., author II. Scassa, Teresa, author III. Currie, Robert J. (Robert John), 1970–, author IV. Title.

KZ4114.C69 2014 341'.0971 C2014-904739-8
C2014-904740-1

The publisher acknowledges the financial support of the Government of Canada through the Canada Book Fund for its publishing activities.

We acknowledge the assistance of the OMDC Book Fund, an initiative of the Ontario Media Development Corporation.

Printed and bound by CPI Group (UK) Ltd, Croydon, CR0 4YY

1 2 3 4 5 18 17 16 15 14

Summary Table of Contents

Detailed Table of Contents

Acknowledgments

This project is something we have been living with over an extended period of time, and as a result, there are many people and organizations that we wish to acknowledge with appreciation.

In 2006, we produced a report for the now defunct Law Commission of Canada titled "Global Reach, Local Grasp: Constructing Extraterritorial Jurisdiction in the Age of Globalization." The report we produced, which was later published in the *Canadian Journal of Law and Technology*,[1] laid the foundation for our project. We are grateful to the Law Commission of Canada for its enthusiasm and interest in the subject, and for the helpful feedback we received from the Commission chair, Yves Le Bouthillier, and from the reviewers of our report.

The project, which has ultimately led to this book, was supported by a three-year Standard Research Grant from the Social Sciences and Humanities Research Council of Canada (SSHRC). Funding from this grant enabled us to hire a number of excellent research assistants. We are very grateful to Kokouvi Akakpo, Stefan Currie-Roberts, Aaron Felt, Carol Fleischhaker, Alex Gorlewski, Jim Janson, Breann Kirincich, Charlotte Morden, Jenny Rodopoulos, Lee Seshagiri, Jenna Wates, and Alexandra Diebel for their research assistance. In particular, we are most appreciative to Alexandra Diebel for her sterling assistance in preparing the manuscript for publication.

1 (2007) 6 CJLT 29–60.

We have all received support in different ways from the institutions with which we are affiliated. Many thanks are due to Sonya Nigam of the University of Ottawa, for her assistance with the preparation of the SSHRC grant application. We also extend our thanks to Lynda Corkum at Dalhousie University. We are grateful for the support of both the Centre for Law, Technology and Society at the University of Ottawa, and the Law and Technology Institute of the Schulich School of Law, Dalhousie University. The support of the Canada Research Chairs Program is also gratefully acknowledged.

We deeply appreciate the insights that we have garnered from a number of our colleagues. Particular thanks are due to Professor Vaughan Black, of the Schulich School of Law, Dalhousie University, whose encyclopedic knowledge of this area of the law and whose thoughtful comments have been invaluable, and to Chris Ram of the Criminal Law Policy Section, Justice Canada.

We are also appreciative of the opportunities we have had along the way to expose our developing thoughts and ideas to a variety of audiences. An earlier and somewhat different version of material that appears in Chapters 4 and 6 of this book was first workshopped at the *Georgetown Journal of International Law* Symposium on International Cyberlaw in Washington, DC on 21 March 2011. The paper presented at this workshop was later published in the *Georgetown Journal of International Law*.[2] Earlier versions of two of the case studies in Chapter 7 were presented at *Unity or Fragmentation of International Law: The Role of International and National Tribunals* held in Oslo, Norway in May 2009 by the University of Oslo and the University of Amsterdam Centre for International Law; this was eventually published as "Flux and Fragmentation in the International Law of State Jurisdiction: The Synecdochal Example of Canada's Domestic Court Conflicts Over Accountability for International Human Rights Violations" in *The Practice of International and National Courts and the (De-) Fragmentation of International Law*.[3] Other parts of this project were presented at: several of the annual conferences of the Canadian Council on International Law; *International Law: The*

2 (2011) 42:4 Geo J Int'l L 1017–82.

3 "Flux and Fragmentation in the International Law of State Jurisdiction: The Synecdochal Example of Canada's Domestic Court Conflicts Over Accountability for International Human Rights Violations" in O-K Fauchauld & A Nollkaemper, eds, *The Practice of International and National Courts and the (De-) Fragmentation of International Law* (Oxford: Hart Publishing 2012), 217–43.

Trickle-Down Effect, a symposium held by the International Law Discussion Group, University of Edinburgh Law Faculty, May 2011; *Globalization of Crime: Criminal Justice Responses*, the 24th international conference of the International Society for the Reform of Criminal Law and the 20th anniversary conference of the International Centre for Criminal Law Reform and Criminal Justice Policy, Ottawa, August 2011; and at the IT.Can Conference in Halifax, Nova Scotia in 2008. We are grateful for the comments and insights shared with us by the participants of these different conferences and workshops.

We would also very much like to thank Jeff Miller at Irwin Law for his warm reception of our manuscript, as well as Alisa Posesorski, Lesley Steeve, and Heather Raven for their assistance in preparing it for publication.

We would like to express our deep appreciation for the enduring encouragement of each of our families. We would not have accomplished this project without their licence to spend time away from them and their backing to go forward with it.

Last, but certainly not least, each of the authors appreciates the support and forbearance of all the others. This project has engaged four colleagues who might not ordinarily work together (because individually, our special interests lie in widely different areas of law), and it has been a truly collaborative project at each step of the way. As a result, we have each had to explain legal ideas and technical terms peculiar to our specialties to the others, taking time to unravel misunderstandings and misconceptions between us and, in turn, to learn about and come to a common understanding of legal norms and procedures that were unknown to us before we began. We have been delighted by the positive impact of this experience: it has been a greatly stimulating interaction, which we hope has enlightened the text of our book to the benefit of its readers.

Steve Coughlan
Robert J. Currie
Hugh M. Kindred
Halifax, Nova Scotia

Teresa Scassa
Ottawa, Ontario
30 January 2014

CHAPTER 1

Introduction: The Contours of Jurisdiction

Law has a limited reach. The capacity of a country like Canada to make and apply law depends on the scope of its jurisdiction. Traditionally, one state's jurisdiction has been geographically limited to its national territory as a matter of mutual recognition of, and coexistence with, other states. But the rapid increase in human activities across state boundaries, together with a growing appreciation of the finite and unitary nature of the world — captured in the term "globalization" — has rendered territorial jurisdiction insufficient. States find they need to act transnationally and internationally in order to protect their populations and their public interests, and to advance their national policies. In short, an expanded concept of geographic jurisdiction across state boundaries has now become indispensable but has to be developed without unduly interfering in the national authority of other states.

This book is about the reach of law beyond state borders from a deliberately Canadian perspective. Our purpose is to investigate the scope of the legal and practical power of Canada to assert (and to respond to foreign assertions of) extraterritorial jurisdiction. Ultimately, we articulate a theoretical and analytical framework to aid decision making by law- and policy-makers when Canada is faced with the issue of whether to act extraterritorially.

Our book revisits Canadian jurisdictional principles and practices in a way that we hope will resonate with lawyers and legal policy-makers of all kinds, whether as private practitioners, academics, civil servants, or legislators. Its genesis was a paper written for the now-defunct Law

Commission of Canada as part of an extensive inquiry it began into the effects of globalization on the Canadian legal system. In a discussion paper[1] published early in its work, the Commission had taken the perspective that globalization was increasingly affecting law, law making, and law enforcement, and that study and democratic discussion were necessary in order to identify and deal with these forces of change. It questioned the continuing role of state sovereignty, the legitimacy of state law-making, and whether the interaction of the national and the international was leading to "uneven access to just outcomes."[2]

Our study paper for the Commission, descriptively titled "Global Reach, Local Grasp: Constructing Extraterritorial Jurisdiction in the Age of Globalization," was uploaded onto its website and received more than 2,000 hits in the first week—a clear testament to the topicality and interest that is attached to the subject matter.[3] Although the Law Commission was shut down shortly afterwards, our paper was published elsewhere[4] and within a few months it was cited by the Supreme Court of Canada.[5]

Alert to the high degree of interest, and aware there was much more that needed to be said about extraterritoriality than could be put into a short research paper cum journal article, we quickly decided to expand our study into a book-length treatment that would maintain the overall framework of the initial paper, but would explore the topic with greater breadth and depth. Our work has convinced us that the exercise of extraterritorial jurisdiction is not only a timely, fascinating legal

---

1 Law Commission of Canada, *Crossing Borders: Law in a Globalized World — Discussion Paper* (Ottawa: Law Commission of Canada, 2006), online: Government of Canada Publications http://publications.gc.ca/site/eng/287260/publication.html.

2 *Ibid* at 11.

3 We learned from informal communications that a number of national justice ministries/departments were working on similar issues. In 2009, the International Bar Association released a major study on the topic: International Bar Association, *Report of the Task Force on Extraterritorial Jurisdiction* (London: International Bar Association, 2008).

4 See Stephen Coughlan, Robert J Currie, Hugh Kindred, & Teresa Scassa, "Global Reach, Local Grasp: Constructing Extraterritorial Jurisdiction in the Age of Globalization" (2007) 6:1 CJLT 29.

5 See *R v Hape*, 2007 SCC 26. See also *Re Canadian Security Intelligence Service Act (Canada)*, 2008 FC 301 and *R v Klassen*, 2008 BCSC 1762, the latter of which also cited with some thoroughness the prior foundational work of Robert J Currie & Steve Coughlan, "Extraterritorial Criminal Jurisdiction: Bigger Picture or Smaller Frame?" (2007) 11 Can Crim L Rev 141.

topic, but that it is also a subject on which there is a pressing need for engagement by jurists and academic and practising lawyers, as well as policy-makers and legislators.

The exercise of extraterritorial jurisdiction is a topic that is both conceptually complex and practically challenging, and one with ramifications for — quite literally — the entire world. It is full of logical problems and intersecting considerations to be weighed and counter-balanced. More importantly, perhaps, it presents issues and potentialities that cannot be ignored, particularly by lawyers, law-makers, and policy-generators. A great deal has been written already on the jurisdictional challenges facing courts and legislatures, in particular, in the age of globalization and the Internet,[6] and a number of authors have addressed specific topics that are also the subject of case studies that we examine in this book.[7] However, it is less common to find works that not only take a comprehensive approach to extraterritorial jurisdiction, but that do so from a Canadian perspective. One recent book of note is Clarkson and Wood's *A Perilous Imbalance*,[8] which examines the challenges posed by globalization to governance issues in Canada. Our book is concerned with many of these governance issues, but the particular perspective we have sought to adopt is one that focuses on the power of the state to act extraterritorially and the meaning of extraterritorial action. From that broader discussion, we seek to develop a framework that can guide law-

---

6 See, for example, Andrea Slane, "Tales, Techs, and Territories: Private International Law, Globalization, and the Legal Construction of Borderlessness on the Internet" (2008) 71:3 Law & Contemp Probs 129; Uta Kohl, *Jurisdiction and the Internet: Regulatory Competence Over Online Activity* (Cambridge: Cambridge University Press, 2007); Bert-Jaap Koops & Susan Brenner, *Cybercrime and Jurisdiction: A Global Survey* (The Hague: TMC Asser, 2006); Jack L Goldsmith & Tim Wu, *Who Controls the Internet? Illusions of a Borderless World* (Oxford: Oxford University Press, 2006).

7 See, for example, François Larocque, *Civil Actions for Uncivilized Acts: The Adjudicative Jurisdiction of Common Law Courts in Transnational Human Rights Litigation* (Toronto: Irwin Law, 2010); Marko Milanovic, *Extraterritorial Application of Human Rights Treaties* (Oxford: Oxford University Press, 2011); Christopher Kuner, "Data Protection Law and International Jurisdiction on the Internet (Part 1)" (2010) 18 Int'l JL & IT 176; Naomi L Svensson, "Extraterritorial Accountability: An Assessment of the Effectiveness of Child Sex Tourism Laws," Notes & Comment, (2006) 28 Loy LA Int'l & Comp L Rev 641; Jeff Leblanc, "The Pursuit of Virtual Life, Liberty and Happiness and its Economic and Legal Recognition in the Real World" (2008) 9 Fla Coastal L Rev 255.

8 Stephen Clarkson & Stepan Wood, *A Perilous Imbalance: The Globalization of Canadian Law and Governance* (Vancouver: UBC Press, 2010).

and policy-makers in Canada in finding appropriate ways to respond to the challenges of globalization and technological development that are consistent with international law principles and that also meet the public policy imperatives of Canadian society.

The grounding of our work in international law is fundamental to what we seek to achieve, and is worth a word of explanation at the outset. Implicit within any project that explores the reach of laws beyond state borders is the need to distinguish between that which falls within and that which lies outside a state's boundaries. This is because territory, and specifically the sovereignty of states over their territories, is the essential basis of what is often called the "Westphalian" system of international law that orders interstate affairs.[9] Put in legal terms, it is necessary to separate the exercises of jurisdiction that are "territorial" and those that are "extraterritorial," because a more restrictive set of rules attaches to the latter than to the former. This can be challenging, as the concept of territoriality has shifted under pressure from both globalization and technological innovation. This shift is manifested in a number of ways; increasingly, though, the executive, legislative, judicial, and administrative branches exercise authority *domestically* in a way that nonetheless has an impact beyond their state's frontiers. Although there may not be extraterritorial action in the traditional sense, the domestic exercise of jurisdiction may have extraterritorial effects. In this book, then, we talk of territorial and extraterritorial action, but also of an intermediate category of territorial action with extraterritorial effects.

As noted, the Westphalian concept of exclusive territorial sovereignty conceives of nation states as sovereign actors each with respect to its own national territory. It is an idea that relies upon the physicality of state borders, and in turn upon physical events and activities that occur within and outside of those borders. Our discussion is, in part, rooted in these physical concepts of borders and actions, but as our intermediate category of territorial action with extraterritorial effects suggests, our analysis is premised on the assumption that something has occurred to destabilize either this notion of state sovereignty or the concept of state

9 See Antonio Cassese, *International Law*, 2d ed (Oxford: Oxford University Press, 2005) at 5–6 and ch 2. While the proper international law term of art is "state," we will refer variously and synonymously to "states," "nation-states," and "countries." References to "national" or "domestic" will similarly refer to matters existing at the state level.

borders — or perhaps both. The discussions that follow briefly explore the driving forces behind this destabilization, but spend more time analyzing what it looks like when it appears, what the legal implications are or might be, and what lacunae have resulted. There is often particular emphasis on the Internet, since it is perhaps the single most significant factor in the changing concepts of territoriality and extraterritoriality.

This first chapter is followed by seven others. Chapter 2 introduces and interrogates the proposition that "globalization" — which we conclude is a very polyvalent and not altogether lucid term — has been the major driver of the increase in use and importance of extraterritorial jurisdiction. It also discusses the role that technology has played in the overall trends. Chapter 3 is the doctrinal cornerstone of the book, providing some definitional and explanatory scope for extraterritorial jurisdiction as it exists in international law and in Canadian law and practice. The focus on Canada becomes particularly tightly drawn at this point; every state has its own domestic (often constitutional) legal framework for dealing with extraterritorial jurisdiction, and we will present Canada's in fairly close detail as a base upon which to explore both domestic and international developments in the rest of the book. The chapter closes by commenting on the intriguing point that trying to do detailed comparative analysis of state practice regarding extraterritoriality is largely an exercise in futility, as state practice varies so incredibly wildly between states even of the same legal tradition, and states themselves change their practices depending on the subject matter being dealt with. The only practical comparative analysis is driven by the subject matters themselves, and even then thorough treatment is elusive at best.

Chapter 4 amplifies one of the central arguments of this book: that the notion of "territory" and how it figures in the law of jurisdiction generally is being destabilized. It does this by describing and analyzing the principle of "extended territoriality," which provides that a state may have lawful jurisdictional claims over matters that touch its territory in some way, even if in the purely kinetic sense the event happens in whole or in part in another state. An understanding of this principle is part of the necessary backbone of any discussion of extraterritoriality in general, or extraterritorial jurisdiction in particular, and yet it is one of the most poorly understood concepts in the field. We seek to clarify it so that our discussion will be properly focused and to help those dealing with extraterritoriality not to be misled, since, as we will argue, its importance is mounting.

Chapter 5 continues on the theme that traditional notions of territory and territorial jurisdiction are being challenged, but with a specific focus on the Internet. We consider how well the older legal approaches can be extended to regulate Internet-based activities by examining a range of legislative and adjudicative approaches to various issues. We also address the challenges of these activities to the political and normative order and how this reflects changing state attitudes towards jurisdiction.

Chapter 6 enters the policy realm, noting through observation and explanation of Canadian practice that there may be a gap between when states *can* exercise extraterritorial jurisdiction (both lawfully and unlawfully), and when they *should* do so. The emphasis is on the exercise of legislative jurisdiction, but we also highlight the implications for the enforcement of these extraterritorial claims and the problems and issues that may arise from their adjudication. The first and larger part of the discussion focuses on the disincentives for using extraterritorial jurisdiction, and identifies the factors that determine how strong a disincentive might be in any given case by drawing two sets of distinctions: the *justifications* for acting extraterritorially (which we identify as: (a) the extraterritorial conduct has a strong connection to Canada; (b) the conduct occurs extraterritorially but is an aspect of the public face of Canada; (c) extraterritorial action is needed to avoid lawless territory; and (d) there is an international agreement to be implemented); and the *functions* for which extraterritorial action is taken (which we identify as: (a) prohibiting behaviour, (b) controlling behaviour, and (c) facilitating behaviour). We then turn to the incentives for acting extraterritorially. Here we do not seek to suggest particular policy points for which extraterritoriality might be an appropriate tool, as that is the job of policy-makers themselves. Rather, we consider incentives within the context of the norm-creating potential that extraterritorial action carries with it, and suggest that Canada could be incentivized (or not) based on a determination of how it might or will react to other states' similar exercises of extraterritoriality.

Chapter 7 presents seven case studies, all of which concern areas of law that bear the marks of the twin pressures of globalization and technological change. We examine the following: extraterritorial compliance with human rights law; extraterritorial accountability for human rights abuses; transnational data protection; international terrorism; child sex tourism; Internet gambling; and virtual worlds. The case studies are presented to substantiate the framework regarding extraterritorial jurisdiction that we develop in this book. Also, in contrast to work on extraterritorial jurisdiction that explores the jurisdictional angles of discrete topics, this collection of case studies allows us to illustrate in sharp comparative relief the disarray that exists both within the international legal order and in Canadian law.

Chapter 8 concludes the book by emphasizing and exploring the theme emerging from the earlier chapters: that exercises of extraterritorial jurisdiction should only be the product of measured, restrained, and judicious decision making. We offer an original proposal in the form of an analytical framework that can be used to guide decision making both as to whether extraterritorial jurisdiction should be exercised, and what considerations could and should be taken into account in a given situation. We provide this framework in the form of a series of questions that ought to be asked by policy-makers in deciding whether to act extraterritorially, presented in the form of sequential steps towards a decision. This decision-making process, we propose, must always take into account three important variables: the intrusiveness, the nature, and the subject of the extraterritorial action being proposed. As noted above, we do not seek to prescribe that this kind of action be taken with regard to particular matters or interests, the determination of which is the role of policy-makers. Rather, our goal is to provide a decision-making matrix that will allow for the most sound and informed judgments to be made in deciding whether and how to use this most useful yet sometimes risky tool of policy implementation.

Extraterritorial jurisdiction is a large, encompassing, and changing idea that affects, and in turn is affected by, the behaviours of states in their law-making and law-enforcing capacities. This book introduces and consolidates the concepts underpinning jurisdiction, as well as providing an analysis of current trends in their development. It also provides not just a forecast, but also a prescriptive approach for the determination in the future of when it would be legitimate and appropriate to advance a particular Canadian policy by the assertion of extraterritorial jurisdiction and the extension of law beyond Canada's borders.

CHAPTER 2

State Jurisdiction: Drivers of Change in Canadian Practice

Prior to engaging in our discussion of Canada's approach to extraterritorial action, we must first explore two phenomena — globalization and technological development — that have been drivers of change around the world. Both these phenomena have resulted in a multiplication of the circumstances in which states may be forced to decide whether and how to act extraterritorially. The dramatically increased mobility of persons and capital, and the increased reliance upon digital communication technology for transactions, communications, leisure, and even criminal activity, create contexts in which states are often confronted by a need to take action, alone or in concert with other nations. Both globalization and technological change have also contributed to another phenomenon which runs like a thread through this book: the destabilization of the Westphalian notion of exclusive territorial sovereignty.

A. GLOBALIZATION

The dominant contemporary destabilizing force is commonly described as globalization. This term has proved difficult to define adequately, in part because it links together a series of phenomena and processes that are vast, complex, and ongoing.[1] The phenomena described by global-

1 Rajneesh Narula, *Globalization and Technology: Interdependence, Innovation Systems and Industrial Policy* (Cambridge, UK: Polity Press, 2003) at 1 [Narula]. John Tomlinson describes it as "the rapidly developing and ever-densening network of interconnections and interdependences that characterize modern social life." (John

ization can include the rise of global markets,[2] the migration of both capital and labour,[3] international trade,[4] the rise of multinational corporations,[5] transborder criminal activity,[6] and the globalization of culture[7] — the list is virtually endless. The term "globalization" can have a variety of meanings, as well as different features and salient characteristics, depending upon which phenomena are implicated in one's use of the term.

In their book on the impact of globalization on Canada's domestic and international legal role, Clarkson and Wood suggest that globalization "refers to the increasing breadth, intensity, and speed of worldwide interconnectedness in all aspects of social life and its consequences for human conduct."[8] They go on to summarize the phenomenon as "a pervasive, heterogeneous, dynamic, interactive, and contested intensification of interconnectedness in all aspects of human affairs, at all geographic scales."[9] According to this view, globalization is a phenomenon that includes just about everything. Sjolander argues that "globalization needs to be seen as an economic, political, social, and ideological phenomenon which carries with it unanticipated, often contradictory

---

Tomlinson, *Globalization and Culture* (Chicago: University of Chicago Press, 1999) at 1 [Tomlinson]).

2 Narula, *ibid* at 18–19. Ewell E Murphy Jr describes transnational investment as the "second powerful accelerator of economic globalization." The first is technology. See Ewell E Murphy Jr, "The Lessons of Seattle: Learning from the Failed Third WTO Ministerial Conference" (2000) 13:2 Transnat'l Law 273 at 284 [Murphy].

3 Aneesh notes that globalization has resulted both in the physical migration of bodies as well as in virtual migration, where innovations in the field of telecommunications have led to virtual outsourcing of call centre, help desk, and a variety of other jobs. See A Aneesh, *Virtual Migration: The Programming of Globalization* (Durham: Duke University Press, 2006) at 1–2.

4 The World Trade Organization (WTO), which is dedicated to removing trade and tariff barriers to foster international trade, has been identified as a force of globalization and a lightning rod for anti-globalization protests. See Murphy, above note 2.

5 Narula, above note 1 at 20.

6 Transborder criminal activity is allegedly rampant. According to Interpol (www.interpol.int), such activities include money laundering, intellectual property counterfeiting, drug trafficking, organized crime, hacking and other high-tech crime, terrorism, and human trafficking.

7 See, generally, Tomlinson, above note 1.

8 Stephen Clarkson & Stepan Wood, *A Perilous Imbalance: The Globalization of Canadian Law and Governance* (Vancouver: UBC Press, 2010) at 6 [Clarkson & Wood].

9 *Ibid* at 9.

and polarizing consequences."[10] Slane describes globalization as constituting "that vague collection of trends that purportedly erase, or at least significantly compromise, the authority of intermediary levels of social, political, economic, and legal orders such as the nation, state or province."[11] As these definitions demonstrate, globalization can be a remarkably sloppy concept.[12]

Since any attempt to define or discuss globalization is inherently conditioned by the context in which the definition is offered, it is important to be forthright about the context in which we write. This is a book written by law professors about shifting notions of territoriality and extraterritorial state action. International law, therefore, provides the lens through which we see globalization. In this context, there are a variety of phenomena that are generally remarked upon as being markers of globalizing forces, and which tend to manifest themselves in changes in domestic and international norms, institutional roles, and governance issues. It is readily observable in the field of law that the last few decades have seen a steep rise in international trade agreements—and in the scope and impact of these agreements.[13] At the governance level, we see the growing prominence of international and supranational organizations and the drive to harmonize legal norms and processes across

---

10 Claire Turenne Sjolander, "The Rhetoric of Globalization: What's in a Wor(l)d" (1995–1996) 51:4 Int'l J 603 at 604.

11 Andrea Slane, "Tales, Techs, and Territories: Private International Law, Globalization, and the Legal Construction of Borderlessness on the Internet" (2008) 71:3 Law & Contemp Probs 129 at 129 [Slane].

12 Twining complains of the hyperbolic way in which globalization is often described, involving "exaggerated, misleading, meaningless, superficial, ethnocentric, or just plain false statements about processes and phenomena." William Twining, "Diffusion and Globalization Discourse" (2006) 47 Harv Int'l LJ 507 at 508.

13 While the major international trade agreement remains the *General Agreement on Tariffs and Trade 1994*, 15 April 1994, 1867 UNTS 187; 33 ILM 1153 [*GATT*] overseen by the WTO, regional and multilateral trade agreements have become common. Such agreements include the *North American Free Trade Agreement*, 17 December 1992, Can TS 1994 No 2, 32 ILM 289 and 605 [*NAFTA*], the *Asia-Pacific Trade Agreement*, 2 November 2005 (previously known as the *First Agreement on Trade Negotiations Among Developing Member Countries of the Economic and Social Commission for Asia and the Pacific (Bangkok Agreement)*, 31 July 1975), and the *Central European Free Trade Agreement (CEFTA) 2006*, 19 December 2006 (entered into force on 1 May 2007). A list of the many regional, bi-, and multilateral trade agreements can be found, online: WTO http://rtais.wto.org/UI/PublicAllRTAList.aspx.

a broad range of social and economic activity.[14] The greater mobility of persons and capital has led to attempts to establish or harmonize norms around international financial transactions, human trafficking, and other areas. A sharp rise in transborder criminal activities and in international terrorism has also led states to think globally in developing norms and institutions to address these issues. The dramatic increase in trade of a global nature, including a shift in the loci of manufacturing and production, and the dynamic growth of the importance of intellectual property rights, has led to the development of new trade and intellectual property agreements. There is increasing convergence of corporate ownership, a rise in multinational corporations (often exercising significant normative power in their own right), and an increasing harmonization of culture and communications internationally.[15] All of these changes can be described as part of "globalization"; from a lawyer's point of view, all are reflected in the development of new norms and institutions both domestically and at the international level.

Although "globalization is everything" is not a particularly satisfying definition, from a pragmatic legal perspective it might be enough to observe that there are certain global forces driving change, and then move on to the task of analyzing the normative and institutional manifestations of this change. Indeed, it is evident that international and domestic legal systems are in a process of fundamental change, that the changes are pervasive, and that they are the result of a variety of forces. Clarkson and Wood offer four themes through which globalization should be assessed from a legal viewpoint: governance (how societies govern themselves); law (how norms are derived); sovereignty (the relationships between states); and legitimacy (how political authority, whether national or international, achieves and maintains legitimacy).[16] These are core questions for legal scholars, framed in the language of law. They are ones that are of interest to us as well in our own work, which focuses on the elusive concepts of territoriality and extraterritoriality.

---

14 More established international and supranational bodies include the United Nations and its many agencies, the WTO, the Organisation for Economic Cooperation and Development (OECD), and the World Intellectual Property Organization (WIPO). There are many others.

15 David Held & Anthony McGrew, "Globalization at Risk?" in David Held & Anthony McGrew, eds, *Globalization Theory: Approaches and Controversies* (Cambridge, UK: Polity Press, 2007) 1 at 4 [Held & McGrew].

16 Clarkson & Wood, above note 8 at 23–41.

1) Sovereignty

Sovereignty is the key issue in a discussion of territorial and extraterritorial action. Indeed, both territoriality and extraterritoriality are premised on state sovereignty. The terms "territorial" and "extraterritorial" describe actions in terms of the notional boundaries of a sovereign state's jurisdiction. Taubman writes:

> The concept of sovereignty is dependent on territoriality, precisely because it concerns absolute or predominant authority of the sovereign powers within the territory of the state, exclusion of external authority and comity between states. Conventional notions of sovereignty are therefore dependent on the integrity of the capacity to exercise control within a well-defined territory.[17]

In our discussion of extraterritoriality in this book, we explore as well the concept of "extended territorial jurisdiction." This is where a state engages in territorial actions based upon an expanded vision of its territory. Largely articulated through the real and substantial connection doctrine, territorial jurisdiction is seen to extend to incidents, actions, and actors that have a real and substantial connection to the state. The phenomenon of globalization gives rise to a sharply growing number of instances of extended territorial jurisdiction. This in turn reshapes our understanding of "territory," which is at the heart of the concept of sovereignty. As both the definitions of territory and the capacity to exercise control are undermined,[18] traditional notions of territoriality and territorial sovereignty come under pressure. Thus, globalization as a phenomenon is important to our discussion as it is descriptive of shifts in the locus of power that undermine traditional notions of sovereignty upon which state jurisdiction is built.[19]

---

17 Antony Taubman, "International Governance and the Internet" [Taubman] in Lilian Edwards & Charlotte Waelde, eds, *Law and the Internet*, 3d ed (Portland: Hart Publishing, 2009) 3 at 27.

18 Notions of "territory" are undermined, for example, by the increasing engagement of a country's citizens in a wide range of activities that are carried out in "cyberspace." This in turn undermines the capacity of states to control citizen activity.

19 See, for example, Saskia Sassen, *Territory, Authority, Rights: From Medieval to Global Assemblages*, rev ed (Princeton: Princeton University Press, 2006) [Sassen, *Territory*]; Chris Brown, "Reimagining International Society and Global Community" in Held & McGrew, above note 15 at 171.

2) Governance

Linked to the issue of sovereignty is the theme of governance. The term "globalization" describes a set of transformations that involve institutional changes as well as shifts in fundamental social and economic dynamics. Sassen argues that the concept of globalization reflects two different dynamics, the first of which is directly related to governance. This dynamic involves the development of institutions or processes that are global in nature — supranational organizations and tribunals, for example.[20] International organizations now exercise increasing authority over a wide range of subject matter, including communications, intellectual property, international trade, finance, environment, marine affairs, health, human rights, and crime. International tribunals have also grown in number and address issues ranging from law of the sea to human rights and war crimes.[21] These new institutions may reflect a shift in competence or jurisdiction from the national to the international. Certainly in our discussion of extraterritoriality, it becomes clear that international treaty making plays a fundamental role in shaping action with respect to problems or issues faced by multiple states. While not all of these treaties establish new institutions of governance, many do; others establish mechanisms for the enforcement of state obligations arising under the treaties.[22]

Governance issues do not just arise through a reconfiguration of how competence is shared between individual states and international bodies established through interstate co-operation. There is a notable emergence of alternative governance models, some of which either marginalize or avoid state involvement. An early example is the regulation of letters of credit that support the flow of international trade. They are nearly always governed by the Uniform Customs and Practice for Documentary Credits maintained by the Commission on Banking Technique and Practice of the International Chamber of Commerce without

20 Saskia Sassen, "The Places and Spaces of the Global: An Expanded Analytic Terrain" in Held & McGrew, above note 15, 79 at 82 [Sassen, "Places and Spaces"].

21 Examples of international tribunals include: the International Criminal Court, international criminal tribunals for Rwanda and Yugoslavia, the European Court of Human Rights, the International Tribunal for the Law of the Sea, and the Permanent Court of International Justice.

22 Consider, for example, the mechanisms provided for in the *GATT*; see, generally, Robert E Hudec, *Enforcing International Trade Law: The Evolution of the Modern GATT Legal System* (Salem, NH: Butterworths, 1993).

any state government involvement at all. A contemporary and unusual example is the governance of Internet infrastructure through the Internet Corporation for Assigned Names and Numbers (ICANN), a private company incorporated under the laws of California. The role of states in relation to this governance body is a work in progress.[23] It offers an interesting example of a supranational governance body established to deal with a novel technological issue that has come to play an extremely important role in managing perhaps the most important global communications infrastructure.

ICANN was formed in October 1998 as the oversight body for domain name registrations.[24] It replaced a private sector company that was under contract with the United States government's National Science Foundation. ICANN's twenty-one member board of directors reflects its international constituency. ICANN has also developed a governance structure[25] designed to involve a variety of stakeholders. Its primary role is to manage the "technical coordination, technical management and operational stability of the Internet."[26] ICANN is a private corporation that performs extremely important Internet oversight functions, and in this sense it may be characterized as a new—and controversial—international governance model.[27]

The governance role of ICANN has been and continues to be challenged by national governments who would prefer to see control over the infrastructure of the Internet in the hands of a more conventional international organization.[28] The World Summit on the Information

---

23 The particular situation of ICANN is discussed later in Chapter 5.

24 ICANN is a non-profit corporation incorporated under the laws of California, and with its headquarters in that state.

25 ICANN, "ICANN Organizational Chart," online: ICANN www.icann.org/en/structure.

26 WIPO, *The Recognition of Rights and the Use of Names in the Internet Domain Name System: Report of the Second WIPO Internet Domain Name Process* (Geneva: WIPO, 2001) at 25, online: www.wipo.int/amc/en/processes/process2/report/html/report.html.

27 DelBianco and Cox argue that ICANN should be thought of as "the Internet's manager—not as its governor." See Steve DelBianco & Braden Cox, "ICANN Internet Governance: Is it Working?" (2008) 21 Pacific McGeorge Global Business & Development Law Journal 27 at 28 [DelBianco & Cox]. However, this does not stop ICANN from being considered a governance body, and from generating international debate over its composition and its role.

28 The threats to ICANN at the international level are discussed in DelBianco & Cox, ibid at 39–40. See also Milton Mueller, Networks and States: The Global Politics of Internet Governance (Cambridge, MA: MIT Press, 2010) at 60–63.

Society (WSIS), a global United Nations summit initiated in 2002 and which concluded in 2005, was the locus of significant challenges to ICANN's role in Internet governance.[29] Part of the resistance/reaction was to the perceived hegemony of the United States, as it had transferred its authority over Internet governance to what is, in essence, a US-based corporation. Mueller argues that the resistance to ICANN goes deeper. He describes ICANN's institutional design as one that "marked a revolutionary departure from traditional approaches to global governance."[30] As ICANN manages issues that are central to communication and information policy, it is radical indeed to have the locus of decision making situated outside the structure of the nation-state and outside traditional international organizations.[31]

ICANN is a novel governance structure not just because it is a not-for-profit corporation not controlled by national governments, but also because the infrastructure it governs does not lend itself to control at the state level. Whether proprietary or open standards are adopted, what top level domains are available for domain name registration and by whom, are important questions.[32] The ability to control the infra-

---

29 Although WSIS did not manage to displace ICANN, it did result in the establishment of the Internet Governance Forum (IGF). Although the IGF is more explicitly international than ICANN, it is still a novel international institution because of its structure. IGF places government representatives "on roughly equal terms with civil society and business participants." (Mueller, *ibid* at 107) Indeed, it describes itself as "a new forum for multi-stakeholder policy dialogue." (IGF, "About the Internet Governance Forum," online: IGF www.intgovforum.org/cms/aboutigf.)

30 Mueller, *ibid* at 60–61.

31 Under ICANN's articles of incorporation, government representatives may not sit on its board. Note that DelBianco & Cox, above note 27 at 29, argue that if an intergovernmental body were to take over the functions of ICANN, its ability to act effectively to regulate Internet infrastructure would be diminished. They write: "[q]uarreling nations would find it impossible to agree on anything but the most trivial technical decisions. Developing nations would press for changes in Internet management to advance their economic development goals. Special interests would seek Internet-enabled social programs to address perceived disadvantages." Perhaps ironically, in advancing their reasons why states should not involve themselves in the management of Internet infrastructure, the authors seem to be saying that it is because they would act like governments.

32 ICANN's governance role is oriented towards technical standards and operational management of Internet infrastructure. The importance of the choices made in this respect, however, go beyond mere technical matters. Indeed, Lessig maintains that the Internet is regulated by code — by software and hardware. (Lawrence Lessig, *Code and Other Laws of Cyberspace* (New York: Basic Books, 1999) at 6 [Lessig, *Code*].) Technical norms and specifications, their evolution, and the laws that constrain

structure of the Internet is a matter of great state interest. Governance issues therefore represent a critical dimension with respect to state sovereignty.[33] Indeed, the recent and controversial negotiations regarding Internet governance, under the auspices of the United Nations' International Telecommunications Union, have brought into sharp relief various fracture points among state positions on the propriety and scope of Internet regulation.[34]

There has also been a growing diversion of dispute resolution arenas within public and national institutions, such as courts or administrative tribunals, to private and international fora, such as international arbitration bodies.[35] While some of these arbitration bodies are established by international agreement,[36] other arbitration processes, such as those created to resolve Internet domain name disputes, international commercial disputes, and even business-consumer disputes, are relatively independent from either domestic or international state involvement. If state jurisdiction is conceived of as a set of puzzle pieces with each state as a piece whose boundaries reflect the limits of their territorial sovereignty, then the principles of international law represent the big picture which both frames and unites all the pieces. These new governance bodies and dispute resolution processes (which often develop their own normative principles) are extra pieces; ones that disrupt the established logic of the puzzle.

---

them, become part of the architecture of cyberspace that may limit and constrain it. In this context, states play a normative role, but so do private actors — those who control the code and architecture. See *ibid*; Joel R Reidenberg, "Lex Informatica: The Formulation of Information Policy Rules through Technology" (1998) 76:3 Tex L Rev 553.

33 Taubman, above note 17 at 7, notes that although the United States has tended to favour a private-sector based approach to Internet governance structures, other governments have sought to play a more active role. He writes that the economic, political, and cultural impact of the Internet have raised "concerns that are reflected in a debate over whether the Internet should be governed through genuinely international structures with distinct legal personality under international law, or whether the legal roots of the Internet should remain embedded in the fertile soil from where it was first cultivated, in the domestic jurisdiction of the US."

34 See "US and UK Refuse to Sign UN's Communications Treaty" *BBC News* (14 December 2012), online: BBC News www.bbc.co.uk/news/technology-20717774.

35 This is reflected in international domain name dispute resolution processes as well as in international commercial arbitrations.

36 This is the case, for example, with arbitration panels under the *GATT*, above note 13 and the *NAFTA*, above note 13.

Linked to the shift of authority over governance, norm-setting, and adjudication away from state actors is the rise of a new kind of actor — the multinational corporation. Not only do multinational corporations exert significant influence over domestic and international law making, they often do so outside of the recognized contexts for law and policy development. Further, they have increasingly become difficult entities to regulate as they are not easily tied to a single jurisdiction from a regulatory point of view. Multinational actors may have significant influence in determining the norms by which they are governed simply due to their economic clout.[37] In addition, their transnational structure permits them to "locate activities in nation states in which the regulation poses the least, or no, obstacle to the activity in which the multinational wishes to engage."[38]

3) Law

The challenges to sovereignty discussed above, and the novel forms of governance, are also reflected in the shift of legal normative authority from national to international levels. Sassen observes that the institutional shift from national to international is not simply a process of stripping nations of their power or sovereignty; in most instances, nation states participate in this process of globalization not just by negotiating the international treaties that establish international institutions or international norms, but also by enacting the laws, in national legislatures, that "implement" or internalize the new norms or that transfer authority to the new international organizations. In this sense, globalization is not just something that "happens" to states; it is something in which they actively participate. Thus sovereignty is still exercised but to different ends. It is probably fair to say that old notions of territorial sovereignty still hold strong in that there continues to be resistance to the notion of individual states engaging in extraterritorial action, particularly in a unilateral manner.[39] However, at the same time, there

---

37 See, for example, Patrick Macklem, "Corporate Accountability under International Law: The Misguided Quest for Universal Jurisdiction" (2005) 7:4 International Law FORUM Du Droit International 281 at 281; Douglas M Branson, "The Social Responsibility of Large Multinational Corporations" (2002) 16:1 Transnat'l Law 121 at 131–32.

38 Branson, *ibid* at 133.

39 This resistance, which reflects the historical development of the international law norms regarding extraterritorial jurisdiction, is discussed in further detail in Chapter 3.

may be greater recognition or acceptance of the need for states to act collectively to address common issues or problems, particularly where purely territorial action would no longer be effective in addressing the problems. This trend towards international treaty making as a means of addressing issues of importance to Canada that occur wholly or partly beyond its borders is a recurring theme in this book. With international treaty making, the underlying authority of the actors is not changed; what changes is how, when, and for what ends their capacities are exercised. Sassen notes that one of the challenges in identifying processes and actors within the broader phenomenon of globalization "is the need to decode at least some of what continues to be experienced and represented as national."[40]

This shift in what is "experienced and represented as national" is evident as well in changing state attitudes towards the actions of their citizens abroad. This is a complex phenomenon. As the global mobility of both persons and capital increases, the nationals of countries (both citizens and legal corporations) increasingly engage in a wide range of activities in foreign countries. While the phenomenon is not new, the scale is much greater than it has been historically. In recent years we have seen attempts by a number of countries to criminalize acts by their citizens abroad, even where those acts are not necessarily illegal in the countries where they take place. This phenomenon is discussed in more detail in our case study on child sex tourism in Chapter 7, Section E. Similarly, there has been pressure brought to bear on governments in various countries, including Canada, to take action to impose legal restraints or obligations on domestic corporations that engage in business activities abroad. In Canada, for example, concerns have been raised about the behaviour of mining and petroleum companies operating in developing countries.[41]

The fact that jurists continue to think in terms of a "national" and an "international" suggests that globalization may not really be about the dismantling of the nation state or its growing irrelevance. Instead,

---

40 Sassen, "Places and Spaces," above note 20 at 82. This point is made equally with respect to the formation of activist groups across borders, which Sassen construes as, in parallel to the internationalization of state action, a kind of internationalization of national activism on issues that increasingly traverse frontiers, such as the environment, human rights, fair trade, and even globalization itself.

41 See, for example, Robert McCorquodale & Penelope Simons, "Responsibility beyond Borders: State Responsibility for Extraterritorial Violations by Corporations of International Human Rights Law" (2007) 70:4 Mod L Rev 598.

the impact of globalization may be a reconfiguration of the national. Issues that have always traversed national boundaries now occur more frequently and on a bigger scale than they once did. For example, there has always been transborder crime, and there has long been means by which states agree to address these issues. The challenge today is one of scale, both in terms of the volume of activity and the ease with which it can take place.

The same issues of scale can be seen in other substantive areas as well. The Berne Convention,[42] which dates back to 1883, aimed to harmonize certain aspects of the copyright regime, and to provide for national treatment, in order to offer creators of works protection on an international scale. Today, international protection remains a value, but the scale has been altered. Harmonization is now not only of norms but of enforcement mechanisms, the norms are more extensive and less flexible, trade sanctions give teeth to treaty obligations, and new international bodies play a role in oversight and enforcement. While the "national" remains important (states negotiate international treaties, the nation is the locus for implementation, and national courts remain an important enforcement mechanism), some of what was once more exclusively national has shifted to the international or global levels. Thus there is less room to develop independent domestic norms in the intellectual property area; there is less room to avoid the implementation of negotiated treaties; and other, more global fora, are emerging as sites for enforcement and dispute resolution.

In addition to reconfiguring the "national," globalization may also be shifting the underlying assumptions of domestic and international actors. At one point, for example, it was accepted in Canada (and elsewhere) that extraterritorial legislative action ought to be rare. This assumption has likely not changed dramatically, in the sense that states still seek to avoid unilateral extraterritorial action. However, there is, perhaps, a greater tendency to seek international consensus on how to proceed in addressing a much wider variety of issues. Thus although unilateral extraterritorial action remains rare, unilateral domestic action on matters which might have impact outside the state is becoming less common. This affects not just the executive and legislative branches. Judges too have shown a greater inclination to look to the out-

42 *Berne Convention for the Protection of Literary and Artistic Works*, 9 September 1886, 828 UNTS 221.

side world, even when interpreting domestic norms.[43] For example, in the *Harvard College* case, Justice Binnie of the Supreme Court of Canada wrote: "The mobility of capital and technology makes it desirable that comparable jurisdictions with comparable intellectual property legislation arrive (to the extent permitted by the specifics of their own laws) at similar legal results . . . ."[44] This shift in attitude—call it a globalized mentality—does not change the roles or abilities of the actors, but it may increase the willingness of those actors to exercise certain powers or to adopt particular approaches to issues.

The "globalized mentality" may also be reflected in a growing tendency of states to co-operate with each other in a variety of ways. While bi- and multilateral treaty negotiations are high level and highly visible examples of this, there are also less overt layers of interstate co-operation. Memoranda of Understanding, for example, reflect agreements to share resources, to work together on issues, to give another state assistance in pursuing investigations or inquiries, and so on. Our case study on transnational data protection in Chapter 7, Section C, in fact explores how various modes of co-operation can be used to address challenging issues of data protection with transborder data flows. This more globalized "attitude of mind" may also affect a state's perceptions of the conduct of its own nationals while they are in other countries.[45]

In this discussion of "law," we have focused on national and international institutions and their changing roles. Yet it is important to keep in mind that law as normative ordering is not confined to these institutions. The second dynamic of globalization described by Sassen[46] involves a more organic set of processes at both the state and the non-state level. Sassen gives as examples the formation of "monetary and fiscal policies critical for the constitution of global markets"[47] and the formation of networks of activists across borders. In both instances, institutions and processes shift from the national to more international contexts. Clarkson and Wood also describe law in terms of legal plur-

---

43 There is a large and interesting literature on this trend. See Anne-Marie Slaughter, "Judicial Globalization" (2000) 40 Va J Int'l L 1103; Carl Baudenbacher, "Judicial Globalization: New Development or Old Wine in New Bottles?" (2003) 38 Tex Int'l LJ 505.

44 *Harvard College v Canada (Commissioner of Patents)*, 2002 SCC 76 at para 13.

45 See, for example, our case study on child sex tourism in Chapter 7, Section E.

46 See text accompanying footnote 20, above in this chapter.

47 Sassen, *Territory*, above note 19 at 20.

alism. They emphasize the growing diversity of sites of normative ordering and the increasingly important role that they play.[48]

4) Legitimacy

The fourth theme identified by Clarkson and Wood is legitimacy, which they describe as the "popular approbation that comes when decisions affecting people are made by appropriate authorities, in acceptable ways, with acceptable results."[49] Framed in this way, legitimacy is a multi-faceted inquiry. It is necessary to consider not just the legitimacy of the actor that makes the decision, but also the legitimacy of the process by which the decision is arrived at, and the legitimacy of the results. While legitimacy is an age-old issue and one that is not exclusive to periods of globalization, there is no question that globalization makes issues of legitimacy more challenging. Below we consider three different types of legitimacy: that of actors, that of process, and that of outcomes.

a) Actor Legitimacy

National governments may face issues of legitimacy when their legislative policies are dictated by international accords that might not be perceived as being in the best interests of the citizenry.[50] Indeed, the rise in grassroots protests against the G20, against treaties such as the *Anti-Counterfeiting Trade Agreement*,[51] and the "occupy" movement all reflect popular challenges to government policies dictated by international agreements. It is not just national governments that face challenges to their legitimacy—international organizations can face questions of legitimacy as well. As noted earlier, ICANN has faced considerable challenges to its legitimacy from both national governments and civil society organizations. More recently, the politics of international bodies

---

48 Clarkson & Wood, above note 8 at 26.

49 *Ibid* at 31.

50 See, for example, "ACTA Copyright Treaty in Doubt As EU Suspends Ratification" *Canadian Press* reprinted in Huffington Post (22 February 2012), online: huffingtonpost.ca www.huffingtonpost.ca/2012/02/22/acta-copyright-treaty-eu-suspends-ratification_n_1293198.html.

51 The final text of the *Anti-Counterfeiting Trade Agreement* (ACTA) can be found, online: Ministry of Foreign Affairs of Japan www.mofa.go.jp/policy/economy/i_property/pdfs/acta1105_en.pdf.

such as the United Nations Human Rights Council has also led to challenges to the legitimacy of its actions and processes.[52]

b) Process Legitimacy

Not only is there now a multiplicity of organizations that exercise authority (including national governments, international organizations, and even multinational corporations), there is a proliferation of processes. One only needs to look to litigation in Canada to see the process-legitimacy challenge. In *Dell Computer Corp v Union des consommateurs*,[53] for example, the Supreme Court of Canada considered arguments about whether an arbitration clause in a standard-form consumer contract that prescribed dispute resolution in the United States under US rules could be used to preclude recourse in Quebec for Quebec consumers under that province's consumer protection legislation. In a globalized and technology-facilitated economy, the issue of which institution has the right to resolve disputes and under the laws of which country is increasingly contentious. Issues of process legitimacy arise in other contexts as well. The debates swirling around the detention of prisoners at Guantanamo Bay, for example, raise profound issues of process legitimacy that touch on the scope of authority of domestic norms and institutions and the construction of space that is controlled by a national government but not constrained by its laws.

c) Outcome Legitimacy

Outcome legitimacy considers the extent to which outcomes of particular processes carried out by particular actors are considered acceptable. As will be seen in the chapters which follow, state institutions have their own mechanisms for rejecting outcomes they consider to be illegitimate where these are the result of perceived illegitimate extraterritorial actions by other states or their institutions. Thus, Canadian courts can refuse to enforce foreign judgments,[54] and the Canadian government can also enact its own laws to rebuff the extraterritorial reach of other states.[55]

---

52 See, for example, Adrian Humphreys, "'A Spectacle of Hypocrisy and Farce': North Korea, Iran Attack Canada's Human Rights Record at UN Forum" *The National Post* (26 April 2013), online: National Post http://news.nationalpost.com/2013/04/26/north-korea-iran-attack-canadas-human-rights-record-at-un-forum.

53 2007 SCC 34.

54 See the discussion in Chapter 3.

55 See the discussion of Canada's response to the Helms-Burton legislation, in Chapter 6.

Globalization, therefore, when seen through a legal lens, reflects domestic and international institutional changes, new laws and policies, and what might be described as a more fluid or "virtual" notion of the state's territorial boundaries. These are all phenomena that we consider in this book, and they point us to the questions at the heart of our work. The scope of the legal and practical power of Canada to assert (and to respond to foreign assertions of) extraterritorial jurisdiction is situated within this dynamic global environment.

B. TECHNOLOGY

From a lawyer's perspective, globalization is reflected in institutional changes, in attitudinal shifts at the law- and policy-making level, and in shifting concepts of state sovereignty and territorial limits. Concurrent with and often facilitating these institutional and dynamic changes,[56] contemporary society is experiencing breathtaking technological development.[57] Building on the work of Archibugi, Narula argues that the globalization of technology occurs through the international exploitation of technology produced at the national level; the global generation of innovation, typically by multinational corporations; and global technological collaborations.[58] Knowledge economies breed globalized workforces, and radical transformations of communications technologies change how people interact, communicate, collaborate, and network.[59] They also change how culture is formed and communicated.[60]

---

56 Held, for example, argues that the changing infrastructure of global communications is a driver of globalization. See David Held, "Global Governance: Apocalypse Soon or Reform!" in Held & McGrew above note 15, 240 at 243. Narula, above note 1 at 2, argues that technology and innovation are "determinants of globalization."

57 Narula defines technology in terms of the "application of scientific knowledge for practical aims" (Narula, *ibid* at 2).

58 Narula, *ibid* at 5, citing Daniele Archibugi & Simona Iammarino, "The Policy Implications of the Globalisation of Innovation" (1999) 28 Research Policy 317; Daniele Archibugi & Jonathan Michie, "The Globalization of Technology: A New Taxonomy" (1995) 19(1) Cambridge Journal of Economics 121.

59 See, for example, the discussion of this phenomenon in Cass Sunstein, *Infotopia: How Many Minds Produce Knowledge* (New York: Oxford University Press, 2006); Yochai Benkler, *The Wealth of Networks: How Social Production Transforms Markets and Freedom* (New Haven: Yale University Press, 2006) [Benkler].

60 There is a vast literature on this subject. We note in particular that much has been written from a copyright perspective on the impact of contemporary forces on the creation and sharing of cultural works protected by copyright. See, for example,

Innovations in biotechnology transform health and agriculture into industries with global economic, legal, and political dimensions.

In spite of the transformative effect of technological change, such change is only one part of the phenomenon of globalization and the stresses placed on notions of territorial sovereignty. As Taubman writes in the case of the Internet: "The classical notion of sovereignty was already under threat, well before the advent of mass Internet usage, in a direct practical sense because of the rise of global business patterns and globalized communication and cultural exchanges; as well as from a theoretical perspective."[61] Thus technology is a distinct and important factor in a discussion of globalization, but it is not on its own the sole or even driving force behind it.

Technological innovation in all its varied forms, from biotechnology to engineering, computer science, applied physics, nanotechnology — the list is endless — is both globalized (through the activities of multinational corporations and international research collaborations) and globalizing. Of the globalizing dimensions of technology, the impact of the Internet is perhaps the most important. This is not simply because of the importance of the technological infrastructure for social, political, cultural, and economic activities, but also because of the way in which this technology has given rise to its own unique governance issues.

The technological infrastructure of the Internet — a global communications network that continues to expand and change — presents its own distinct challenges to state jurisdiction and national sovereignty. These arise in part because the Internet facilitates the building of alliances, networks, and commercial relationships across borders in ways that are virtually unmediated by the state and, in practice, are often elusive to state control. Internet-based disputes, harms, and conflicts have challenged states in terms of either defining the boundaries of their own competence to act, or in terms of acting in ways that can be practically

---

Lawrence Lessig, *The Future of Ideas: The Fate of the Commons in a Connected World* (New York: Vintage Books, 2002); Kembrew McLeod, *Freedom of Expression: Overzealous Copyright Bozos and Other Enemies of Creativity* (New York: Doubleday, 2005). See also the discussion by Benkler of the proliferation of non-market cultural production in Benkler, *ibid* at ch 3. See, as well, the discussion in Robert Rattle, *Computing our Way to Paradise?: The Role of Internet and Communications Technologies in Sustainable Consumption and Globalization* (Lanham, MD: Altamira Press, 2010).

61 Taubman, above note 17 at 27.

enforced. In many cases, solutions lie only through interstate and more broadly international collaborations. Slane writes:

> The legal handling of the Internet's capacity for uncontrolled crossing of territorial borders informs and shapes our understanding of the Internet in two ways: first, by framing the substantive issues arising from the application of local law as a conflict between a cosmopolitanism that embraces global community and a parochialism that thwarts global community; second, by framing procedural issues as a contest between simple and complex approaches to determining the significance of new legal circumstances arising from the technology or the relationships it enables, or both.[62]

From a legal outlook, the challenge of the Internet operates on both a national and international level. It involves a challenge to shape or extend existing laws to cover Internet-based conduct, and to test the boundaries of courts' willingness to assert jurisdiction over disputes. Concurrently, there is a new layer of international normative collaboration around Internet-based activities in a variety of fields, from intellectual property treaties[63] to the Council of Europe's *Convention on Cybercrime*.[64]

At the same time, the Internet has created its own governance challenges, as it is itself a decentralized global network with an infrastructure that is not easily controlled by any one state. As discussed earlier, ICANN has emerged as a novel international governance body. It is a corporation that is not controlled by states, although compromises have been made to permit increasing levels of state input. This new form of governance, which is discussed in greater detail in Chapter 6, is not without controversy, but it illustrates a kind of ad hoc innovation in traditional modes of international governance.

---

62 Slane, above note 11 at 129.

63 For example, two WIPO treaties are commonly referred to as the Internet treaties: *WIPO Copyright Treaty*, 20 December 1996, 36 ILM 65, Art 5 (entered into force 6 March 2002), online: WIPO www.wipo.int/treaties/en/ip/wct/trtdocs_wo033.html; and *WIPO Performances and Phonograms Treaty*, 20 December 1996, 36 ILM 76 (entered into force 20 May 2002), online: WIPO www.wipo.int/treaties/en/ip/wppt/trtdocs_wo034.html.

64 EC, 23 November 2001, ETS No 185, 41 ILM 282 (entered into force 7 January 2004). See, generally, Mike Keyser, "The Council of Europe *Convention on Cybercrime*" (2002–2003) 12:2 J Transnat'l L & Pol'y 287.

The Internet has other implications for governance as well. With digitization and the Internet has come a school of thought that increasingly views code—computer programs—as a vehicle for normative ordering.[65] As we show in the case study in Chapter 7, Section C, on transnational data protection, the role of code as law is of growing significance, both in private ordering (shaping how consumers interact with goods or with companies offering services) in domestic regulation (where governments limit citizen access to certain online sites or activities),[66] and in international regulation (through the setting and adoption of international technological standards). The role of code has become important enough that Aneesh has coined the word "algocracy" to refer to the rule of the algorithm.[67]

Through its decentralized structure that evades state control, the Internet has also become a powerful vehicle for the formation of non-governmental networks and alliances. While some of these are terrorist or criminal networks, others are peaceful networks formed along social or political lines. The Internet has been identified as a powerful vehicle for movements to destabilize governments,[68] and it has been used as an organizing tool for global movements, including that against neoliberal globalization.[69] The Internet has also become a vehicle for col-

---

65 Lessig, *Code*, above note 32; Benkler, above note 59; Tim Wu, *The Master Switch: The Rise and Fall of Information Empires* (New York: Alfred A Knopf, 2010).

66 For example, see Jonathan Zittrain, *The Future of the Internet and How to Stop It* (New Haven, CT: Yale University Press, 2008) at 113; Jonathan Zittrain & Benjamin Edelman, "Documentation of Internet Filtering in Saudi Arabia" Berkman Center for Internet and Society (12 September 2002), online: Berkman Centre for Internet and Society http://cyber.law.harvard.edu/filtering/saudiarabia. Kohl discussed the willingness of some corporations to create country-specific sites to address state censorship requirements. See Uta Kohl, *Jurisdiction and the Internet: A Study of Regulatory Competence over Online Activity* (Cambridge, UK: Cambridge University Press, 2007) at 29.

67 Aneesh, above note 3 at 5.

68 See for example, "Social Media, Cellphone Video Fuel Arab Protests" *The Independent* (27 February 2011), online: The Independent www.independent.co.uk/life-style/gadgets-and-tech/social-media-cellphone-video-fuel-arab-protests-2227088.html; Mark Sedra, "Revolution 2.0: Democracy Promotion in the Age of Social Media" *The Globe and Mail* (2 February 2011), online: The Globe and Mail www.theglobeandmail.com/commentary/revolution-20-democracy-promotion-in-the-age-of-social-media/article564610.

69 See for example, Claudine Beaumont, "G20: Protesters Use Twitter, Facebook and Social Media Tools to Organise Demonstrations" *The Telegraph* (1 April 2009), online: The Telegraph www.telegraph.co.uk/finance/g20-summit/5090003/G20-

laborative knowledge projects, cultural initiatives, and other activities that were once state-centred and often state-funded or controlled. Indeed, the phenomenon of crowd-funding has developed rapidly from an experimental way to fund entrepreneurial or cultural innovation to an increasingly popular alternative to fund all manner of activity, including compensating victims of harms,[70] raising money for charitable purposes,[71] and even raising money to buy potentially explosive evidence of wrong-doing by political figures.[72] It is perhaps beyond the scope of this book to discuss these changes and movements, but it is important at least to note their existence and their potential to further subvert traditional notions of domestic jurisdiction and state sovereignty.

The Internet, then, is at once the subject of new international governance frameworks, the object of increasingly harmonized state norms regarding infrastructure and conduct, and a venue by which individuals shape and form alliances and movements that transcend national boundaries. It is a case study of the challenges to the Westphalian concept of territorial state jurisdiction, and of the ways in which states continue to define or redefine their territorial boundaries, and find new ways to act within them. It is both a driver and a marker of globalization; at the same time, technology itself is producing tangible changes to norms and governance structures.

C. CONCLUSION

This discussion of globalization and technological change provides a backdrop for the following discussions of both how the choice to act extraterritorially can and should be made, as well as the often more dif-

---

summit-Protesters-use-Twitter-Facebook-and-social-media-tools-to-organise-demonstrations.html.

70 See, for example, Paul Hilder, "How a Crowd Came to the Aid of Bullied Bus Monitor Karen Klein" *The Guardian* (25 June 2012), online: The Guardian www.guardian.co.uk/commentisfree/2012/jun/25/karen-klein-bus-monitor-bullied-online-campaign.

71 See, for example, Brett Zongker, "Hurricane Sandy Relief Gets Boost from Crowd-funding Efforts" The Huffington Post (22 December 2012), online: Huff Post Impact Canada www.huffingtonpost.com/2012/12/28/crowdfunding-sandy-relief_n_2376704.html.

72 See, for example, Megan O'Toole, "Rob Ford Crack-Cocaine Video Crowd-Funding Campaigns Spring up to Purchase Alleged Tape" *The National Post* (17 May 2013), online: National Post http://news.nationalpost.com/2013/05/17/several-crowd-funding-campaigns-spring-up-to-purchase-video-allegedly-showing-rob-ford-smoking-crack-pipe.

ficult exercise in determining the limits of any state's territorial jurisdiction. While the discussion in the chapters that follow draws on long-standing bedrock principles of international law, and, in that sense, represents a normative continuity and stability, the context in which these principles are interpreted and applied is considerably less stable. As this book moves towards the exposition of a contemporary framework for decision making around extraterritorial action, we will strive to adapt the established norms to a shifting global context.

CHAPTER 3

The Jurisdictional Status Quo in Canada and Internationally

The goal of this chapter is to be both descriptive and analytical. We will attempt to describe the current state of international law regarding the exercise of extraterritorial jurisdiction by states, expanding on some of the basic definitional material in Chapter 1. We will also examine where and how that law is implemented into Canadian law and state practice, which we will then briefly compare to the law and practice of other states and/or groups of states. This exercise is also necessarily analytical, in that it deals with bodies of international and domestic law that are symbiotically linked, but at the same time encompass a broad range of diverse and sometimes inconsistent principles and practices. Accordingly, we will adapt, formulate, and use some terms and categories that will allow us to frame the overall discussion and help the reader to follow the thread of the arguments through this book.

A. JURISDICTION IN INTERNATIONAL LAW

1) Jurisdiction Defined

The term "jurisdiction" has multiple meanings and layers within meanings, all of which are driven by the context in which it is used. Generally the term "describes the limits of legal competence of a state or other regulatory authority . . . , to make, apply, and enforce rules of conduct upon persons."[1] Domestically speaking, jurisdiction is the ability of the

1 Vaughan Lowe & Christopher Staker, "Jurisdiction" in Malcolm Evans, ed, *International*

state, whether via the legislature, the executive, or the courts, to exert power over persons, places, and things.

A discussion of extraterritoriality, however, necessarily engages the state's ability to exert its power in ways that involve and affect people, places, and things that are beyond its borders. In the international legal system, the state is essentially a territorial entity and each state enjoys plenary jurisdiction within, and exclusive control over, its territory.[2] Any act that exerts power outside the state's territory necessarily implicates the interests of other states. This is manifestly so where the act in question affects another state's territory or citizens, as this quite directly engages the interests of the second state. It is equally true, however, even for areas such as the high seas or outer space. Because no state has plenary jurisdiction in these areas, all states have at least a conceptual interest in regulating the manner in which any other state acts, so as to safeguard their own interests.

Accordingly, the focus here must be on jurisdiction in its international law meaning. This invokes a number of different concepts and relationships. Most importantly, jurisdiction at international law "reflects the basic principles of state sovereignty, equality of states and non-interference in domestic affairs."[3] As explored in the next section, it is an overarching concept that provides a legal basis for states to sort out what each may do, and not do, particularly outside their borders.

2) Jurisdictional Actors: A Public Law Concept

In this book we discuss the justifications for, and limitations upon, acting extraterritorially. It is vital at the outset to recognize that jurisdiction

---

Law, 3d ed (Oxford: Oxford University Press, 2010) 313 at 313 [Lowe & Staker]. And see Bruno Simma & Andreas Müller, "Exercise and Limits of Jurisdiction" in James Crawford & Martti Koskenniemi, eds, *The Cambridge Companion to International Law* (Cambridge, UK: Cambridge University Press, 2012) 134 [Simma & Müller].

2 See, generally, Hugh M Kindred & Phillip M Saunders, eds, *International Law: Chiefly as Interpreted and Applied in Canada*, 7th ed (Toronto: Emond Montgomery, 2006) ch 2 [Kindred & Saunders].

3 Malcolm N Shaw, *International Law*, 6th ed (Cambridge, UK: Cambridge University Press, 2008) at 645. Indeed, Simma and Müller offer the intriguing observation that "it should not come as any surprise that the relations privileged by [the law of jurisdiction] reflect fundamental normative choices underlying the international legal order itself. In other words, in the micro-discipline of jurisdiction the macro-principles of contemporary international law become manifest" (Simma & Müller, above note 1 at 137).

is an inherently public law concept. One of the building blocks of the literature regarding the law of jurisdiction has, for many decades,[4] been the division of the state into three entities for the purpose of exercising jurisdiction.[5] These familiar branches are: the *legislative* or *prescriptive* branch, which refers to the ability of the state to make and apply laws to subject matter, whether that subject matter involves wholly domestic matters or touches on matters outside the state's territory; the *enforcement* or *executive* branch, which refers to the state's ability to act in such a manner as to give effect to its laws (including the ability of police or other government actors to investigate a matter, which the Supreme Court of Canada has referred to[6] as *investigative jurisdiction*); and the *judicial* or *adjudicative* branch, which refers to the ability of a state's courts to adjudicate cases, and particularly for our purposes, those with foreign elements. Here, we will use the terms legislative, enforcement, and adjudicative to categorize state actions.

Accordingly, any action taken by a state that can be called an exercise of jurisdiction must ultimately go through one or more of these branches. The exercise of jurisdiction operates across a spectrum of subject matter, and jurisdiction is a function of the level of state interaction with or intrusion into the subject matter. Depending on the subject matter, there may be an exercise of legislative, executive, or judicial jurisdiction—or there may be a combination of any two or three of them. In fact, it is rarely an action of only one branch of the state that is implicated. For example, as is often noted, while a state may nominally extend legislative jurisdiction, a practical exercise of that jurisdiction is not possible unless the state can lawfully gain both legislative and en-

4 For the classic exposition see Michael Akehurst, "Jurisdiction in International Law" (1972–73) 46 Brit YB Int'l L 145 at 145. See also FA Mann, "The Doctrine of Jurisdiction in International Law" (1964-I) 111 Rec des Cours 1 and Stephen Coughlan et al, "Global Reach, Local Grasp: Constructing Extraterritorial Jurisdiction in the Age of Globalization" (2007) 6:1 CJLT 29 [Coughlan et al].

5 Other international law writing and jurisprudence often refers to two categories, "prescriptive" and "enforcement" jurisdiction, with adjudicative jurisdiction being, at most, a sub-principle of enforcement (for a recent example, see Gideon Boas, *Public International Law: Contemporary Principles and Perspectives* (Cheltenham, UK: Edward Elgar, 2012) at 246). In our view, that typology is better suited for purely criminal law matters.

6 In *R v Hape*, 2007 SCC 26 at para 58 [*Hape*], the Court adopted this term as used by the current authors in Coughlan et al, above note 4.

forcement jurisdiction.[7] For example, if an individual murders his victim in Winnipeg and flees to Colorado, Canada has legislative jurisdiction over the murder, which took place in its territory, by way of the *Criminal Code*. However, it can exercise neither enforcement jurisdiction by arresting the murderer, nor adjudicative jurisdiction by trying him, at least until he is extradited to Canada or otherwise reappears. Further, as will be explored here, the *law* of jurisdiction changes depending upon which branch of the state is engaged in a particular exercise of jurisdiction; so, for example, the rules governing legislative jurisdiction are different from those regarding enforcement jurisdiction. It is important to understand this, not least because proposals for law reform should reflect a holistic idea of what kind of state action is being contemplated.

Criminal law, as explored in more detail below, is the domain from which the international law of jurisdiction originally emerged, and it is our primary source for examining the range of jurisdictional action and justification for extraterritorial action. It is therefore worth being aware that, at various stages, an exercise of criminal jurisdiction can involve all three state branches. The executive might sign a treaty with other states, agreeing to criminalize a particular act and exercise jurisdiction over it. Most such treaties are not self-executing[8] and will require an exercise of legislative jurisdiction (the passing of a law) to both criminalize the act and establish jurisdiction over it. The police, an arm of the executive branch of the state, exercise enforcement jurisdiction by investigating the crime and arresting suspects. The courts exercise adjudicative jurisdiction, first by determining whether they have the jurisdiction to adjudicate (either by looking to their inherent jurisdiction or determining whether the legislature has awarded them the power to adjudicate this particular matter) and then by trying and sentencing the perpetrator.[9]

---

7 Kindred & Saunders, above note 2 at 548; Sharon A Williams & Armand LC de Mestral, *An Introduction to International Law*, 2d ed (Toronto: Butterworths, 1987) at 125.

8 They are not self-executing because either the states themselves are dualist and require implementation of treaties into national laws (such as Canada) or, even in those states which directly incorporate treaties into the national law, the treaty provisions themselves tend to be framed on a general level, requiring some level of domestic interpretation and implementation in order to effectively translate them into domestic law. See on this point Neil Boister, "Transnational Criminal Law?" (2003) 14 EJIL 953.

9 For further explanation of adjudicative jurisdiction in the Canadian context, see Robert J Currie, "*Libman* at 25; or, Canada and Qualified Territoriality: Do We Understand Jurisdiction Yet?" in Chios Carmody, ed, *Is Our House in Order? Canada's Imple-*

Not all three branches need be involved in every exercise of extraterritorial jurisdiction. Not all treaties are concerned with prohibiting behaviour, for example, and so legislation might be necessary simply to empower the executive to act, without any enforcement function being needed. The *Civil International Space Station Agreement Implementation Act*, as one instance, primarily exists to grant the executive the ability to carry out Canada's obligations with regard to the Civil International Space Station: its focus is neither prohibitory nor regulatory.[10]

Indeed, depending on the subject matter, a specific exercise of jurisdiction might involve only one branch, with little or no activity from the other two. The executive in particular may engage in unilateral exercises of its jurisdiction, such as making diplomatic communications, imposing trade embargoes, or signing treaties or memoranda of understanding. This possibility is apparent in such statutes as the *Health of Animals Act*,[11] which allows the Minister of Agriculture to enter into agreements with or license agencies overseas. The courts in common law jurisdictions, when exercising their inherent powers, sometimes administer the (court-made) common law and act to resolve a dispute between parties that touches on more than one country, without any input from the legislature — though even then, attempts to enforce a civil judgment will likely involve the machinery and compulsory powers of the executive. In similar circumstances, civil law states would see various kinds of interaction between executive-level activity, legislative creation of the civil code, and judicial interpretation and enforcement of the code's provisions.

It is important, too, to recognize that an act of jurisdiction is still public, even if it is with regard to a subject matter thought of as "private." The courts may adjudicate public *law* (for example, criminal, regulatory, privacy, and so on), but they may also preside over private law disputes between parties. Those parties bring a private right of action that they possess before the court, and the court (in an act of adjudicative jurisdiction) determines whether it can adjudicate and proceeds to resolve the dispute. However, the court, as a branch of government, is a public law actor, and the act of adjudication itself is public. This is true even for private international law, with courts deciding whether they have jurisdic-

---

mentation of International Law (Montreal, Kingston: McGill-Queen's University Press, 2010) 199.

10 SC 1999, c 35.

11 SC 1990, c 21.

tion to hear disputes with foreign aspects or whether to enforce foreign awards or other judgments.[12]

In addition to all of these governmental, public law roles, there is also an aspect of extraterritoriality that primarily concerns private actors. An exceptional situation may exist where private parties (including the state, when it is acting as a private litigant) agree to submit a dispute to a private arbitral body of some sort, essentially contracting out of their legal and/or constitutional rights to have the courts hear the dispute. One might question whether the ability of the private body to deal with the matter should strictly be referred to as "jurisdiction" (a better term might be "competence," given the public law content and connotation of the word "jurisdiction"), but there is no question that the effect can be to resolve a dispute with an extraterritorial component. Even in this context, it is worth noting that public law jurisdiction is in the background of private dispute mechanisms. Governments may choose to outlaw these private mechanisms, or more realistically, may regulate access to them by statute[13] or civil code, or pass laws regarding when arbitral awards will and will not be enforced, including the enforcement of contracts containing mandatory arbitration clauses.[14]

3) The International Law of Jurisdiction: Customary and Treaty-Based

The previous section has dealt with the ways in which an exercise of jurisdiction is made manifest. This section will dig into the substance of the law of jurisdiction. While, as noted in Chapter 1, every state has its own domestic (and often constitutional) law dealing with the exercise of jurisdiction, jurisdiction in the sense we mean here is primarily

---

12 See *Beals v Saldanha*, 2003 SCC 72, with regard to enforcement of foreign monetary awards. See also *Pro Swing Inc v Elta Golf Inc*, 2006 SCC 52 for enforcement of foreign non-monetary awards. Even with enforcement of judgments, there is a public, executive element contemplated, insofar as execution on assets goes. For example, a US national is awarded a civil judgment against a Canadian national, and applies to the Canadian courts to order the award enforced (adjudicative jurisdiction). The court decides in favour, and the litigant has the award enforced by the sheriff executing upon the judgment debtor's assets in Canada (executive jurisdiction).

13 Most Canadian provinces have some sort of statutory regulation of arbitration, for example, Ontario's *Arbitration Act, 1991*, SO 1991, c 17.

14 See the discussion of private arbitration of extraterritorial disputes in Chapter 7, Section G.

a creature of customary international law.[15] The international customary rules on jurisdiction are binding on all states and establish a set of overarching principles that provides a legal basis for states to determine what each may do, and not do, inside and outside their borders. Given the potential for conflict between states as they exercise jurisdiction, it has been accurately stated that the purpose of this body of law "is to safeguard the international community against overreaching by individual [state]s."[16]

The starting point in international law is territoriality: in the international legal system, the state is essentially a territorial entity and each state enjoys plenary jurisdiction within, and exclusive control over, its territory.[17] A state's plenary jurisdiction over its territory, and every person and thing within it, is a function of state sovereignty. As other states are equally sovereign, it follows that as soon as one state exerts power in a way that purports to regulate or actively affect matters outside its borders, it will face, at least nominally, some limitations. This is captured in the inelegant but standard phrase, "extraterritorial jurisdiction."

The international law regarding the exercise of jurisdiction by states can be expressed simply: one state's exercise of sovereign power cannot infringe upon the sovereignty of another state or states. This is easy enough to assert, but nebulous and nuanced in application because judging where the line is crossed is a complex exercise. As explained below, the rules differ as between legislative and enforcement jurisdiction as well. The central point of conflict will be situations of *concurrent*

---

15 Customary international law refers to those rules of international law that are derived from the practices of states and the formal recognition by states that this state practice is obligatory (*opinio juris*). Customary international law principles bind all states, even those that have not formally consented to be bound. This is distinguished from treaty law, under which obligations arise by way of formal agreement between states. See, generally, Kindred & Saunders, above note 2 at 107–82.

16 Hannah L Buxbaum, "Transnational Regulatory Litigation" (2006) 46 Va J Int'l L 251 at 304. It is, in some ways, important not to understate the dangers presented by jurisdictional conflict. As Chris Ram has noted, in matters of jurisdiction, "[s]tates and intergovernmental organizations act with caution, deliberation and consensus because the consequences of precipitous unilateral actions can be dire. The First World War started, in part, because one State insisted on the right to conduct a criminal investigation into the murder of one of its officials on the sovereign territory of another." See Chris D Ram, "The Globalization of Crime as a Jurisdictional Challenge" (Paper delivered at the 2011 Annual Conference of the Canadian Council on International Law, Ottawa) [copy on file with authors] at 1.

17 See, generally, Kindred & Saunders, above note 2 at 13–106.

jurisdiction; that is, where two or more states have some legal claim to exercise jurisdiction over a particular matter.

It is worth noting that, as in all international legal disputes, resolution can be reached on an ad hoc basis; states can agree on where primary jurisdiction should lie on a case-by-case basis. For example, if a French citizen murders an American citizen in the territory of the United States, France may have a claim to jurisdiction over its national.[18] However, it is likely to defer to the United States since the United States is the state where the act occurred and probably where all of the evidence is located, as well as being the more aggrieved state of the two. Simply because a state notionally has jurisdiction over a matter does not necessarily mean that it will have any interest in exercising it.

Earlier in this chapter, we explained that a state may exercise three forms of jurisdiction: legislative, enforcement, and adjudicative. In the following discussion we consider the principles developed in international law that are applicable to the exercise of each kind of jurisdiction in turn.

a) Legislative Jurisdiction

International law has developed several principles concerning legislative jurisdiction to allow states to mitigate the conflict that may result from concurrent claims to jurisdiction. This system of "allocat[ing] competences"[19] is a direct outgrowth of the need to manage interstate relations, and while it is normative in character, it is functionalist in practice. As Professor Brownlie wrote, "the sufficiency of grounds for jurisdiction is an issue normally considered relative to the rights of other states and not as a question of basic competence."[20]

The starting point, of course, is the *territorial principle*, which renders territorial sovereignty (as discussed above) one of the bedrock jurisdictional notions. It is accepted that a state can assert jurisdiction over its territory, including the territorial sea, internal waters, airspace, and cer-

18 This falls under the "nationality principle," explained in Section A(3)(a)(i), below in this chapter.

19 Rosalyn Higgins, *Problems and Process: International Law and How We Use It* (Oxford: Clarendon Press, 1994) at 56 [Higgins]. By this phrase, Professor Higgins (as she then was) was referring to the use of principles of jurisdiction to determine which states had claims of jurisdiction over a matter and determining the relative strength of those claims (*ibid*).

20 Ian Brownlie, *Principles of Public International Law*, 7th ed (Oxford: Oxford University Press, 2008) at 299 [Brownlie].

tain maritime zones.[21] In the context of criminal jurisdiction, it is not unusual (and is increasingly typical) that a crime may take place in more than one state, either by way of elements of the crime occurring in more than one state, or where the crime is completed in one state but has effects in another. This has led to the development of a subclass of the territoriality principle, called *extended territoriality*, which is becoming more prominent both within and outside the criminal realm. The importance and complexity of separating this kind of case from those involving extraterritorial jurisdiction lead us to deal with it separately in Chapter 4.

Since territoriality is the starting point, it follows that the other jurisdictional principles are geared towards managing claims of extraterritorial jurisdiction—that is, they provide support for a state's ability to lawfully legislate regarding persons, things, or matters that are outside its territory. Four principles have gained some acceptance in international law as supporting legislative jurisdiction on an extraterritorial basis.

i) Nationality Principle

States may assert jurisdiction over the acts of their nationals, wherever the act might take place. This principle is employed more often by civil law than by common law states, but has nearly equal status with territoriality as a fairly universally accepted valid ground of jurisdiction.[22]

ii) Protective Principle

A state may assert jurisdiction "over acts committed abroad that are prejudicial to its security, territorial integrity, and political independence."[23] Examples of such acts are treason, espionage, and counterfeiting of state currency.

iii) Universal Principle

States may assert jurisdiction over certain criminal acts that are deemed to be offensive to the international community at large and thus justify broad jurisdictional permissiveness. This jurisdiction can be exercised even when the crime takes place outside the asserting state's territory, and neither the victims, evidence, nor any other aspect of the crime has any connection to the asserting state. Some examples are genocide,

---

21 Robert J Currie, *International & Transnational Criminal Law* (Toronto: Irwin Law, 2010) at 60–61 [Currie].

22 Currie, *ibid* at 66–68.

23 Kindred & Saunders, above note 2 at 559.

crimes against humanity, war crimes, and piracy.[24] Currently controversial is whether international law permits "absolute" universal jurisdiction, which allows a state to initiate proceedings against an individual for one of these crimes without having the individual in custody. A more common practice for those states that prosecute on this basis is to exercise "custodial" universal jurisdiction, prosecution being conditional on the apprehension of the accused in the territory of the asserting state.[25]

Certain treaty regimes oblige member states that apprehend an individual accused of the relevant crime to prosecute the individual regardless of whether there is any connection between the crime and the apprehending state. If the state does not wish to prosecute, then it is obliged to extradite the individual to a treaty partner state that indicates a willingness to prosecute (referred to in the literature as *aut dedare, aut judicare*, "extradite or prosecute").[26] This kind of jurisdiction is called "conditional" universal jurisdiction, and it can be distinguished from the broader notion of universality both by its mandatory character and by the fact that it applies only between the parties to the relevant treaty.

iv) Passive Personality Principle

Some states have, from time to time and controversially, asserted jurisdiction over acts that injured their nationals, regardless of territorial location.[27] It is increasingly accepted that passive personality jurisdiction can be used, though usually as a subsidiary principle, in cases of terrorist violence. The United States makes extensive use of this principle in anti-terrorism legislation.[28]

Exercising extraterritorial jurisdiction, then, is not necessarily prohibited under international law. In terms of international law methodology, it is controversial whether the law is permissive, in the sense that each state is free to exercise jurisdiction unless there is a prohibitive rule to the contrary,[29] or restrictive, requiring a state to justify its assertion of

---

24 Currie, above note 21 at 104–52 and 281–88.

25 This is the Canadian approach; see the *Crimes Against Humanity and War Crimes Act*, SC 2000, c 24 [*Crimes Against Humanity Act*].

26 Currie, above note 21 at 96–99.

27 *Ibid* at 68–69.

28 See, generally, Christopher L Blakesley, "Extraterritorial Jurisdiction" in M Cherif Bassiouni, ed, *International Criminal Law*, vol 2, 3d ed (Leiden: Martinus Nijhoff, 2008) at 83 [Blakesley].

29 An approach that is grounded in the famous *Lotus* case. See SS *"Lotus" (France v Turkey)* (1927), PCIJ (Ser A) No 10 [*Lotus*].

jurisdiction on some recognizable legal basis.[30] As Professor Ryngaert has noted, "it is unclear which doctrine has the upper hand,"[31] and in any event, the question is essentially one of burden of proof. The important point is that each of the jurisdictional principles above has the effect of legitimizing, to a greater or lesser extent, a state's claim to exercise jurisdiction over persons, places, and things beyond its territory. As there are no real rules regarding priority of jurisdiction under international law, these principles are essentially tools used by states to broker conflicts, usually in situations of concurrent jurisdiction. Moreover, there is one sense in which these principles are definitely permissive: no state is bound under customary international law to use any of them, and would only be required to do so under a treaty obligation to that effect.[32]

Recently, the principles described above have been employed as criteria within a more global test for the legality of an exercise of jurisdiction: whether there is "a substantial and bona fide connection between the subject-matter and the source of the jurisdiction."[33] Brownlie, among others, has posited that state jurisdiction over an extraterritorial act will be lawful where this primary test is met.[34] In a similar vein is the American rule of jurisdiction known as "reasonableness," which is set out in the *Restatement (Third) of US Foreign Relations Law*,[35] though the extent to which it reflects accepted international law principles is debatable.[36]

b) Enforcement Jurisdiction

Given the state sovereignty concerns at play when actual enforcement of law is concerned, the rules regarding the exercise of enforcement juris-

30 Lowe & Staker describe it as a need for a "clear connecting factor, of a kind whose use is approved by international law," above note 1 at 320.

31 Cedric Ryngaert, *Jurisdiction in International Law* (Oxford: Oxford University Press, 2008) at 21 [Ryngaert].

32 See, for example, *Case Concerning Questions of Interpretation and Application of the 1971 Montreal Convention Arising from the Aerial Incident at Lockerbie (Libya v United Kingdom)*, Order of 14 April 1992, [1992] ICJ Rep 3.

33 Brownlie, above note 20 at 311.

34 Brownlie would also require that in exercising jurisdiction, the state is not intervening in the domestic or territorial jurisdiction of another state, and that "elements of accommodation, mutuality, and proportionality" are applied (*ibid*).

35 American Law Institute, *Restatement of the Law Third: The Foreign Relations of the United States* (St. Paul, MN: American Law Institute, 1987) § 403.

36 See Jordan Paust, "International Law before the Supreme Court: A Mixed Record of Recognition" (2005) 45 Santa Clara L Rev 829 at 845.

diction are much more restrictive. As the Permanent Court of International Justice (PCIJ) wrote in the still-influential *Lotus* case, a state:

> may not exercise its power in any form in the territory of another State. In this sense jurisdiction is certainly territorial; it cannot be exercised by a State outside its territory except by virtue of a permissive rule derived from international custom or from a convention.[37]

Accordingly, not only will states not enforce the public (particularly criminal) laws of other states,[38] but absent exceptional circumstances, no state may enforce its own laws upon the territory of a second state without some clear legal authorization to do so.[39] This extends to both investigative jurisdiction[40] (so, for example, the police of one state cannot investigate in another state without the latter's permission[41]) and jurisdiction over the person (for example, the police of one state cannot arrest an individual in another state, again without the latter's permission).[42] In civil actions, a court cannot effect a subpoena on a witness in another state for lack of jurisdiction over the person. Likewise in civil matters, while a court of State A may grant judgment against a defendant, the successful plaintiff could not access the enforcement mechanisms of State A to execute that judgment against the defendant's assets in State B. Rather, the plaintiff would have to bring his judgment to a court in State B, which (incidentally, in an exercise of adjudicative juris-

---

37 *Lotus*, above note 29 at 18–19.

38 See *The Antelope*, 23 US (10 Wheat) 66 (1825), Marshall J.

39 As the Supreme Court of Canada has written, "[t]he general rule that a state's criminal law applies only within its territory is particularly true of the legal procedures enacted to enforce it; the exercise of an enforcement jurisdiction is 'inherently territorial'. . . .": *R v Terry*, [1996] 2 SCR 207 at para 17 [*Terry*].

40 In *Hape*, above note 6, the Supreme Court of Canada was dealing with a co-operative investigation between police officers of Canada and the Turks & Caicos, and identified "investigative jurisdiction" as a sub-principle of enforcement jurisdiction, involving "the ability of police or other government actors to investigate a matter." (*Ibid* at para 58, citing Coughlan et al, above note 4.)

41 As a recent example, in 2013 a dispute emerged regarding accusations by US police that Canadian police were operating an agent on US soil without the permission of the American government. See John Nicol & Dave Seglins, "L.A. Cocaine Bust Threatens Canada-U.S. Police Relations" *CBC News Canada* (12 February 2013), online: CBC www.cbc.ca/news/canada/story/2013/02/11/canada-us-police-relations.html.

42 Brownlie, above note 20 at 309; Higgins, above note 19 at 70; John Dugard, *International Law: A South African Perspective*, 2d ed (Kenwyn, SA: Juta & Co, 2000) at 173.

diction) would authorize its enforcement in State B through the sheriff or other state enforcement mechanism.

It is because of the prohibition on extraterritorial exercises of enforcement jurisdiction that states have developed co-operative mechanisms by which they exercise enforcement jurisdiction on each others' behalf, usually under treaty arrangements. The paradigmatic example is extradition, whereby states transfer individuals for criminal justice purposes (either to face prosecution or to serve previously imposed prison sentences), at the request of a state that seeks to exercise jurisdiction over the individual. Another example is mutual legal assistance, another typically treaty-based regime whereby states transfer evidence at the request of their partner states for use in criminal prosecutions.

A modern variety of co-operation in investigative jurisdiction is the establishment of arrangements whereby officials from one state are actually given authorization to operate on the territory of the co-operating state. This can have varying degrees of formality. For example, in the *Hape* case,[43] the Supreme Court of Canada focused on a joint investigation between RCMP officers and the local police in Turks & Caicos, and the evidence indicated that the Canadians had simply been given permission to investigate by a high-ranking police official in the area. More formally, in 2009 Canada and the United States concluded the *Framework Agreement on Integrated Cross-Border Maritime Law Enforcement Operations*,[44] a treaty that essentially authorizes each state's maritime enforcement personnel to exercise enforcement jurisdiction in the other state's waters (and in limited circumstances, on the other state's territory). Other kinds of co-operation are co-ordinated by intergovernmental policing networks such as Interpol and Europol.

c) Adjudicative Jurisdiction

The actions of any adjudicative bodies in a state (courts, paradigmatically) are driven by the domestic legal or constitutional order, and domestic courts do not view themselves, nor are they typically viewed, as

43 *Hape*, above note 6.

44 The *Framework Agreement on Integrated Cross-Border Maritime Law Enforcement Operations between the Government of Canada and the Government of the United States*, 26 May 2009, Can TS 2012 No 25 (entered into force 11 October 2012), online: Public Safety Canada www.publicsafety.gc.ca/cnt/rsrcs/pblctns/frmwrk-grmnt-ntgrtd-crss-brdr/index-eng.aspx, as implemented by the *Integrated Cross-Border Law Enforcement Operations Act*, SC 2012, c 19, s 368, online: Justice Laws Website http://laws-lois.justice.gc.ca/eng/acts/I-14.7.

actors on the international plane. That said, the actions of a court in choosing to exercise jurisdiction over a particular dispute, and making a decision or issuing a judgment about that dispute, can obviously have extraterritorial effects, and the actions of a domestic court are treated as the actions of its parent state to the extent of any such effects. Moreover, courts are definitely charged with discovering, assessing, and applying the legal rules (both domestic and international) about their exercises of jurisdiction over matters with extraterritorial aspects. As these rules encapsulate both legislative and enforcement activities, courts will generally view themselves as being constrained by both sets of rules,[45] and assessment by other states of any actions they take will be made pursuant to those rules. As one commentary explains it:

> Where a national court asserts that its domestic laws are applicable to particular conduct occurring outside its state's territory, it is exercising [legislative] jurisdiction and should be subject to those principles. Where it convicts, sentences and punishes an offender, it is exercising enforcement jurisdiction and should accordingly be subject to the enforcement rules.[46]

Thus, a court's exercise of adjudicative functions may depend in part on the legislative and enforcement powers of the state over the particular matter in dispute.

4) The Principles Applied

These rules emerged from the criminal law stable, and as a result they are quite broad in scope and fairly permissive in nature. On the whole they are not well-developed, and certainly not as well-developed as rules relating to extended territorial and extraterritorial jurisdiction that have evolved in the courts of various states for use in their domestic legal systems.[47] Historically, they have worked fairly well in the criminal

---

45 That is, unless the state is authorized to exceed or violate international law under the domestic constitutional order. This is the case for Canada — Parliament is constitutionally competent to exercise its jurisdiction in excess of international law. See the text surrounding note 79, below in this chapter.

46 International Bar Association, *Report of the Task Force on Extraterritorial Jurisdiction* (6 February 2009) at 10 [*IBA Report*]. The report also notes that the rules, if any, are less clear regarding courts that apply the law of foreign states or apply international law, *ibid.*

47 Blakesley, above note 28 at 94–95.

law sphere, where the reasonably rare interstate conflicts have tended to be resolved via negotiation between prosecutorial authorities or governments; one does not see a surfeit of cases before the International Court of Justice regarding criminal jurisdiction.[48]

Also, there are two other limiting factors that temper or otherwise guide states' exercises of extraterritorial jurisdiction. The first is the concept of international comity or *comitas gentium*. Comity has been described as encompassing "the rules of politeness, convenience and goodwill observed by States in their mutual intercourse without being legally bound by them."[49] It is "an attitude of respect and deference as between states, and a firm determination not to act in a manner that interferes with this respect and deference unless strictly necessary, despite there being no obligation to defer in this way."[50] Comity, then, can be employed in all three exercises of extraterritorial jurisdiction. Legislatively, a legislature may enact statutes that are designed to accommodate the interests of other states, or that avoid particular techniques so as not to tread on any comity toes. The executive will naturally have myriad ways to entertain comity concerns in the exercise of the state's foreign affairs power. The judiciary will use comity, as the Supreme Court of Canada framed it, as a principle of interpretation that guides courts in how to exercise adjudicative jurisdiction.[51]

The second limiting factor is awareness on the part of a state as to how a particular exercise of jurisdiction may have an impact on the formation or interpretation of international law norms themselves. While this is not the place for an extended discussion of the methodology regarding customary international law, a customary international law norm is one

---

48 However, they are not unheard of. See *Case Concerning Questions of Interpretation and Application of the 1971 Montreal Convention Arising from the Aerial Incident at Lockerbie (Libya v United States)*, Order of 14 April 1992, [1992] ICJ Rep 114; *Case Concerning the Arrest Warrant of 11 April 2000 (Congo v Belgium)*, [2002] ICJ Rep 3; *Questions Relating to the Obligation to Prosecute or Extradite (Belgium v Senegal)*, [2012] ICJ Rep 422, online: International Court of Justice www.icj-cij.org/docket/index.php?p1=3&p2=3&code=bs&case=144&k=5e.

49 Brownlie, above note 20 at 29 citing L Oppenheim, *International Law: A Treatise*, vol I, 8th ed, by H Lauterpacht (London: Longmans, Green & Co, 1963) at 34. As Brownlie noted, "comity" is also used "in four other ways: (1) as a synonym for international law; (2) as equivalent to private international law (conflict of laws); (3) as a policy basis for, and source of, particular rules of conflict of laws; and (4) as the reason for and source of a rule of international law." (Brownlie, above note 20 at 29 [citations omitted].)

50 Currie, above note 21 at 40.

51 *Hape*, above note 6 at para 47.

that arises from some practice that is consistent among a large majority of states (state practice), accompanied by a demonstrable recognition on the part of states that this practice incurs a legal obligation (*opinio juris*).[52] When a state undertakes a particular exercise of jurisdiction that is not expressly permitted under customary international law, it is creating new state practice. If a number of other states either do likewise or acquiesce to this exertion of jurisdiction, the practice may crystallize into a rule of law. Thus, a rationally acting state will consider that, while it may be in its immediate self-interest to exercise jurisdiction in a particular case, caution might be called for on the basis that other states may follow suit, which may not be in the first state's medium- to long-term interest.[53]

However, the customary principles of jurisdiction have worked less well for private law disputes. Certainly they are binding upon all state exercises of jurisdiction in private international law, whether it be legislative, enforcement, or adjudicative.[54] However, in private international law cases, the interests presented are more economic than public-order oriented, and thus the major players reasonably desire and demand predictability.[55] As a result, national systems of private international law (or conflicts of law) are much more detailed and nuanced than the more indeterminate and malleable public international law rules,[56] in "recognition that civil jurisdiction is not merely an exercise of State power,

52 Kindred & Saunders, above note 2 at 148; Gibran van Ert, *Using International Law in Canadian Courts*, 2d ed (Toronto: Irwin Law, 2008) at 21–24.

53 States will also consider whether their act might trigger an act of repulsion by a state that is affected by an exercise of extraterritorial jurisdiction, a topic that is discussed below.

54 While this proposition has some historic controversy attached to it, "[t]he weight of opinion supports the proposition that the existence of the State's right to exercise jurisdiction is determined by public international law (which, accordingly, provides the standard by which municipal rules can be measured) and that public international law regulates the consequences of the wrongful exercise of [civil] jurisdiction" (Jonathan Hill, "The Exercise of Jurisdiction in Private International Law" in Patrick Capps, Malcolm Evans, & Stratos Konstadinidis, eds, *Asserting Jurisdiction: International and European Legal Perspectives* (Oxford: Hart, 2003) 39 at 43–44).

55 "The fundamental significance of jurisdiction is to enable the parties to foresee the extent of their liability and assess the legal and practical expense of defending a dispute in a particular jurisdiction." Lorna Gillies, "Addressing the "Cyberspace Fallacy": Targeting the Jurisdiction of an Electronic Consumer Contract" (2008) 16:3 Int'l JL & IT 242 at 245, citing Adrian Briggs, *The Conflict of Laws* (Oxford: Oxford University Press, 2002).

56 Ryngaert, above note 31 at 17.

but also a means of resolving private disputes."[57] Public international law principles have informed the growth and development of private international law principles, particularly in those areas where public law legislation is privately enforced, such as securities, anti-competition, and intellectual property laws. There are also specific public international law treaties that facilitate interstate co-operation in private law disputes, though these are more in the way of basic machinery[58] rather than assisting in jurisdictional selection. On the whole, however, most commentators note that there has been a commingling and confluence between the rules of jurisdiction as they apply purely to public matters and as they apply to private law matters[59] — particularly, as we will explore later,[60] regarding the Internet.[61] Accordingly, we will discuss jurisdiction in various areas of substantive law throughout this book, but always with an eye to their impact on the overall international law of extraterritorial jurisdiction.[62]

Another relevant point is that states often seek to manage the exercise of jurisdiction and head off disputes by concluding treaties, both bilateral and multilateral, which contain obligations regarding the co-ordination of exercising jurisdiction over particular matters. Again, the most prominent of these emerge from the criminal law field and are often referred to as the "suppression conventions,"[63] examples being the

57 Oren Bigos, "Jurisdiction Over Cross-Border Wrongs on the Internet" (2005) 54:3 ICLQ 585 at 586.

58 See, for example, *Hague Convention on the Service Abroad of Judicial and Extrajudicial Documents*, 15 November 1965, TIAS No 6638, 20 UST 361, online: Hague Conference on Private International Law www.hcch.net/index_en.php?act=text.display&tid=44.

59 Christopher Kuner, "Data Protection Law and International Jurisdiction on the Internet (Part 1)" (2010) 18 Int'l JL & IT 176 at 183, citing in particular Alex Mills, *The Confluence of Public and Private International Law* (Cambridge, UK: Cambridge University Press, 2009) at 298.

60 See Chapter 5.

61 Uta Kohl, *Jurisdiction and the Internet: A Study of Regulatory Competence over Online Activity* (Cambridge, UK: Cambridge University Press, 2007) at 19.

62 It may also be worth noting that we are specifically trying to avoid the use of jurisdictional terminology that has emerged from US private international law jurisprudence, which is very popular in the literature — i.e., the concepts of "subject matter jurisdiction" or "personal jurisdiction." We avoid them because they have very specific meanings within that body of law, whereas we are discussing the overall international law. References to that terminology, if any, will be found only within specific discussions of US private international law.

63 Currie, above note 21 at 96–99.

UN *Convention on Transnational Organized Crime*[64] and the *Terrorist Bombings Convention*.[65] These treaties typically provide that each state party is obliged to criminalize a particular act; exercise jurisdiction over it on a number of bases (including those set out above); agree to the exercise of extraterritorial jurisdiction by other states parties over the relevant offences, even if a given state does not typically exercise such jurisdiction; and participate in processes (often consultative) to resolve jurisdictional conflicts short of adjudication. States forestall conflicts and co-ordinate prosecutions in this way. Efforts to co-ordinate extraterritorial jurisdiction over private law areas have been less successful.[66]

5) Distinguishing Extraterritorial Effects from Extraterritorial Jurisdiction

As we have shown, jurisdictional conflicts can arise where more than one state is able to claim jurisdiction concurrently, which must mean that one or both claims have some extraterritorial element. A final but important distinction to be made is between an exercise of jurisdiction that may be properly said to be extraterritorial, and a domestic action that may have extraterritorial effects but is not an assertion of extraterritorial jurisdiction. As a matter of domestic policy, states may take actions that will have, or are even designed to have, extraterritorial effects of some kind, but cannot be said to be an exercise of extraterritorial jurisdiction.

For example, the European Union has put into place a ban on the importation of seal products from Canada, due to domestic distaste for the seal hunt.[67] This is simply a matter of closing borders to products that a state (or states) does not wish to have come into the country. As a matter of jurisdictional reach, it is a wholly domestic measure. Yet it is designed to have an impact outside the EU, specifically to pressure the Canadian government into ending or more assiduously regulating the seal hunt. Essentially, one domestic exercise of jurisdiction is being used in such a way as to convince another state to make a particular ex-

---

64 *Convention against Transnational Organized Crime*, 15 November 2000, 2225 UNTS 209, TIAS No 13127.

65 *International Convention for the Suppression of Terrorist Bombings*, 15 December 1997, 2149 UNTS 256, Can TS 2002 No 8.

66 *IBA Report*, above note 46 at 89–92.

67 See EC, *Trade in Seal Products* (11 March 2011), online: European Commission Environment http://ec.europa.eu/environment/biodiversity/animal_welfare/seals/seal_hunting.htm.

ercise of jurisdiction on its own. However, in our view, this is more of a political tactic than a legal one. Were the EU to put in place directives that its member states pass laws purporting to regulate the Canadian seal hunt or prosecute Canadian sealers, that would be an exercise of extraterritorial jurisdiction (specifically legislative).

Another example of measures having extraterritorial effect is the 1995 passage of the EU Data Protection Directive,[68] which established norms for the protection of the processing of personal information of EU residents. One of the most controversial aspects of the directive was the set of rules it established around the transfer of data for processing to a third country. Such transfers were only to be permitted where that country could ensure an "adequate" level of protection.[69] As a result of this directive, other countries whose businesses wanted to continue to be able to process European data had to act to set data protection norms that would meet the standard of "adequate" as assessed by the EU. In the end a handful of countries, including Canada, Switzerland, and Argentina, enacted legislation that was found to meet the EU standards.[70] In the United States, while new data protection legislation was not forthcoming, a "safe harbour" agreement was negotiated which permitted US companies to qualify as "safe harbours" for EU data so long as they met certain standards for the processing of data.[71] Although there was nothing explicitly extraterritorial about the EU Data Protection Directive, it nevertheless had an extraterritorial effect, as it compelled foreign governments either to enact new laws or to negotiate new agreements.

---

68 EC, *Directive 95/46/EC of the European Parliament and of the Council of 24 October 1995 on the protection of individuals with regard to the processing of personal data and on the free movement of such data*, [1995] OJ L 281 at 31.

69 *Ibid*, art 25.

70 Lilian Edwards, "Privacy and Data Protection Online: The Laws Don't Work?" in Lilian Edwards & Charlotte Waelde, eds, *Law and the Internet*, 3d ed (Portland: Hart, 2009) 443 at 454.

71 Note that an EU review of safe harbour was generally dissatisfied with the level of protection offered. See EC, *The Implementation of Commission Decision 520/2000/EC on the Adequate Protection of Personal Data Provided by the Safe Harbour Privacy Principles and Related Frequently Asked Questions Issued by the US Department of Commerce*, SEC (2004) 1323 final (20 October 2004), online: European Commission Justice http://ec.europa.eu/justice/policies/privacy/docs/adequacy/sec-2004-1323_en.pdf. Edwards notes that data processing outside the European Union in non-approved countries may still take place if the data subject consents, or if special contractual clauses are in place. She observes that the use of contractual terms in the export of data for processing is increasingly common. Edwards, *ibid* at 455.

B. CURRENT CANADIAN APPROACHES TO EXTRATERRITORIAL JURISDICTION

1) Introduction: Asserting and Responding to Extraterritorial Action

To comprehend the practice of extraterritorial jurisdiction of a particular state, one must focus on three things: (1) the constitutional arrangement of the state in terms of whether and to what extent any branch of government is empowered to act extraterritorially; (2) the manner in and extent to which international law principles are implemented into the domestic law framework; and (3) the state's actual extraterritorial assertions of jurisdiction in various areas of law, both public and private. This is what this section seeks to do vis-à-vis Canada.

The international principles of jurisdiction discussed in Section A have been exercised by Canada in the country's own distinctive ways. As explained above, extraterritorial jurisdiction may be asserted by any organ of government—legislative, executive, or judicial. Extraterritorial power can be expressed by legislating to criminalize foreign behaviour, by executive orders-in-council to impose trade embargoes on foreign ports, or by judicial orders for the service of process abroad. As noted in Chapter 1, the ultimate authority for any branch of government to act extraterritorially depends on the Canadian Constitution and its grants and limitations of power. In addition to the unilateral assertion of extraterritorial authority, Canada may also exercise jurisdiction abroad through agreements with foreign states. Such agreements may take the form of bilateral agreements, multilateral treaties, or United Nations obligations.

Just as Canada may assert extraterritorial jurisdiction, it must also expect that other states will also try to exercise extraterritorial power that may, deliberately or coincidentally, have impacts on Canada and its interests. This prospect should moderate Canada's own assertion of extraterritorial jurisdiction, which ought to be rational and measured so as not to undercut Canadian diplomacy regarding excessive claims of extraterritorial jurisdiction by other states. In short, the probability of like — even reciprocal — assertion of extraterritorial authority by states demands a degree of comity.

The impacts on Canada of foreign extraterritorial actions may be excessive and objectionable or reasonable and unobjectionable. Many such actions occur pursuant to bilateral or multilateral treaties that reciprocally permit states parties to exercise jurisdiction. In such instances, Canada may assert jurisdiction extraterritorially but, equally, has accepted by agreement in advance that the other states parties may exercise their jurisdiction in or against Canada (for example, via the criminal suppression conventions, discussed above in Section A). In situations not subject to treaty arrangements, the independent assertion of jurisdiction by foreign authorities may still be reasonable (such as enforcement of choice of forum clauses in commercial contracts). Then Canada, on grounds of comity, may decide it would be more appropriate to defer to the foreign jurisdiction and not to exercise its own territorial authority. But sometimes the exercise of extraterritorial jurisdiction by foreign states has negative impacts for Canada. In response, Canada has found it expedient and necessary to repulse such foreign actions by unilateral, domestic responses (such as blocking and clawback legislation) for the protection of Canadian interests.

Since the mechanisms used by Canada to assert or to respond to extraterritorial action have been developed through practise and experience, they follow no set pattern or order. There is often considerable overlap of legislative, enforcement, and adjudicative functions between the legislative, executive, and judicial organs of any government, and of course this is true for Canada. For example, the executive government may prescribe regulations (subsidiary legislation), the legislatures may call witnesses and hold individuals in contempt, and judges regularly deliver court orders after adjudications. For each organ, the cited actions are examples of the principal function of another organ, but that does not invalidate them. Further, extraterritorial jurisdiction need not be exercised by each organ of government independently; frequently, the participation of two or more will be required to achieve the desired extraterritorial outcome. For instance, Parliament's proscription of crimes against humanity[72] even outside Canada was an act of legislative extraterritorial jurisdiction. Yet it has no effect unless, upon commission of such a crime, the police and prosecutors (elements of the executive branch of government exercising enforcement jurisdiction) investigate the offence and interview the witnesses at the foreign site, and then a Canadian court (in its adjudicative capacity) executes the extraterritorial jurisdiction over the foreign crime, granted to it by the same legislation, to hear the case against the accused.

What follows is a set of illustrative examples representing a cross-sectional review of the mechanisms Canada has used, first in asserting

---

72 In the *Crimes Against Humanity Act*, above note 25.

extraterritorial jurisdiction, and then in responding to its exercise by foreign states. The responsive mechanisms are divided into two sections to reflect the acceptance and the repulsion of foreign extraterritorial action. For convenience of appreciation, all three sections explain the means employed by Canada to exercise, accept, or repel extraterritorial jurisdiction under the legislative, executive, and judicial processes separately.

2) Means to Assert Jurisdiction Extraterritorially

a) Legislation

Parliament's extensive power to prescribe laws will only result in their enforcement when Canada has jurisdiction over both the act and the actor. While Parliament has the sovereign capacity to legislate extraterritorially, the application of its enactments to foreign events and persons, as explained in Section A(3)(b), above in this chapter, may not be enforced in a foreign state without the authorization of that state. Parliament, however, does not always address the issue of enforcement, but leaves statutes to be applied by the other organs of government, namely the executive and the courts. Extraterritorial legislation exists in five jurisdictional forms:

1) Jurisdiction over extraterritorial subject matter. This arises where Parliament has enacted specific legislative provisions that apply to events that take place outside its borders. For example, the *Competition Act*[73] section 46 prohibits anti-competitive agreements made abroad by domestic Canadian corporations. Similarly, the child sex tourism provision of the *Criminal Code*[74] applies to conduct by Canadians abroad.
2) Jurisdiction over extraterritorial persons of any nationality. Parliament may enact legislative provisions that apply to anyone, regardless of nationality, outside its territorial borders. For example, the *Criminal Code* section 477.1 prescribes offences on board Canadian ships at sea, some of which may be committed by Canadians, and others by foreigners.
3) Jurisdiction over extraterritorial persons who are Canadian officials. In this case, Canadian law would apply to the acts of Canadian officials overseas, such as RCMP or military personnel on operations abroad.[75]

---

73 RSC 1985, c C-34 [*Competition Act*].

74 RSC 1985, c C-46, s 7(4.1) [*Criminal Code*].

75 For example, the *National Defence Act*, RSC 1985, c N-5, s 67.

4) Jurisdiction over extraterritorial acts by extraterritorial actors. In this instance, Parliament enacts laws that apply to conduct outside Canada, regardless of the nationality of the actor. For example, the *Crimes Against Humanity and War Crimes Act*,[76] especially sections 6 and 8, deal with offences committed outside Canada and give Canada jurisdiction over the perpetrators.
5) Jurisdiction over extraterritorial places outside other states' territory. Parliament may enact laws that apply in certain locations outside of Canadian territory such as Antarctica and space.[77]

Most legislation is mandatory in its prescriptions — that is, it acts directly to compel performance or to criminalize misbehaviour or non-compliance — and territorial in its ambit. Yet legislation may also be used as a persuasive tool to affect the conduct of its addressees extraterritorially. This is a particularly effective means to assert legislative influence over the extraterritorial conduct of individuals and corporations who reside, do business, or hold property within Canada. Various pieces of economic sanctions legislation not only prohibit certain types of trade with certain countries, but also impose duties on affected businesses to determine on a continuing basis whether they control property of designated foreign interests and to disclose information known to them about such property or transactions in it.[78] This type of legislative activity reflects the distinction, made above, between an exercise of extraterritorial jurisdiction and an exercise of domestic jurisdiction that has some extraterritorial effect.

In addition, although international law may express limits on a state's jurisdiction, as discussed in Section A above, Parliament is constitutionally capable of enacting legislation in contravention of international law.[79] The particular circumstances of the occasion will determine how wise or unwise such a parliamentary course of action will

---

76 Above note 25.

77 For example, the *Antarctic Environmental Protection Act*, SC 2003, c 20; the *Space Station Agreement Act*, above note 10; and the *Remote Sensing Space Systems Act*, SC 2005, c 45.

78 For example, *Regulations Implementing the United Nations Resolution on Eritrea*, SOR/2010-84 ss 11 & 12 made under the *United Nations Act*, RSC 1985, c U-2. See also the *Special Economic Measures Act*, SC 1992, c 17 [*Economic Measures Act*] and regulations; and the *Criminal Code*, above note 74, ss 83.01–83.05 and *Regulations Establishing a List of Entities*, SOR/2002-284.

79 *Attorney General for Canada v Attorney General for Ontario*, [1937] AC 326 (JCPC); *Hape*, above note 6 at paras 53–56.

be. A classic instance occurred in 1970 when Canada adopted regulatory and managerial powers over large areas of the Arctic seas by enactment of the *Arctic Waters Pollution Prevention Act*.[80] Many states, including the United States, objected to this assertion of authority as excessive and in contravention of the international law of the sea at the time. However, Canada asserted that the environmental fragility of the area demanded special protective laws and it successfully carried this argument in the UN Conference on the Law of the Sea, which was then underway. As a result the United Nations *Convention on the Law of the Sea*[81] contains article 234, which vindicates Canada's legislation.

This discussion of the extraterritorial legislative power of Parliament does not apply to the provincial legislatures, which are constitutionally limited to their own territories. Thus a province that wishes to apply its legislation extraterritorially may do so only with the aid of the federal government.[82] Not surprisingly, for political reasons associated with a province's concern for its plenary authority, this has rarely occurred. It is also awkward legally to achieve. One attempt may be seen in the *Oceans Act*,[83] sections 9 and 21, which permit the application of provincial laws outside the province in the coastal waters and other offshore areas within Canadian (federal) jurisdiction. The technique used is to allow the province to request the federal government to pass orders-in-council to extend application of the provincial statute in question to the offshore area adjacent to the province. In other words, the provincial legislation is asserted extraterritorially by fiat of the federal executive. This power in the *Oceans Act* has been exercised to apply Prince Edward Island's laws in the area of the Confederation Bridge from Prince Edward Island to New Brunswick.[84]

b) Executive Action

While legislative organs of government obtain their authority from the Canadian Constitution, executive acts of government are derivative assertions of power. To be valid, all executive and administrative decisions

---

80 RSC 1985, c A-12.

81 *United Nations Convention on the Law of the Sea*, 10 December 1982, 1833 UNTS 3 (entered into force 16 November 1994).

82 On this point see Armand de Mestral & Evan Fox-Decent, "Rethinking the Relationship between International and Domestic Law" (2008) 53 McGill LJ 573 at s E.

83 SC 1996, c 31.

84 *Confederation Bridge Area Provincial (PEI) Laws Application Regulations*, SOR/97-375.

must be clothed with the authority of some enabling statute or Crown prerogative power. Nonetheless, the Government of Canada is a principal source of extraterritorial action. Moreover, the action may be prescriptive or executory. Frequently a statute gives a minister of the Crown prescriptive authority to make regulations (i.e., to exercise subordinate legislative power) establishing rules, standards, and policies of operation, as well as enforcement power to appoint officials to administer the regulations, either by directly executing them for the government or by policing their performance by their addressees. The powers of the Minister of Fisheries and Oceans under the *Fisheries Act*[85] are good examples of this combined legislative and enforcement authority to regulate fishing in the extraterritorial seas off Canada's coasts.

The range of means of taking extraterritorial action is great. For convenience, the techniques may be divided between unilateral measures and participatory acts, which may be either bilateral or multilateral in nature. Unilateral measures are obviously within the exclusive force and control of the government. They are typically addressed to both natural and juridical persons abroad, whether they are Canadians or foreigners. For example, ministers may make discretionary orders about foreigners, such as decisions involving migrants under the *Immigration and Refugee Protection Act*[86] on humanitarian and compassionate grounds or out of public policy considerations.[87] Or the government may promote codes of good conduct for Canadians abroad, such as corporate social responsibility and human rights standards for Canadian companies and their officers when investing and operating in developing countries.[88]

Unilateral acts may also be addressed to foreign states and their governments. Thus, the Canadian government may make demands or requests of a foreign government for its assistance in reaching persons extraterritorially, as it does when it asks for the extradition of fugitive offenders under the *Extradition Act*.[89] It may also try to influence the actions and policies of foreign governments in order to have them respect Canada's rights and interests or to protect Canadians present in the

85 RSC 1985, c F-14, s 43.

86 SC 2001, c 27.

87 *Ibid*, ss 25.1 & 25.2.

88 See the Canadian government's Office of the Extractive Sector Corporate Social Responsibility (CSR) Counsellor online: Foreign Affairs and International Trade Canada www.international.gc.ca/csr_counsellor-conseiller_rse/index.aspx.

89 SC 1999, c 18.

foreign state. Thus, the Canadian government may impose economic sanctions against a foreign state or its property under the *Economic Measures Act*[90] for grave breaches of international peace and security. Less forcefully, the government may pursue diplomatic avenues to influence a foreign state's policies or actions that affect Canada. Representations at rising diplomatic levels of contact with a foreign government may be made on behalf of Canadians subjected to mistreatment in its territory. Maher Arar's detention and torture in Syria as a supposed terrorist was a much-publicized instance. The subsequent formal inquiry into the conduct of various Canadian government bodies in the affair disclosed, *inter alia*, that efforts were made to obtain his return to Canada initially by the actions of consular officials, then by representations of the Canadian ambassador to Syria, followed by an intervention of the Minister of Foreign Affairs, and ultimately a letter from the prime minister.[91]

When extraterritorial issues between Canada and foreign states are not confrontational, comity and co-operation may be better ways to resolve them. Such participatory means to control extraterritorial jurisdiction may be bilateral or multilateral. For example, Canada has written a number of bilateral memoranda of understanding (MOUs), that is, reciprocal non-binding statements of policy, with other states for the better administration of practical, everyday matters between them. So, for example, Canada has a MOU with the United States concerning indigenous peoples and the north that sets out mutual objectives for co-operative efforts over a range of northern affairs, including the preservation of the cultures and the sustainable development of indigenous communities.[92] Another arrangement between Canada and France pro-

---

90 Above note 78.

91 Commission of Inquiry into the Actions of Canadian Officials in Relation to Maher Arar, *Report of the Events Relating to Maher Arar: Analysis and Recommendations* (Ottawa: Public Works and Government Services Canada, 2006) at 32–45, online: Security Intelligence Review Committee www.sirc-csars.gc.ca/pdfs/cm_arar_rec-eng.pdf. A similar course of negotiations was ultimately successful in freeing Abdullah Khadr from mistreatment and detention at the hands of Pakistan's intelligence agency (which was done, in turn, at the behest of the CIA): *United States of America v Khadr*, 2011 ONCA 358, leave to appeal to SCC refused, [2011] SCCA No 316.

92 Aboriginal Affairs and Northern Development Canada, *Memorandum of Understanding between the Department of Indian and Northern Affairs Canada and the Department of the Interior of the United States of America concerning Indigenous and Northern Issues* (29 March 2010), online: Aboriginal Affairs and Northern Development Canada www.aadnc-aandc.gc.ca/eng/1100100014184.

vides for mutually satisfactory performance of inspection, maintenance, airworthiness, and operation of aircraft leased between them.[93]

Multilateral techniques are even better solutions to conflicting extraterritorial claims because they reflect a common interest among a broader range of contending states to resolve the claims. It has proved effective and efficient for Canada to promote multilateral negotiations with foreign states to harmonize their national laws internationally in line with Canadian standards and interests. Canadian government initiatives of this kind within the International Maritime Organization have produced uniformity of regulation of the international shipping industry in many ways, to the mutual benefit of Canadian overseas traders and all other users of its services. Agreements on the law governing international sales contracts and the requirements for intercountry adoptions are further examples of the application of multilateral solutions to conflicts of extraterritorial jurisdiction.[94]

However, there is some risk to Canada in pursuing such multilateral paths — specifically, that other more powerful states, such as the United States and the European Union, may overpower Canadian influence and turn the negotiations away from Canadian interests and objectives. In addition, a spirit of co-operation and mutual benefit is an essential condition for the success of these participatory techniques of handling extraterritorial tensions. Proof is evident in the failure to date of nation states, Canada among them, to negotiate a treaty to criminalize terrorism generally. Only specific types of terrorism have been outlawed internationally because, as it is quipped, one state's terrorist is another state's freedom fighter.[95]

c) Judicial Process

Courts, as the interpreters of legislation and reviewers of administrative action, are frequently the arbiters of the jurisdiction of the other organs

---

93 Transport Canada, *Memorandum of Understanding on the Lease of Aircraft Between Direction Générale de l'Aviation Civile (France) and Aviation Group, Department of Transport (Canada)* (18 March 1991), online: Transport Canada www.tc.gc.ca/eng/civilaviation/standards/int-memoranda-france-3684.htm.

94 See *United Nations Convention on Contracts for the International Sale of Goods*, 11 April 1980, 1489 UNTS 3, Can TS 1992 No 2 and Convention on Protection of Children and Co-operation in Respect of Intercountry Adoption, 29 May 1993, Can TS 1997 No 12 (entered into force 1 May 1995).

95 For a discussion of international anti-terrorism efforts, see the case study in Chapter 7, Section D.

of government. But to exercise their own adjudicative authority, they must have effective control over both the acts and the actors involved. In other words, as discussed above, they require both prescriptive jurisdiction over the subject matter and executory power over the persons involved. When any one of these elements of a case is outside Canada, the courts have to find a legitimate basis for stretching the reach of their territorial jurisdiction. This is not a problem when some statute grants such authority. An example already mentioned is the *Crimes Against Humanity and War Crimes Act*, [96] by which the courts are empowered to try offenders for extraterritorial offences.

Ordinarily, a Canadian court cannot proceed with a case without personal jurisdiction over the parties. In criminal cases, if the accused is outside Canada, the usual procedure is to seek her extradition, but this process normally requires that an extradition treaty exists between Canada and the foreign state where the fugitive is located. In civil cases, a foreign defendant might submit to the jurisdiction of the Canadian court voluntarily, by counterclaiming against the plaintiff, or by prior agreement, such as a choice of forum clause in a transnational or extraterritorial contract. If the defendant does not attorn to the court in one of these three ways, he may be served with process *ex juris* if he ordinarily resides in Canada or if the case is sufficiently connected to Canada.[97] Exceptionally, foreign defendants may be pressured to appear by attachment of their property within the forum, such as the arrest of a ship that enters a Canadian port.

The required degree of association of a case with Canada to found jurisdiction in both criminal and civil proceedings is now a common standard. The test determines whether the subject matter of the case has a "real and substantial connection" to the forum.[98] In criminal cases, even if this test is satisfied, the court must still obtain control over a for-

96 Above note 25.

97 See, generally, Stephen GA Pitel & Nicholas S Rafferty, *Conflict of Laws* (Toronto: Irwin Law, 2010).

98 *R v Libman*, [1985] 2 SCR 178 (criminal) and *Morguard Investments Ltd v De Savoye*, [1990] 3 SCR 1077 [*Morguard Investments*] (civil) as modified in *Club Resorts Ltd v Van Breda*, 2012 SCC 17 [*Club Resorts*]. See also Uniform Law Conference of Canada, *Court Jurisdiction and Proceedings Transfer Act* (adopted in 1994), online: ULCC/CHLC www.ulcc.ca/en/uniform-acts-en-gb-1/183-court-jurisdiction-and-proceedings-transfer-act/1092-court-jurisdiction-proceedings-transfer-act [*CJPTA*]. Even though this test is met, the court's jurisdiction in civil actions may still be subject to *forum non conveniens* and state immunity claims, discussed in Chapter 4, Section C.

eign accused. In civil suits, the plaintiff who satisfies the real and substantial connection test will usually be permitted to serve process on the absent defendant *ex juris*.

This approach has allowed courts to assert jurisdiction over a great variety of claims involving transnational features, including, for example, the breach of an Ontario probation order that took place in Cuba;[99] a Canadian answering machine message that referred callers to a hate message broadcast by way of an American phone number;[100] an alleged libel on an Illinois website which was downloaded, read, and republished in three newspapers in Ontario;[101] an electronic contract for the purchase and sale of a computer that included a link to an international arbitration clause;[102] and a copyright issue regarding "international Internet transmissions."[103] It bears reiterating, however, that the assertion of jurisdiction in these cases was made on the basis of their territorial connection to Canada. Though the cases included extraterritorial facts, the jurisdiction applied was *not* extraterritorial.[104] A truly extraterritorial assertion of civil jurisdiction might be mounted in exceptional cases when Canada is the forum of last resort.[105]

Even when a Canadian court has complete jurisdiction over the parties and the events in issue between them, it may face difficulties in proceeding with the hearing if the evidence is extraterritorial. If foreign witnesses do not appear voluntarily, a subpoena directed abroad can be issued — but can also be ignored. An order for taking testimony abroad is also possible, but it requires the co-operation of foreign authorities for its fulfillment. Similarly, orders for the production of information and documents abroad, and letters rogatory to foreign courts are also judicial assertions of extraterritorial authority that may readily be rebuffed. In criminal matters, these extraterritorial limitations on the judicial process are increasingly alleviated nowadays by interstate agreements for mutual legal assistance, as discussed further in this subsection. In

99 *R v Greco* (2001), 155 OAC 316 (CA).

100 *Canada (Canadian Human Rights Commission) v Canadian Liberty Net*, [1998] 1 SCR 626.

101 *Breeden v Black*, 2012 SCC 19.

102 *Dell Computer Corp v Union des consommateurs*, 2007 SCC 34.

103 *Society of Composers, Authors and Music Publishers of Canada v Canadian Assn of Internet Providers*, 2004 SCC 45 at para 60.

104 This crucial distinction is fully explored in Chapter 4.

105 *Charron Estate v Village Resorts Ltd*, 2010 ONCA 84 but on further appeal *sub nom Club Resorts*, above note 98, the Supreme Court deliberately did not comment on the doctrine. However it is included in the *CJPTA*, above note 98, s 6.

civil litigation, co-operative arrangements have been reached in some areas where the government is involved (for example, in mutual legal assistance in civil competition matters[106]), but private Canadian plaintiffs must seek to satisfy Canadian orders with the aid of foreign courts as best they can.

The application of the *Canadian Charter of Rights and Freedoms* in extraterritorial situations has presented some special complications. The Supreme Court of Canada has taken a cautious approach in criminal matters where its general stance has been to confine the *Charter* to Canadian territory. In extradition cases, for example, the Court has drawn careful lines: while the *Charter* (especially section 7's requirement of respect for fundamental justice) applies to the domestic extradition process, the criminal process and penalties in the requesting state are not subject to *Charter* scrutiny, as this would amount to impermissible extraterritorial application.[107] The possible fate of the accused in the requesting state is nonetheless relevant to the section 7 inquiry in Canada. The courts have blurred the distinction slightly by finding that extradition to face a foreign criminal process or punishment that would "shock the conscience" of Canadians constitutes a violation of section 7 by the Canadian state.[108]

In cases where criminal evidence was gathered on foreign soil, the Supreme Court has consistently held that the *Charter* will not be applied

---

106 See the *Competition Act*, above note 73, Part III. Canada has concluded agreements with the Republic of Korea, Japan, the United States, Mexico, Europe, Australia, New Zealand, the United Kingdom, Chile, Costa Rica, and Brazil, online: Competition Bureau www.competitionbureau.gc.ca/eic/site/cb-bc.nsf/eng/h_00128.html#a5.

107 *United States of America v Burns*, 2001 SCC 7 [*Burns*].

108 It has been ventured that it is misplaced concern about extraterritorial application of the *Charter* that has caused this blurriness; see Robert J Currie, "*Charter* without Borders? The Supreme Court of Canada, Transnational Crime and Constitutional Rights and Freedoms" (2004) 27 Dal LJ 235. The "shocks the conscience" bar is high, and has only been reached in a small number of cases. Chief among these are *Burns* itself (*ibid*), where the accused would have faced the death penalty; *Philippines (Republic) v Pacificador* (2002), 60 OR (3d) 685 (CA), leave to appeal to SCC refused, [2002] SCCA No 390, where the accused would have been deprived of essentially every procedural right; *Doyle Fowler c Canada (Ministre de la Justice)*, 2011 QCCA 1076, where the accused would have faced a life sentence without parole for a crime allegedly committed while he was a minor; and *United States of America v Leonard*, 2012 ONCA 622, where the Aboriginal accuseds would have faced sentencing laws that did not take their Aboriginal heritage into account, and could easily have been tried in Canada.

directly to the acts of foreign authorities, even where they are the subject of adjudication in the Canadian trial.[109] Constitutional scrutiny of the acts of Canadian officials on foreign soil, however, has been a much more contentious matter. In its 1998 decision of *R v Cook*,[110] the Court was willing to apply the *Charter* to the acts of Canadian police who had questioned a suspect detained in the United States, but only because they had obtained the consent of American authorities to do the questioning and therefore did not interfere with the foreign state's exercise of its own territorial sovereignty. However, in 2007, the Court reversed itself in the case of *R v Hape*,[111] finding that the *Charter* could not apply extraterritorially to the actions of Canadian police who were involved in a joint investigation in Turks & Caicos. To do so, the Court ruled, would be an act of extraterritorial enforcement jurisdiction, which would violate the sovereignty of the foreign state. However, the Court did leave open two exceptions: where the foreign state had given its permission for the application of Canadian law to its territory; and "where the participation of Canadian officers in investigative activities sanctioned by foreign law would place Canada in violation of its international obligations in respect of human rights."[112] The latter "human rights exception" has come into play in the Court's major post-*Hape* jurisprudence, all of which involves the role Canadian state officials played in the fate of Omar Khadr, a Canadian imprisoned at the US detention facility in Guantanamo Bay.[113]

The *Hape* line of cases has been quite controversial, and offers some interesting insights into the interplay between domestic and international laws on the exercise of extraterritorial jurisdiction; accordingly, it is the subject of a case study in Chapter 7, Section A. It is worth

---

109 *Terry*, above note 39; *R v Harrer*, [1995] 3 SCR 562; *Schreiber v Canada (AG)*, [1998] 1 SCR 841. In each of these cases, however, the Court noted that any unfairness to the trial that resulted from the manner in which the foreign officials gathered the evidence could be remedied during the trial, and thus strictly territorially, under ss 7 and 11(d) of the *Charter*.

110 [1998] 2 SCR 597 [*Cook*].

111 Above note 6.

112 *Ibid* at para 101.

113 *Canada (Justice) v Khadr*, 2008 SCC 28; *Canada (Prime Minister) v Khadr*, 2010 SCC 3. See Robert J Currie, "A Tale of Two Brothers: The Impact of the *Khadr* Cases on Canadian Anti-Terrorism Law" in C Forcese & F Crépeau, eds, *Terrorism, Law and Democracy: Ten Years After 9/11* (Montreal: Canadian Institute for the Administration of Justice, 2012) 307.

remarking that in other kinds of police co-operation cases, the courts have sometimes strayed very near to extraterritorial application of the *Charter*. In *Purdy v Canada (Attorney General)*,[114] for example, the British Columbia Court of Appeal ruled that an individual was entitled to a remedy for breach by the RCMP of his section 7 right to full answer and defence, even though the trial was to be held in Florida.

Personal status is another matter that presents transnational jurisdictional problems for the courts. International recognition of an individual's marriage, divorce, custody, adoption, or legitimacy is crucial. A Canadian court may become involved in making determinations about the status of a person who is or goes abroad. Conversely, the courts may have to decide whether to recognize an individual's status as determined in a foreign jurisdiction. In some situations, multilateral treaties protect an individual's status between Canada and other states parties.[115] In other circumstances, the application of conflicts of law rules, either Canadian or foreign, may sort out the issue of extraterritorial recognition.[116] Even so, disputing parties may seek to challenge the decision of a Canadian court beyond its reach in a foreign forum, when restraint and comity become the only safeguards against conflicting orders determinative of extraterritorial status.[117]

Even when a Canadian court has full jurisdictional control over a case, extraterritorial problems may still arise over fulfillment of its judgment. In civil actions, ordinarily the winner of a case against a foreign defendant must seek to enforce the Canadian judgment against the foreign loser in the foreigner's courts. However, on occasion, it may be possible to obtain a Canadian court order for execution of the sanction

---

114 2003 BCCA 447.

115 For example, *Convention on the Nationality of Married Women*, 20 February 1957, 309 UNTS 65, Can TS 1960 No 2.

116 This can become quite controversial. Consider the matter of a same-sex couple who had been married in Toronto but were domiciled in Florida and the United Kingdom. When they sought a divorce from the Ontario courts, the Government of Canada intervened and argued that, because under the conflicts of law rules the marriage had to be valid under the laws of both the state of marriage and the state of domicile, their marriage had in fact not been valid. See Janyce McGregor, "Same-sex Divorce Options Explored by Harper Government" *CBC News* (12 January 2012), online: CBC News www.cbc.ca/news/canada/toronto/story/2012/01/12/pol-harper-same-sex-marriage.html?cmp=rss.

117 See for example, *Thomson v Thomson*, [1994] 3 SCR 551, in which parents struggled over custody of their child in both Scottish and Canadian courts under the *Convention on Civil Aspects of International Child Abduction*, 25 October 1980, Can TS 1983 No 35.

or remedy when it is capable of being levied against some property of the foreigner found within Canada,[118] or may be enforced by compulsory transfer of title to movable property of the foreigner that is subject to Canadian control, such as the registration of ships. In criminal cases, judgments against property are not common, but when made are subject to the same kind of principles. Thus personal property used in the commission of crime and seized by the police in Canada may be declared forfeit to the Crown.[119]

Judgments and court orders for penalties and remedies against an absconding defendant pose other extraterritorial problems. Fines for criminal convictions and damages in civil suits may not be collectable if the individual leaves Canada, but court orders may be made to freeze or seize any local assets left behind. Personal remedies of maintenance, specific performance, injunction, and accounting, when granted by Canadian courts against fugitive or foreign defendants, may not be honoured unless the plaintiff can enlist the aid of a foreign court to enforce them.

d) Bilateral Agreement

Rather than act unilaterally, Canada's extraterritorial objectives may be more readily achieved through co-operation and agreement with foreign states. Bilateral agreements may be ad hoc arrangements or permanent treaties. Seeking the ad hoc consent of foreign authorities is a quick and straightforward way to deal with particular extraterritorial incidents.[120] For example, in *R v Cook*,[121] Canada sought and received permission from US authorities for the RCMP to interview Deltonia Cook in jail in New Orleans. The permission of the foreign state allows Canadian authorities to act in a "sovereign" manner without infringing upon the sovereignty of the host.

Permanent treaties for the allocation of extraterritorial authority come in several forms as follows:

1) *Standing agreements for mutual assistance and co-operation over extraterritorial matters.*

   By these treaties, Canada may request and expect a treaty partner to exercise its territorial powers to perform the extraterritorial

118 For example, *Zschiegner v United States of America*, 2001 NSCA 74.

119 *Criminal Code*, above note 74, s 490.1.

120 The reverse is also possible: a foreign government might ask the Canadian government to provide police or military aid in Canada.

121 Above note 110.

action desired by Canada. These treaties are typically both mutual and reciprocal. Classic examples are the Canada-US Agreement Regarding the Application of Their Competition and Deceptive Marketing Practices Laws[122] and the Canada-US Treaty on Mutual Legal Assistance in Criminal Matters.[123] Their titles explain their intended functions. The latter has been implemented by the *Mutual Legal Assistance in Criminal Matters Act*,[124] for reciprocal application in favour of US extraterritorial requests to Canada. Canada also has a series of bilateral agreements with various states about taxation.[125] In addition to limiting the double taxation of Canadians on their foreign income, these agreements also organize the mutual and reciprocal exchange of information to prevent fiscal evasion and prohibit discriminatory tax practices.

2) *Standing agreements for reciprocal extraterritorial authority.*
The treaties in this class permit Canada to operate its legal system or some part of it, such as enforcement of Canadian laws by federal officials, within the jurisdiction of the other state party. An example is the Exchange of Notes (that is, a treaty) between Canada and the United States regarding the application between them of the NATO Status of Forces Agreement.[126] Another arrangement with the

---

122 *Agreement between the Government of Canada and the Government of the United States of America Regarding the Application of Their Competition and Deceptive Marketing Practices Laws*, 3 August 1995, Can TS 1995 No 15, 36 ILM 311.

123 *Treaty between the Government of Canada and the Government of the United States of America on Mutual Legal Assistance in Criminal Matters*, 18 March 1985, Can TS 1990 No 19 (entered into force 24 January 1990).

124 RSC 1985, c 30 (4th Supp).

125 For example, *Convention between the Government of Canada and the Government of the United Kingdom for the Avoidance of Double Taxation and the Prevention of Fiscal Evasion with respect to Taxes on Income and Capital Gains*, 8 September 1978, Can TS 1980 No 25 (entered into force 17 December 1980); *Convention between the Government of Canada and the Government of the French Republic for the Avoidance of Double Taxation and the Prevention of Fiscal Evasion with respect to Taxes on Income and on Capital*, 2 May 1975, Can TS 1976 No 30 (entered into force 29 July 1976).

126 *Exchange of Notes Constituting an Agreement Between the Government of Canada and the Government of the United States to Facilitate Co-operation Between Military Services of the Two Countries*, 19 August 1994, Can TS 1994 No 34, with reference to *Agreement Between the Parties to the North Atlantic Treaty Regarding the Status of their Forces*, 19 June 1951, Can TS 1953 No 13 [*NATO Status of Forces Agreement*].

United States is the Agreement on Air Transport Preclearance,[127] by which Canada has obtained (on a reciprocal basis) legal authority to apply its customs, immigration, and border controls to travellers to Canada on the territory of the United States. Still another example is the co-operation between the US and Canadian governments regarding cross-border policing, most recently exemplified in the implementation of an agreement[128] allowing US police to exercise enforcement powers in Canada (and vice versa), via the *Integrated Cross-Border Law Enforcement Operations Act*.[129]

3) *Standing agreements for mutual extraterritorial authority.*
In this category of treaties, the states parties exercise a shared jurisdiction over a transnational activity. One example is the International Joint Commission over use and abuse of Canada-US boundary waters pursuant to the 1909 Boundary Waters Treaty.[130] Another occurs under NAFTA when bilateral panels hear claims between states parties, and when Canadian courts review arbitral awards of Chapter 11 claims by US or Mexican corporations of unlawful expropriation in each other's territories.[131]

e) Multilateral Agreement

Multilateral treaty making offers the greatest opportunity for the widest resolution of conflicting assertions of extraterritorial jurisdiction. They fall into the following two categories:

1) *Multi-party treaties granting reciprocal extraterritorial authority.*
These are not yet common, though one example is the UN Fish Stocks Agreement.[132] Under article 21 on enforcement of regional fisheries

---

127 *Agreement on Air Transport Preclearance Between the Government of Canada and the Government of the United States*, 18 January 2001, Can TS 2003 No 7 (entered into force 2 May 2003) [*Canada-US Agreement on Air Transport Preclearance*].

128 Above note 44.

129 *Ibid.*

130 *Treaty between the United Kingdom and the United States of America relating to Boundary Waters and Questions arising along the Boundary between Canada and the United States*, 11 January 1909, UKTS 1910 No 23.

131 *North American Free Trade Agreement*, Can TS 1994 No 2, 32 ILM 289 and 605 implemented in Canada by the *North American Free Trade Agreement Implementation Act*, SC 1993, c 44. For a Chapter 11 example, see *Canada (AG) v SD Myers, Inc*, 2004 FC 38.

132 *Agreement for the Implementation of the Provisions of the United Nations Convention on the Law of the Sea of 10 December 1982 relating to the Conservation and Management of*

rules, Canada may exercise boarding, inspection, and detention powers against foreign fishing vessels on the high seas, as regulated by the *Coastal Fisheries Protection Act*.[133]

2) *Multi-state organizations exercising mutual extraterritorial authority.* A host of specialized agencies of the United Nations take concerted action on extraterritorial problems in specific sectors of human concern. Canada participates in a variety of such intergovernmental organizations which maintain: (a) bodies for overseeing the implementation of the organization's purposes (for example, the Conference of the Parties to the Convention on International Trade in Endangered Species (CITES),[134] and the Conference of the Parties to the Convention on Biological Diversity[135]), (b) entities for inspecting, monitoring, verifying, and reporting compliance of states parties with the organization's rules and standards (for example, the International Atomic Energy Agency's oversight of nuclear facilities), and (c) organs with supranational decision-making authority (for example, the World Trade Organization's Dispute Settlement Board).

The United Nations Organization (UNO) deserves special mention because of the universality of its functions and membership and the uniqueness of its supranational powers in many areas. Multilateral attention by UNO to extraterritorial concerns has become a very significant part of its work as the central world body in the current transition to globalism within so many fields of human interest and endeavour. As a member of UNO, Canada bears responsibility, along with all the other member states, to fulfill its duties under the *UN Charter*. From time to time, these may include collective measures of the organization or, in other words, extraterritorial action by Canada in association with other member states in the name of UNO. Under UNO's authority, Canada may act extraterritorially when:

1) Canada implements UNO's obligations incurred under a mandatory decision of the Security Council to sanction foreign states, for in-

---

Straddling Fish Stocks and Highly Migratory Fish Stocks, 4 August 1995, 2167 UNTS 3, 34 ILM 1542 (ratified by Canada 3 August 1995).

133 RSC 1985, c C-33, as amended by SC 1994, c 14; *Coastal Fisheries Protection Regulations*, CRC, c 413.

134 *Convention on International Trade in Endangered Species of Wild Fauna and Flora*, 2 July 1974, 993 UNTS 243, Can TS 1975 No 32.

135 *Convention on Biological Diversity*, 11 June 1992, Can TS 1993 No 24, 31 ILM 822.

stance by orders made under the *United Nations Act*;[136] and

2) Canada voluntarily participates in measures authorized by Security Council resolution under the *United Nations Charter*, Chapter VII (peacekeeping missions to foreign states).

3) Responses to Extraterritorial Action against Canada

Obviously, extraterritorial jurisdiction is not only exercised by Canada. Other states also take extraterritorial action, which sometimes impacts Canada. These impacts may be intrusive yet benign, or excessive and objectionable. Canada responds in different ways to foreign extraterritorial acts depending whether or not they are acceptable. Therefore, it will be convenient to discuss the means of accepting or repulsing foreign acts of state separately.

a) Accepting Foreign Extraterritorial Acts

i) Legislation

Extraterritorial actions of foreign states that are acceptable to Canada are mostly taken according to the terms of a prior reciprocal arrangement with Canadian treaty partners. Such arrangements, like the examples given below, usually need to be implemented by legislation in Canadian law. The legislation may authorize foreign officials to exercise specific powers within Canada, such as the authority granted to US customs and immigration officers to apply the US border regime within Canada to passengers to the United States under the *Preclearance Act*.[137] Statutes may also be enacted to grant a foreign state jurisdiction over particular places or subject matter within Canada. For example, the *Visiting Forces Act*[138] sets out the criminal and civil jurisdiction that the United States may exercise on its agreed military bases in Canada.

ii) Executive Action

The federal government's responsibility for the conduct of Canada's foreign affairs, under the prerogative power of the Crown, gives the executive considerable freedom of action in dealing with foreign states,

---

136 RSC 1985, c U-2.

137 SC 1999, c 20, which implements the *Canada-US Agreement on Air Transport Preclearance*, above note 127.

138 RSC 1985, c V-2, pursuant to the *NATO Status of Forces Agreement*, above note 126.

including issues of extraterritorial jurisdiction. A frequent unilateral action is to welcome a foreign head of state to Canada with the liberty of full immunity from the jurisdiction of the Canadian legal system. The executive's power to make treaties with foreign states enables it to handle matters at the interface of their respective jurisdictions in amicable ways. There are also examples of bilateral agreements, such as the arrangements for the construction of bridges between Canada and the United States,[139] and of multilateral conventions, like the *Convention on International Civil Aviation*[140] and the *Convention on the International Regulations for Preventing Collisions at Sea*, widely known as *COLREGS*.[141]

Executive power to make decisions whether to accept or reject foreign extraterritorial applications of law to Canada may also arise from the provisions agreed in the conclusion of bilateral or multilateral treaties. For instance, where an extradition agreement is in force between Canada and a foreign state, the Minister of Justice must decide, in accordance with the *Extradition Act*,[142] whether to fulfill a request for the extradition of a fugitive in Canada. Similarly, under multilateral conventions, Canada is bound to protect the interests of a variety of foreign rights holders. Thus Canadian officials are required to accept compliant applications from foreigners, along with Canadians, for the registration of their trademarks and plant breeders' rights.[143]

iii) Judicial Process

The adjudicative power of Canadian courts, even when they appear to have territorial jurisdiction, may be limited or restrained by competing foreign extraterritorial claims. There are, in other words, situations in which the courts consider it appropriate, or are even compelled by law, to recognize the priority of the jurisdiction of some foreign state. These situations are mostly of two kinds.

---

139 Implemented by legislation in *An Act Respecting the Buffalo and Fort Erie Public Bridge Company*, SC 1934, c 63, the *Campobello-Lubec Bridge Act*, SC 1958, c 23 and the *Blue Water Bridge Authority Act*, SC 1964-65, c 6.

140 7 December 1944, 15 UNTS 295, Can TS 1944 No 36 and its multiple subsequent Protocols.

141 20 October 1972, Can TS 1977 No 45 (entered into force 15 July 1977).

142 Above note 89. The minister's discretionary decision may only be taken upon a committal order following an extradition hearing by a Canadian superior court.

143 See the *Trade-marks Act*, RSC 1985, c T-13 and the *Plant Breeders' Rights Act*, SC 1990, c 20.

First is the challenge in civil cases against the inconvenience of the forum. Upon a finding of sufficient connection of a case with Canada to found extended territorial jurisdiction, the defendant may still argue that the Canadian court is *forum non conveniens*.[144] If it is shown that a foreign court is a "clearly more appropriate forum" to adjudicate the case,[145] the Canadian court will likely, out of comity, dismiss the action.

Second, foreign states, their leaders, officials, and representatives are entitled to immunity from the jurisdiction of the courts in Canada. Under international law, a foreign state that is recognized by Canada is a sovereign equal and consequently it may not be subjected to the Canadian legal system. The principle applies equally to Canada within foreign states. The privilege of the foreign state is sourced in customary international law. It is no longer a blanket immunity—there are exceptions. The rules are impressed in Canadian law by the *State Immunity Act*.[146] In consequence, Canadian courts will dismiss cases brought against a foreign state or its officers and representatives respecting acts done in their official capacities, unless the circumstances fall within one of the limited exceptions. The practice with regard to foreign diplomats has been codified in a multilateral treaty—the *Vienna Convention on Diplomatic Relations*[147]—to which Canada is a subscribing party. As a result, claims against such persons or wrongs committed by them while accredited to Canada may not be pursued within a Canadian court. Equally, a Canadian court may not issue any kind of process or order against such individuals either within or outside Canada.

Canadian courts also have responsibilities regarding various requests from foreign state organs for assistance in the extraterritorial execution of their functions. The courts must decide whether to accede to and enforce in Canada such applications as a foreign government's request for the extradition of a fugitive,[148] a foreign police force's approach for legal assistance in a criminal investigation,[149] and the petition of a

---

144 *Morguard Investments*, above note 98; *Club Resorts*, above note 98; and *CJPTA*, above note 98, s 11.

145 *Club Resorts*, *ibid* at paras 108–9.

146 RSC 1985, c S-18.

147 18 April 1961, 500 UNTS 95, Can TS 1966 No 29, implemented by the *Foreign Missions and International Organizations Act*, SC 1991, c 41.

148 This is done under an extradition treaty and the *Extradition Act*, above note 89. This is a combined function of the courts and the Minister of Justice.

149 Pursuant to the conditions of the *Mutual Legal Assistance in Criminal Matters Act*, above note 124.

foreign court's letters rogatory.[150] In addition, Canadian courts have to determine how to respond to the requests of successful plaintiffs for the enforcement of their foreign judgments, as a matter of comity or bilateral treaty,[151] and their foreign arbitral awards, pursuant to the New York Convention.[152]

iv) International Agreement

Treaties, by definition, are mutual and often are also reciprocal. The classes of international agreements concluded by Canada in sections B(2)(d) & (e) above on means to assert jurisdiction extraterritorially by bilateral and multilateral agreement not only entitle Canada to exert its legal authority extraterritorially, but also oblige Canadian organs of government to recognize and accede to reciprocal extraterritorial acts and requests by the treaty partner in Canada. Provided the foreign state party complies with the provisions and procedures of the particular treaty, its application of extraterritorial power will be acceptable to Canada.

b) Repulsing Foreign Extraterritorial Acts

i) Legislation

Foreign state assertions of extraterritorial jurisdiction that Canada considers excessive are likely to be parried or repulsed in one way or another. Legislatively, Canada may enact measures to counter the impacts of objectionably intrusive foreign state acts in order to protect or provide remedies to affected Canadians. These often take the form of "blocking" and "clawback" statutes. An example is the federal *Foreign Extraterritorial Measures Act*,[153] which permits the attorney general, upon finding

---

150 Pursuant to the *Canada Evidence Act*, RSC 1985, c C-5, s 46; *OPSEU Pension Trust Fund v Clark* (2006), 270 DLR (4th) 429 (Ont CA), sets out the standard for enforcement of letters rogatory.

151 For example, *Convention between the Government of Canada and the Government of the United Kingdom providing for the Reciprocal Recognition and Enforcement of Judgments in Civil and Commercial Matters*, 24 April 1984, Can TS 1987 No 29, UKTS 1988 No 74 [*Canada-United Kingdom Convention*].

152 *Convention on the Recognition and Enforcement of Foreign Arbitral Awards*, 10 June 1958, Can TS 1986 No 43 (entered into force 7 June 1959) [*New York Convention*] as implemented by the *United Nations Foreign Arbitral Awards Convention Act*, RSC 1985, c 16 (2d Supp).

153 RSC 1985, c F-29. Similar legislation has been enacted by provinces, for example, Ontario's *Business Records Protection Act*, RSO, 1990, c B.19 and Quebec's *Business Concerns Records Act*, RSQ c D-12.

that Canadian trade and commercial interests are adversely affected by a foreign state's actions, to do the following:

1) to prohibit natural or legal persons in Canada from (a) following that state's executive directives and judicial orders, or (b) supplying any requested or required documents and information;
2) to prohibit the enforcement of any judgment of that state's courts in Canada;
3) to permit the Canadian defendant to sue the foreign plaintiff in the Canadian courts for recovery of an equal sum where the judgment is executed against local assets of the Canadian defendant in the foreign state.

Parliament has also enacted legislative overrides of foreign choice of forum or choice of law clauses in transnational contracts. An example is the *Marine Liability Act*,[154] by which Canadian shippers/exporters and importers/consignees of goods by sea may be given (a) the choice of a Canadian court or arbitration regardless of the terms of any choice of forum clause, and (b) the benefit of Canadian law irrespective of any contracted choice of foreign law.

ii) Executive Action

Acting through its delegated powers, the executive can respond in several ways to jurisdictional overreach by foreign states. One mechanism is the discretionary ministerial order, available under many different types of legislation. A good example of this is the *Extradition Act*,[155] which empowers the attorney general to refuse to extradite a person in Canada to a foreign state on several grounds, including where the requesting state is exercising extraterritorial jurisdiction over the offence that forms the basis of the request.[156]

In its exercise of the federal foreign affairs (prerogative) power, the executive may also make diplomatic responses to the foreign state's extraterritorial actions. These can be "soft" or conciliatory options (for example, ambassadorial representations, state-to-state negotiations) or "hard" options (for example, unilateral withdrawal of trade and aid). The

---

154 SC 2001, c 6, s 46 (plus Part 5 & Schedule 3) [*Marine Liability Act*].

155 Above note 89.

156 *Ibid*, s 47(e). In practice no such refusals are made, though see *Romania (State) v Cheng* (1997), 158 NSR (2d) 13 (SC), aff'd (1997), 162 NSR (2d) 395 (CA) for a similar case.

executive can also make orders for countermeasures, such as temporary non-performance or suspension by Canada of obligations to a foreign state commensurate with the injury suffered from its excessive extraterritorial acts.[157]

iii) Judicial Process

The judiciary has neither the range nor the scope of power enjoyed by the legislative and executive branches of government to respond to extraterritorial acts by foreign states, and, in any event, tends to be leery of adjudicating cases that may affect them. Comity commends Canadian courts to be respectful of the sovereignty of foreign states.

As guardians of their own process and the ultimate arbiters of applicable law, however, the courts are fully empowered to handle foreign claims, usually made by private actors, for the primacy of some foreign jurisdiction. In response, procedural tools may be used to control such attempts to oust Canadian jurisdiction. Thus the Canadian court might reject a foreign choice of forum clause or a foreign choice of law clause in a multinational contract. However, this power is not commonly exercised, due to the common law's reluctance to interfere with contractual relations any more than necessary[158] unless a statute authorizes it.[159] Another procedural weapon that may be employed when the Canadian court has determined that it is *forum conveniens* but the (foreign) defendant persists in commencing proceedings in a foreign court is to issue an anti-suit injunction. Such an order is directed to the defendant in the Canadian court, not against the foreign court, and so is not an affront to the territorial sovereignty of the foreign state. But a Canadian court has no means to enforce such an injunction in a foreign court, which may decide to ignore its effects.

---

157 See International Law Commission, *Draft Articles on the Responsibility of States for Internationally Wrongful Acts*, in Report of the International Law Commission on the Work of its Fifty-third Session, UNGAOR 56th Sess, Supp No 10, UN Doc A/56/10, (2001) arts 49–52 and *Vienna Convention on the Law of Treaties*, 23 May 1969, 1155 UNTS 331 (1969), Can TS 1980 No 37, art 60.

158 See *ZI Pompey Industrie v ECU-Line NV*, 2003 SCC 27; and *Momentous.ca Corp v Canadian American Association of Professional Baseball Ltd*, 2012 SCC 9.

159 For example in contracts for the carriage of goods by sea by virtue of the *Marine Liability Act*, above note 154.

Canadian courts may also rebuff foreign court orders or government demands that wade too deeply into Canadian jurisdiction. The refusal to recognize or enforce foreign court judgments and arbitral awards is one way Canadian courts can control the assertion of foreign extraterritorial jurisdiction, though they may be subject to treaties[160] that usually limit this power. Further, Canadian courts, though they may acknowledge a decision of a foreign state's court, will not generally assist in the execution of the foreign state's penal, fiscal, and confiscatory laws, nor any foreign law that contravenes a fundamental rule of Canadian public policy.[161]

iv) International Agreement

All of the bilateral and multilateral treaties mentioned in sections B(2)(d) & (e) above on means to assert jurisdiction extraterritorially by bilateral and multilateral agreement operate reciprocally, affording the same rights of extraterritorial actions by foreign treaty partners where Canada asserts extraterritorial jurisdiction against them. The treaties, however, also set limits on the exercise of extraterritorial authority, and therefore provide reciprocal protection for Canadian interests. Should a foreign state breach a convention's negotiated standards by an excessive exercise of extraterritorial power, Canada may respond defensively by using any of the techniques discussed in this section. Typically, it would proceed from a soft stance, such as expressions of displeasure and negotiations, through progressively firmer measures up to the hard realities of international countermeasures and protective domestic legislation. Canada might also respond offensively with "equal and opposite" measures, that is, by asserting similar extraterritorial jurisdiction against the offending foreign state, as well as by pursuing international law remedies for breach of treaty.

---

160 For example, the *Canada-United Kingdom Convention*, above note 151 and the *New York Convention*, above note 152.

161 See *Laane v Estonian State Cargo & Passenger Steamship Line*, [1949] SCR 530.

Table 3.1. Means of Asserting Canadian Jurisdiction Extraterritorially (ET)

Type of Action	*Type of Jurisdiction*	*Example*	*Comments*
Legislation	Prescription		
	1) Over ET subject matter	Child sex tourism	Led international initiative
	2) Over ET persons (nationals and aliens)	Offences on board Canadian ships	Avoids lawless territory
	3) Over ET persons (Canadian officials)	RCMP and military personnel acting abroad	Control of public face of Canada
	4) Over ET acts and actors	Crimes against humanity	Pursuant to universal jurisdiction
	5) Over ET places	Antarctica and outerspace	Avoids lawless territory
Executive Action	Enforcement		
	1) Unilateral		
	a) Requests	Protection of Canadians abroad and extradition requests	Normal interstate relations
	b) ET orders	Imposition of economic sanctions	Usually pursuant to a decision of an IGO
	c) ET decisions	Discretionary immigration decisions	International law respects national choices
	2) Bilateral	MOU with United States over Northern affairs	Mutual administrative convenience
	3) Multilateral	Harmonization of national laws on international sales of goods	Convenience and efficiency
Judicial Process	Prescription and Enforcement		
	1) Under legislation		
	a) Enforcement of ET statutes	Crimes against humanity	Pursuant to universal jurisdiction
	2) By common law powers		
	a) Prescription		

Type of Action	*Type of Jurisdiction*	*Example*	*Comments*
Judicial Process (cont'd)	i) Over ET subject matter	Court of last resort	Exceptional
	ii) Over ET persons	Service of process abroad	When court has jurisdiction over subject matter
	b) Enforcement		
	i) Against ET persons	Seizure of property in Canada	Limited means of enforcement
	ii) ET interlocutory actions	• Limited ET application of *Canadian Charter* • Letters rogatory and issuance of subpoenas	• Restraint in face of foreign sovereignty • Need foreign state assistance
Bilateral Agreement	Prescription and Enforcement		
	1) Ad hoc ET assistance	Consent for RCMP to act in foreign state	Administrative convenience
	2) Standing ET assistance	Canada-US Treaty on Mutual Legal Assistance	Mutual administrative convenience
	3) Reciprocal ET authority	Canada-US status of forces agreement and double taxation treaties	Jurisdictional clarity
	4) Mutual ET authority	1909 *Boundary Waters Treaty*	Mutual solution
Multilateral Agreement	Prescription and Enforcement		
	1) Reciprocal ET authority	UN Fish Stocks Agreement	Exceptional extension of jurisdiction
	2) Mutual ET authority	Through IGOs, e.g., COP of CITES	Mutual solutions
	a) Implementation	IAEA inspections	
	b) Compliance	NAFTA panel system	
	c) Adjudication	WTO Dispute Settlement Board	

Table 3.2. Means of Accepting Foreign Assertions of Extraterritorial (ET) Jurisdiction

Type of Action	*Type of Jurisdiction*	*Example*	*Comments*
Legislation	Prescription		
	1) Over persons	*Preclearance Act*	Mutual administrative convenience
	2) Over subject matter and places	*Visiting Forces Act*	Criminal and civil jurisdictional clarity
Executive Action	Enforcement		
	1) Unilateral	Invitation to foreign head of state	Prerogative power over foreign affairs
	2) Bilateral	• Extradition of accused offender • Limitation of state immunity	Discretionary power of response
	3) Multilateral	Foreign rights registration in Canada, e.g., trademarks	Mutual benefit
Judicial Process	Prescription and Enforcement		
	1) Prescription		
	a) Over ET incidents	*Forum (non) conveniens*	Comity
	b) Over foreign states and officials	State immunity	Customary international law
	c) Over foreign diplomatic and consular representatives	*Foreign Missions & International Organizations Act*	Pursuant to multilateral treaties
	2) Enforcement		
	a) Over foreign state acts and requests	• Mutual legal assistance in criminal law • Extradition • Letters rogatory • Enforcement of foreign judgments	• Multilateral treaty • Bilateral treaties • Comity • Bilateral treaties and comity
	b) Over foreign arbitrations	Enforcement of awards	*New York Convention*
International Agreement	Prescription and Enforcement	See bi- and multilateral treaties in Table	Mutual solutions

Type of Action	*Type of Jurisdiction*	*Example*	*Comments*
International Agreement (cont'd)		3.1 — all operate reciprocally to protect, as well as extend, Canadian jurisdiction	

Table 3.3. Means of Repulsing Excessive Foreign Assertions of Extraterritorial (ET) Jurisdiction

Type of Action	*Type of Jurisdiction*	*Example*	*Comments*
Legislation	Prescription		
	Blocking/clawback	*Foreign Extraterritorial Measures Act*	Exceptional
	Override	Court/arbitration choice under the *Marine Liability Act*	Uncommon
Executive Action	Enforcement		
	1) Unilateral a) Orders	Countermeasures for breach of international law	Uncommon
	2) Bilateral a) Objection b) Decisions	Diplomatic transactions Refusal to fulfill extradition request	Normal interstate relations Discretionary
Judicial Process	Prescription and Enforcement		
	1) Prescription a) Procedural restrictions	• Anti-suit injunctions • Rejection of choice of law clauses	• Uncommon • Infrequent
	2) Enforcement a) Remedial restrictions	Non-enforcement of foreign judgments	Infrequent
International Agreement	Prescription and Enforcement	See bi- and multilateral treaties in Table 3.1 — all operate reciprocally to protect, as well as extend, Canadian jurisdiction. If breached, apply executive action above.	Mutual solutions

C. TRANSNATIONAL COMPARISON OF EXTRATERRITORIAL JURISDICTION

The reader might well wonder at the significant generality of the so-called rules of international law regarding the exercise of extraterritorial jurisdiction that are described in Section 3(A), above. However, this generality stems from the fact that the international law on point emerges from a system of state practice that has never been uniform, and that has become more fractured as various fields of law grow increasingly specialized. As a result of the dual impacts of globalization and technological change, discussed in Chapter 2, the pressure points of jurisdiction emerge in increasingly divergent types of places and problems. A recent wide-ranging study on extraterritorial jurisdiction carried out by the International Bar Association[162] examined the practice of states in six different areas of law (antitrust, tort, criminal, bribery and corruption, securities, and insolvency). The resultant report reveals a dizzying divergence of practice in the exercise of extraterritorial jurisdiction and even in conceptions as to what "extraterritoriality" means[163] and what the governing norms are or should be. Similarly, in Chapter 7 of this book we present a number of case studies that illustrate that some developing areas of law (or, concurrently, developments in some areas of law) present challenges of various sorts for future state practice. While there is sometimes a certain amount of unity in state practice, this is not always the case — and moreover, the problems change depending on the area of law being dealt with or its subject matter.

While surveying comparative state practice is often a fruitful inquiry for transnational problems, on this topic we can only offer a few crass generalizations regarding approaches to the exercise of extraterritorial jurisdiction. Anglo-American practice, and common law states generally, tend to adhere most closely to the territorial principle[164] and

---

162 *IBA Report*, above note 46.

163 For example, a great deal of the literature and descriptions of state practice regarding "extraterritorial jurisdiction" is actually concerned with states exerting jurisdiction over matters that have some extraterritorial aspects, but that also have ties with or effects upon the exerting state's territory. This is more appropriately labelled "extended territorial jurisdiction," a distinction that we take up in some detail in the next chapter.

164 This is often ascribed to the fact that both the United Kingdom and the United States were "dominated by sea-frontiers," which reduced the state's need for concern over what happened beyond its borders; Williams & de Mestral, above note 7.

view extraterritorial jurisdiction as being significantly exceptional, to the point where common law principles of legislative interpretation usually contain some version of a presumption against extraterritorial jurisdiction.[165] European civil law states, by contrast, historically took a broader view because the geography of the continent meant that cross-border conduct would need to be dealt with more frequently; this, combined with an historical constitutional aversion to extraditing nationals, meant that the nationality principle in particular, and forms of extraterritorial jurisdiction generally, were uncontroversial from an early date.[166] The jurisdictional focus, it might be said, was on person *and* place in the civilian tradition, in contrast to the common law preference for *locus*.

In the twentieth and early twenty-first centuries, the United States emerged as something of an outlier in this field, the legislature aggressively asserting extraterritorial jurisdiction over certain forms of crime, such as narcotics and especially terrorism, "in a manner inconsistent with . . . fundamental international law principles."[167] Post 9/11, this was complemented by belligerent exertions of extraterritorial executive jurisdiction that were driven by the rhetoric of the "global war on terror," the most noteworthy example of which was the practice of "extraordinary

---

This notion has been questioned, however: see Michael Hirst, *Jurisdiction and the Ambit of Criminal Law* (Oxford: Oxford University Press, 2003) ch 1.

165 For example, Ruth Sullivan & Elmer A Driedger, *Sullivan and Driedger on the Construction of Statutes*, 4th ed (Markham, ON: Butterworths, 2002) at 594; Pierre-André Côté, Stéphane Beaulac, & Mathieu Devinat, *The Interpretation of Legislation in Canada*, 4th ed (Toronto: Carswell, 2011) at 212–20.

166 Professor Ryngaert notes the contrast between the European approach to criminal matters, which is to set out a generalized set of jurisdictional principles applying to all criminal laws, as opposed to the United States and the United Kingdom, who apply extraterritorial jurisdiction only to specific offences (Ryngaert, above note 31 at 85–87).

167 Blakesley, above note 28 at 137. Blakesley's piece is quite authoritative, yet overlooks other very expansionist American assertions of extraterritorial jurisdiction, such as how the United States exerts (in 18 USC § 7(7)) extraterritorial criminal jurisdiction over collisions between ships on the high seas, even if neither the ship nor its officers is American. This directly contravenes the international law rules governing high seas collisions. For a case where Canadian authorities encountered this practice, see *R v ALT Navigation Ltd* (2002), 96 CRR (2d) 155 (NLSCTD). For comment on this aspect of the case, see Chantelle MacDonald, "U.S. Breaking Law in Virgo Case, Says International Law Expert" *The Lawyer's Weekly* (24 January 2003).

rendition."[168] On the other hand, international horror at the 9/11 attacks and enthusiasm for combating terrorism[169] led to a large number of states adopting much more robust assertions of extraterritorial jurisdiction over various forms of terrorism, to the point where some of the earlier American positions may have attracted sufficient consensus to give them normative force.[170] Sometimes, today's exceptionalism can be tomorrow's customary international law.

Outside the common law world, particularly in English language literature, state practice is harder to track. There are common law and civil law states among the post-colonial states in Asia and Africa, all of which share to some greater or lesser extent the jurisdictional preferences of the former colonial legal systems. Sharia law states do use extraterritorial jurisdiction to some extent, but such laws are driven primarily by the interest in ensuring that Muslims worldwide adhere to religious edicts as manifest in the form of laws, which on a state level usually emerges as nationality-based jurisdiction.[171] However, these states, as well, are not unwilling to make assertions of extraterritorial legislative and enforcement jurisdiction, as can be observed from the fatwas placed on author Salman Rushdie[172] and the Danish newspaper *Jyllands-Posten*,[173] which purported to provide legal authority for Muslims worldwide to kill the impugned individuals for breaking religious laws despite any lack of connection to the states in question.

---

168 Regarding which see Open Society Justice Initiative, *Globalizing Torture: CIA Secret Detention and Extraordinary Rendition* (New York: Open Society Foundations, 2013) and Leila N Sadat, "Extraordinary Rendition, Torture and Other Nightmares from the War on Terror" (2007) 75 Geo Wash L Rev 1200. European involvement in the practice should not be discounted; see Amnesty International, *State of Denial: Europe's Role in Rendition and Secret Detention* (London: Amnesty International, International Secretariat, 2008).

169 Led, it should be said, by some law-making efforts on the part of the UN Security Council; regarding which, see Kent Roach, *The 9/11 Effect: Comparative Counter-Terrorism* (Cambridge, UK: Cambridge University Press, 2011) ch 2.

170 This development is the subject of a case study in Chapter 7, Section D.

171 See Khaled Abou El Fadl, "Striking a Balance: Islamic Legal Discourses on Muslim Minorities" in Yvonne Yazbeck Haddad & John L Esposito, eds, *Muslims on the Americanization Path?* (Oxford: Oxford University Press, 1998) 47.

172 Kenin Malik, *From Fatwa to Jihad: The Rushdie Affair and Its Aftermath* (Brooklyn, NY: Melville House, 2010); "Iran Adamant Over Rushdie Fatwa" *BBC News* (12 February 2005), online: BBC News news.bbc.co.uk/2/hi/4260599.stm.

173 Naser Khader & Flemming Rose, "Reflections on the Danish Cartoon Controversy" (2007) 14:4 Middle East Quarterly 59.

This chapter has sought to explain the incomplete rules of jurisdiction under international law, as well as the ways they have been interpreted and applied in the Canadian practice of extraterritorial jurisdiction. As we have shown, this practice is not neat and orderly; indeed, its diversity has often led to confusion over the meaning and scope of the very concept of extraterritoriality. We have already drawn a distinction between extended territoriality and true extraterritoriality, yet we think the difference between them is such a centrally important matter, and is so frequently misunderstood, that we give it separate attention in the next chapter.

CHAPTER 4

Extended Territoriality versus Extraterritoriality: A Key Jurisdictional Distinction

A. INTRODUCTION

When dealing with complex subject matter, it is appropriate to carefully distinguish the concepts that are being dealt with from those that are not. In the case of this book, we consider it necessary to explore a key distinction. That distinction is between the exercise of *extraterritorial* jurisdiction by the state, which as we have shown involves the state exerting its power over persons, places, and things that are wholly outside the state's territory; and the exercise of *extended territorial* jurisdiction, which involves an exertion of jurisdiction, usually adjudicative, over a matter that has some extraterritorial elements or aspects, but also has significant links to the state's territory. It is the latter elements or aspects that form the basis of the jurisdictional claim.

While this distinction could be rolled out reasonably quickly—and indeed, it gets only a few paragraphs of discussion in most international law textbooks—we feel it requires extended discussion here for two reasons. First, from a practical perspective, research and experience tell us that the distinction between an extraterritorial matter and one with extraterritorial aspects is easily confused, particularly due to the factual and doctrinal complexity that attaches to it. It is an extremely important distinction because, as we explore below, it determines whether entire bodies of law and interpretive norms attach to a particular matter. Nonetheless, mistakes are easily made and confusion is not uncommon, even at the highest levels.[1]

1 For example, in *Society of Composers, Authors and Music Publishers of Canada v Canadian Assn of Internet Providers*, 2004 SCC 45 [*SOCAN*], the Supreme Court of Canada

Second, the key to all of these questions is the determination of where, for legal purposes, something happened, or something or someone is located, and in the context of globalization and in a highly networked environment, this has become particularly complex. Many matters that might attract the attention of a state, and thus cause it to exercise its jurisdiction, have elements or aspects that occur in a number of other states. This is particularly so in the context of the Internet, where something that is accessible via the World Wide Web may be said to be "occurring" or "located" in every country connected to the Internet — that is, everywhere. Yet this is hardly a sensible notion upon which to found legal claims to jurisdiction over that thing, and the principle of extended territoriality has become increasingly important to help a state sort out whether the thing is within its territory for legal purposes, or whether it must resort to extraterritorial jurisdiction. Thus, while extended territoriality is slightly outside the overall scope of this book, we feel it deserves attention as a further exploration of the pressures that globalization has put upon jurisdictional dynamics in the international community.

Accordingly, this chapter will provide a brief explanation of the principle of extended territoriality, followed by an account of how it is exercised in Canadian criminal and civil proceedings. The latter discussion will yield the interesting insight that, on an international law level, much of what is called "private international law" actually only provides for detailed inquiry into whether jurisdiction should be asserted on an extended territorial basis. The penultimate section will investigate the

---

was considering whether Canada had jurisdiction over music transmitted into Canada via the Internet for the purposes of applying the *Copyright Act*, and framed the matter as avoiding the exertion of extraterritorial jurisdiction. However, as the Act had no extraterritorial effect, the question was in fact whether Canada could exert territorial jurisdiction (on an extended territoriality basis) over the transmissions in question. See discussion in Stephen Coughlan et al, "Global Reach, Local Grasp: Constructing Extraterritorial Jurisdiction in the Age of Globalization" (2007) 6:1 CJLT 29 at 42–43. In *R v Greco* (2001), 155 OAC 316 [*Greco*], the Ontario Court of Appeal analyzed the offence of breaching a probation order as both a matter of extraterritorial jurisdiction and extended territorial jurisdiction, without expressly finding that it was either. Nor, to be fair, is this confusion limited to the courts, and practically speaking much of the confusion likely stems from the way in which cases are argued by litigants. Confusion was avoided in *R v Klassen*, 2008 BCSC 1762, where the accused argued unsuccessfully that a law providing for extraterritorial jurisdiction over sexual assault of children was *ultra vires* because it did not have a "real and substantial connection" to Canada — which, as the court recognized and as discussed below, is the test for whether there is *extended* territoriality over the offence.

pressures that the Internet has put upon courts in determining territoriality, and the increasing use of extended territoriality as a tool for this purpose, after which a few conclusions will be offered.

B. INTERNATIONAL LAW PRINCIPLES AND THE CONTINUUM OF TERRITORIALITY

Recall that a state's entitlement to exercise jurisdiction over persons, places, and things within its territory is a foundational aspect of state sovereignty and a firmly established principle of customary international law. From early days, however, states had to deal with matters, particularly criminal offences, which occurred partly within but partly outside one state's territory. This led to the development of *extended territorial jurisdiction*,[2] which is sometimes thought of as a subset of the principle of territorial jurisdiction. This principle accommodates a problem that is simply stated, but is legally complex in a system based on exclusive state sovereignty over territory: some acts, conduct, and transactions take place in the territory of more than one state. The classic international law textbook example is that of A, standing in state X, who fires a gun across a border into state Y, killing B. Clearly the entire crime of murder did not occur within a single state, so which state has jurisdiction to prosecute? In the modern day of transnational transactions and porous borders, this simple example has been supplanted by complex multi-state narcotics trafficking activities, money-laundering techniques that see funds running through ten banks in ten countries in as many minutes, and various kinds of terrorist acts.

Influential American legal nomenclature describes "objective territoriality" (the offence starts in one state but finishes in the forum state) and "subjective territoriality" (the offence begins in the forum state but is completed elsewhere).[3] Both of these tend to be recognized as legitimate bases for claiming territorial jurisdiction over a matter. In American antitrust law, the controversial "effects doctrine" has been asserted,

---

2 The principle is known by a number of labels, including "qualified territorial jurisdiction" (Robert J Currie, *International & Transnational Criminal Law* (Toronto: Irwin Law, 2010) at 62 [Currie]; Ilias Bantekas, *International Criminal Law*, 4th ed (Oxford: Hart, 2010) at 333). We prefer "extended" as being the most evocatively descriptive label—the state is, in a figurative sense, extending its jurisdiction out to cover some acts that took place beyond its borders. And see Kate Brookson-Morris, "Conflicts of Criminal Jurisdiction" (2007) 56:3 ICLQ 659.

3 Reviewed in Currie, *ibid* at 62–64.

imposing liability on individuals outside the United States whose activities have had economic impact within the United States.[4] In the practice of some states, extraterritorial conspiracies can be prosecuted if any acts to complete them have been done within the forum state,[5] or even if they have not.[6] The central idea, however, is that the forum state is asserting jurisdiction because something significant has been done on its territory that can ground a claim that the act in question actually *happened there*; the claim is one of territorial jurisdiction, and not extraterritorial jurisdiction. So, for example, in an American case,[7] a US citizen was prosecuted for a first-degree murder that took place in Mexico on the basis that the element of premeditation had taken place in Arizona. In the Canadian case of *R v Reyat*, the accused was convicted of manslaughter and possession and use of explosives for planting a bomb on an airplane in Vancouver that exploded and caused the deaths in Tokyo, Japan.[8]

An assessment of the territoriality of a particular thing or matter is therefore not absolute, but is better understood as operating on a continuum or scale, as illustrated below:

Figure 4.1

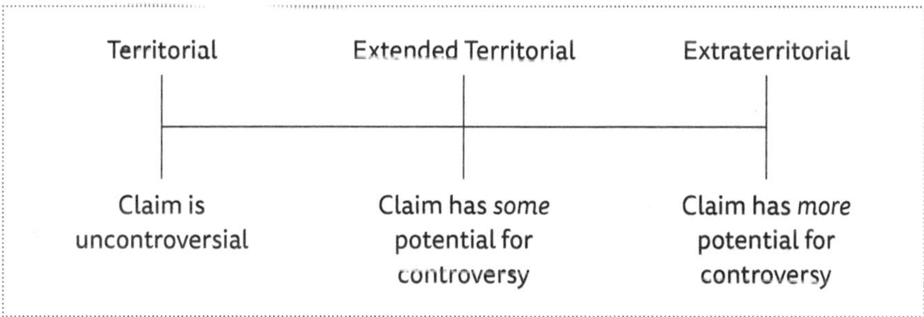

Alternatively, it can be illustrated in Venn diagram form:

---

4 *Ibid* at 64.

5 *Director of Public Prosecutions v Doot*, [1973] AC 807 (HL).

6 *Liangsiriprasert v Government of the United States of America*, [1991] 1 AC 225 at 251C (PC). See also *R v Bow Street Metropolitan Stipendiary Magistrate, Ex parte Pinochet Ugarte (No 3)*, [1999] 2 All ER 97 at para 125 (HL), Hope LJ; the Canadian *Criminal Code*, RSC 1985, c C-46, s 465(4); and *United States v Noriega*, 746 F Supp 1506 (SD Fla 1990). See Joshua Blackmore, "The Jurisdictional Problem of Extraterritorial Conspiracy" (2006) 17:1 Crim LF 71.

7 *State of Arizona v Willoughby*, 181 Ariz 530 (1995).

8 (1993), 40 WAC 161 (BCCA).

Figure 4.2

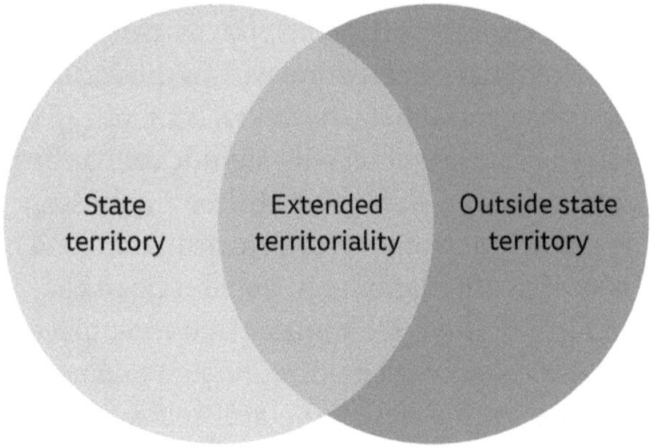

Extended territoriality, then, helps to set the outer boundaries of the territoriality principle. It is an accepted jurisdictional principle in customary international law, even though its precise scope is vague.[9] It is unsurprising that it emerged from the criminal law practice of states, as it embodies the powerful public policy objective that the forum in which a crime is committed should be able to prosecute it, even if, strictly speaking, the crime did not occur wholly in one state. This principle has a stretching effect on the concept of territorial jurisdiction that is of mutual benefit to states in ensuring that there is not impunity for crime, effectively by way of increasing the number of states which are competent to prosecute. As a matter of custom, it is similar to the principles of extraterritorial jurisdiction outlined in Chapter 3, in that it is permissive — states are not compelled to exercise jurisdiction on this basis, but are permitted to if they choose. The flip side of this permissiveness is that other states can only object to the use of this principle if its use is somehow excessive or the offence is too remote from the claiming state, because otherwise the claim is recognized as one of territorial jurisdic-

9 To be specific, its scope is vague because state practice differs on the point. For example, compare the Canadian approach to criminal jurisdiction, reviewed in Section C, below in this chapter, with the US Supreme Court's decision in *Morrison v National Australia Bank Ltd*, 130 S Ct 2869 at 2883 (2010), and the Australian authorities reviewed in Belinda Wells & Michael Burnett, "When Cultures Collide: An Australian Citizen's Power to Demand the Death Penalty under Islamic Law" (2000) 22 Sydney L Rev 5 at 26–27. And see Cedric Ryngaert, "Territorial Jurisdiction Over Cross-frontier Offences: Revisiting a Classic Problem of International Criminal Law" (2009) 9:1 Int'l Crim L Rev 187.

tion with all of the solidity that such a claim entails. One can imagine any number of conflicts that might arise in such situations, but generally none do. This is in no small part because prosecutorial authorities tend to broker their jurisdictional claims via negotiation, behind the scenes and often prior to charges being laid.[10]

Moreover, the extended territoriality principle is sometimes used as a mandatory or optional basis for jurisdiction in crime suppression treaties. For example, in the OECD *Convention on Combating Bribery of Foreign Public Officials in International Business Transactions*,[11] article 4 requires each signatory state to establish jurisdiction over the relevant offence "when the offence is committed in whole or in part on its territory."

C. EXTENDED TERRITORIALITY IN CANADIAN CRIMINAL PROCEEDINGS

Canada has traditionally been oriented towards territorial jurisdiction, and this is reflected in section 6(2) of the *Criminal Code*, which states: "Subject to this Act or any other Act of Parliament, no person shall be convicted . . . of an offence committed outside Canada." This provision enacts a presumption against extraterritorial jurisdiction over criminal offences, but is silent on its face about how to determine whether a cross-border offence is considered to be committed *inside* Canada. However, in the leading decision of *R v Libman*,[12] the Supreme Court of Canada applied the extended territoriality principle and generated an influential test for courts to use in making this determination.[13]

In *Libman* itself, the accused had been committed for trial for fraud and conspiracy to commit fraud and applied to have his committal

10 Currie, above note 2 at 64–65.

11 17 December 1997, Can TS 1999 No 23.

12 *R v Libman*, [1985] 2 SCR 178 [*Libman*].

13 In methodological terms, the Supreme Court was acknowledging that the customary international law principle of extended territoriality (which the decision, authored by Gerard La Forest J, did not explicitly name) was part of the common law of Canada. The Court was more explicit on the point that customary international law is incorporated as part of Canadian law in the later case of *R v Hape*, 2007 SCC 26 [*Hape*]. A more detailed discussion can be found in Robert J Currie, "*Libman* at 25; or, Canada and Qualified Territoriality: Do We Understand Jurisdiction Yet?" in Chios Carmody, ed, *Is Our House in Order? Canada's Implementation of International Law* (Montreal/Kingston: McGill-Queen's University Press, 2010). And see Troy Lavers, "Jurisdictional Issues in Extraterritorial Criminal Law" in Christopher PM Waters, ed, *British and Canadian Perspectives on International Law* (Leiden: Martinus Nijhoff, 2006).

quashed on the basis that the alleged crimes occurred outside Canada. Libman had employed a number of people in Toronto to sell what were apparently worthless shares in two fictitious mining companies. The sales were made by telephone to US residents, who also received promotional material from Panama and Costa Rica. The purchasers sent their money to offices operated by Libman's associates in Panama and Costa Rica, to which countries Libman would travel to obtain his share of the proceeds; he would then return to Canada with the money and pay his salespeople.[14]

Though not framed this way by the Supreme Court, Libman's argument was essentially that subsection 6(2) (then 5(2)) of the *Criminal Code* should apply and defeat the charges. Importantly, Libman had been charged with conspiracy under section 423(1)(d)[15] of the *Criminal Code*, which covered conspiracies to commit an offence in Canada, and not under section 423(3),[16] which explicitly covered conspiracies to commit an offence outside Canada. The fraud provisions at the time contained no extraterritorial language. The factual question to be answered was whether the alleged acts had occurred in Canada, for if they had not, then Canadian courts had no jurisdiction. The legal question was what factors the courts should use to determine whether a cross-border offence could be said to have occurred in Canada.

Writing for the Court, La Forest J began by noting that criminal jurisdiction was primarily territorial, but that "states increasingly exercise jurisdiction over criminal behaviour in other states that has harmful consequences within their own territory or jurisdiction . . . ."[17] His review of the "doctrinal confusion"[18] in past English and Canadian cases emphasized that the courts of neither country had felt bound by strict territoriality. Both English and Canadian legal systems had demonstrably taken jurisdiction over criminal conduct that had taken place in whole or in part in foreign countries, where it had unlawful or harmful consequences domestically, as well as over offences where the victim and impact were abroad.[19] Subsection 6(2) of the *Criminal Code*, La Forest

14 *Libman*, above note 12 at 181–82.

15 Now s 465(1)(d).

16 Now s 465(4), which came into effect only after some of the transactions were complete; *Libman*, above note 12 at 183.

17 *Ibid* at 184.

18 *Ibid* at 186.

19 *Ibid* at 208–9.

J noted, "does not say that criminal law is confined to Canadian territory; it says rather that no person 'shall be convicted in Canada for an offence committed outside of Canada.'"[20]

Drawing on various aspects of the older cases, as well as on academic writings, La Forest J then formulated a two-part test to determine when Canada could take criminal jurisdiction over transnational crimes. First,

> all that is necessary to make an offence subject to the jurisdiction of our courts is that a significant portion of the activities constituting that offence took place in Canada. As it is put by modern academics, it is sufficient that there be a "real and substantial link" between an offence and this country, a test well known in public and private international law . . . .[21]

Second if a "real and substantial link" was established, "[o]ne must then consider whether there is anything in those facts that offends international comity,"[22] and specifically, whether there is anything "in the requirements of international comity that would dictate that this country refrain from exercising its jurisdiction."[23]

Analyzing the facts before the Court in *Libman*, La Forest J concluded that the links between Canada and the offence were "ample."[24] He agreed with a lower court finding that the preparatory activities in which Libman had engaged in Toronto to perpetrate the frauds would alone support territorial jurisdiction, though he also emphasized the fact that the profits generated were brought to Canada. He further held that the fact that the harm to victims occurred outside Canada made no difference to the analysis.[25] Nothing in relation to international comity would preclude Canada from prosecuting the crime, and in fact, La Forest J suggested that international comity compelled Canada to do so.[26] The committal for both fraud and conspiracy was upheld.

The *Libman* test has seen some development in both lower courts and the Supreme Court's own jurisprudence, though the reported cases do not always display a uniform approach. The test is best understood

---

20 *Ibid* at 209.
21 *Ibid* at 212–13.
22 *Ibid* at 211.
23 *Ibid* at 214.
24 *Ibid* at 213.
25 *Ibid* at 210–12.
26 *Ibid* at 213–14.

by separating out its two elements: "real and substantial connection" (as the phrase usually goes[27]), and "international comity."

1) "Real and Substantial Connection"

Again, the purpose of the *Libman* test is to determine whether a cross-border offence took place in Canada, and the bulk of that determination lies in ascertaining whether there is a "real and substantial connection." Since this is a test for *territorial* jurisdiction, the connection must be between some aspects of the offence and the territory of Canada. In *R v Ouellette*,[28] Béliveau J of the Quebec Superior Court framed "real and substantial connection" in a way that still reflects the current practice of the courts, describing it as a:

> test of varying content which is assessed in relation to the circumstances and, in particular, the importance of the elements of the offence linked to Canada, the relevant facts which arose in Canada and the harmful consequences which were caused, or which could have been caused, in Canada.[29]

In *Libman* itself, the Supreme Court was clearly suggesting a generous approach to this question, and the case makes clear that it is not necessary that particular elements of the crime have taken place in Canada, since this was the formal, "mechanical" approach of the past that the Court was specifically rejecting. Rather, the focus was to be on "all relevant facts that take place in Canada" — for example, the fact that the proceeds of the fraud were brought to Canada.[30]

Such relevant facts may, of course, include any formal elements of the crime that took place in Canada,[31] but also any facts relating to "the

---

27 There is no particular distinction to be made between "real and substantial links," which is the phrase used in *Libman* itself, or "real and substantial connection," which is how La Forest J rephrased the test for application in other contexts (for example, *Morguard Investments Ltd v De Savoye*, [1990] 3 SCR 1077 [*Morguard Investments*], regarding assumption of jurisdiction in civil matters, discussed in the next section). The latter phrase is most frequently used now, and will be used here.

28 (1998), 126 CCC (3d) 219 (Qc Sup Ct) [*Ouellette*].

29 *Ibid* at 229.

30 *Libman*, above note 12 at 211. Though see *R v Drakes*, [2005] OTC 577 (SCJ), distinguishing *Libman* on its facts.

31 See *Canada (Canadian Human Rights Commission) v Canadian Liberty Net*, [1998] 1 SCR 626 [*Canadian Liberty Net*].

formulation, initiation, or commission of the offence."[32] In *R v Vézina*,[33] the Supreme Court held that *Libman* would support jurisdiction over a conspiracy and attempt to defraud, where the scheme was launched in Canada but the victim would be in another state.[34] On the other hand, in *R v Dos Santos*,[35] the accused was convicted of illegal fishing in Canadian waters even though he never left his ship, which was outside Canada's 200-mile limit—he accomplished the fishing by sending his crew in small boats to drop nets within Canada's fisheries waters. Justice Barry ruled that "[w]hile the planning and evolution of the offence may have occurred outside the 200 mile limit, the culmination of the offence occurred [inside],"[36] which satisfied the *Libman* test; therefore, the accused had committed his offence in Canada. In general, then, the analysis should be shaped by the nature of the offence with which the accused has been charged.[37]

In some cases, a real and substantial connection has been found on the basis that, while the harmful act took place outside Canada, some consequences of that act were felt in Canada. In *R v Ouellette*,[38] the accused was charged with manslaughter after assaulting the victim while in the Dominican Republic. The victim died from injuries sustained during the assault after returning home to Canada. Justice Béliveau held that there was a real and substantial connection for the manslaughter charge, based *inter alia* on the fact that the victim had died in Canada and the harmful consequences of the offence occurred in Canada. He emphasized that the death of the victim was an element of the crime of manslaughter, and while it was a "secondary aspect" of the crime, it was the "determinant element" for the jurisdictional inquiry.[39] Similarly, in R

---

32 *R v OB* (1997), 99 OAC 313 at para 12 (CA) [*OB*]. See also *R v Hammerbeck* (1993), 26 BCAC 1 (CA) (child abducted from Canada to the United States); *R v Doiron* (1989), 93 NBR (2d) 444 (CA) (accused imported narcotics into Canada where he "caused" them to be transported over the border by picking up the drugs and leaving them 250 metres from the border for transport by associates).

33 [1986] 1 SCR 2.

34 *Ibid* at 20.

35 (1992), 96 Nfld & PEIR 13 (Nfld SCTD).

36 *Ibid* at para 65. Regarding the bracketed word, while the case report reads "outside" it is clear from the context that Barry J meant to say "inside."

37 See *Libman*, above note 12 at 210.

38 Above note 28.

39 *Ibid* at 100. Justice Béliveau also cited the accused's interest in being tried in Canada as a relevant factor.

v Greco,[40] the accused was charged with breach of probation for assaulting his girlfriend while in Cuba. The Ontario Court of Appeal found a real and substantial connection, based on the facts that the "treatment, protection and safety of the victim . . . who lives in Canada" had substantial impacts within Canada;[41] that only Canada had any interest in ensuring compliance with orders made by Canadian courts;[42] and that the offence arose out of a breach of a Canadian probation order.[43]

It has also become clear that the *Libman* test does not just apply to purely criminal offences, but also to offences under federal regulatory legislation.[44] This was most recently underscored by the Ontario Court of Appeal in *R v Stucky*,[45] where the accused was charged under section 52 of the federal *Competition Act* with making misleading representations "to the public," where his only targets were people in the United States. The court held that "the meaning of 'the public' is not restricted to the Canadian public where there is a real and substantial link or connection between the offence and Canada."[46] Due to the evidence that at the time of the offence, the accused was in Canada, initiated his alleged misrepresentations in Canada, and received his profits here, "[t]here is a real and substantial connection between the offence alleged and Canada, notwithstanding the fact that the 'public' to whom the representations were made was located outside Canada."[47] In fact the court went further, noting that *Libman* "has general application" and "is part of our general law concerning jurisdiction."[48]

---

40 *Greco*, above note 1.

41 *Ibid* at para 25.

42 *Ibid* at paras 41–42.

43 *Ibid* at para 42. *Greco* is often referred to as the leading case regarding the application of *Libman*, though as has been noted elsewhere, the judgment appears to confuse and intermingle extraterritorial and extended territorial jurisdiction (see Currie, above note 2 at 421–22). However, the result is consistent with the overall policy of *Libman*, and may overturn the court's more conservative finding in *OB*, above note 32. See also *R v Rattray*, 2008 ONCA 74, and *R v Stanny*, 2008 ABQB 746.

44 See *Canadian Liberty Net*, above note 31; *SOCAN*, above note 1; *R v Karigar*, 2013 ONSC 5199.

45 2009 ONCA 151.

46 *Ibid* at para 24.

47 *Ibid* at para 32.

48 *Ibid* at para 33.

2) International Comity

The basic idea behind international comity is that states owe each other a certain duty to accommodate each others' interests — "out of, politeness, convenience and goodwill, rather than strict legal obligation . . . ."[49] In applying the *Libman* test, courts must inquire whether there is anything in the interests of comity that suggests Canada should not take jurisdiction over a particular case. Notably, in *Libman*, La Forest J took a modern and expansive view of comity, expressing the opinion that comity may in some cases compel Canada towards taking jurisdiction over a transnational offence in order to serve the mutual interest of states in crime suppression. "In a shrinking world," he memorably declared, "we are all our brother's keepers."[50]

The comity portion of the test has not seen any significant development, as there has been no case to date where any evidence was presented on comity that required consideration. This is not surprising, however, given that the Crown will typically make certain decisions in the background prior to proceeding with a prosecution. Prosecutors may satisfy themselves that there are no other states that wish to prosecute the particular offence, or may even negotiate with their foreign counterparts to ensure that the accused is prosecuted in the state which has the best chance of conviction. A finding that taking jurisdiction in a particular case would offend international comity would notionally be made in a situation where another state wished to prosecute and did not wish Canada to do so; evidence thereof might take the form of an outstanding extradition request[51] or a formal diplomatic protest to Canada's exercise of jurisdiction. A court might then be called upon to compare the strength of Canada's "real and substantial connection" to the case with that of the competing state(s).[52] Again, if such a situation were to exist, the Crown would be more likely to deal with it through background diplomatic negotiation and it probably would not reach the court.

---

49 *Hape*, above note 13 at para 47.

50 *Libman*, above note 12 at 214.

51 *R v Larche*, 2006 SCC 56 at para 64.

52 *R v Cook*, [1998] 2 SCR 597 at para 136, Bastarache J, concurring.

D. EXTENDED TERRITORIALITY IN CANADIAN CIVIL LITIGATION

The jurisdiction of civil courts in Canada is driven by the international principles discussed previously,[53] as well as their constitutional authority and limits, and practical considerations about enforceability. Typically those courts limit themselves territorially and rarely assert genuine extraterritorial jurisdiction. They must, however, handle a growing proportion of cases that have extraterritorial features — cases, in other words, that involve transnational transactions. Perhaps a party is resident, or the incident occurred, abroad. Increasingly, courts are faced with issues where Internet or electronic transactions make it difficult to determine where a given incident took place. Ordinarily a Canadian court must have jurisdiction over each party and over the subject matter of the suit.[54] Jurisdiction over plaintiffs can be assumed since, by instituting actions, they attorn to the court's authority. Jurisdiction over defendants cannot be assumed if they are outside the court's territorial reach. They must voluntarily submit to the court's jurisdiction or the plaintiffs must satisfy the criteria for service out of the jurisdiction, that is, extraterritorially. Similarly, jurisdiction over the civil wrong is automatic when done within the court's territorial ambit, but may require the court's permission to pursue the action if it was committed extraterritorially.

In Canadian practice, the courts in common law provinces[55] have developed sets of principles to guide their discretion in asserting jurisdiction in transnational situations. More recently, some provinces have replaced these principles with a statutory set of rules by enacting the model *Court Jurisdiction and Proceedings Transfer Act* (*CJPTA*),[56] which was developed by the Uniform Law Conference of Canada (ULCC). The model act is similar in approach to the common law principles since the ULCC sought to harmonize and regularize the diversity of provin-

53 See Chapter 3, Section A(3).

54 See Chapter 3, Section A(4).

55 Quebec has statutory rules on court jurisdiction found at arts 3134–63 CCQ. The jurisdiction of the Federal Courts, as statutory courts, is also established by their constitutive legislation: *Federal Courts Act*, RSC 1985, c F-7, ss 17–28.

56 Uniform Law Conference of Canada, *Court Jurisdiction and Proceedings Transfer Act* (adopted in 1994), online: ULCC/CHLC www.ulcc.ca/en/uniform-acts-en-gb-1/183-court-jurisdiction-and-proceedings-transfer-act/1092-court-jurisdiction-proceedings-transfer-act [*CJPTA*]. See, generally, Vaughan Black, Stephen GA Pitel, & Michael Sobkin, *Statutory Jurisdiction: An Analysis of the Court Jurisdiction and Proceedings Transfer Act* (Toronto: Carswell, 2012).

cial practices. The approach to jurisdiction common to all these acts and principles involves the degree of association that the parties and the facts in a dispute bear to Canada. However, a court's readiness to assume jurisdiction at common law or under the *CJPTA* may be restrained either out of comity towards foreign states and their jurisdictional authority, or by international law regarding the sovereign immunity of foreign states, their officials and representatives.

The main features and divergences of the common law and statutory designs for civil jurisdiction will be briefly explored in turn, followed by an outline of the restraints that are placed on the courts.

1) Civil Jurisdiction at Common Law

Since the Supreme Court of Canada plays an unifying role in the Canadian legal system across civil and criminal law, perhaps it is not surprising that the common law principles concerning jurisdiction in civil actions, under the guise of conflicts of law rules, have developed in a similar fashion and over much the same time period as the criminal law practice founded in *R v Libman* in 1985.[57] However, the jurisprudence on the civil side is separate from the criminal experience discussed above in Section C because the basic principles for determining the connection of a transnational transaction to Canada have to be suited to private actions as opposed to public prosecutions.

The leading decision on the common law principles of adjudicative jurisdiction in civil litigation was delivered by the Supreme Court of Canada in the case of *Morguard Investments Ltd v De Savoye*[58] in 1990. It propounded a two-part test: whether Canada has a "real and substantial connection" with the injurious incident suffered by the plaintiff, and whether, as a result of that inquiry, the acceptance or rejection of jurisdiction would respect order and fairness between the plaintiff and the defendant.[59]

---

57 Above note 12. A significant reason for these contemporaneous developments in transnational criminal and civil law was the strong influence of La Forest J, known to be wise in matters of international law, during his time on the SCC.

58 *Morguard Investments*, above note 27, was not the first civil case to discuss the degree of association between the circumstances of the action and the forum as the basis for determining the court's jurisdiction, but it formally anointed the standard of "real and substantial connection."

59 "The concept of order and fairness is integral to the question of determining whether there is real and substantial [connection] . . . ." (*O'Brien v Canada (Attorney General)*, 2002 NSCA 21 at para 20) and "The concept of fairness in determining jurisdiction

The test of a real and substantial connection to Canada expresses two complementary aspects of a court's jurisdiction. First, the reach of the court is not wholly limited territorially. But, secondly, the extraterritorial features of a case must have an association with the court's territorial scope of operation. In short, the court's jurisdiction may be exercised over a matter beyond its territory provided an appropriate degree of connection to its territory can be demonstrated. This is, in truth, "extended territorial jurisdiction" as explained earlier in this chapter.[60] Fully extraterritorial actions, such as a suit between foreign parties over an incident abroad, are typically turned away by the courts for lack of Canadian connections, except when the foreign defendant submits to the court or perhaps when the Canadian forum is the court of last resort, which is the subject of a case study on extraterritorial accountability for human rights abuses in Chapter 7, Section B.

The flexibility inherent in the real and substantial connection test gave the courts wide discretion but little practical guidance in its application. It was the Ontario Court of Appeal in *Muscutt v Courcelles*[61] that first provided assistance with a list of eight factors to consider and weigh in order to determine whether a sufficient connection to the jurisdiction exists.[62] Yet even with this guidance, courts continued to experience difficulty and variance in assessing the relationship between the different factors and the relative weight to be given to them. After seven years of judicial experience with the *Muscutt* list of factors, the Ontario Court of Appeal took the opportunity in *Charron Estate v Village Resorts Ltd*[63] to appoint a five-judge panel to review them. Then in a further appeal, *sub nomine Club Resorts Ltd v Van Breda*,[64] the Supreme Court of Canada, for the first time, gave directions on how the real and substantial connection test should be applied, and in the process substantially reconfigured the previous approach under *Muscutt*. Justice LeBel spoke for the whole court in stating that if the real and substantial connection test is to operate in an orderly and fair way, it cannot be so flexible as to depend

should be considered from the point of view of both the respondent [plaintiff], as well as the appellants [defendants]" (*Oakley v Barry* (1998), 166 NSR (2d) 282 at para 95 (CA)).

60 See Section B, above in this chapter.

61 (2002), 60 OR (3d) 20 [*Muscutt*].

62 *Ibid*, listed and discussed in paras 75–110.

63 2010 ONCA 84 [*Charron Estate*].

64 2012 SCC 17 [*Club Resorts*]. See also *Éditions Écosociété Inc v Banro Corp*, 2012 SCC 18, and *Breeden v Black*, 2012 SCC 19 [*Breeden*].

on a case-by-case assessment of connecting factors such as the *Muscutt* approach encouraged:

> Justice and fairness are undoubtedly essential purposes of a sound system of private international law. But they cannot be attained without a system of principles and rules that ensure security and predictability in the law governing the assumption of jurisdiction by a court. Parties must be able to predict with reasonable confidence whether a court will assume jurisdiction in a case with an international or interprovincial aspect. The need for certainty and predictability may conflict with the objective of fairness. An unfair set of rules could hardly be considered an efficient and just legal regime. The challenge is to reconcile fairness with the need for security, stability and efficiency in the design and implementation of a conflict of laws system.[65]

The real and substantial connection test, LeBel J wrote, must produce predictable results in objectively verifiable circumstances:

> Jurisdiction must . . . be established primarily on the basis of objective factors that connect the legal situation or the subject matter of the litigation with the forum. The [Ontario] Court of Appeal was moving in this direction in the cases at bar. This means that the courts must rely on a basic list of factors that is drawn at first from past experience in the conflict of laws system and is then updated as the needs of the system evolve.[66]

Justice LeBel indicated that predictability should be attained by a presumptive approach to jurisdiction. In short, if the circumstances of the plaintiff's claim are connected to the forum by a factor the courts have previously determined to be sufficient, the real and substantial connection test will be presumed to be satisfied. Justice LeBel stated:

> In my view, identifying a set of relevant presumptive connecting factors and determining their legal nature and effect will bring greater clarity and predictability to the analysis of the problems of assumption of jurisdiction, while at the same time ensuring consistency with the objectives of fairness and efficiency that underlie this branch of the law.[67]

---

65 *Club Resorts*, *ibid* at para 73.

66 *Ibid* at para 82.

67 *Ibid* at para 78.

If a case does not exhibit an existing presumptive connecting factor, the plaintiff may move the court to recognize a new one.[68] The presence of either an existing or a new presumptively real and substantial connection will allow the court to assume jurisdiction unless the defendant objects and is able to rebut the presumption on the facts.[69] The defendants' right to try to rebut may be seen partly as a continuing concern for fairness in the otherwise now ordered and predictable process of determining jurisdiction.

So far the Supreme Court has recognized four presumptive connecting factors applicable in tort actions:

(a) the defendant is domiciled or resident in the province;
(b) the defendant carries on business in the province;
(c) the tort was committed in the province; and
(d) a contract connected with the dispute was made in the province.[70]

The central features of these connecting factors are obvious and well established, but the presumptions they raise will not always automatically and immediately allow the court to assume jurisdiction. Though one aim of the Supreme Court was to simplify the process of determining jurisdiction, the practical application of each presumptive connecting factor is likely to require further consideration by the courts. For example, in a case involving a transnational tort, the court will have to first elicit rules for determining the place of the wrong, and then consider the evidence of the plaintiff that the presumption attaches, and of the defendant, in rebuttal, that it does not. In addition, connecting factors in other areas of law, such as contracts and property, will need to be recognized by the courts in future cases as presumptively sufficient to found jurisdiction.[71]

---

68 *Ibid* at paras 80, 91–92, and 100.

69 *Ibid* at paras 80–81 and 93–100.

70 *Ibid* at para 90.

71 A word should be said about *Unifund Assurance Co v Insurance Corp of British Columbia*, 2003 SCC 40 [*Unifund*], and the potential ambiguity it engenders. The issue in *Unifund* was the extent to which the Ontario *Insurance Act* was applicable to an accident occurring in British Columbia but involving Ontario residents. The Court there, in essence, allowed for three possibilities: that the Ontario legislation was *ultra vires*; that it was *intra vires* and applicable: or that it resided in a middle ground that it was *intra vires* but constitutionally inapplicable to the action in British Columbia. They found the third to be true in that particular case.

It bears reiteration, however, that the assumption of jurisdiction pursuant to the real and substantial connection test is always an exercise of territorial authority, albeit in an extended mode. The Supreme Court mentioned three other separate bases of civil jurisdiction, and it is only these grounds that might occasionally give rise to Canadian adjudication of truly extraterritorial wrongs.

First, LeBel J affirmed two existing grounds of personal jurisdiction over defendants: by their submission to the court, and by service of process upon them while within the territorial reach of the court.[72] If a foreign

---

Unifund creates potential confusion because it deals with analogous questions to *Libman*, above note 12 and *Club Resorts*, above note 64, but does not use the same terminology in doing so. That is, it considers whether legislation can be applicable outside its territory (legislative jurisdiction, as in *Libman*) or whether a court might simply have jurisdiction to hear a matter (adjudicative jurisdiction, as in *Club Resorts*). The Court holds that different tests govern those two situations. For example, at para 58 they hold that "a 'real and substantial connection' sufficient to permit the court of a province to take jurisdiction over a dispute may not be sufficient for the law of that province to regulate the outcome." *Unifund* requires a "sufficient connection," which is more than just a real and substantial connection, for a province to be able to regulate the outcome.

This creates the potential for ambiguity because of the terminology used. *Unifund* uses "sufficient connection" to describe legislative jurisdiction — exactly the concept under discussion in *Libman*, which does *not* use that term. On the face of it, it could appear that *Libman* and *Unifund* both create tests meant to apply to the same circumstances, but use different terminology to do so and do not acknowledge one another's existence.

No unproblematic solution to this difficulty exists, because it has not yet been clearly recognized by courts. A likely solution is that *Unifund* (because of its reliance on "the demands of Canadian federalism") was meant to apply specifically to *interprovincial* applicability of legislation, which is a subset of extraterritorial application of such legislation. However, the Supreme Court has not explicitly said that, and lower courts have not always understood the case in that way. See, for example, *Ontario College of Pharmacists v 1724665 Ontario Inc (cob Global Pharmacy Canada)*, 2013 ONCA 381, in which the Ontario College of Pharmacists was found to have jurisdiction over Internet sales of generic prescription drugs which were shipped from India to the United States by a Belizean company, based on sales from a call centre in Ontario. The Ontario Court of Appeal reached this conclusion not by asking whether the *Libman* test was met (though it seems that it would be), but rather on the basis that there was a "sufficient connection" as required by *Unifund*.

Adding to the ambiguity is the uncertain status of *Unifund* itself. Subsequent cases seem to have treated similar situations as settled by whether provincial legislation was *intra vires* or not, ignoring *Unifund*'s middle ground of being *intra vires* but constitutionally inapplicable. See *British Columbia v Imperial Tobacco Canada Ltd*, 2005 SCC 49.

72 *Club Resorts*, above note 64 at para 79.

defendant submits to the court's jurisdiction, as opposed to appearing to contest it, clearly the court will have authority to hear the action. Similarly if the defendant is served with process within the forum, the court will have jurisdiction over both parties and so may proceed. So, for example, the victim of a tortious injury at the instance of a foreign resident and in a foreign place may found jurisdiction for an action in a Canadian court by service of process on the tortfeasor if and when he should happen to enter the geographic territory of the court. The procedure is not dependent on habitual (or any) residence of the defendant, and thus may offer an opportunity for a suit for an extraterritorial tort, however fleeting the foreign defendant's presence within the forum may be.

The third and potentially most significant basis for the exercise of civil jurisdiction extraterritorially is the concept of court of last resort. The authority of a court to take jurisdiction on this basis was set forth by the Ontario Court of Appeal in *Charron Estate* in stating: "Where there is no other forum in which the plaintiff can reasonably seek relief, there is a residual discretion to assume jurisdiction."[73] However, on appeal to the Supreme Court, LeBel J repeatedly refused to pass any comment on the concept,[74] so its validity and operation at common law have yet to be definitively determined.

2) Civil Jurisdiction under the *Court Jurisdiction and Proceedings Transfer Act*

In recent years, even as the common law principles affecting jurisdiction have been elaborated by the senior courts, a movement towards legislative reform has been felt across Canada. As noted earlier, the ULCC took up the subject of adjudicative jurisdiction and developed a model *CJPTA*.[75] As of August 2013, the model act was operative in some form in British Columbia,[76] Saskatchewan,[77] and Nova Scotia,[78] and had been enacted, though not brought into force, in the Yukon Territory.[79] Thus it

73 Above note 63 at para 100. See also para 54, *ibid.*

74 *Club Resorts*, above note 64 at paras 59, 82, 86, and 100.

75 Above note 56.

76 *Court Jurisdiction and Proceedings Transfer Act*, SBC 2003, c 28.

77 *Court Jurisdiction and Proceedings Transfer Act*, SS 1997, c C-41.1.

78 *Court Jurisdiction and Proceedings Transfer Act*, SNS 2003 (2d Sess), c 2.

79 *Court Jurisdiction and Proceedings Transfer Act*, SY 2000, c 7 [not yet in force].

has hopped and skipped across Canada, while other provinces are also engaged in the process of reviewing their jurisdictional practices.[80]

The contents of the *CJPTA* were constructed by the ULCC from research into and consensus upon what is good and useful about the judicial practice of civil jurisdiction across Canada, together with a measure of progressive development that seemed necessary and would likely be generally acceptable. As the ULCC's introductory comments explain, the *CJPTA* is intended:

> (1) to replace the widely different jurisdictional rules currently used in Canadian courts with a uniform set of standards for determining jurisdiction;
> (2) to bring Canadian jurisdictional rules into line with the principles laid down by the Supreme Court of Canada in *Morguard Investments Ltd v De Savoye* . . .
> (3) by providing uniform jurisdictional standards, to provide an essential complement to the rule of nation-wide enforceability of judgments in the uniform *Enforcement of Canadian Judgments Act* . . . .[81]

However, there is a sharp difference in the form and status of the jurisdictional rules of the *CJPTA*. Where the model is adopted, its provisions have legislative force. This means the Act's jurisdictional rules not only override the local common law principles by reason of their statutory force, but are also expressly made the exclusive basis for the courts' adjudicative authority in civil cases.[82] As a result, courts subject to the *CJPTA* face an abrupt change in roles. They no longer have control of their civil jurisdiction through the malleable method of the common law. The courts' powers under the *CJPTA* are now reduced to the more limited role of interpreting the meaning of the legislation.

Under the *CJPTA*, jurisdiction over a "person" in the form of the defendant depends upon a connection to the province/territory or its legal system sufficient to found something called "territorial competence."[83] The choice of this phrase clearly indicates the basis for jurisdiction

80 Alberta, Manitoba, and Ontario: see *Charron Estate*, above note 63 at para 53.

81 *CJPTA*, above note 56.

82 *Ibid*, s 2(2).

83 *Ibid*, s 1. According to the ULCC Introductory comments to the *CJPTA*, the legislative intention is that jurisdiction must be established "by the existence of defined connections between the territory or legal system of the enacting jurisdiction, and a party to the proceeding or the facts on which the proceeding is based." (*Ibid*, s 0.2.)

under the *CJPTA*. It does not offer much scope for jurisdiction over extraterritorial parties or incidents, as explained below.

"Persons" expressly include foreign countries[84] as well as corporations, partnerships, and associations since these bodies are also referred to in the Act. Proceedings against persons are allowed on four grounds only:

1) If the defendant accepts the court's jurisdiction by submission, counter claim, or choice of forum agreement,[85]
2) If the defendant is "ordinarily resident" in the province/territory,[86]
3) If a "real and substantial connection" exists between province/territory and the facts in the case,[87] or
4) If the province/territory is the forum of last resort for the plaintiff.[88]

The circumstances in which a person or state is "ordinarily resident" are not defined in the *CJPTA*. Presumably the requirement will inhibit the initiation of suits against individuals or state representatives who pass through or are otherwise temporarily present in the province/territory.[89] Thus it is no longer possible to found jurisdiction by serving process on defendants when they happen to change transportation, stop over en route, or stay just long enough for a meeting in the province/territory, as continues to be possible under the common law pursuant to the Supreme Court's judgment in *Club Resorts*.[90]

Alternatively, if the court finds the suit has "a real and substantial connection" with the province/territory, the third ground is satisfied and jurisdiction may be asserted over the defendant even though she may not be ordinarily resident. In these circumstances, a plaintiff may serve a passing or temporary resident or even sue an absent defendant outside Canada.[91] A real and substantial connection is presumed in twelve described situations.[92] Most instances concern property or events

84 *Ibid*, s 1(b).
85 *Ibid*, ss 3(a)–(c).
86 *Ibid*, s 3(d).
87 *Ibid*, s 3(e).
88 *Ibid*, s 6.
89 The ULCC Comments to *CJPTA* s 3 indicate this is the drafters' intention of s 3(d) (*ibid*, s 3.2).
90 Discussed above at note 64.
91 Subject to the court's rules of procedure for service of process *ex juris*.
92 Above note 56, s 10. The presumptive approach in the *CJPTA* influenced the SCC's new perspective on the application of the real and substantial connection test in *Club Resorts*, above note 64 at paras 52, 64, and 75–77.

within the province/territory. The presumption also attaches to foreign contracts that contain choice of law clauses naming the province/territory, and to the enforcement of foreign judgments and arbitral awards.[93]

This list is not exclusive, so the plaintiff may try to prove that the individual circumstances of the case establish a sufficient connection to the province/territory.[94] What criteria the court should apply to the evidence a plaintiff produces is not indicated in the *CJPTA*. The experience of the courts in the application of their respective enactments of the *CJPTA* so far seems to favour resorting to the common law factors listed in *Muscutt*,[95] but whether this practice will continue or change in light of the Supreme Court's fresh approach in *Club Resorts* towards the real and substantial connection test remains to be seen.[96]

In sum, to sue foreign defendants for foreign activities, plaintiffs must establish, either by application of a presumptive association or by their own evidence, that a real and substantial connection exists between the factual circumstances of their claim and the province or territory of Canada in which their actions are brought. By doing so, the plaintiff has in fact affirmed the suit is within the extended concept of the court's territorial jurisdiction and is not an exercise of extraterritorial jurisdiction.[97]

The only opportunities for the exercise of extraterritorial jurisdiction by a court under the *CJPTA* arise under the first or fourth grounds — that is, when the foreign defendant chooses to submit to the court's jurisdiction, or when the court is the forum of last resort.[98] A case has yet to be

---

93 Presumably under the 1958 UN *Convention on the Recognition and Enforcement of Foreign Arbitral Awards*, 10 June 1958, Can TS 1986 No 43 (entered into force 7 June 1959) [New York Convention] as legislatively implemented across Canada, for example, *United Nations Foreign Arbitral Awards Convention Act*, RSC 1985, c 16 (2d Supp).

94 As the ULCC Comments to s 10 explain, the defendant also has the right to try and rebut the presumption (above note 56).

95 See *Olney v Rainville*, 2008 BCSC 753 at para 32; *Cameron v Equineox Technologies Ltd*, 2009 BCSC 221 at para 25; and *Bouch v Penny (Litigation Guardian of)*, 2009 NSCA 80. But see *Stanway v Wyeth Canada Inc*, 2009 BCCA 592, especially the comment at para 73.

96 See, for example, *Kilderry Holdings Ltd v Canpower International BV*, 2013 BCCA 82, in which the court considered LeBel J's enunciation of the law on jurisdiction in *Club Resorts* to be consistent with the *CJPTA* as applied in British Columbia.

97 As explained in Section B, above in this chapter.

98 *CJPTA*, above note 56, ss 3 and 6. Section 6 (court of last resort) was not enacted in the Saskatchewan legislation.

heard by a court as the forum of last resort under the *CJPTA* so the actual operation of that criterion remains uncertain. But at least the existence of the plaintiff's right to move the court to assume jurisdiction on this statutory basis is certain,[99] unlike under common law, where the concept has been supported by the Ontario Court of Appeal, but not ruled on by the Supreme Court.[100] Even so, in neither of these two instances can the complainant compel an action to judgment. A suit, once begun, may still be dismissed if the defendant does not choose to submit to the court or the court does not exercise its discretion to accept jurisdiction as the forum of last resort.[101]

3) Restraints on Civil Jurisdiction

Both the common law and statutory principles for asserting jurisdiction are themselves subject to restraints of two kinds. First, a Canadian court has an overarching discretionary power not to accept jurisdiction in transnational situations when it considers it to be *forum non conveniens*. Secondly, a court may not assert jurisdiction over a foreign defendant who has a right to sovereign immunity.

The concept of *forum non conveniens* reflects the demands of interstate comity, as outlined in Section C(2), above in this chapter.[102] It developed at common law as part of the conflicts of law or private international law to provide suitable acknowledgment and allowance for the foreign sovereign interests involved in transnational situations. The court's responsibility is permissive, not mandatory, reflecting the non-binding nature of comity. The power is typically engaged when the courts of another state are asserted to be a more appropriate location for adjudication of the case. In the Supreme Court's judgment in *Club Resorts*, LeBel J observed:

> When it is invoked, the doctrine of *forum non conveniens* requires a court to go beyond a strict application of the test governing the recognition and assumption of jurisdiction. It is based on a recognition that

---

99 Subject to a possible constitutional challenge that this provision of the *CJPTA* is *ultra vires* the enacting province because it exceeds the territorial reach of provincial authority. See LeBel J's remarks on the constitutional aspects of the determination of civil adjudicative jurisdiction in *Club Resorts*, above note 64 at paras 31–34.

100 Discussed at note 71, above in this chapter.

101 *CJPTA*, above note 56, s 6.

102 Above at note 49. And see Chapter 3, Section A(3)(d).

> a common law court retains a residual power to decline to exercise its jurisdiction in appropriate, but limited, circumstances in order to assure fairness to the parties and the efficient resolution of the dispute.[103]

The Supreme Court also made clear that the assertion of *forum non conveniens* must be put forward by the defendant and may not be invoked by the court of its own initiative.[104] Further, the Supreme Court confirmed the standard for declaring *forum non conveniens* is the existence of an alternative forum which the defendant demonstrates is "clearly more appropriate."[105] Courts have developed lists of factors that might go towards making this decision, but in *Club Resorts* LeBel J cautioned that:

> the factors that a court may consider in deciding whether to apply *forum non conveniens* may vary depending on the context and might include the locations of parties and witnesses, the cost of transferring the case to another jurisdiction or of declining the stay, the impact of a transfer on the conduct of the litigation or on related or parallel proceedings, the possibility of conflicting judgments, problems related to the recognition and enforcement of judgments, and the relative strengths of the connections of the two parties.[106]

The *CJPTA* retains the limitation on the civil court's freedom to take jurisdiction when it is *forum non conveniens.*[107] In order to make this discretionary decision, the *CJPTA* indicates the court:

> *must* consider the circumstances relevant to the proceeding, including:
> (a) the comparative convenience and expense for the parties to the proceeding and for their witnesses, in litigating in the court or in any alternative forum,
> (b) the law to be applied to issues in the proceeding,
> (c) the desirability of avoiding multiplicity of legal proceedings,
> (d) the desirability of avoiding conflicting decisions in different courts,
> (e) the enforcement of an eventual judgment, and

---

103 Above note 64 at para 104.
104 *Ibid* at paras 102 & 103.
105 *Ibid* at paras 103 and 108–9, as first stated in *Amchem Products Inc v British Columbia (Workers' Compensation Board)*, [1993] 1 SCR 897.
106 Above note 64 at para 110.
107 Above note 56, s 11(1).

(f) the fair and efficient working of the Canadian legal system as a whole.[108]

This list of factors bears some similarity to the list of considerations under common law as enumerated by the Supreme Court in *Club Resorts*, but is not similarly indicative only. In light of its statutory force, the court "must" consider all these factors. As the Supreme Court observed on another occasion, "[s]ection 11 of the *CJPTA* was intended to codify the *forum non conveniens* test, not to supplement it."[109]

This discretionary power should not be exercised by a court until after it has determined that it may take extended territorial jurisdiction over a suit.[110] As a result, even if the extraterritorial features of a civil suit are adjudged to be within the extended territorial reach of the court, the action may still be dismissed as more appropriately pursued abroad.

Secondly, the willingness of a court to take jurisdiction over a transnational case may yet be inhibited where the defendant is a foreign state or one of its organs, agents, officials, or representatives. The prohibition is grounded in international law,[111] which grants the privilege of foreign sovereign immunity from local court jurisdiction, whether that is based on extended territorial or extraterritorial principles. The restriction is recognized and enforced in Canada principally through the *State Immunity Act*[112] and applies in all Canadian courts whether they take a common law or statutory approach to the determination of their civil jurisdiction. The *State Immunity Act* obviously overrides the common law principles about civil jurisdiction and is made to predominate over the statutory rules in the *CJPTA* by the latter's direction that, in the event of conflict between the *CJPTA* and another statute, federal or provincial, the other enactment shall prevail.[113] As a result, the immunities of foreign sovereign defendants as legislated in the *State Immunity Act*[114] will persist, regardless of the court's willingness to exercise its jurisdiction, whether on an extended territorial or an extraterritorial basis.

---

108 *Ibid*, s 11(2) [emphasis added].

109 *Teck Cominco Metals Ltd v Lloyd's Underwriters*, 2009 SCC 11 at para 22. See also the discussion of these factors in *Breeden*, above note 64.

110 *Club Resorts*, above note 64 at para 101.

111 As explained in Chapter 3, Section B(3)(a)(iii).

112 RSC 1985, c S-18, the operation of which is discussed in the case study on extraterritorial accountability for human rights abuses in Chapter 7, Section B.

113 Above note 56, s 12.

114 Above note 112.

E. EXTENDED TERRITORIALITY IN THE INTERNET CONTEXT

The principle of extended territoriality is of some usefulness in the global Internet context. States around the world have faced the challenge of addressing Internet-based activities.[115] They do so as activity normally within their sphere of authority moves into online forms (the migration of commerce to the Internet, for example). They also do so as the Internet embraces roles previously played by heavily regulated industries such as telecommunications and broadcasting. Civil wrongs also find their way onto the Internet: defamation and infringement of copyright or trademarks serve as examples. Many forms of criminal conduct have also migrated to the Internet (illicit gambling, distribution of child pornography, and fraud, to give but a few examples). States also react to other crimes and threats to national security posed by the Internet, such as hacking, malware, the sabotage of systems and networks, and the use of the Internet by terrorist and criminal organizations.[116] In all of these contexts, states assert the jurisdiction they have always asserted over similar activities within their borders. The difference is, of course, that these activities are no longer confined to their borders. The harmful conduct may originate outside national boundaries; it may originate inside the country, but be targeted elsewhere. States that act through an exercise of legislative, executive, or judicial authority do act territorially in one sense, but their actions often have extraterritorial effects or dimensions. As Held writes, "developments at the local level — whether economic, political or social — can acquire almost instantaneous global consequences and vice versa."[117]

There is a distinction, therefore, between two types of normative ventures that states might undertake: (1) where states collaborate to set new norms to govern conduct that spans borders; and (2) where a state must decide whether conduct has taken place substantially within its territorial jurisdiction and is thus subject to its laws. The principle of extended territoriality is of some use in legitimating such exercises of state

---

115 See the case studies on Internet gambling and virtual worlds in Chapter 7, Sections F & G, respectively.

116 For example, in the United States, see the *Computer Fraud and Abuse Act of 1986*, 18 USC § 1030 (1986), as well as provisions of the *USA PATRIOT Act*, Pub L 107-56, 115 Stat 272 (2001).

117 David Held, "Global Governance: Apocalypse Soon or Reform!" in David Held & Anthony McGrew, eds, *Globalization Theory* (Cambridge: Polity Press, 2007) 240 at 243 [citations omitted].

jurisdiction, but it is not always easy to negotiate the boundary between traditional notions of territorial (however extended) and extraterritorial action. In Section B of this chapter, we distinguished between assertions of extraterritorial jurisdiction, which ran the risk of infringing the sovereignty of other states, and domestic acts with extraterritorial effects, which generally did not. This traditional distinction is becoming blurred. If territorial action increasingly has extraterritorial effect, what is the level of impact or effect that warrants characterizing an act as extraterritorial? Is extraterritorial effect now a routine by-product of territorial action, and if so, does this embolden states to take actions within their territories that have explicit extraterritorial consequences? Clearly the notion of comity has some limiting power here, but the challenges are real. In the next section we explore various ways in which courts have faced up to those challenges.

1) Extended Territoriality and the Courts

With Internet-based matters more frequently coming before both criminal and civil courts, those courts increasingly struggle to come to terms with how to articulate the boundaries of their jurisdiction in a manner that is respectful of the principles of territoriality and comity. Courts are used to considering whether they have jurisdiction over both the subject matter (the dispute, the act, the crime) and the parties involved. As explained earlier in this chapter, these considerations have become merged into a more globalized assessment of whether there is an association that the Supreme Court of Canada has called a real and substantial connection to the jurisdiction.[118] This test accepts that the Internet may present various points of connection, but it measures the strength of these connections in order to avoid an inappropriate assertion of jurisdiction.

Subject matter jurisdiction relates to the court's authority over the subject matter of the dispute. To use an illustration from the context of intellectual property, jurisdiction over copyright matters is purely national in scope.[119] Thus, to have jurisdiction over a copyright dispute, the

---

118 *Libman*, above note 12. The *Libman* formulation of the test has been influential (see, for example, *R v Smith*, [2004] EWCA Crim 631), but courts in different states use varying terminology to describe essentially the same test.

119 See the useful discussion of this point in Lee Ann W Lockridge, "Intellectual Property in Outer Space: International Law, National Jurisdiction, and Exclusive Rights in Geospatial Data and Databases" (2006) 32:2 J Space L 319 at 342–43.

alleged act of infringement must have taken place within the state in which the court is located. An author whose book is copied by an American citizen in the United Kingdom cannot sue for infringement in the United States. Under British law, the lawsuit must be brought in the United Kingdom. Where there is no subject matter jurisdiction, a court will not hear a case. The principles are the same in the context of the Internet, though their application is more challenging as the locus of an act of infringement that takes place over the Internet may be more difficult to determine. The principles of subject matter jurisdiction and of national treatment between states established under international treaties remain constant; it is the relationship of the acts to state "territory" that are contested.

With some types of activity, territorial connection may be superficially obvious. For example, with the tort of defamation over the Internet, it is possible to say that a key element of the tort — publication and the ensuing harm of damage to reputation — occurred wherever the offending materials were viewed.[120] Yet this connection potentially exists wherever there is Internet access, and courts have increasingly tended to require "something more" in order to ground a connection to a state's territory.[121] The fact that a website might be accessed by residents of one jurisdiction does not necessarily mean that it has been,[122] or that consequences

---

120 Although some courts require that there be genuine harm in the jurisdiction where the material was viewed. See, for example, *Dow Jones & Co Inc v Jameel*, [2005] EWCA Civ 75, appealed to the House of Lords on a different issue, where the court found that its jurisdiction over the matter depended on the number of people who had viewed the online publication. It was established that only five had done so in England; this was considered insufficient and the court threw out the claim of defamation. See also *Al Amoudi v Brisard*, [2006] EWHC 1062 (QB) [*Al Amoudi*]. In Canada, the Supreme Court recently held that publication for defamation purposes occurred "when the impugned statements [documents on a US website] were read, downloaded and republished in Ontario by three newspapers" (*Breeden*, above note 64 at para 20).

121 Andrea Slane identifies this as an approach by courts, which she labels as "the Internet is 'here, there and everywhere'"; the ubiquity of the Internet is used by the courts to *restrain* their exercises of jurisdiction. "[C]ourts can claim that if the public addressed by the defendant's activity *meaningfully includes* the population of the forum jurisdiction, then the forum court may be entitled to exercise jurisdiction and to apply local law" (Andrea Slane, "Tales, Techs and Territories: Private International Law, Globalization, and the Legal Construction of Borderlessness on the Internet" (2008) 71:3 Law & Contemp Probs 129 at 144).

122 See *Crookes v Newton*, 2008 BCSC 1424, aff'd 2009 BCCA 392, appeal dismissed (without comment on this point), 2011 SCC 47.

should flow if it has. Thus courts have rejected jurisdiction in cases where, in spite of the fact that the material could have been viewed from within their domestic jurisdiction, there was an insufficient nexus between the parties and the jurisdiction.[123] By the same token, a company that does not target its wares or services to a particular jurisdiction does not infringe upon the trademarks of a trader in that jurisdiction simply because it uses the same or a similar trademark on its website.[124] Recent cases have looked at the extent to which a website targets a particular market.[125] Thus, the territorial connection for subject matter must be more than simply the ability to access content from a particular location.

The case of *eBay Canada Ltd v Canada (MNR)*[126] offers an interesting example of how a court reworked the notion of "territory" in the Internet age. In that case, Canada's Federal Court of Appeal considered an appeal regarding the obligation of eBay Canada to provide certain information about its Canadian "PowerSellers" to the Canada Revenue Agency (CRA). The CRA sought this information so as to determine whether these individuals had properly declared their income from their eBay activities. eBay Canada had resisted disclosure of this information, which was contained in electronic records stored on a server located in the United States and owned by eBay Inc, a US company. eBay Canada is a wholly owned subsidiary of eBay International, which in turn is a wholly owned subsidiary of eBay US. eBay Canada argued that the information being sought by the CRA was "foreign-based" information that could not be disclosed to the CRA under Canada's *Income Tax Act*.[127]

---

123 In *Al Amoudi*, above note 120, the court found that it was insufficient to simply show that the publication could have been accessed from the United Kingdom; it was necessary to show that a sufficient number of people had actually accessed it.

124 *Pro-C Ltd v Computer City, Inc* (2001), 55 OR (3d) 577 (CA). In *Zippo Manufacturing Company v Zippo Dot Com, Inc*, 952 F Supp 1119 (WD Pa 1997), a US court set out a "sliding scale" test for jurisdiction in Internet cases that looked at the degree of interactivity of the website. This test has been influential in many other cases, though it has become increasingly controversial. The test distinguishes between active and passive websites, and degrees of activity and passivity in between.

125 *Hy Cite Corporation v BadBusinessBureau.com*, 297 F Supp 2d 1154 (WD Wis 2004).

126 2008 FCA 348 [*eBay*].

127 RSC 1985, c 1 (5th Supp). Two provisions of the *Income Tax Act* were relevant in this dispute. The first, s 231.2(1), authorizes the Minister of National Revenue (MNR) to require any person to produce information "for any purpose related to the administration or enforcement of this Act. . . ." Section 231.2(2) governs the particular case of information relating to unnamed persons. In cases where information about unnamed persons is sought, the MNR is required to obtain judicial authorization.

A key issue was thus whether the information was properly characterized as "foreign-based." Justice Evans noted that section 231.6 of the *Income Tax Act*, which defines and addresses "foreign-based information," was enacted in 1988, a technological dark age, relatively speaking. At that point in time, it might have been reasonable to conclude that a document was located where it was situated. However, the court was of the view that technology changed the situation. Thus, Evans J stated:

> In order to determine the parameters of the concept of "location" on the present facts, it is helpful to consider whether the rationale for a separate statutory regime governing requirements to produce "foreign-based information or document" applies to information in electronic form which is accessible through computers situated far from the servers on which the information is stored.[128]

Justice Evans was of the opinion that courts should "interpret legislation in light of contemporary technology and, if necessary, should 'transpose' its terms to take into account the changed technological environment in which it is to be applied."[129] He concluded that the scheme under section 231.6 was directed at a situation where it might be "unduly onerous for a person to be required to produce material located outside Canada and in the possession of another person . . . ."[130] Justice Evans noted that there may also have been a legislative concern about the law having an unduly extraterritorial effect. From this he construed the set of facts before him. He declined to find that the information at issue was foreign-based. He noted that the information was accessible in Canada to employees of the appellants "with the click of a mouse."[131] In such

---

Judicial authorization will be forthcoming where "the person or group is ascertainable" (s 231.2(3)(*a*)) and where "the requirement is made to verify compliance by the person or persons in the group with any duty or obligation under this Act" (s 231.2(3)(*b*)). It was under this provision that the MNR had proceeded. Section 231.6 of the Act deals specifically with "foreign-based" information or documents, which are defined as information or documents located outside Canada. This section permits the MNR to require any person resident in Canada to supply it with foreign-based information or documents. Section 231.6 notably makes no provision for obtaining foreign-based information about unnamed persons. In fact, where foreign-based information is required, it is sought by requiring the person to whom the information relates to produce it.

128 *eBay*, above note 126 at para 43.

129 *Ibid* at para 42.

130 *Ibid* at para 47.

131 *Ibid* at para 48.

circumstances, he ruled that it would be nonsensical "to insist that information stored on servers outside Canada is as a matter of law located outside Canada for the purpose of section 231.6 because it has not been downloaded."[132] He noted that people did not travel to the site of servers in order to read the information stored in them. Further, he noted that if eBay Canada chose to download the information it could view on its screens, the information would be located in Canada. He expressed the view that "it is formalistic in the extreme for the appellants to say that, until this simple operation is performed, the information which they lawfully retrieve in Canada from the servers, and read on their computer screens in Canada, is not located in Canada."[133] Essentially, as no one outside the country was compelled to act (the documents could be accessed from eBay Canada's computer system in Canada), there was no extraterritorial action, and, in the court's view, any extraterritorial effect would be minimal.[134]

The issue is still open in Canada, as the Supreme Court has not taken a definite stance either way. Some language consistent with *eBay*'s slight stretching of territory can be found in the Supreme Court's 2008 decision in *Tele-Mobile Co v Ontario*.[135] The case dealt with "production orders" (a court order which compels third parties in possession of information relevant to a criminal investigation to produce documents or data for use in criminal investigations) and the dispute was unrelated to any issue about territoriality. However, the Court quoted the following text from the explanation given by the federal government to Parliament upon introduction of the law:

> Law enforcement agencies and crown prosecutors have been asking for a new investigative tool for some time and with *the proliferation of the Internet and the widespread adoption of new communications technologies*, the timing is right for this form of investigative tool.
>
> The production orders will solve a number of nagging issues for investigators including extraterritorial searches and timing issues. Under these new orders, persons who have possession or control of

132 *Ibid.*

133 *Ibid* at para 50.

134 The court noted as well that agreements between the appellants and PowerSellers provide that eBay may disclose "confidential 'eBay System Information.'" Thus the agreements between eBay Canada and its top sellers contemplated that such disclosures might take place (*ibid* at para 49).

135 2008 SCC 12.

> documents, data or information will have to produce that information whether it resides in Canada or abroad. Thus, as long as they have possession or control over the relevant information, they will be required to produce it no matter where it is located. *This solves the problem that has in part been created by inexpensive overseas data warehousing.*[136]

On the other hand, in the criminal case of *R v Morelli*,[137] the accused had been charged with possession of pornographic images of children, though not with the related offence of *accessing* child pornography. For the majority of the Supreme Court of Canada, Fish J ruled that "possession" had to mean more than the accused having accessed or viewed a file on the Internet — rather, the file must have been downloaded:

> [27] . . . viewing and possession should nevertheless be kept conceptually separate, lest the criminal law be left without the analytical tools necessary to distinguish between storing the underlying data file and merely viewing the representation that is produced when that data, residing elsewhere, is decoded . . . .
>
> [29] Without storing the underlying data, however, an image on a screen cannot be transferred. The mere possibility of sharing a *link* to a Website or enlarging the visual depiction of a Website, as one could "zoom in" on a TV screen image, is insufficient to constitute control over the content of that site. It is indeed the underlying data file that is the stable "object" that can be transferred, stored, and, indeed, possessed. More broadly, the object possessed must itself have some sort of permanence.
>
> [30] Thus, while it does not matter for the purposes of criminal possession how briefly one is in possession of the object, the thing said to be culpably possessed cannot — like a broadcast image flickering across a TV screen or a digital image displayed transiently on-screen — be essentially evanescent.
>
> [31] Plainly, the mere fact that an image has been accessed by or displayed in a Web browser does not, without more, constitute possession of that image.[138]

---

136 *Ibid* at para 40 [emphasis in original].

137 2010 SCC 8.

138 *Ibid* at paras 27 and 29–31. The Court also ruled that even a cached file could usually not amount to possession, though this was because caching was automatic and not

Justice Fish noted that by defining "possession" in this way, the Court did not intend to limit or circumscribe the concept of "constructive possession," and allowed for the possibility that, for example, saving a file into an external e-mail account could amount to constructive possession, even without the file ever being downloaded.[139]

There is no hard and fast rule that defines a state's territorial boundaries on the Internet. The High Court of Australia in *Dow Jones v Gutnick* noted that a single rule has not emerged "because the rules pay insufficient regard to the different kinds of tortious claims that may be made."[140] Tortious conduct on the Internet manifests itself in different ways. Hörnle notes that:

> not all torts committed by information disseminated through the Internet can be located by reference to the same action (such as uploading or downloading information) or by reference to the location of the same connecting factor (such as the server hosting the information, the establishment of the person producing the information, etc.).[141]

Courts have also used jurisdiction over persons or parties as a means of determining whether to take jurisdiction over a dispute even where there is a connection to the court's territorial jurisdiction. A single act can have legal consequences in more than one country, and redress may be more appropriate in some jurisdictions than in others. While Internet-based acts may span the globe, individuals remain fairly closely and predictably tied to particular places (by residence or by operation of a business, for example). Thus, inquiries into personal jurisdiction may allow courts to limit the circumstances in which they will assume jurisdiction over a dispute. In American private law cases, this concept is expressed in terms of the *de minimis* principle; in other words, a defendant must meet a certain minimum threshold for contact with the jurisdiction.[142] Therefore, where

---

normally the result of any intentional action on the part of the accused (and thus intent could not be proven) (*ibid* at paras 34–37).

139 *Ibid* at paras 32–33.

140 *Dow Jones & Co Inc v Gutnick*, [2002] HCA 56 at para 43 [*Gutnick*]. In *Gutnick*, the High Court found that the tort of defamation occurred in Australia when material harmful to the reputation of the Australian plaintiff was downloaded in Australia, even though it was hosted on a server located in the United States.

141 Julia Hörnle, "The Jurisdictional Challenge of the Internet" in Lilian Edwards & Charlotte Waelde, eds, *Law and the Internet*, 3d ed (Portland: Hart, 2009) 121 at 136.

142 *Milliken v Meyer*, 311 US 457 at 463 (1940); *International Shoe Co v Washington*, 326 US 310 at 316 (1945); Hörnle, *ibid* at 143–44.

the defendant has no real connection with the state, the court may decline to take jurisdiction over the matter in dispute. A defendant's place of residence and place of business may be relevant factors in establishing whether she has sufficient connection to the jurisdiction.[143] Again, however, while the principles are long established, the Internet destabilizes the concept of an individual's connection to a territory. Whereas a brick and mortar storefront is connected to a state in a real and physical manner, an Internet website may not be—particularly where it is not hosted on a server within the court's jurisdiction, but has merely been a site through which a few sales have been made in that jurisdiction.

Of course, at some point jurisdiction over parties and subject matter jurisdiction begin to fuse. In "locating" acts on the Internet, it is relevant to consider both physical points of contact and the relationship of the actor to the territory. It is not surprising, therefore, to view the emergence of more hybrid tests. For example, in Canada, the real and substantial connection test has evolved, and it requires the court to examine a range of factors before deciding to take jurisdiction. These factors blend considerations of both personal and subject matter jurisdiction.[144]

An important check to courts' exercise of adjudicative jurisdiction has always been the discretionary power of national courts to refuse the enforcement of a court decision from another jurisdiction. This power provides an interesting buffer that allows courts to reject undue reach into their jurisdiction by the laws of another country. In other words, through this aspect of adjudicative jurisdiction in the private international law arena,[145] national courts have a means of assessing the appropriateness of a foreign state's decision that it has both personal and subject matter jurisdiction regarding the acts of a defendant located in the national court's jurisdiction. A court asked to enforce such a decision will only do so if it is of the view that the deciding court had proper

---

143 See, for example, *Panavision International, LP v Toeppen*, 141 F3d 1316 at 1321 (9th Cir 1998); *American Information Corporation v American Infometrics, Inc*, 139 F Supp 2d 696 (D Md 2001); *Nissan Motor Co Ltd v Nissan Computer Corporation*, 89 F Supp 2d 1154 (CD Cal 2000), aff'd without opinion 246 F3d 675 (9th Cir 2000).

144 See Section D(1), above in this chapter.

145 It is well-established, indeed axiomatic, that courts will not enforce the public laws of other states: Sharon A Williams & Armand LC de Mestral, *An Introduction to International Law: Chiefly as Interpreted and Applied in Canada*, 2d ed (Toronto: Butterworths, 1987) at 125–26.

jurisdiction over both the subject matter and the parties. Where it is not persuaded that this was the case, it will not give effect to the judgment.[146]

Where a national court has been too quick to take personal jurisdiction over individuals, a decision to not enforce the judgment will serve as a means by which another court places a check on its extraterritorial reach. The court in the jurisdiction in which a foreign decision is sought to be enforced may decline to order its enforcement if it is of the view that the foreign court was not properly seized of the dispute.

It is in this way that courts play an important role in defining the territorial boundaries of state action. They can extend those boundaries through interpretation of laws (by finding that a law empowers, through the exercise of legislative jurisdiction, investigations into events that take place in whole or in part outside of the country); events (by finding, for example, that an Internet communication occurs both at the point of transmission and the point of reception, instead of one or the other); or facts (by finding that individuals have sufficient ties to the jurisdiction). They can restrict the boundaries by the same means. Finally, they can limit the reach of other states' laws by refusing to enforce judgments against their residents, nationals, or corporations where they are of the view that the foreign court was not properly seized of jurisdiction.

F. CONCLUSION

The jurisdiction of both the civil and the criminal courts of Canada is in general limited by their geographic or territorial scope. In criminal cases, the *Criminal Code* only applies within Canada unless a particular offence or jurisdictional provision prescribes its extraterritorial reach. Likewise, in civil cases the courts ordinarily must have territorial authority over the parties and the subject matter. Extraterritorial civil jurisdiction is limited to actions in which the foreign defendant becomes personally subject to the court by submission to or service within the forum, and suits before a Canadian court as the forum of last resort. But transnational crimes, contracts, torts, and other cross-border transactions are becoming so frequent in our globalized world that both civil and criminal courts have had to refine the means to determine when a situation is sufficiently associated with Canada that it can be said to be within Canadian territorial jurisdiction. This is the concept of "extended territorial

146 See, for example, *Lucasfilm Ltd and Others v Ainsworth*, [2009] EWCA Civ 1328.

jurisdiction" for which the Supreme Court of Canada (led by La Forest J) has developed the test of a real and substantial connection to the Canadian forum. Introduced for criminal cases in *Libman* in 1985 and "formally adopted"[147] for civil suits in *Morguard Investments*[148] in 1990, it is now of general application to cases involving extraterritorial features, whether they are criminal or regulatory prosecutions, civil claims, or requests for the enforcement of foreign judgments. Deciding whether an action passes the test of having a real and substantial connection to Canada is a fact-dependent determination for which the Supreme Court of Canada has given individual directions in criminal and civil actions.

Thus extended territorial jurisdiction has emerged as the judicial vehicle that drives curial authority — reach of the court — over transnational cases. It is *not* extraterritorial jurisdiction, but it is designed to deal with cases involving some extraterritorial aspects. Even so, the application of extended territorial jurisdiction does not always empower the court to hear a case as it is subject to other external restraints.

Comity exerts a non-binding admonition on courts to exercise their discretion not to assert jurisdiction out of respect for the sovereign authority of the foreign state involved in the transnational situation. In criminal matters, comity is part of the *Libman* test, a formalized and mandatory inquiry as to whether the Crown should be prevented from prosecuting a particular case because of its foreign elements, and the interest of other states therein. In civil actions, the concept has become formalized in the conflict of laws — or private international law — principle of *forum non conveniens*. In addition, foreign state immunity is a deeply rooted privilege in international law that extends to foreign sovereign acts, personnel, and property in both criminal and civil circumstances. Canadian courts have a legal duty to respect the immunity from their jurisdiction of foreign states and their governments, agencies, officials, and representatives.

Similar principles govern the question whether or not foreign court judgments should be respected and enforced by Canadian courts. Substantial territorial connection of the foreign forum with the parties and the subject matter of the case will be looked for by the Canadian court, subject to the tempering influence of comity and respect for Canadian state immunity.

---

147 Justice LeBel in *Club Resorts*, above note 64 at para 24.

148 Above note 27.

Particularly through the choices made by courts in their exercise of adjudicative jurisdiction, the practices of Canada and other states reviewed in this chapter have demonstrated the stress that is still being placed on the notion of territorial jurisdiction in the face of globalization and the ubiquity of the Internet. Further, these practices also illustrate the continued currency of the notion of territoriality as the foundation for the exercise of state power. Problem areas, of course, remain, and the law of jurisdiction is often shaped according to the body of substantive law that is being dealt with and the kinds of problems that law raises, but courts and legislatures have proven remarkably adaptable and creative. Territoriality may be becoming a much more fluid concept than in years past, but for the moment, the ongoing development of "extended territoriality" as a jurisdictional sub-principle illustrates that it seems to be able to bend without breaking.

CHAPTER 5

Jurisdiction over the Internet?

States typically regulate matters arising within their territorial sovereignty, but that practice is inadequate to govern the Internet. Since Internet-based activities occur instantaneously both within and outside of a state's territory — they are at once national, transnational, and global — the boundaries of the state's jurisdiction, whether legislative, executive, or adjudicative, are severely strained. In this chapter, we address these issues of jurisdictional reach by considering how existing national laws, often enacted prior to the introduction of the Internet, may be extended to apply to Internet-based activities. We also consider the corollary — how Internet-based activities are eroding political sovereignty and state jurisdiction.

A. THE REACH OF STATE JURISDICTION OVER THE INTERNET

When jurisdiction over the Internet and its uses is at issue, states have to consider whether the acts or conduct that they seek to control, regulate, or modify are appropriately linked to their territory. The challenge is by no means a small one. In the early days of the Internet, Johnson and Post observed that the Internet:

> is destroying the link between geographical location and: (1) the *power* of local governments to assert control over online behaviour; (2) the *effects* of online behaviour on individuals and things; (3) the *legitimacy*

of a local sovereign's efforts to regulate global phenomena; and (4) the ability of physical location to give *notice* of which sets of rules apply.[1]

These challenges remain. Not only is Internet-based activity difficult to regulate, its effects are distributed and difficult to measure, and the laws of individual states are unlikely to have much effect without some form of global co-operation. Internet-based activities raise deep concerns for states since they affect important matters of local and national governance, such as cultural and linguistic policy, economic policy, social policy, criminal law, and morality.[2]

1) Culture, Language, and Expression

Cultural and linguistic policies are being increasingly disrupted by the Internet. For example, the Quebec government's legislation requiring businesses operating in Quebec to offer a French language option to consumers encountered significant hurdles with the rise of e-commerce.[3] Businesses with premises in Quebec must ensure that they have a French language version of their website in order to comply with the law. However, there is no way to stop businesses anywhere else in the world from selling their wares or services to Quebeckers over the Internet in any language they choose.[4] Cultural policies might also be at risk. Federal Canadian content regulations[5] have long required radio and television undertakings to meet certain quotas for Canadian broadcast content. The federal regulator has so far hesitated to apply such rules

---

1 David R Johnson & David Post, "Law and Borders: The Rise of Law in Cyberspace" (1996) 48 Stan L Rev 1367 at 1370 [emphasis in the original].

2 Thomas Schultz, "Carving up the Internet: Jurisdiction, Legal Orders, and the Private/Public International Law Interface" (2008) 19:4 EJIL 799 at 801, argues that it is the area of protection of local values in which one sees the strongest assertion of state jurisdiction over Internet activity [Schultz].

3 The legislation is known as the *Charter of the French Language*, RSQ c C-11. It provides that the language of business in Quebec is French. Section 58 of the law requires all public signs and advertising to be in French.

4 This is effectively conceded by the fact that the Office québécois de la langue française indicates that only those businesses with an address in Quebec must have a French version of their website. See Office québécois de la langue française, *Information and Communication Technologies in French*, online: Gouvernment du Québec www.oqlf.gouv.qc.ca/ressources/bibliotheque/depliants/20100212_depliant6fva.pdf at 4.

5 See, for example, *Radio Regulations, 1986*, SOR/86-982 [*Radio Regulations*].

in the context of the Internet.[6] In many countries, broadcasters have also had to account for certain standards of "decency," including restrictions regarding profanity, nudity, and violence.[7] These restrictions functioned so long as the state could exercise control over the broadcasters. In a decentralized, distributed system such as the Internet, consumer choice governs, and it will be increasingly difficult for states to impose cultural and other agendas.[8]

The regulation of citizen expression also becomes more challenging on the Internet. There are numerous instances of national governments attempting to transpose limits on various types of expression from traditional media to the Internet, often with great difficulty. Examples include attempts in Canada and Germany to address the dissemination of hate propaganda over the Internet,[9] attempts in China to limit cer-

---

6 Canadian Radio-television and Telecommunications Commission (CRTC), *Broadcasting Regulatory Policy* CRTC 2009-329 (4 June 2009), online: CRTC www.crtc.gc.ca/eng/archive/2009/2009-329.htm.

7 In Canada, the CRTC may refuse to renew the licence of a broadcaster that does not comply with prescribed standards of decency. This is a system that works reasonably well in the context of a broadcasting network where licences are required in order to operate a broadcast undertaking. It does not work at all in the context of the Internet. The regulations relating to content standards are found in the *Radio Regulations*, above note 5, ss 3(c) (obscene or profane content) and 3(b) (hate speech), and *Television Broadcasting Regulations, 1987*, SOR/87-49, ss 5(1)(c) (obscene or profane content) and 5(1)(b) (hate speech). In 2011, the CRTC attracted international media attention when it ruled that Canadian radio stations could not play the Dire Straits song "Money for Nothing" unless a certain word, considered homophobic, was edited out. The decision is currently under review: "CRTC Asks the Canadian Broadcast Standards Council to Review Decision to Ban Dire Straits Song" (21 January 2011), online: CRTC www.crtc.gc.ca/eng/com100/2011/r110121.htm.

8 For a discussion of content regulation on the Internet in the European Union, see Elizabeth Newman, "EC Regulation of Audio-visual Content on the Internet" in Lilian Edwards & Charlotte Waelde, eds, *Law and the Internet*, 3d ed (Portland: Hart, 2009) 159.

9 The Canadian Human Rights Commission (CHRC), acting under s 13 of the *Canadian Human Rights Act*, RSC 1985, c H-6 [*CHRA*], has struggled to address hate speech on the Internet, with a great deal of controversy. A report commissioned by the CHRC recommended that extreme forms of hate speech be dealt with under *Criminal Code* provisions and not under the *CHRA*. See Richard Moon, *Report to the Canadian Human Rights Commission Concerning Section 13 of the Canadian Human Rights Act and the Regulation of Hate Speech on the Internet* (Ottawa: Canadian Human Rights Commission, 2008). Moon argued that ISPs should play some role in limiting hate speech over the Internet through the application of acceptable use policies to customer activity (*ibid* at 41). In June 2013, private member's Bill C-304 resulted in the repeal of s 13 (Bill C-304, *An Act to Amend the Canadian Human Rights Act (Protecting*

tain types of discourse by imposing technological constraints on infrastructure,[10] attempts in countries such as Iran to block access to certain Internet services,[11] and attempts to apply French law to the sale of Nazi memorabilia on eBay.[12]

Economic policy is also difficult to apply to the Internet. Governments that have sought to facilitate electronic commerce, to regulate competition, and to impose taxation on online goods and services have all quickly realized that little can be done without international co-operation.[13] Economic policy is also reflected in international trade treaties, and these have proliferated in recent years in regional, bi-, and multilateral forms.[14]

Even social policy with Internet dimensions pose challenges to concepts of territoriality. For example, Canada has a shorter term of protec-

---

Freedom), 1st Sess, 41st Parl, 2013 (assented to 26 June 2013)). This effectively leaves Internet-based hate speech regulation to the field of criminal law. In Germany, the German High Court took jurisdiction over an Australian citizen who posted holocaust-denial material online. See *Töben*, BGH (12 December 2001) 1 StR 184/00 LG Mannheim, reproduced at (2001) 8 Neue Juristiche Wochenschrift 624 [*Töben*].

10 Subjects that are banned include democracy, the Dalai Lama, and the Falun Gong. See, for example, Jack Linchuan Qiu, "Virtual Censorship in China: Keeping the Gate between the Cyberspaces" (1999–2000) 4 Int'l J Comm L & Pol'y 1. However, Zittrain argues that these technological measures are imperfect, and work-arounds are generally possible. See Jonathan Zittrain, *The Future of the Internet and How to Stop It* (New Haven, CT: Yale University Press, 2008) at 106. See also Yochai Benkler, *The Wealth of Networks: How Social Production Transforms Markets and Freedom* (New Haven, CT: Yale University Press, 2006) at 268–69.

11 For example, Iran has banned access to the Internet services of both Facebook and Twitter. See Saeed Kamali Dehghan, "Iran Tightens Online Censorship to Counter US 'Shadow Internet'" *The Guardian* (13 July 2011), online: The Guardian www.guardian.co.uk/world/2011/jul/13/iran-tightens-online-censorship.

12 See the discussion of the litigation arising in this matter, below.

13 In fact, there is a great deal of effort at the international level to harmonize norms in order to facilitate electronic commerce. See, for example, Charles H Martin, "The Electronic Contracts Convention, the CISG, and New Sources of E-Commerce Law" (2008) 16:2 Tul J of Int'l & Comp L 467. For a discussion of the challenges of taxation of the Internet, see Ken Griffin, Mark McMurtrey, & LeaAnn Smith, "To Tax or Not to Tax? Foreign and Domestic Taxation of the Internet" (2008) 12:1 Proceedings of the Academy of Legal, Ethical and Regulatory Issues 1. In the competition or antitrust context, see Daniel D Sokol, "International Antitrust Institutions" in Andrew T Guzman, ed, *Cooperation, Comity and Competition Policy* (Oxford: Oxford University Press, 2010) 186, online: Oxford University Press www.oxfordscholarship.com/view/10.1093/acprof:oso/9780195387704.001.0001/acprof-9780195387704-chapter-010.

14 Perhaps the most notable of these has been the *Final Act Embodying the Results of the Uruguay Round of Multinational Trade Agreements*, 15 April 1994, 1867 UNTS 3 (December 1993 text) and 33 ILM 1143 (1994) (April 1994 text).

tion for copyright than does either the United States or the EU member states.[15] This means that works fall into the public domain in Canada twenty years before they do in those other jurisdictions. Yet a Canadian website that seeks to make public domain works freely available online might well run into difficulties if those works can be accessed and downloaded in countries where the term of copyright protection has not yet expired.[16] Further, Canadians would not benefit from more general access to works in the public domain in Canada from internationally hosted websites; effectively, their access to works from such sites would be limited to those works in the public domain in those countries with longer terms of protection than in Canada. In this way, the Canadian policy decision to have a shorter period of copyright protection is undermined in the context of the Internet by the different policy decisions of other countries.

The now infamous sale of Nazi memorabilia on the website Yahoo.com offers an illustration of another challenge to state jurisdiction posed by the Internet. It is a challenge that manifests itself in many ways and across a range of subject matter. In the Yahoo! case, advocacy groups in France brought a complaint against both Yahoo! (the company) and the Yahoo! France website (which served to provide access to Yahoo.com) over the sale of hundreds of objects of Nazi memorabilia through Yahoo's auctions page. A French court found that Yahoo! had violated French law, as both the illegal objects and related hate propaganda materials could be accessed and viewed in France. The court was of the view that as the auction site could identify French visitors to the site well enough to display French language banner advertisements to them, it was clearly targeting them. One part of the court's order was for Yahoo! to limit both the hosting of and the access to offensive content in France.[17] The court

---

15 In Canada, the term of protection is the life of the author plus fifty years. In the European Union and the United States, it is the life of the author plus seventy years.

16 This has proven to be a significant challenge, for example, for those who have tried to create online archives of public domain works. See, for example, Hannibal Travis, "Building Universal Digital Libraries: An Agenda for Copyright Reform" (2005–2006) 33 Pepp L Rev 761 at 792ff.

17 Trib gr inst Paris, 22 May 2000, *Association Union des Etudiants Juifs de France, la Ligue contre le racisme et l'Antisémitisme (LICRA) contre société YAHOO! Inc et société YAHOO FRANCE*. Available in French, online: lexinter.net www.lexinter.net/JPTXT/licra_yahoo.htm. An English translation of the decision, by Richard Salis is available, online: Juriscom.net http://lthoumyre.chez.com/txt/jurisfr/cti/yauctions 20000522.htm.

found that since it was technologically possible to block access to certain content to visitors from France, Yahoo! was required to adopt such measures to avoid breaching the law.[18] This interim ruling was confirmed by a second decision rendered after the court considered a study by a team of Internet experts who assessed the technological feasibility of blocking French users from accessing the disputed content.[19]

Following the French court order, Yahoo! sought declaratory relief from the US District Court for the Northern District of California, asking that the court decline to recognize or enforce the French court orders. Judge Fogel essentially found that the French court's decision could not be reconciled with the First Amendment protection for freedom of speech.[20] A US-based company could not be forced to comply with the regulation by another country of speech protected under the First Amendment in the United States. Thus the ruling turned on the difference in values between the two countries. In France, the goals of fighting racism and anti-Semitism justified restrictions on speech, whereas such restrictions would not be justifiable in the United States. The decision underlines a fundamental challenge with the exercise of state jurisdiction in relation to the Internet.

The decision was appealed to the 9th Circuit Court of Appeals.[21] The *en banc* court reversed the decision and remanded it with directions to

---

18 Note that Uta Kohl is critical of this decision and argues that it was not evident that the Yahoo! content had "a substantial effect on French territory so as to make an assertion of regulatory competence reasonable." Uta Kohl, *Jurisdiction and the Internet: A Study of Regulatory Competence over Online Activity* (Cambridge, UK: Cambridge University Press, 2007) at 100.

19 Trib gr inst Paris, 20 November 2000, Ordonnance de Référé. Available in French, online: Lapres & Associes www.lapres.net/ya2011.html; English translation available, online: Lapres & Associes www.lapres.net/yahen11.html. Note that Schultz, above note 2 at 821, argues that using filtering as a means of restricting the liability of companies online has consequences for a free and open flow of information on the Internet.

20 *Yahoo! Inc v La Ligue Contre Le Racisme Et L'Antisemitisme*, 169 F Supp 2d 1181 (ND Cal 2001). For a discussion of this case, see Evan Scheffel, "*Yahoo, Inc. v. La Ligue Contra Le Racisme et L'Antisemitism*: Court Refuses to Enforce French Order Attempting to Regulate Speech Occurring Simultaneously in the U.S. and in France" (2003) 19:2 Santa Clara Computer & High Tech LJ 549; Sakura Mizuno, "When Free Speech and the Internet Collide: Yahoo! – Nazi – Paraphernalia Case" (2001) 10 Currents 56.

21 *Yahoo! Inc v La Ligue Contre Le Racisme Et L'Antisemitisme*, 433 F3d 1199 (9th Cir 2006) [*Yahoo II*]. For comments on the appellate court decision, see, for example, Andrew M Pickett, "Much Yahoo! About Nothing: The Ninth Circuit, Jurisprudential Schizophrenia, and The Road Not Taken in *Yahoo! v. La Ligue Contre le Racisme et*

dismiss the action, although the court was not united in its reasons for judgment. A majority of judges found the District Court had personal jurisdiction over the defendants, but the matter was not ripe for decision. A minority of the judges held the matter was ripe, but the court below lacked personal jurisdiction. The case went no further because the US Supreme Court did not grant *certiorari*.

In ruling that the decision was not yet ripe, the majority of the 9th Circuit Court of Appeals noted that it was not clear from the facts whether Yahoo!, in changing its practices, had already substantially complied with the French court's orders. If there were substantial compliance, there might be no attempt to enforce the judgment in the United States. In addition, if Yahoo! were already in substantial compliance, the argument that the enforcement of the French court's orders would violate the First Amendment would be difficult to assess. The court noted that there did remain an issue of whether the First Amendment had extraterritorial effect, and thus whether denying access to certain content to French users amounted to a violation of the First Amendment even if US-based users were not affected by any changes. However, the majority noted that without knowing if Yahoo!'s policy changes brought it into substantial compliance, there was no way to know whether there would actually be a First Amendment issue, and without knowing what further steps would need to be taken, it would be impossible to tell whether any such argument would be based on the infringement of rights in the United States and France, or simply in the United States alone. The majority concluded that, "First Amendment issues arising out of international Internet use are new, important and difficult. We should not rush to decide such issues based on an inadequate, incomplete or unclear record."[22] Thus, although the case does not resolve these interesting and important issues, it does expose some of the challenges of determining the limits of state jurisdiction in the context of the Internet.

---

l'Antisémitisme" (2006) 8 Tul J Tech & Intell Prop 231; Robert T Razzano, "Error 404 Jurisdiction Not Found: The Ninth Circuit Frustrates the Efforts of Yahoo! Inc. to Declare a Speech-Restrictive Foreign Judgment Unenforceable" (2004–2005) 73 U Cin L Rev 1743.

22 *Yahoo II*, *ibid* at 1223.

2) Morality

It has always been the case that some activities may be regulated differently in some jurisdictions than in others. This is particularly the case with so-called moral questions—those involving gambling and pornography, for instance, both of which are the subject of case studies in Chapter 7. It is also the case with speech-related activities: hate crimes, sedition, and other forms of subversive speech are treated quite differently in different jurisdictions, as the Yahoo! case illustrates. A state seeking to control or restrict these forms of speech within its own borders may wish to target those engaging in these forms of speech in other countries.[23] Conduct may be perfectly legal in the jurisdiction where a site is hosted, even though it is not legal in all of the jurisdictions where the particular wares or services offered are consumed. Where this is the case, a country may seek to assert jurisdiction over the offshore Internet host or actor on the basis that their activities spill over into their jurisdiction, where they are illegal.[24] Or, they may seek various compromise solutions that reflect the limitations on their ability to enforce their laws; for example, the European Union regulates foreign gambling only where there is "equipment" in place in the particular member state, while Australia essentially concedes and prohibits unlicensed gambling only by Australian residents.[25] A state may also seek to have their own

---

23 *Töben*, above note 9. In *Citron v Zündel (No 4)* (2002), 41 CHRR D/274 (CHRT), the CHRC found Canadian citizen Ernst Zündel to have violated the *CHRA*, above note 9, by ordering an employee based in California to upload hate propaganda to a website hosted on a server also located in California. Here, the national jurisdiction was exercised not by pursuit of offshore actors, but by pursuing someone in Canada for directing certain activities in another country.

24 See, for example, *People v World Interactive Gaming Corp*, 714 NYS2d 844 (1999). In this case, a company based in Antigua (but with a Delaware-incorporated parent company) operated an online gambling website from Antigua. The New York court took criminal jurisdiction over the matter because the gambling site was accessed by many residents of New York. The court stated that a "computer server cannot be permitted to function as a shield against liability, particularly in this case where respondent's activity targeted New York as the location where they conducted many of their allegedly illegal activities" (at 850). Note, however, that in this case the location of the company in Antigua may have been deliberate so as to evade the reach of US authorities. For other offshore gambling cases in which US courts have taken jurisdiction, see *United States v American Sports, Ltd*, 286 F3d 641 (3d Cir 2002) and *United States v Ross*, 1999 WL 782749 (SDNY Dist Ct 1999).

25 See Joseph J McBurney, "To Regulate or to Prohibit: An Analysis of the Internet Gambling Industry and the Need for a Decision on the Industry's Future in the United States" (2005–2006) 21 Conn J Int'l L 337 at 355.

national law limitations (such as a minimum age requirement for participation in the activity) implemented by the offshore site.[26] It is also a peculiarity of the Internet context that in some cases, the limitations required may be achievable through the use of technology. The French court in Yahoo!, for example, looked at ways in which Yahoo! could modify its system so as to block access to offensive content to French users without affecting access by US users. This capacity to implement different state norms through adaptations of computer code represents another interesting dimension of state jurisdiction over the Internet. More recently, states have negotiated directly with major multinational technology companies to have their (often repressive) policies implemented within the technology as a condition of operation within their borders.[27]

3) National Law and Transborder Companies

Significant challenges can arise where a state sets norms of conduct within its own jurisdiction that are infringed by Internet-based companies located elsewhere, whose services are nonetheless available to its citizens. The battle between Facebook and the Privacy Commissioner of Canada offers an interesting illustration of the extent to which Canadian law can reach, however informally, outside the boundaries of the state. Facebook, which operates a hugely popular social networking site internationally, was the subject of a complaint to the Privacy Commissioner in 2008.[28] The complaint alleged that the site operators violated

---

26 See, more generally, the case study in Chapter 7, Section F.

27 For example, Research in Motion was forced to address security concerns raised by the Chinese and Indian governments in order to continue offering its services in those countries. See "Blackberry Server in China? India Wants a Monitoring Unit Too" *The Times of India* (29 July 2010), online: The Times of India http://articles.timesofindia.indiatimes.com/2010-07-29/india/28316801_1_security-agencies-blackberry-server-security-concerns. After facing controversy over its co-operation with Chinese authorities over censorship issues, Google first pulled out of China, and later returned to that market but under different terms. See Amir Efrati & Loretta Chao, "Google Softens Tone on China" *Wall Street Journal Online* (12 January 2012), online: The Wall Street Journal http://online.wsj.com/article/SB10001424052970203436904577155003097277514.html.

28 The original complaint made against Facebook to the Privacy Commissioner is in a letter from the Canadian Internet Policy and Public Interest Clinic (CIPPIC) to the Privacy Commissioner of Canada (30 May 2008), online: CIPPIC www.cippic.ca/uploads/CIPPICFacebookComplaint_29May08.pdf. Privacy and extraterritoriality are considered in greater detail in the case study in Chapter 7, Section C.

Canadian data protection laws by not ensuring that the collection, use, and disclosure of personal information were in accordance with those laws. The Privacy Commissioner, emboldened by a court decision that found that she had jurisdiction to investigate complaints involving foreign companies so long as the collection, use, or disclosure of information took place in Canada,[29] investigated, and found that Facebook was not compliant.[30] Interestingly, Facebook chose to work with the Commissioner to attempt to change their system to her satisfaction.[31] The alternative was to face an enforcement action in Canadian Federal Court. It is not clear what effect any decision of the Federal Court could or would have had on Facebook, which is based in California.[32]

The case offers interesting insights into the effect that a national law setting data protection norms can have on the practices adopted by a for-

29 *Lawson v Accusearch, Inc (cob Abika.com)*, 2007 FC 125. In this case, the Federal Court ruled that while the *Personal Information Protection and Electronic Documents Act*, SC 2000, c 5, did not have extraterritorial effect, the Office of the Privacy Commissioner of Canada did have the power to investigate the collection, use, and disclosure of personal information by a US-based company where the collection, use, or disclosure was linked to Canada, essentially on the basis of qualified territoriality. See the case study in Chapter 7, Section C; and see Donna L Davis, "Tracking Cross-Border Data Flows: A Comment on *Lawson v Accusearch Inc.*" (2007) 6:2 CJLT 119.

30 The Privacy Commissioner's findings with respect to the complaint are available in Elizabeth Denham, "Report of Findings into the Complaint Filed by the Canadian Internet Policy and Public Interest Clinic (CIPPIC) against Facebook Inc under the *Personal Information Protection and Electronic Documents Act*" (16 July 2009), online: Office of the Privacy Commissioner of Canada www.priv.gc.ca/cf-dc/2009/2009_008_0716_e.pdf.

31 The Commissioner later reviewed the changes made by Facebook in response to the complaint, and ruled that the matter was resolved. See "Privacy Commissioner Completes Facebook Review" (22 September 2010), online: Office of the Privacy Commissioner of Canada www.priv.gc.ca/media/nr-c/2010/nr-c_100922_e.cfm.

32 Though in terms of the exercise of enforcement jurisdiction, at least, it is interesting to note that privacy authorities in various states have begun to co-operate in their investigations — a good example of which is a recent case involving co-operation between the Privacy Commissioner of Canada and her Dutch counterparts; see Office of the Privacy Commissioner of Canada, News Release, "WhatsApp's Violation of Privacy Law Partly Resolved after Investigation by Data Protection Authorities: Canadian and Dutch Data Privacy Guardians Release Findings from Investigation of Popular Mobile App" (28 January 2013), online: Office of the Privacy Commissioner of Canada www.priv.gc.ca/media/nr-c/2013/nr-c_130128_e.asp and the Dutch Data Protection Authority, News Release, "Canadian and Dutch Data Privacy Guardians Release Findings from Investigation of Popular Mobile App" (28 January 2013), online: Dutch Data Protection Authority www.dutchdpa.nl/Pages/en_pb_20130128-whatsapp.aspx.

eign company. Similar issues arise in the European Union in the case of the data protection regime and some Internet companies. For example, Google (like other search engines) may retain IP addresses associated with search data. Google has had the practice of retaining this data indefinitely. However, if the data qualifies as personal information, the retention of the data indefinitely is not permitted under EU data protection norms governing the retention and reuse of personal information.[33] Google did agree to reduce its period of data retention under pressure from the European Union;[34] however, the reduced retention period remained controversially high, resulting in a complaint against Google by the Article 29 Data Protection Working Party.[35] Like the Facebook case, the issue is one of national norms or standards pushing multinational Internet-based companies to make changes to how they operate. However, the changes tend to be voluntary, and might only meet the regulator halfway. Enforcement beyond this point remains problematic, as the jurisdictional complexities will be challenging for any court that tries to render a decision on the violation of domestic norms that can be enforced without limiting or denying its nationals access to a global site or service.

It is to be noted that states have clearly not abdicated their territorial jurisdiction when it comes to Internet-based activities that touch on social, cultural, or "public order" issues. Indeed, Schultz argues that "[t]he protection of such local values lies at the heart of modern conceptions of political sovereignty . . . ."[36] More specifically, he argues that the principles of jurisdiction arose to ensure that one state, in the regulation of matters within its borders, does not unduly encroach on the sovereign-

---

33 EC, *Directive 2006/24/EC of the European Parliament and of the Council of 15 March 2006 on the retention of data generated or processed in connection with the provision of publicly available electronic communications services or of public communications networks and amending Directive 2002/58/EC*, [2006] OJ, L 105/54 online: EUR-lex http://eur-lex.europa.eu/LexUriServ/LexUriServ.do?uri=OJ:L:2006:105:0054:0063:EN:PDF [*Data Retention Directive*].

34 Edwards & Waelde, eds, above note 8 at 458. See also Christopher Kuner, "Data Protection Law and International Jurisdiction on the Internet (Part 1)" (2010) 18:2 Int'l JL & IT 176.

35 See letter from Article 29 Data Protection Working Party to Mr Page (16 October 2012), online: European Commission http://ec.europa.eu/justice/data-protection/article-29/documentation/other-document/files/2012/20121016_letter_to_google_en.pdf.

36 Schultz, above note 2 at 807.

ty of another.[37] It is not surprising, therefore, that it is in this soft area of values that we find some of the more contentious exercises of jurisdiction, as well as a rising tide of regulatory approaches that mandate technological boundaries to online activities.

B. THE EROSION OF STATE JURISDICTION

Not only does the Internet pose new challenges for states in terms of how to determine when and how they should exercise their jurisdiction, but the Internet and the related phenomenon of globalization discussed in Chapter 2 have an eroding effect on jurisdiction. Jurisdiction is, of course, an essential element of state sovereignty as it is defined as the ability of states to govern that which concerns their territory. Yet there are a number of forces and factors that undermine both the concept of territory and the ability of the state to truly regulate what occurs within its borders. Sassen notes that "globalization has brought strong pressures for the deregulation of a broad range of markets, economic sectors, and national borders and, furthermore, for the privatization of public sector firms and operations."[38] These are clearly phenomena that erode state jurisdiction by effectively removing certain subject matter from state authority.[39]

The globalization of commerce — first between businesses, and more recently with the rise of e-commerce, between business and individuals — has given rise to two other phenomena that erode state jurisdiction through the choices of private actors.[40] The first is the ubiquity of choice of law clauses that require parties to contracts to settle disputes in one jurisdiction over all others with connections to the agreement. These choice of law clauses thus limit state jurisdiction over a

37 *Ibid* at 808. Schultz writes: "To reconcile these two imperatives — to protect local values without encroaching on the territory of other states — is the fundamental problem of state intervention on the Internet."

38 Saskia Sassen, *Territory, Authority, Rights: From Medieval to Global Assemblages*, revised ed (Princeton: Princeton University Press, 2006) at 222 [Sassen].

39 Schultz, above note 2 at 801, comments on the rise of transnationalism as a phenomenon that contributes to the undermining of national jurisdictions.

40 Schultz, *ibid* at 805, argues that "online communities of various kinds, albeit primarily of a commercial nature, will further the development of their social norms into private legal systems."

wide range of transactions that might otherwise have been considered to fall within the jurisdiction of their national courts.[41]

In addition to choice of law clauses, mandatory arbitration clauses have found their way into business and consumer contracts. By agreeing to mandatory arbitration of disputes, the parties move any potential disputes over the agreement to a private dispute resolution provider instead of the national courts of any one country. Schultz describes these regimes as causing "their normative environments to be largely divorced from public legal systems: a private dispute resolution mechanism applies privately developed norms and the outcome of the procedure is enforced through private means."[42] In some cases, such as with domain name registrations, the arbitration clause does not necessarily remove the jurisdiction of the courts.[43] Yet the arbitration mechanism, while not definitively relocating all disputes, still moves the vast number of them out of national courts.[44]

Domain name disputes centre on the issue of bad faith registration of domain names, the notional "addresses" of Internet websites. Yet implicit in domain name disputes is the protection of trademark

41 For example, in *Dell Computer Corp v Union des consommateurs*, 2007 SCC 34, the Supreme Court of Canada upheld the validity of an arbitration clause in an online consumer contract that provided that any disputes should be resolved by arbitration provided by a US-based arbitration company. In doing so, it rejected class action proceedings brought under Quebec law. By contrast, in *Seidel v TELUS Communications, Inc*, 2011 SCC 15, the Supreme Court of Canada ruled that a class action law suit could proceed under British Columbia consumer protection law, notwithstanding the existence of a mandatory arbitration clause in the standard-form contract. The BC legislation explicitly stated that consumer rights could not be waived. Some Canadian provinces have similarly legislated to limit the effect of mandatory arbitration clauses in consumer contracts; others have not. See Teresa Scassa & Michael Deturbide, *Electronic Commerce and Internet Law in Canada*, 2d ed (Toronto: CCH Canadian, 2012) at 71–73.

42 Shultz, above note 2 at 831. Schultz notes that there are real advantages to this practice, and that numerous online alternative dispute resolution systems have emerged. He defines these mechanisms broadly, ranging from online mediation or arbitration to credit card chargebacks and trustmarks (*ibid* at 830).

43 The Uniform Domain Name Dispute Resolution Policy [UDRP], for example, provides in paragraph 4(k) that any dispute may be submitted to a court either before the mandatory arbitration process under the UDRP is completed, or after a decision has been reached. (UDRP, as Approved by ICANN 24 October 1999, online: ICANN www.icann.org/en/help/dndr/udrp/policy.) For an example of a Canadian court that rejected the outcome of a mandatory domain name dispute arbitration, see *Black v Molson Canada* (2002), 60 OR (3d) 457 (SCJ).

44 See also the discussion of this issue in the case study in Chapter 7, Section C.

rights — something that normally falls within the domestic law of the state in which the trademark is registered. Domain name registrants agree to submit any disputes to arbitration, which is carried out by panels appointed by private corporations.[45] Such arbitrations are controversial for a number of reasons.[46] One reason relates to jurisdiction, at least in part. While arbitration moves disputes out of any one country's jurisdiction, the panelists nevertheless apply legal principles that derive from trademark law. Although there are commonalities in the trademark law of many countries as a result of international treaties on the subject,[47] the accusation levelled at these dispute resolution panels is that they have allowed US trademark law principles to dominate.[48] This presents an interesting illustration both of the erosion of national jurisdiction, and also of concerns about the internationalization of the legal principles of a single state.

---

45 The domain name dispute resolution system for the Top Level Domains is administered by ICANN, but dispute resolution is contracted out to private dispute resolution providers. A list of approved providers can be found online: ICANN www.icann.org/en/dndr/udrp/approved-providers.htm.

46 Criticisms of the UDRP have included allegations that panelists show a bias towards trademark owners. See, for example, Michael Geist, "Fair.com?: An Examination of the Allegations of Systemic Unfairness in the ICANN UDRP" (August 2001), online: uOttawa http://aix1.uottawa.ca/~geist/geistudrp.pdf; Michael Geist, "Fundamentally Fair.Com? An Update on Bias Allegations and the ICANN UDRP," online: uOttawa http://aix1.uottawa.ca/~geist/fairupdate.pdf; and Milton Mueller, "Rough Justice: An Analysis of ICANN's Uniform Dispute Resolution Policy," V2.1, online: The Centre for Convergence and Emerging Networking Technologies http://dcc.syr.edu/PDF/roughjustice.pdf. More comprehensive critical studies include: Annette Kur, "UDRP: A Study by the Max-Planck-Institute for Foreign and International Patent, Copyright and Competition Law" (Munich: Max-Planck-Institute, 2002) at 65, online: Karlsruher Institut für Technologie www.zar.kit.edu/DATA/projekte/udrp_705937a.pdf; A Michael Froomkin, "ICANN's 'Uniform Dispute Resolution Policy' — Causes and (Partial) Cures" (2002), 67:3 Brook L Rev 605; Laurence R Helfer, "Whither the UDRP: Autonomous, Americanized or Cosmopolitan?" (2004) 12:2 Cardozo J Int'l & Comp L 493; and Kenneth L Port, "Trademark Monopolies in the Blue Nowhere" (2002) 28:3 Wm Mitchell L Rev 1091.

47 See, for example, *Paris Convention for the Protection of Industrial Property*, 20 March 1883, 828 UNTS 305 revised at Stockholm 14 July 1967, amended on 28 September 1979, online World Intellectual Property Organization: www.wipo.int/treaties/en/ip/paris/trtdocs_wo020.html.

48 See, for example, Helfer, above note 46 at 496.

Another eroding effect relates to the role of transnational corporations.[49] These powerful entities lead supranational existences, prompting some to comment on their lack of real accountability to the laws of any particular jurisdiction.[50] Multinational actors may wield enormous power in terms of dictating the norms by which they are governed. Earlier we discussed the case of Facebook and privacy norms. While Facebook has been responsive to some of the privacy concerns raised by national regulators, its changes to its privacy polices might stop short of what the law of some jurisdictions requires.[51] Google offers another interesting example. When faced with the European Directive on data retention,[52] which imposes limits on its retention of user data, it negotiated a compromise that it was prepared to accept, but that was still in excess of the limits sought by the European Union.

Aside from resisting or shaping the normative rules governing Internet activity, corporations also develop and introduce technological layers that may have a significant effect on how the Internet is accessed and used. Sassen refers to the developments in "firewalled intranets for firms, firewalled tunnels for firm-to-firm transactions, identity verification, trademark protection and billing"[53] as examples of technological layers that shift the open and public nature of the Internet towards a private and commercial one. The combination of the power of multi-

49 Sassen speaks of "the power of private corporate interests in shaping the activity space of the Internet." (Sassen, above note 38 at 331.)

50 See, for example, Malcolm J Rogge, "Towards Transnational Corporate Accountability in the Global Economy: Challenging the Doctrine of *Forum Non Conveniens* in *In Re*: Union Carbide, Alfaro, Sequihua, and Aguinda" (2001) 36:2 Tex Int'l LJ 299; Alison Lindsay Shinsato, "Increasing the Accountability of Transnational Corporations for Environmental Harms: The Petroleum Industry in Nigeria" (2005–2006) 4:1 Northwestern Journal of International Human Rights 186; Magdalena Bexell, Jonas Tallberg, & Anders Uhlin, "Democracy in Global Governance: The Promises and Pitfalls of Transnational Actors" (2010) 16:1 Global Governance 81.

51 CIPPIC brought its initial complaint against Facebook to the Office of the Privacy Commissioner of Canada. (The text of the complaint can be found online, above note 28.) Although the Office of the Privacy Commissioner ultimately declared itself satisfied with the changes made by Facebook (Letter from OPC to CIPPIC (25 August 2009), outlining its resolution with Facebook, online: Office of the Privacy Commissioner of Canada www.priv.gc.ca/media/nr-c/2009/let_090827_e.cfm), CIPPIC continues to express concerns that Facebook is not compliant with privacy norms (see letter from CIPPIC to Facebook (28 May 2010), online: CIPPIC www.cippic.ca/uploads/LT_Facebook-Re_Privacy_Response-FINAL-05282010.pdf).

52 *Data Retention Directive*, above note 33.

53 Sassen, above note 38 at 331.

national corporations and the growing global dependence on access, not just to the Internet but to certain ubiquitous tools and services, has an eroding effect on states' capacity to exercise their jurisdiction. The surging interest in cloud computing raises similar concerns; the records and documents of companies in one country may end up stored on servers hosted in another, and may even be subject to the laws of the host country.[54]

The Internet may have other effects on the ways in which governments seek to control their own domestic policies and even their own state "assets." Here, the Internet must be considered both in terms of its architecture and in terms of the global mass communication vehicle that it has become. Increasingly, governments are aware of the potential of the Internet to drive innovation. Both citizens and corporations put pressure on governments to facilitate, rather than impede, activities that encourage collaboration, cross-pollination, and innovation in all fields of endeavour.[55] To do so requires changes to national laws and policies relating to technology and infrastructure, competition, and innovation. These changes are, in a sense, driven from below — it is the architecture of the Internet, the way that it functions, and the way that it has been embraced by citizens and businesses, that pushes governments to adapt and change how they regulate and govern. They are also driven from multiple points globally. Sassen notes that the Internet provides a mechanism by which localized movements "can become part of cross-border networks and move from being subject to specific national/local laws to a global scale where these laws almost cease to be operative . . . ."[56] This globalized network can in turn "function as a political support and resource for the localities that constitute that network."[57]

The open government data movement offers an illustration of this phenomenon. Driven in part by a popular push towards greater transparency in government and in part by arguments of economic necessity — to fuel the information economy by making government data sets

---

54 See, for example, Office of the Privacy Commissioner of Canada, "Cloud Computing for Small and Medium-sized Enterprises: Privacy Responsibilities and Considerations," online: Office of the Privacy Commissioner of Canada www.priv.gc.ca/information/pub/gd_cc_201206_e.asp.

55 Sassen, for example, notes the "strengthening of civic and political groups concerned with the extent to which private corporate interests are shaping Internet access and development . . . ." (Sassen, above note 38 at 331.)

56 Sassen, *ibid* at 338.

57 *Ibid* at 339.

freely available in increasingly standardized digital formats — more and more states are now moving in this direction.[58] Although some have initially tried to retain control over the formats in which information is disseminated and the uses to which it can be put, these efforts are fading in the face of a growing push towards harmonization of standards, interoperability, and open access.[59] As Taubman puts it: "The growth of the Internet increasingly fuels a practical expectation, and bolsters a normative claim, that digital information should flow freely regardless of physical location . . . ."[60]

Other forms of grassroots Internet movements include the organization of major protests that actually take place in specific geographic locations (and that may involve the movement of individuals across borders). Those rallying around a particular cause may network so as to stage protests in major cities around the globe, or they may organize a convergence on a particular point for a particular purpose. This has notably been the case, for example, with the co-ordination of protests against G20 summits.[61] Sassen writes that activism of this kind

---

58 For example, Canada recently joined the other G8 countries in signing the Open Government Charter. See James Vincent, "G8 Open Data Charter Will 'Increase Transparency' and 'Fuel Innovation'" *The Independent* (19 June 2013), online: The Independent www.Independent.co.uk/life-style/gadgets-and-tech/g8-open-data-charter-will-increase-transparency-and-fuel-innovation-8665696.html.

59 For example, both Australia and New Zealand have very recently adopted policies on open government data. See Lindsay Tanner, "Declaration of Open Government" (16 July 2010), online: Australian Government Department of Finance www.finance.gov.au/e-government/strategy-and-governance/gov2/declaration-of-open-government.html; E-Government, New Zealand, "New Zealand Government Open Access and Licensing (NZGOAL) Framework," online: New Zealand Government Department of Internal Affairs http://ict.govt.nz/guidance-and-resources/information-and-data/nzgoal. The United Kingdom has also adopted an open government policy: "UK Government Licensing Framework," online: National Archives www.nationalarchives.gov.uk/information-management/uk-gov-licensing-framework.htm. Canada has also adopted an open government policy, and has set out an action plan on open government. See "Canada's Action Plan on Open Government," online: data.gc.ca www.data.gc.ca/eng/canadas-action-plan-open-government.

60 Antony Taubman, "International Governance and the Internet" in Edwards & Waelde, eds, above note 8 at 27.

61 See the account of such organized protests in: Trevor CW Farrow, "Negotiation, Mediation, Globalization Protests and Police: Right Processes; Wrong System, Issues, Parties and Time" (2002–2003) 28 Queen's LJ 665. More recent accounts of the use of social media in protests include those that were part of the Arab Spring (see Carol Huang, "Facebook and Twitter Key to Arab Spring Uprisings: Report" *The National* (6 June 2011), online: The National www.thenational.ae/news/uae-news/

contributes "to an incipient unbundling of the exclusive authority, including symbolic authority, over territory and people we have long associated with the national state."[62]

Of course, in another fairly simple way, the Internet erodes state jurisdiction by loosening the control a state may have over its citizens. While this is going to be felt more acutely under authoritarian governments, there is a message here as well for all governments regarding the decentralization of sources of information. Benkler notes that "the introduction of Internet communications makes it harder and more costly for governments to control the public sphere."[63] Indeed, he goes on to argue that the Internet provides "avenues of discourse around the bottlenecks of older media, whether these are held by authoritarian governments or by media owners."[64] While a state's jurisdiction is not formally removed in such circumstances, its ability to effectively control certain types of communication within its borders is dramatically reduced.

---

facebook-and-twitter-key-to-arab-spring-uprisings-report) and during the protests in Turkey (see Alex Konrad, "Tools of Victory: The Tech That Helped Turkish Protesters Save Taksim Square" *Forbes* (7 March 2013), online: Forbes www.forbes.com/sites/alexkonrad/2013/07/03/the-tech-that-helped-turkish-protesters.

62 Sassen, above note 38 at 340.

63 Benkler, above note 10 at 270.

64 *Ibid* at 271.

CHAPTER 6

Weighing the Scales about Acting Extraterritorially

A. INTRODUCTION: DISTINGUISHING "CAN" FROM "SHOULD"

We have discussed the international law rules governing when Canada would be seen by other nations as having the ability to act extraterritorially.[1] That question—when Canada can effectively act extraterritorially—matters, but is not the central question. Rather, the more important question (and the question that is the focus of this chapter) is the one that explores when Canada *should* act extraterritorially: When is doing so the right decision? The question of whether Canada *can* effectively act extraterritorially is a relatively easy one. As discussed in Chapter 3, for the most part it depends on the issue of whether a jurisdictional claim would be recognized at international law by other countries. Additionally, it involves the practical consideration of whether any claim Canada might make to act extraterritorially will be enforceable, either unilaterally or through the co-operation of other states. There is also the purely domestic question of when Canadian courts (or administrative bodies) will recognize and implement extraterritorial claims by Parliament or the legislatures.[2]

---

1 See Chapter 3, Section A.

2 In this regard, it is worth noting s 8 of the *Interpretation Act*, RSC 1985, c I-21. The provision was enacted by Parliament and therefore is subject to amendment by that body, but at present it (in general) limits the application of statutes to the territory of Canada, with expansion in some cases to the exclusive economic zone of Canada, and in other cases, to the continental shelf. Finally, it also envisions that

Whether, in general or in a specific situation, Canada *should* act extraterritorially is a much more difficult question that raises many other issues. The nationality principle, for example, might allow Canada to legislate quite broadly over the behaviour of Canadian citizens wherever they might be in the world; it does not follow that it would be a sensible decision for Parliament to exploit the nationality principle to the maximum extent possible. As the Supreme Court has noted:

> While the Parliament of Canada, unlike the legislatures of the Provinces, has the legislative competence to enact laws having extraterritorial effect, it is presumed not to intend to do so, in the absence of clear words or necessary implication to the contrary. This is because "[i]n our modern world of easy travel and with the emergence of a global economic order, chaotic situations would often result if the principle of

---

statutes should be taken to apply extraterritorially where that result "expressly or by necessary or reasonable implication was intended."

The section reads:

> 8. (1) Every enactment applies to the whole of Canada, unless a contrary intention is expressed in the enactment.
>
> (2) Where an enactment that does not apply to the whole of Canada is amended, no provision in the amending enactment applies to any part of Canada to which the amended enactment does not apply, unless it is provided in the amending enactment that it applies to that part of Canada or to the whole of Canada.
>
> (2.1) Every enactment that applies in respect of exploring or exploiting, conserving or managing natural resources, whether living or non-living, applies, in addition to its application to Canada, to the exclusive economic zone of Canada, unless a contrary intention is expressed in the enactment.
>
> (2.2) Every enactment that applies in respect of exploring or exploiting natural resources that are
>
> (*a*) mineral or other non-living resources of the seabed or subsoil, or
>
> (*b*) living organisms belonging to sedentary species, that is to say, organisms that, at the harvestable stage, either are immobile on or under the seabed or are unable to move except in constant physical contact with the seabed or subsoil
>
> applies, in addition to its application to Canada, to the continental shelf of Canada, unless a contrary intention is expressed in the enactment.
>
> (3) Every Act now in force enacted prior to December 11, 1931 that expressly or by necessary or reasonable implication was intended, as to the whole or any part thereof, to have extra-territorial operation shall be construed as if, at the date of its enactment, the Parliament of Canada had full power to make laws having extra-territorial operation as provided by the *Statute of Westminster, 1931*.

> territorial jurisdiction were not, at least generally, respected"; see *Tolofson v Jensen*, [1994] 3 S.C.R. 1022 (S.C.C.), at p. 1051, *per* La Forest J.[3]

In short, Canada should not exercise extraterritorial jurisdiction in every circumstance where it could do so.

At a minimum, the question of whether Canada *should* act extraterritorially requires consideration of: (1) the domestic concerns that might tempt Canada to legislate with extraterritorial effect; (2) the impact on international relations of Canada choosing to act—or not act—extraterritorially; and (3) the attitude Canada should adopt towards other states acting extraterritorially within Canada's jurisdiction. Related to these questions is whether one is discussing unilateral or multilateral extraterritorial action. Whether Canada is attempting to act independently of or in concert with other states is very relevant to when it should act extraterritorially. Equally, whether the discussion is about unilateral action by another state or a joint international effort should affect the Canadian viewpoint of other countries legislating action that will have effect in Canada. Our goal in this chapter, however, is more ambitious than simply listing the relevant considerations. We hope to provide guidance as to how to take those competing considerations into account in any given case.

As the title of this chapter indicates, whether Canada should act extraterritorially in a given situation is settled by weighing the competing interests against one another. There are various disincentives to acting extraterritorially: most notably, that to do so can threaten comity between states, and that laws that overreach the effective grasp of the state might be unenforceable. On the other hand, there are certain incentives to act extraterritorially on some occasions, which will be related to the particular policy goals to be served by that action. Whether Canada should act extraterritorially on any given occasion depends on weighing the incentives against the disincentives in each particular case.

In this chapter, we will discuss both the disincentives and the incentives to acting extraterritorially. As discussed in Chapter 3, each of the legislative, executive, and adjudicative branches exert jurisdiction in some form, and therefore each has the ability to act extraterritorially. The extraterritoriality we discuss and the analysis we put forward in this chapter is predominantly based on legislative action: specific-

---

3 *Society of Composers, Authors and Music Publishers of Canada v Canadian Assn of Internet Providers*, 2004 SCC 45 at para 54.

ally, legislation of Parliament, since, as we noted earlier,[4] the provinces have few means to act extraterritorially. However, the overall structure of the analysis and the considerations that we point to arise in analogous ways for the other branches of government. Further, these instances of legislative action frequently involve further enforcement and adjudicative activity extraterritorially to implement their purposes and provisions. While the following examples of statutes often prescribe offences, they also enable government departments and officials to exercise such prescriptive, investigative, and enforcement powers (that is, all kinds of executive action) extraterritorially as may be necessary to fulfill the objectives of the legislation. Similarly, these statutes also involve the courts in exercising extraterritorial jurisdiction to adjudicate on the extraterritorial reach of the legislation and the appropriateness of the extraterritorial actions of the executive. Therefore, although the focus of discussion will be legislative extraterritoriality, we will, where appropriate, point to ways in which these same considerations arise in other contexts.

The greater part of the discussion will focus on the disincentives: not in order to say that Canada should never act extraterritorially, but rather to point out that those disincentives are not uniform. While they exist strongly in some cases, they are weak or virtually non-existent in others. We propose to more clearly identify the factors that determine how strong the disincentive might be in any given case by drawing two sets of distinctions.

One set of distinctions concerns the *justifications* for acting extraterritorially. By this, we mean the policy goals that have been seen in Canada as making it legitimate for Canada to act extraterritorially. We will argue that four such justifications have been acknowledged so far, and we suggest that those same four should guide future action. Those four justifications are: (1) the extraterritorial conduct has a strong connection to Canada; (2) the conduct occurs extraterritorially but is an aspect of the public face of Canada; (3) extraterritorial action is needed to avoid lawless territory, and; (4) there is an international agreement to be implemented.

The other set of distinctions focuses on the *functions* for which extraterritorial action is taken. There are many ways in which Canada can and does act in pursuit of the justifications above, whether through

4 See Chapter 3, Section B(2).

legislation, executive action, court decisions, or other means, as discussed above in Chapter 3, Section B. Broadly speaking, however, we will argue that all extraterritorial action can be seen as falling within one of three approaches: (1) prohibiting behaviour, (2) controlling behaviour, and (3) facilitating behaviour.

We will also consider the incentives to acting extraterritorially. In large measure, it should be said, the incentive to act extraterritorially is a question for domestic policy-makers. Acting extraterritorially is not the norm and carries certain risks. Against that, how important is it to, for example, make child sex tourism illegal?[5] Is forbidding gender-selection–in vitro fertilization services an important enough issue that Canada should act extraterritorially? Protecting fishing stocks? Preventing environmental degradation? These value judgments are for domestic policy-makers, and our discussion of the incentives does not and can not take account of those assessments.

However, some general insight into the question of incentives can be gained by considering the reverse circumstances. Our primary question is when Canada should have an incentive to act extraterritorially: that is, to act in a way that could have an impact in the territory of another state. To properly assess that, it is necessary also to consider Canada's reaction when other states act in a way that has an impact in Canadian territory. Whenever Canada acts extraterritorially, it contributes to creating an international norm, making it more acceptable to act extraterritorially in such circumstances. The strength of an incentive to do so, therefore, depends in part on when Canada is and is not comfortable with that norm being created.

We turn now to consider the disincentives.

B. DISINCENTIVES TO ACT EXTRATERRITORIALLY

As noted in the introduction, we pursue this issue by drawing two sets of distinctions — one about the existing justifications for acting extraterritorially, the other about the functions for which one would do so. In essence, our argument is a simple one. It is probable that existing exercises of extraterritorial jurisdiction correspond to those circumstances in which the disincentives are least likely to be present. Considering

---

5 See the further discussion of this point in the case study of child sex tourism in Chapter 7, Section E.

when Canada has, in the past, seen acting extraterritorially as justified, and the ways in which it has seen it to be appropriate to exercise that jurisdiction, will therefore help pinpoint those disincentives.

1) Justifications for Extraterritorial Action

This section will discuss the rationales that have, to this point, been seen as a sufficient justification for Canada to choose to exercise extraterritorial jurisdiction. We argue that four can be identified, although the boundaries between them are not necessarily drawn precisely, and more than one justification can be operating at a time. Although Canada is not necessarily bound to continue as it has proceeded in the past, a clear understanding of the motivations that have guided exercises in extraterritoriality until now will be useful.

As listed above in Section A, the four currently observable motivations for acting extraterritorially are: (1) the extraterritorial conduct has a strong connection to Canada; (2) the extraterritorial conduct is an aspect of the public face of Canada; (3) extraterritorial action is needed to avoid lawless territory, and; (4) there is an international agreement to be implemented. Various pieces of legislation might well fall into more than one of these categories, but that is not a concern: the real point of this discussion is to see that these are the justifications that have been sufficient to warrant acting extraterritorially to date.[6] Because Canada has a longer history of acting extraterritorially in the criminal law sphere than in other areas, it will sometimes be useful to distinguish between criminal and non-criminal laws, but these categories should be seen as applying generally.

a) The Extraterritorial Conduct Has a Strong Connection to Canada

In Chapter 4 we discussed the concept of extended territoriality—that is, legislation that affects behaviour outside of Canada's territory, but

---

6 A more complete discussion of these models can be found in Robert J Currie & Steve Coughlan, "Extraterritorial Criminal Jurisdiction: Bigger Picture or Smaller Frame?" (2007) 11:2 Can Crim L Rev 141 [Currie & Coughlan]. The discussion there also includes consideration of exactly to whom various pieces of legislation are made to apply: Canadians only, those found in Canada, anyone, and so on. That aspect of the analysis is not central to the point being pursued here, though we will occasionally make mention of it.

where the jurisdictional claim is based on a real and substantial connection to Canada. It is important to distinguish between that situation and extraterritorial conduct that falls into this first category; there is legislation which is roughly analogous to the "real and substantial connection test," and that is not what we are intending to capture here.

For example, there are some *Criminal Code* provisions that make behaviour illegal even though some of the prohibited conduct takes place outside Canada. In some of those cases (the ones we are not intending to capture in this category), the fact that certain aspects of the offence are not territorially based in Canada is of no real consequence to the offence: the focus of the offence is the behaviour that occurs within Canada. The simplest example of this category is possession of stolen goods.

Under the *Criminal Code* it is an offence to possess property that was obtained from a crime in Canada or from "an act or omission anywhere that, if it had occurred in Canada, would have constituted an offence punishable by indictment."[7] This provision, and others like it, should not really be understood as extraterritorial provisions. They are not aimed at reducing thefts or other offences outside Canada; rather, the point is that if an accused in Canada is in possession of stolen goods, it is irrelevant (as far as the possession offence is concerned) where the goods were stolen from. In many offences, phrases like "whether in or out of Canada" serve the same function as the phrase "directly or indirectly" as a modifier of "apply force" in the assault provisions — not to add a consideration, but to remove one. Falling into this category would be criminal offences such as procuring illicit sexual intercourse,[8] operating unseaworthy vessels,[9] making a false document,[10] gaming in stocks,[11] brokers illegally reducing stock,[12] money laundering offences,[13] and bigamy.[14] In each of these, the objectionable behaviour occurs in Canada, though some ancillary aspect might have occurred outside Canada's borders. We do not regard these offences as genuinely relevant to an extraterritorial discussion.

---

7 *Criminal Code*, RSC 1985, c C-46, s 354 [*Code*].
8 *Ibid*, s 212(a).
9 *Ibid*, s 251.
10 *Ibid*, s 366.
11 *Ibid*, s 383.
12 *Ibid*, s 384.
13 *Ibid*, Part XII.2.
14 *Ibid*, s 290.

However, there are offences that do actually apply extraterritorially, in the sense that the behaviour that is the core of the offence occurs outside Canada, and the legislation consciously intends to forbid that behaviour. Similarly, there are pieces of legislation with non-prosecutorial goals that also focus on behaviour occurring outside Canada's borders. These pieces of legislation are extraterritorial in their effect because the behaviour they concern occurs outside Canada; however, the consideration that justifies the legislation is that that extraterritorial behaviour will in turn have an impact within Canada. To achieve the goal of protecting that concern, there is an incidental need to extend the territorial scope of the legislation. That is what we mean by controlling conduct with a strong connection to Canada.

For example, there are some specific criminal offences that actually aim at prosecuting behaviour that occurs outside Canada's borders, such as treason and high treason,[15] or passport and certificate of citizenship offences.[16] Furthermore, there is a considerable amount of non-criminal legislation that is clearly motivated because the conduct being legislated has a strong connection to Canada. Indeed, probably the most noteworthy difference between the criminal and non-criminal context is that this justification for extraterritoriality is much more pronounced in the latter situation.

Many (though not all) of these provisions create offences, though not in the *Criminal Code*. Various offences related to voting, for example, are proscribed whether committed inside or outside of Canada.[17] The *Security of Information Act* is, in large measure, specifically designed around protecting the interests of the state, and the behaviour proscribed in it is not only an offence wherever in the world it occurs, but will be enforced against anyone who is later in Canada.[18] The *Immigration and Refugee Protection Act* provides that acts which are proscribed by it will be an offence even if committed outside Canada,[19] as does the *Citizenship Act* involving false representations concerning citizenship.[20] All of those statutes create offences relating to behaviour which, wherever it occurs, could

15 *Ibid*, s 46(3).
16 *Ibid*, ss 57 & 58.
17 *Canada Elections Act*, SC 2000, c 9, s 281 [*Canada Elections Act*].
18 RSC 1985, c O-5, s 26.
19 SC 2001, c 27, s 135.
20 RSC 1985, c C-29, s 30.

undermine aspects of the Canadian state, and so they are made offences wherever they are committed.

There are other ways in which legislation could be based on a strong connection to Canada, however. For example, the *Non-smokers' Health Act* obliges Canadian employers generally to prevent their employees from smoking in the workplace: the Act is also extended to apply to workspaces on aircraft, trains, vessels, or motor vehicles being operated between Canada and another country.[21] The *Health of Animals Act* allows the Minister of Agriculture to provide financial or technical assistance to a person or government outside Canada to control or eradicate a disease that could affect persons or animals in Canada.[22] The minister can also designate laboratories outside Canada for the administration of the Act.[23]

In some cases, the strong connection to Canada is found in the fact that something might enter Canada in the absence of action. For example, the *Tobacco Act* prohibits anyone in Canada from publishing or broadcasting cigarette advertisements outside of Canada in order to then have them appear in this country.[24] That provision is supported by the *Foreign Publishers Advertising Services Act*, which provides that:

> 3. (1) No foreign publisher shall supply advertising services directed at the Canadian market to a Canadian advertiser or a person acting on their behalf.[25]

Similar legislation prohibits broadcasting election advertising from outside Canada, or indeed election advertising of any sort by non-Can-

---

21 RSC 1985, c 15 (4th Supp), s 1(2). The Act applies when the intercountry transportation is operated by a Canadian, but not when it is operated by a non-Canadian (*ibid*, s 1(3)).

22 SC 1990, c 21, s 21.

23 *Ibid*, s 30.

24 SC 1997, c 13, s 31(3). Based on their extraterritorial effect, these provisions were challenged at trial but were upheld: see *JTI Macdonald Corp v Canada (AG)* (2002), [2003] RJQ 181 at paras 440–42 (Qc Sup Ct). By the time the matter reached the Supreme Court of Canada, the challenge to this provision was no longer in issue: *Canada (AG) v JTI-Macdonald Corp*, 2007 SCC 30.

25 SC 1999, c 23 [*Foreign Publishers Act*]. See also s 15, which provides that:

> 15. (1) In a proceeding for a contravention of s 3, a foreign publisher who commits an act outside Canada that, if committed in Canada, would be an offence under that section is deemed to commit that act in Canada.

adians.[26] See also the *Quarantine Act*, permitting appropriate officers to conduct screening or bar entry to Canada while acting outside Canada.[27]

Finally, the strong connection to Canada might arise because of the person to whom the law applies. For example, the *Government Employees Compensation Act* provides compensation to Canadian government employees in the case of injury, disease, or death, and does so whether the injury or disease arose in or out of Canada.[28] Similarly, pension benefits can be available to persons who have worked for Canada while outside the country.[29]

The same kinds of considerations can be seen arising in non-legislative contexts. The Supreme Court's decision in *Canada (Justice) v Khadr*,[30] for example, could be looked at as considering whether there is a strong connection to Canada with regard to enforcement and adjudicative jurisdiction. Khadr was detained by American authorities in Guantanamo Bay, but while there he was interviewed by Canadian officials. He sought disclosure from the Crown of the records of those interviews and the information handed over to American authorities, information to which he would have been entitled had the events occurred in Canada's territory. The Court noted that the territorial limits to the application of the *Charter* would normally mean that Khadr's application could not succeed.[31] However, where the actions taken by Canadian officials amounted to a violation of Canada's international obligations with regard to fundamental human rights, a court could apply the *Charter* to

---

26 *Canada Elections Act*, above note 17, ss 330 & 331. The ban on election advertising is not explicitly extraterritorial — it simply prohibits anyone from trying to induce voters unless the person is a Canadian citizen or permanent resident.

27 SC 2005, c 20:

> 53. A screening officer, a quarantine officer or an environmental health officer may exercise any power or perform any duty or function under this Act respecting a traveller or conveyance at an entry point in another country if doing so does not conflict with the laws of that country.

28 RSC 1985, c G-5, s 3(2) [*Government Compensation Act*]. To similar effect see the *Merchant Seamen Compensation Act*, RSC 1985, c M-6, s 7: "This Act applies to accidents happening within or outside Canada."

29 See, for example, the *Canadian Forces Members and Veterans Re-establishment and Compensation Act*, SC 2005, c 21, s 69 [*Canadian Forces Compensation Act*] or the *Royal Canadian Mounted Police Superannuation Act*, RSC 1985, c R-11, ss 32.1 and 32.12 [*Police Superannuation Act*].

30 *Canada (Justice) v Khadr*, 2008 SCC 28 [*Khadr 2008*].

31 *Ibid* at para 17.

the actions of those officials despite the absence of a territorial jurisdictional claim.[32]

b) The Extraterritorial Conduct Is an Aspect of the Public Face of Canada

Another consideration that has been seen to justify having Canadian legislation govern behaviour outside Canada's borders is having that legislation directed at what we are describing as "the public face of Canada." Typically, legislation falling into this category exercises some sort of control over government agencies operating overseas, though that is not the only possibility.

The *Official Languages Act*, for example, requires that a federal office or institution "in Canada or elsewhere" must be able to provide services in either official language where there is reasonable demand.[33] The motivation behind this is to serve the goal of making Canada, and presenting it as, a bilingual nation. Similarly, a provision in the *Canadian Human Rights Act* permits investigations of discriminatory conduct which occurs outside of Canada but where the victim is a Canadian citizen or permanent resident; this legislation seems, at least in practice, to be directed towards the goal of controlling Canada's public face.[34]

Some legislation that we suggest falls into this category is aimed at individuals rather than government agencies; usually this is done by creating an offence. For example, the *Foreign Enlistment Act* makes it an offence for a Canadian, outside Canada, to enlist "in the armed forces of any foreign state at war with any friendly foreign state."[35] This could be seen as an aspect of this category in the sense that it would be an embarrassment to have Canadian nationals as combatants against Canada's allies. In the same way, the *Corruption of Foreign Public Officials Act* (which makes bribery of foreign officials to gain a business advantage an offence), could be seen as serving the goal of controlling Canada's public face.[36] Further, while acting as employees in a place outside Canada, public servants are bound by the *Criminal Code*,[37] and services offence

32 The Court notes: "[I]f Canada was participating in a process that was violative of Canada's binding obligations under international law, the *Charter* applies to the extent of that participation." *Ibid* at para 19.

33 RSC 1985, c 31 (4th Supp), s 22(b).

34 RSC 1985, c H-6, s 40(5)(c) [*Human Rights Act*].

35 RSC 1985, c F-28, s 3.

36 SC 1998, c 34, s 3 [*Corruption of Officials Act*].

37 Above note 7, s 7(4).

provisions in the *National Defence Act*[38] or the RCMP Code of Conduct apply to offences committed outside Canada.[39] Formerly all those employed on Canadian ships overseas were, under the *Canada Shipping Act*, bound by Canadian criminal law, though those provisions have been replaced by somewhat more limited rules in the *Criminal Code*.[40]

c) Extraterritorial Action Is Needed to Avoid Lawless Territory

The third policy justification for asserting extraterritorial jurisdiction that has arisen in Canadian law occurs where there is no competing territorial claim by another state. In most instances of extraterritorial action, there can be the disincentive that the action will interfere with another state's sovereignty. When a territory is not under the control of any government, however, not only is that disincentive absent, there will also be the advantage of avoiding the danger of lawless territories. It is therefore unsurprising that some extraterritorial exercises of Canada's jurisdiction are aimed at that situation.

One of the oldest extraterritorial provisions in the *Criminal Code*, for example, relates to piracy. That offence often occurs on the high seas, and so the *Criminal Code* prohibits it whether it is committed in or out of Canada.[41] In more recent times, outer space has raised the same issue of a jurisdictional gap, and Canada now also asserts (in some circumstances) jurisdiction over offences on the international space station.[42] Similar provisions cover some offences committed on aircraft and on ships or fixed platforms outside the continental shelf of any country.[43] Finally, section 477.1(e) extends jurisdiction to offences committed "outside the territory of any state."

The nature of the jurisdictional claims is not identical in each case, however. In some instances, such as piracy, the offence contains no provision limiting Canada's assertion of jurisdiction — the behaviour is simply declared to be an offence "in or out of Canada." In other cases

---

38 RSC 1985, c N-5.

39 *Royal Canadian Mounted Police Regulations, 1988*, SOR/88-361.

40 *Canada Shipping Act*, RSC 1985, c S-9, ss 610 (repealed SC 1987, c 7, s 65), 611 (repealed SC 1987, c 7, s 65), 612 (repealed 1990, c 44, s 18), and 613 (repealed 1990, c 44, s 18). Section 477.1 of the *Criminal Code* now exerts extraterritorial jurisdiction in some of the circumstances which used to be covered by the *Canada Shipping Act*, in a way more in keeping with the principles of jurisdiction under international law.

41 Above note 7, s 74(2).

42 *Ibid*, ss 7(2.3)–(2.34).

43 *Ibid*, ss 7(1), (2), (2.1), & (2.2).

(such as some hijacking and terrorist offences included in section 7(2) of the *Criminal Code*), the jurisdictional claim rests on the additional condition that the accused is later present in Canada. In yet other cases, such as outer space[44] and section 477.1(e) of the *Criminal Code*, the claim is more limited. In the latter case, Canada claims jurisdiction over the lawless territory for offences committed by Canadians; in the former, over offences by *and* against Canadians.

One consequence of this variety of jurisdictional approaches is that, although Canada regards itself as able to prosecute for these offences, other countries might or might not respect that claim. As a result, in some circumstances Canada might not be able to obtain an accused's extradition to face charges here.

The goal of avoiding lawless territories can also be seen in legislation where the primary focus is not declaring particular behaviour to be an offence. The *Antarctic Environmental Protection Act*, for example, prevents Canadian citizens or companies from being in the Antarctic or interfering with its environment without a permit, which could be issued either by Canadian officials or by some other state with authority to do so.[45] Similarly the *Remote Sensing Space Systems Act* prohibits the operation of satellites that detect raw data from the Earth's surface, and also controls the use of data from such satellites.[46] Once again such activity would be allowed with a licence, though in this case the Act only envisions licences issued by the Minister of Foreign Affairs. The real concern here seems to be avoiding "lawless territory" rather than the presence of a strong connection to Canada — there is no requirement that the sensing done from space be *of* Canada.[47] Indeed, a motivating factor behind the statute was to satisfy the United States that suitable controls were being placed over such remote sensing satellite systems, which were moving from public to private hands.[48] A further exertion of control over territory which is not in any state is found in the provisions

---

44 *Ibid*, ss 7(2.3) & (2.31).

45 SC 2003, c 20.

46 SC 2005, c 45, s 6.

47 The Act, however, only applies to Canadian citizens, permanent residents, corporations, or "members of any prescribed class of persons having a substantial connection to Canada related to remote sensing space systems" (*ibid*, s 6).

48 See the Background to the Bill at Lalita Acharya, "Bill C-25, *An Act Governing the Operation of Remote Sensing Space Systems*" (20 December 2004), online: Parliament of Canada www.parl.gc.ca/About/Parliament/LegislativeSummaries/bills_ls.asp?Language=E&ls=C25&Mode=1&Parl=38&Ses=1&source=library_prb#4end.

of the *Telecommunications Act* for granting international submarine cables licences on the seabed.[49]

The theory behind avoiding lawless territory can also arise with regard to adjudicative jurisdiction, and can be seen in the recently developed notion that a court can have jurisdiction as a "forum of necessity." This basis for jurisdiction allows a court to hear a matter in the absence of any kind of territorial jurisdiction, on the basis that there will otherwise be nowhere that the case can be tried.[50]

d) Extraterritorial Action Is Required by an International Convention

With the arguable exception of piracy, the first 1892 *Criminal Code* contained no extraterritorial provisions based on international agreement. By the time the 1985 Revised Statutes version came into being, there were a significant number, and today there are perhaps twice as many such provisions as in 1985. To the extent that Canada's extraterritorial *criminal* jurisdiction has grown in the past few decades, the growth has

---

49 SC 1993, c 38, ss 17–21.

50 The Ontario Court of Appeal explained the forum of necessity doctrine in *Charron Estate v Village Resorts Ltd.*, 2010 ONCA 84 at para 100 [*Charron Estate*]:

> The forum of necessity doctrine recognizes that there will be exceptional cases where, despite the absence of a real and substantial connection, the need to ensure access to justice will justify the assumption of jurisdiction. The forum of necessity doctrine does not redefine real and substantial connection to embrace "forum of last resort" cases; it operates as an exception to the real and substantial connection test. Where there is no other forum in which the plaintiff can reasonably seek relief, there is a residual discretion to assume jurisdiction.

The Ontario Court of Appeal was there considering whether "forum of necessity" was a basis for assuming jurisdiction at common law, but the Supreme Court of Canada expressly declined to settle that point when deciding the appeal: *Club Resorts Ltd v Van Breda*, 2012 SCC 17. However, the doctrine has a statutory foundation in some provinces. See, for example, the *Court Jurisdiction and Proceedings Transfer Act*, SBC 2003, c 28, s 6:

> A court that under section 3 lacks territorial competence in a proceeding may hear the proceeding despite that section if it considers that
> (a) there is no court outside British Columbia in which the plaintiff can commence the proceeding, or
> (b) the commencement of the proceeding in a court outside British Columbia cannot reasonably be required.

See also art 3136 CCQ. Forum of necessity as a basis of jurisdiction is discussed further in the case study on extraterritorial accountability for human rights claims in Chapter 7, Section B.

occurred entirely in this category. This category has also been the cause of expanded jurisdictional claims in non-criminal areas.

Canada has signed many agreements to prosecute in the case of particular types of crimes. As a result, the *Criminal Code* contains extraterritorial provisions dealing with offences on aircraft;[51] offences committed in relation to an "air navigation facility used in international air navigation"[52] and/or to civil airports outside Canada;[53] offences in relation to cultural property;[54] personal offences against an "internationally protected person";[55] hostage taking;[56] offences involving nuclear material;[57] torture by Canadian officials overseas;[58] offences against United Nations or associated personnel;[59] offences involving explosives or other lethal devices;[60] financing terrorism;[61] and child sex tourism.[62] Provisions now in the *Crimes Against Humanity and War Crimes Act*,[63] most of which were formerly in the *Criminal Code*, permit prosecutions for genocide, war crimes, and crimes against humanity that occurred outside Canada.

As with the other categories, the exact nature of the jurisdictional claim is quite various: sometimes over citizens, sometimes over those found present in Canada, and so on. In each case, the limits on jurisdiction are a reflection of the nature of the treaty to which Canada is a signatory and because of which it has enacted the legislation.

This category readily overlaps with other justifications, which is not surprising — things that Canada sees as justification for acting extraterritorially are frequently seen in that way by other countries as well. For example, the *Antarctic Environmental Protection Act*, discussed as an example of avoiding lawless territory, is also an example of this final category, implementing international agreements. Canada is a signatory to the Protocol on Environmental Protection to the Antarctic Treaty, and

---

51 Above note 7, s 7(1).
52 *Ibid*, s 7(2)(c).
53 *Ibid*, s 7(2)(d).
54 *Ibid*, s 7(2.01).
55 *Ibid*, s 7(3).
56 *Ibid*, s 7(3.1).
57 *Ibid*, ss 7(3.2)–(3.6).
58 *Ibid*, s 7(3.7).
59 *Ibid*, s 7(3.71).
60 *Ibid*, s 7(3.72).
61 *Ibid*, ss 7(3.73)–(3.75). Sections 7(3.74) and (3.75) are somewhat broader than they had to be given the treaty: see the discussion in Currie & Coughlan, above note 6.
62 Above note 7, s 7(4.1).
63 SC 2000, c 24.

the *Antarctic Environmental Protection Act* is our domestic implementation of that Protocol.[64] Similarly, the *Remote Sensing Space Systems Act* was instituted pursuant to the *Agreement Between the Government of Canada and the Government of the United States Concerning the Operation of Commercial Remote Sensing Satellite Systems*.[65]

Many other statutes also fall within this category: the *Migratory Birds Convention Act, 1994*,[66] the *Civil International Space Station Agreement Implementation Act*,[67] the *Chemical Weapons Convention Implementation Act*,[68] and statutes implementing any number of other bilateral or multilateral agreements.[69]

e) Justification-based Disincentives Diagnosed

None of the four categories we outline above is watertight. For example, the concern about avoiding lawless territories is one shared by most nations; laws against piracy or governing the use of the Antarctic that fall into that category are therefore also means of implementing international agreements. Similarly, the prohibition on child sex tourism implements an international agreement, but also reflects concern over Canada's public face as a potential "source" country for tourists rather than a concern as a destination country.[70]

Nonetheless, it is useful to draw a distinction between the categories above based on how intrusive they are on the interests of other states. Comity between states is an important consideration, and the more that Canada intrudes into what other states see as their legitimate (or exclusive) sphere, the stronger the justification must be to act extraterritorially. In considering this point, an important distinction can be drawn between three situations: (1) unilateral extraterritorial action; (2) multi-

---

64 Above note 45, s 3.

65 16 June 2000, Can TS 2000 No 14. See Acharya, above note 48.

66 SC 1994, c 22. For the most part this Act simply applies to the exclusive economic zone of Canada, but there are extensions in some circumstances to the high seas: s 18.3.

67 SC 1999, c 35.

68 SC 1995, c 25.

69 See, for example, the *Preclearance Act*, SC 1999, c 20, allowing travellers or goods to be precleared for entry into Canada while in the United States, the *Corruption of Officials Act*, above note 36, or the *Proceeds of Crime (Money Laundering) and Terrorist Financing Act*, SC 2000, c 17.

70 See the case study discussing child sex tourism in Chapter 7, Section E.

lateral extraterritorial action; and (3) extraterritorial impact without extraterritoriality.

The first of these is obviously more intrusive on the interests of other states than the latter two. When Canada acts based on a real and substantial connection to Canada, typically the jurisdiction of some other state is not being ousted; rather, Canada is asserting an interest in prosecuting actions, for example, which are of little concern to the other state (because it had no connection to that state) or in prosecuting in addition to whatever actions the other state takes. Similarly, when many states have agreed on a joint solution to a shared problem, there is no threat to comity in acting in accordance with that agreement — except, of course, to the extent that states not party to the agreement might also be affected. Unilateral extraterritorial action, on the other hand, has a much greater potential to be intrusive.

Parallel observations can be made about the potential effectiveness of laws assessed against those categories. Where the action taken by Canada is not actually extraterritorial but has an extraterritorial impact, typically one of two things will be true: either the person governed by the legislation will actually be present in Canada at some point and the law will be enforced by that means, or an extradition request will be made. Subject to the ordinary rules of extradition (double criminality, for example), the co-operation of other states in enforcing Canadian laws that are not actually extraterritorial can probably be expected. Similarly, where Canada has acted in accordance with an international agreement, by definition at least those other nations that are party to the agreement can be expected to assist with enforcement of that law. On the other hand, where Canada has unilaterally taken extraterritorial action, there is less of a guarantee that other states would be willing to assist.

These factors are directly relevant to whether extraterritorial action is justified. The more likely it is that extraterritorial action will infringe on another state's territorial jurisdiction, the more difficult it becomes to justify such action; the less likely it is that other states would assist in enforcement of that action, the more difficult it becomes to justify it. Neither factor is determinative: the costs of infringing comity might be assessed as of lower importance than failing to achieve whatever the goal is of the extraterritorial action. Similarly, it might be possible to enforce the action in a way that achieves its goals, even in the absence of co-operation from other states. Nonetheless, it is clearly easier to justify extraterritorial action when these hurdles do not need to be crossed.

It is therefore worth assessing, in general terms, each of the four categories against the question of how intrusive they are on the interests of other states, and how likely it is that other states might assist with enforcement where necessary.

Working backwards, the last category can be regarded as generally non-intrusive. When there is an international agreement to be implemented, by definition it is not an instance of unilateral extraterritorial action. There should be little threat to comity, and there are good reasons to expect assistance from other states with enforcement. Indeed, the treaty partner states are legally obliged to accept the assertion of extraterritorial jurisdiction itself, and are usually obliged to provide various sorts of assistance with enforcement.

When Canada is acting extraterritorially to avoid lawless territory, the problem of infringing on comity is far less likely to arise, precisely because the laws do not apply to any other state's territory. That does not itself mean that other states would assist with enforcement; as a practical matter, however, virtually all extraterritorial Canadian law that deals with lawless territory is pursuant to an international agreement, and so for the most part these two categories overlap.

Extraterritorial action aimed at controlling the public face of Canada raises different issues. On the one hand, actions falling within this category typically arise out of some unilateral exercise of authority, and so in theory will have the potential to infringe on another state's sovereignty. However, by the very nature of the category, laws that are motivated by this concern are less likely to bring about results that, in practical terms, have an effect on other states. Laws that govern the internal operations of Canadian government offices overseas, for example, either by requiring them to offer services in both English and French or by extending benefit programs to cover government employees who work in those offices, are unlikely to offend the state in which those offices are located.

There is no guarantee that this will be so, of course. Consider, for example, the provision in the *Human Rights Act* that permits investigations of discriminatory conduct occurring outside of Canada where the victim is a Canadian citizen or permanent resident.[71] On the face of it, this looks like a very broad exercise of extraterritorial jurisdiction. The section allows investigations into complaints of discriminatory practices within the meaning of the Act where the practice:

71 Above note 34, s 40(5)(c).

> occurred outside Canada and the victim of the practice was at the time of the act or omission a Canadian citizen or an individual lawfully admitted to Canada for permanent residence.

Taken literally, this would seem to extend the protection of the *Human Rights Act* to Canadian citizens or permanent residents anywhere in the world, against anyone. If the law were applied in that way, it likely would offend comity since we would be imposing on other states our cultural values — Canada is one of the few countries in the world to recognize same-sex marriage, for example, and so our views on discrimination based on sexual orientation will not necessarily match up with those of the majority of other states. In practice, however, the section has only been used when the alleged discriminatory practice was undertaken by a Canadian government actor outside the country — a customs official failing to deal appropriately with an application for entry into the country, for instance.[72]

The most complex category is extraterritorial action where the justification is that the conduct has a strong connection to Canada. Some action falling in this category will not in fact interfere with another state's jurisdiction and will not require assistance with enforcement. The *Non-smokers' Health Act*, for example, has extraterritorial effect in that it applies to workspaces on aircraft, trains, vessels, or motor vehicles being operated between Canada and another country.[73] However, its motivating concern is much like that behind the "public face of Canada" in the sense that it only attempts to control the "element" of Canada that is travelling through another state, and so it is unlikely to have a great impact there. Similarly, it is likely that Canada can exercise effective control, at least for the purposes of preventing employees from smoking, without assistance from any other state.

On the other hand, some extraterritorial action within this category is quite explicitly aimed at preventing action by non-Canadians not in Canada. Various bans on advertising from outside Canada in a way which will enter Canada, for example, are aimed primarily at actions

72 See, for example, *Canada (AG) v McKenna*, [1999] 1 FC 401 (CA) or *Canada (Secretary of State for External Affairs) v Menghani*, [1994] 2 FC 102 (TD). In this same regard, note that the *Corruption of Officials Act*, above note 36, (which was previously silent on the point) was amended in June 2013 to expressly state that it applies only to Canadians citizens, permanent residents, or entities created under the laws of Canada.

73 Above note 21, s 1(2). The Act applies when the intercountry transportation is operated by a Canadian, but not when it is operated by a non-Canadian (s 1(3)).

and actors outside Canadian borders.[74] Similarly, the *Citizenship Act* creates various offences concerning citizenship certificates (such as using one to personate another person or trafficking in them) and states:

> 30. (1) An act or omission that would, if committed in Canada, be an offence under this Act is, if committed outside Canada, an offence under this Act.[75]

The *Immigration and Refugee Protection Act* contains a similar provision.[76] These provisions potentially infringe comity to the extent that they purport to directly govern the behaviour of foreign nationals while they are in other states; whether they actually do so realistically depends on the extent to which other states would see this as a legitimate step for Canada to have taken, which may be driven in part by whether those states have similar provisions. The degree of assistance that might be obtained with enforcement rests on that same consideration. (See the further consideration of this issue below, in the discussion of incentives.)

It is possible, it should be noted, to fall between these two positions. The *Security of Information Act*, for example, does not contain a broad and general assertion of extraterritorial application. Instead, it contains a deeming provision which is more limited in scope:

> 26. (1) A person who commits an act or omission outside Canada that would be an offence against this Act if it were committed in Canada is deemed to have committed it in Canada if the person is
> (*a*) a Canadian citizen;
> (*b*) a person who owes allegiance to Her Majesty in right of Canada;

---

74 See the *Tobacco Act*, above note 24, s 31(3) and the *Foreign Publishers Act*, above note 25. See also the *Canada Elections Act*, above note 17, s 330(2):

> (2) During an election period, no person shall broadcast, outside Canada, election advertising with respect to an election.

and s 331:

> 331. No person who does not reside in Canada shall, during an election period, in any way induce electors to vote or refrain from voting or vote or refrain from voting for a particular candidate unless the person is
> (*a*) a Canadian citizen; or
> (*b*) a permanent resident within the meaning of subsection 2(1) of the *Immigration and Refugee Protection Act*.

75 Above note 20, s 30.

76 Above note 19, s 135.

(*c*) a person who is locally engaged and who performs his or her functions in a Canadian mission outside Canada; or

(*d*) a person who, after the time the offence is alleged to have been committed, is present in Canada.[77]

In essence, the extraterritorial application of this Act is limited to circumstances in which Canada likely has an effective means to enforce the law because it has some practical method of control over the person alleged to have committed the offence. This might not directly address the comity issue, but it does dramatically limit the question of the need for assistance in enforcement.

What these examples demonstrate is that Canada primarily acts extraterritorially in concert with other states, which has historically been the case, and acting to implement an international agreement is the largest "growth area." That is hardly surprising, and it is a reflection in part of the fact that the disincentives to act extraterritorially are either dramatically reduced or are absent where there is an international agreement — there is little to no risk of offending other states, and there is reason to expect co-operation from other states in enforcement. However, that is not the exclusive situation in which Canada has acted extraterritorially, and it need not be the sole situation moving forward. Other considerations are also relevant, particularly when Canada is acting in the absence of an international agreement. The issues arising there can be seen in the second set of distinctions it is necessary to draw — those concerning the reasons for which extraterritorial action is taken.

2) Functions of Extraterritorial Action

As noted in the Introduction to this chapter, we argue that extraterritorial action can be seen as falling within one of three approaches: (1) prohibiting behaviour; (2) controlling behaviour; and (3) facilitating behaviour. As with the previous set of distinctions, these are not watertight compartments, but they are a useful conceptual tool. We shall here briefly describe each of these three categories, then turn to assess how placing an action into one of these categories affects the policy justification for extraterritoriality.

---

77 Above note 18, s 26.

a) Prohibiting Behaviour

Some extraterritorial action is concerned with prohibiting particular kinds of behaviour. Most obviously, extraterritorial criminal laws fall within that sphere, such as prohibitions on piracy, torture, or treason. There are, however, also pieces of non-criminal legislation that have the same goal. Bans on election advertising or tobacco advertising from other countries appearing in Canada are examples of prohibitory legislation.[78] Legislation making it an offence for Canadians to enlist in the armed forces of unfriendly nations, or to bribe foreign public officials, also falls into this category.[79]

Prohibitory legislation, by its nature, raises the most difficult enforcement issues, and so depends not just on the action of the legislative branch in creating the law, but also the executive branch in investigating it, and the judicial branch in adjudicating disputes.

b) Controlling Behaviour

A second motive for acting extraterritorially is not to forbid behaviour but to control the manner in which it occurs. Consider again for a moment the *Antarctic Environmental Protection Act*.[80] Much of the Act consists of prohibitions preventing persons or vessels from being in the Antarctic or interacting with the environment without a permit. On the other hand, it is equally important that the Act *allows* for the possibility of permits. That is, the Act is also a way of authorizing particular types of behaviour by Canadians in areas that are not part of Canada's territory.

The same is true of many of the other statutes which can be considered controlling. Rather than forbidding behaviour, much of that legislation lays down rules for how particular activities are to be carried on. That is the extraterritorial role of the *Official Languages Act*,[81] for example, or of the *Human Rights Act*[82] — to say that services will be offered in both English and French, and in a non-discriminatory way.

In some ways this category can overlap with the prohibitory approach, of course — legislation that permits certain activities with a li-

---

78 See the *Canada Elections Act*, above note 17, s 330, the *Foreign Publishers Act*, above note 25, s 3, and the *Tobacco Act*, above note 24, s 31(2).

79 See the *Foreign Enlistment Act*, above note 35, s 3, and the *Corruption of Officials Act*, above note 36, s 3.

80 Above note 45.

81 Above note 33.

82 Above note 34.

cence (such as the *Remote Sensing Space Systems Act*[83]) regulates ways in which activity can occur but does so by prohibiting other ways. However, that is not necessarily the case. The *Official Languages Act* regulates an aspect of how government offices overseas will operate, but does not create any offences as a means of doing so.[84] Other pieces of legislation enable particular activities elsewhere—licensing laboratories outside Canada under the *Health of Animals Act*,[85] for instance.

In any event, the notion of controlling behaviour extraterritorially should be seen as broader than just dealing with matters that have a licensing requirement. We consider this category to include any legislation aimed at collecting taxes or fees of any type. Yet other pieces of legislation—such as those dealing with pensions or compensation—grant benefits based on some measure of extraterritoriality, so they too would fall within this category. The important feature for this category is that the extraterritorial action "sets the rules" in some way, but this need not be a formal licensing requirement. So, for example, we include in this category legislation such as the *Government Compensation Act* (which can provide compensation for injuries suffered outside of Canada[86]) or various pension plans.[87]

We have referred primarily to legislation, but extraterritorial action to control behaviour could involve branches of government other than the legislature. Where a licensing scheme is in place, there will need to be a body (whether part of the executive or executing authority delegated to it) to grant them, and likely some body to deal with appeals where a licence is denied. There would also need to be procedures in place to grant benefits or to hear appeals from those *denied* benefits. To the extent that extraterritorial action in this category is "enforced," it would be through those means. It is therefore worth observing that those means do not themselves have a very pronounced extraterritorial impact. There would be no question of seeking extradition or interfering directly with behaviour in the territory of another state, for example.

Accordingly it is possible that the executive/enforcement branch will be called upon (but that is not necessarily the case), and if the ju-

---

83 Above note 46.

84 Above note 33, s 22(b).

85 Above note 22.

86 Above note 28, s 3(2).

87 See, for example, the *Canadian Forces Compensation Act*, above note 29, s 69, or the *Police Superannuation Act*, above note 29, ss 32.1 and 32.12.

dicial/adjudicative branch is involved, it is more likely to be through administrative decision makers than through the more formal court process.

c) Facilitating Behaviour

Our final category, facilitating behaviour, covers provisions that simply permit particular entities to operate extraterritorially. The point that distinguishes this from the previous category is that the legislation makes no attempt to govern how the entity will operate.[88] The *Bank Act*, for example, provides that:

> Subject to this Act, a bank has the capacity to carry on its business, conduct its affairs and exercise its powers in any jurisdiction outside Canada and in the manner that the laws of that jurisdiction permit.[89]

Similar language can be found in the *Trust and Loan Companies Act*,[90] the *Insurance Companies Act*,[91] the *Cooperative Credit Associations Act*,[92] the *Canada Cooperatives Act*,[93] the *Museums Act*,[94] the *Canada Business Corporations Act*,[95] and others.[96] The extraterritorial effect of this legislation is entirely facilitative. It makes no attempt to forbid any type of conduct, but it also does not regulate; it merely allows the particular private entity (a creature of statute and therefore having only the abilities given it by legislation) to operate extraterritorially, provided it does so in accordance with the laws of the foreign jurisdiction. Similar legislation permits extraterritorial action by government actors in certain defined situations.[97]

---

88 See the *Museums Act*, SC 1990, c 3, s 16 or the *Bank Act*, SC 1991, c 46, s 15(4).

89 *Bank Act*, *ibid*.

90 SC 1991, c 45, s 14(4).

91 SC 1991, c 47, s 15(4).

92 SC 1991, c 48, s 16(4).

93 SC 1998, c 1, s 27(1).

94 Above note 89, s 16.

95 RSC 1985, c C-44, s 15(3).

96 See also the *Asia-Pacific Foundation of Canada Act*, RSC 1985, c A-13, s 6. In addition see the *International Development Research Centre Act*, RSC 1985, c I-19, s 4(2), which grants the Centre the power to do various things (carry out research, support conferences, hold real property, and so on) "in Canada or elsewhere."

97 See, for example, the *Bank of Canada Act*, RSC 1985, c B-2, s 4(2):

> (2) The Bank may establish branches and agencies and appoint agents or mandataries in Canada and may also, with the approval of the Governor in Council, establish branches and appoint agents or mandataries elsewhere than in Canada.

See also the *National Housing Act*, RSC 1985, c N-11, s 77(1):

Legislation that only facilitates extraterritorial action, then, does not raise many issues domestically or abroad. It imposes few demands, because it does not require either enforcement or licensing. It is minimally intrusive extraterritorially, because the requirement that the laws of the other jurisdiction be complied with eliminates (or all but eliminates) any concerns about comity.

d) Function-based Disincentives Diagnosed

When we discussed the justifications for acting extraterritorially, we identified the two major considerations as the inability to enforce legislation and the concern for comity. We observed there that multinational action is less likely to raise these concerns, while unilateral extraterritorial action is more likely to raise them. However, in applying this distinction to the functions of extraterritorial action, it becomes clear that those concerns do not arise equally in all contexts.

Where Canada hopes to forbid behaviour in the territory of other states, those issues would loom large; enforcement will be a practical consideration, and the pressure of comity will be strong. It is easy to imagine that the United States, for example, might be unsympathetic on free speech or economic grounds to the prohibition in the *Foreign Publishers*

---

77. (1) The Corporation may . . .
    (*b*) support and participate in the development of, and investigate, housing, housing finance, living environments and community planning outside Canada, either directly or through other persons, including foreign governments or agencies of foreign governments and non-governmental organizations.

A further example is the *Canadian Transportation Accident Investigation and Safety Board Act*, SC 1989, c 3, s 3:

3. (1) This Act applies in respect of aviation occurrences
    (*a*) in or over Canada;
    (*b*) in or over any place that is under Canadian air traffic control; and
    (*c*) in or over any other place, if
        (i) Canada is requested to investigate the aviation occurrence by an appropriate authority, or
        (ii) the aviation occurrence involves an aircraft in respect of which, or that is operated by a person to whom, a Canadian aviation document has been issued under Part I of the *Aeronautics Act*.

Finally, see the *Federal Real Property and Federal Immovables Act*, SC 1991, c 50, s 5(3):

(3) In a jurisdiction outside Canada, federal real property may be granted, and federal immovables may be conceded, by any instrument or act by which, under the laws in force in that jurisdiction, real property and immovables may be transferred.

Act on non-Canadian publications including advertisements directed at the Canadian market.[98] They could see that (or any similar future legislation) as an inappropriate attempt to interfere in their ability to regulate their domestic marketplace, and refuse to assist in prosecutions.

Where the goal of extraterritorial action is only to exert some form of control over behaviour, however, concerns over comity and enforcement might still exist, but in a diminished form. The *Non-smokers' Health Act*[99] illustrates this point. Although the Act does contain some offences, they are incidental to and only a means of achieving the goal of the Act: that work spaces be generally smoke-free, that there be designated (and ventilated) smoking areas, and so on. Particularly as the extraterritorial effect of that scheme is limited to Canadian carriers operating outside of Canada, setting workplace rules does not impose a great threat to any other state and greatly diminishes enforcement concerns.

Similarly, some extraterritorial action in the "controlling behaviour" category involves providing a benefit through a pension or other compensation scheme. It is difficult to find any basis upon which another state could have jurisdictional concerns that a Canadian worker receives compensation from a Canadian source for an injury incurred while working for Canada, simply because the accident occurred in that other state.[100] By the same token, enforcement issues are likely to be minimal at best, since in all likelihood any benefit can be provided without the need for another state's co-operation.

Finally, where extraterritorial action falls into the "facilitating behaviour" category, comity and enforcement concerns should be minimal to non-existent. As we noted earlier, the norm is for such facilitative provisions to expressly require the entity to act in accordance with the laws of the jurisdiction, and so comity is respected. Enforcement issues will not arise, because not even offences in incidental support of a regulatory scheme will be present.

---

98 Above note 25. See also s 15 of the Act, which provides that:

> 15. (1) In a proceeding for a contravention of section 3, a foreign publisher who commits an act outside Canada that, if committed in Canada, would be an offence under that section is deemed to commit that act in Canada.

99 Above note 21.

100 See the *Government Compensation Act*, above note 28, s 3(2).

3) Conclusions Regarding Disincentives

Combining discussion of these two sets of distinctions, we can begin to see much more clearly when extraterritorial action will and will not raise disincentives. We observed first that there are relatively few disincentives to extraterritorial action that implements international agreements or is otherwise part of multilateral action. The category that was potentially the most problematic was action taken on account of a strong connection to Canada, because such conduct is typically unilateral.

Even there, however, not all action will be equal. Some instances in this category—for example, using secret information for the benefit of a foreign power in the *Security of Information Act*,[101] citizenship certificate fraud in the *Citizenship Act*,[102] advertising from outside Canada contrary to the *Foreign Publishers Act*[103]—are unambiguous attempts to prohibit behaviour by non-Canadians while they are not on Canadian soil. Those laws raise the greatest concerns, and so carry with them the strongest disincentives. That is, there would need to be a particularly strong policy incentive on the other side of the scale to justify acting extraterritorially in this way.

On the other hand, some instances of extraterritorial action, although motivated by a strong connection to Canada, only attempt to regulate or are merely facilitative. Canada has chosen to pay pensions to armed forces or RCMP members even if their time in the service was spent out of the country.[104] As observed earlier, such action raises few concerns, and so there is less—potentially far less—disincentive to acting extraterritorially in this way. Accordingly, action of this sort can be justified without the need for as strong an incentive. A much clearer picture emerges, then, of the situations in which extraterritorial action will be either controversial or mundane, in need of strong justification or easily accepted.

Even this, however, is not the end of the analysis. The discussion to this point has helped isolate when the disincentives to act extraterri-

---

101 Above note 18, s 26.

102 Above note 20, s 30.

103 Above note 25. See also s 15 which provides that:

> 15. (1) In a proceeding for a contravention of section 3, a foreign publisher who commits an act outside Canada that, if committed in Canada, would be an offence under that section is deemed to commit that act in Canada. (*Ibid.*)

104 *Canadian Forces Compensation Act*, above note 29, s 69; *Police Superannuation Act*, above note 29, ss 32.1 and 32.12.

torially are likely to be present in greater or lesser degrees. However, even within the most controversial category (unilateral extraterritorial action to prohibit behaviour), there are distinctions that need to be drawn. Two points must be made.

The first concerns another variable that was referred to in discussing some pieces of legislation: to whom will the extraterritorial action apply? Some laws explicitly target the world — the prohibition on forging citizenship certificates in the *Citizenship Act* not only applies anywhere in the world, but to anyone in the world.[105] Some laws only target those whom Canada has a reasonable prospect of prosecuting — individuals who are physically present in Canada, for example.[106] Other laws target only Canadians.[107]

This variable could obviously be relevant to how easy or difficult it might be to justify extraterritorial action. The enforcement question becomes easier if the person subject to the law is already present in Canada. If the person is not, the assistance of another state is likely to be necessary, and so this becomes in some ways as much of a "can" question as it is a "should" question. To have some reasonable prospect of obtaining the assistance of other states, Canada's claim to jurisdiction must have some prospect of being recognized as acceptable state practice.

The second point may be made by comparing the impacts of two extraterritorial prohibitions in Canadian law: "do not steal our military secrets" and "do not advertise tobacco to our residents." The latter, as noted above, could be controversial; other states might quite plausibly not see that as a legitimate goal — or at least not as a legitimate enough goal for Canada to act extraterritorially in pursuit of it. On the other hand, every state will acknowledge it as legitimate for another state not to want its military secrets stolen,[108] and as outlined in Chapter 3,

---

105 Above note 20, s 30.

106 See, for example, the *Code*, above note 7, s 7(1)(b), exerting jurisdiction over anyone committing an offence on an aircraft while it is in flight "if the flight terminated in Canada." See also the *Security of Information Act*, above note 18, s 26(1).

107 *Foreign Enlistment Act*, above note 35, s 3.

108 This opinion can coexist perfectly plausibly with the desire to *obtain* that other state's military secrets. Indeed, it is the combination of those two beliefs that leads to espionage: "of course they don't want us to know it, but we want to know it." It is perhaps for that reason that s 26(1)(d) of the *Security of Information Act*, above note 18, does not purport to make the Act enforceable against the world, but only against "a person who, after the time the offence is alleged to have been committed, is present in Canada."

Section A(3), this recognition is implemented by way of the protective principle.

In other words, states are likely to recognize some exercises of extraterritoriality by other states as reasonable and justified, even if those actions are not undertaken pursuant to a multilateral agreement. Really, this is a way to begin to discuss the next major consideration: the incentives to act extraterritorially. Where the goal served by extraterritorial action is one widely understood and accepted, that amounts to saying that there is a strong incentive to act in that way. It is to that topic we now turn.

C. INCENTIVES TO ACT EXTRATERRITORIALLY

The preceding section looked at the disincentives to acting extraterritorially. It did so essentially by the process of elimination: by considering the circumstances in which Canada has been willing to act extraterritorially, we were able to show more clearly when those disincentives are absent, and therefore what they are. This section will proceed in much the same way.

As we said in the introduction, the main incentive in any particular situation to acting extraterritorially will be the policy goals of the action, which are not for us to assess. However, it is possible to consider the way in which those policy goals would be perceived by other states, which ought to be a relevant consideration any time Canada considers acting extraterritorially.

The focus of this discussion will be Canada's response to extraterritorial action by other states. The simple argument is reminiscent of the "golden rule": we have an incentive to act as we would want others act. Extraterritoriality is the exception rather than the norm, but it can be part of a harmonious global approach. Accordingly, we will consider extraterritorial actions by other states that have or can have an impact on Canada, in order to assess which are acceptable to Canada and which incite its reaction. We suggest that Canada has an incentive to engage in extraterritorial action where it invites that by others, but should avoid contributing to a new international norm in other circumstances. In other words, if policy goals of the government of the day correspond to situations where extraterritorial action by other states is perceived as legitimate, then there is a greater incentive to pursue those particular policy goals extraterritorially.

To begin, it is worth noting that Canada's main response to extraterritorial action by other states, at least in the circumstances where such action actually occurs, is one of acquiescence and co-operation.[109] We have noted in the previous section that the greatest growth in Canada's own assertions of extraterritoriality have come pursuant to international conventions, which lead us not only to assert jurisdiction in some cases, but to cede it in others. We claim the ability to prosecute a French citizen for actions on a US-registered plane so long as the flight lands in Canada,[110] but by the same token we agree that other states could prosecute Canadians for actions on a Canadian-registered aircraft if the flight lands elsewhere. Whenever we sign an international agreement that shares responsibility for prosecuting, we are accepting that the other signatories have the same legitimacy in acting extraterritorially as we do. In some circumstances this can have extraterritorial impact on Canada, and we accept that.

This same attitude of co-operation can also be seen in some contexts where extraterritorial action by other states does not rest upon prior international agreement. We discussed above various Canadian statutes that prohibit behaviour even when that behaviour occurs outside our borders: offences dealing with citizenship fraud, immigration fraud, treason, or official secrets. Not surprisingly, Canada is not the only country to have such legislation and to give it extraterritorial effect.[111] It is reasonable to suggest that Canada sees those laws of other countries as generally uncontroversial.[112] That is so, we suggest, because no real

---

109 See Chapter 3, Section B.

110 See, for example, *R v Minot*, 2011 NLCA 7.

111 See, for example, with regard to voting fraud, the *Representation of the People Act 1983* (UK), c 2, s 178; with regard to espionage, the *Crimes Act 1961* (NZ), 1961/43, 1 RS 635, ss 78–78A, the *Official Secrets Act 1989* (UK), c 6, s 15, or the *Official Secrets Act 1972* (Malaysia), Act 88, s 25; or with regard to citizenship, the *Australian Citizenship Act 2007* (Cth), ss 50 & 51.

112 It is difficult to demonstrate that something is *not* an issue, but to the extent it can be done, it is by looking at circumstances where questions would arise if there were any. Accordingly, see, for example, *United States of America v Ibrahim*, 2011 BCSC 357. The actual issue in that decision concerned disclosure, but the underlying cause of the action against Ibrahim, a Canadian citizen, was that the United States wanted to prosecute him in connection with fraudulent immigration applications. Despite extensive litigation over various issues by Ibrahim (see also *United States of America v Ibrahim*, 2010 BCSC 1777 and *United States of America v Ibrahim*, 2009 BCSC 1090), the suggestion that the immigration fraud offences could not be made extraterritorial did not arise. See also *United States of America v Vreeland* (2002), 20 Imm LR (3d)

issue of conflicting policy goals arises in this situation; each state sees it as legitimate for other states to take those steps necessary to preserve itself as a state.

Put another way, the extraterritorial effect of these laws is essentially circumstantial. In discussing disincentives to act extraterritorially, we classified these laws as falling in the category of action with a strong connection to Canada, which is really the main point of concern. The policy concern of laws such as these is an entirely domestic one: the security and control of the state. That it is peripherally necessary to act extraterritorially to protect those objectives does not alter the fact that the objectives themselves are domestic ones.

Such laws, whether Canada's or those of other countries, are justified at international law under the protective principle, but that is not the key point. Our observation from the beginning has been that "should" is a separate question from "can," and so the fact that international law permits such domestic laws to have extraterritorial application is not sufficient. In essence, it is important here to see the direction that causation runs: it is not "the protective principle applies, therefore all states see it as acceptable," but rather, "all states see it as acceptable, therefore the protective principle applies."[113]

This general attitude of co-operation also extends to the investigative branch. Canada is a signatory to many mutual legal assistance treaties, and police forces in Canada routinely carry out investigations on Canadian soil for the benefit of prosecutions in other countries pursuant to requests under the treaties. Indeed, it is not even necessary for there to be a formal request under the terms of the relevant treaty — police forces

---

299 (Ont SCJ), where the applicant (described by the judge as an "imaginative and manipulative person who has little regard for the truth," at para 24) argued that the extradition application for fraud he was subject to was a ruse, and that the United States actually wanted to prosecute him for treason. It was argued that special protections might be needed because treason is a capital offence in the United States, but the suggestion that the law could not be extraterritorial did not arise.

113 An analogous point is made in *Suresh v Canada (Minister of Citizenship and Immigration)*, 2002 SCC 1 at para 60 [*Suresh*]:

> International treaty norms are not, strictly speaking, binding in Canada unless they have been incorporated into Canadian law by enactment. However, in seeking the meaning of the Canadian Constitution, the courts may be informed by international law. Our concern is not with Canada's international obligations *qua* obligations; rather, our concern is with the principles of fundamental justice. We look to international law as evidence of these principles and not as controlling in itself.

are entitled to co-operate with one another on an informal basis without such a request.[114]

Similarly, Canadian courts will (subject to exceptions to be discussed below) assist courts of other countries with their processes. Canada is a signatory to the Hague *Convention on the Service Abroad of Judicial and Extrajudicial Documents in Civil or Commercial Matters*,[115] under which Canada will serve documents within its territory on behalf of foreign courts. Equally, Canadian courts will normally enforce letters rogatory (or a "letter of request," as it is termed in some legislation) issued by courts of other countries, compelling witnesses to appear and give evidence or produce documents as an investigative technique for proceedings in other jurisdictions.[116] It has been found that such requests can be enforced even when the entity to be examined in Canada is a Crown corporation.[117]

The judiciary and the executive also co-operate in the extraterritorial application of the laws of other states through the extradition process. Extradition takes place under the *Extradition Act*[118] and the terms of the relevant extradition treaty. After a requesting state makes a request for a person's extradition, there are two stages. At the first stage, the judicial stage, a judge will hold an extradition hearing to inquire whether

---

114 See *R v Dorsay*, 2006 BCCA 117 at para 65. See also various cases where German police discovered a child pornography ring and (via Interpol) gave IP addresses to police forces in other countries, including Canada: *R v Ward*, 2008 ONCJ 355; *R v McNeice*, 2010 BCSC 1544; *R v Verge*, [2009] OJ No 6300 (Ct J); or *R v Hutchings*, 2010 ONCJ 214. We note, however, that cases are emerging where unfettered informal policing co-operation is attracting *Charter* claims; see *United States of America v Wakeling*, 2012 BCCA 397, leave to appeal to SCC granted, [2012] SCCA No 534; *United States of America v Fafalios*, 2012 ONCA 365.

115 15 November 1965, Can TS 1989 No 2.

116 See, for example, *Canada Evidence Act*, RSC 1985, c C-5, s 46, or similar provisions in various provincial acts. Note that the *Canada Evidence Act* permits a Canadian court to compel a witness to appear and testify by video-link before the court in the other jurisdiction. Interestingly, Canada is not a signatory to the Hague *Convention on the Taking of Evidence Abroad in Civil or Commercial Matters*, 18 March 1970, 847 UNTS 231, though these provisions largely accomplish what that Convention would require.

117 *Lantheus Medical Imaging Inc v Atomic Energy of Canada Ltd*, 2013 ONCA 264. The Ontario Court of Appeal there observed that "comity refers to mutual respect between sovereign nations and holds that, generally, [Letters of Request] from foreign courts should be enforced in Canada" (at para 40).

118 SC 1999, c 18. Extradition need not concern the extraterritorial substantive application of another state's laws, but it can do so, and at a minimum requires Canada to participate in sending a person to be dealt with under the laws of another state.

a *prima facie* case against the accused can be made out by the requesting state.[119] Presuming this is met, then at the second stage, the executive stage, the Minister of Justice makes a discretionary decision whether to order extradition.[120]

Generally speaking, Canada has been very willing to grant extradition requests. The extradition treaty between Canada and the United States, for example, permits the minister to prosecute rather than extradite, to refuse extradition on the basis that the offence was of a political character, or to seek assurances that the death penalty would not be imposed. No minister has ever chosen to do either of the first two, and no minister ever sought assurances regarding the death penalty until the Supreme Court ordered in *Burns* that they were required to do so.[121] Canada has extradited fugitives even when there is a significant difference in the penalties here and in the requesting state.[122]

The norm, then, is for Canada to co-operate with requests from other states for assistance, even when those requests amount to assisting that state in acting extraterritorially. Canada does so out of respect for comity between nations; it is important to note, however, that that respect is not unlimited. As the Supreme Court has observed:

> It is upon this comity of nations that international legal assistance rests. Thus the courts of one jurisdiction will give effect to the laws and judicial decisions of another jurisdiction, not as a matter of obligation but out of mutual deference and respect. A foreign request is given full force and effect *unless it be contrary to the public policy of the jurisdiction to which the request is directed . . . or otherwise prejudicial to the sovereignty or the citizens of the latter jurisdiction*.[123]

Therefore, although the norm is co-operation, we also find circumstances in which Canada does not defer to the requests or efforts of other states. Not all requests for letters rogatory are enforced, for example.[124] Similarly, not all requests for extradition are granted.

---

119 *Ibid*, s 24.

120 *Ibid*, s 40.

121 Gary Botting, *Extradition between Canada and the United States* (Ardsley, NY: Transnational Publishers, 2005) at 20.

122 See, for example, *United States of America v Emery*, 2005 BCSC 1192.

123 *Zingre v The Queen*, [1981] 2 SCR 392 at 401 [*Zingre*] [emphasis added].

124 See, for example, *Presbyterian Church of Sudan (Re)* (2006), 275 DLR (4th) 512 (Ont CA) [*Presbyterian Church*]. Declining to grant a letter of request issued by a United States District, the Court of Appeal refused the request for assistance because it

In the context of extradition, for example, the "double criminality" rule requires that the behaviour that is to be prosecuted by the requesting state must be something that would also have been a crime in Canada.[125] Further, the *prima facie* case standard is meant to guarantee that a person will only be made to face trial in another country when there is some real basis to think that that person has committed an offence. As the Supreme Court has held, "[i]nternational comity does not require the extradition of a person on demand or surmise."[126]

There have also been exceptional circumstances in which Canada has refused extradition requests even though the *prima facie* criteria for extradition have been met. For example, in a set of companion cases, prosecutors in the United States sought the extradition of a number of Canadians who were alleged to have taken part in a scheme to defraud

---

had not been adequately shown that relevant evidence was likely to be produced, nor that the evidence was necessary or otherwise unobtainable.

125 In fact the rule is stricter than just that the behaviour is illegal in both countries: it must have been a sufficiently serious offence in both countries. Section 3 of the *Extradition Act* provides:

> 3. (1) A person may be extradited from Canada in accordance with this Act and a relevant extradition agreement on the request of an extradition partner for the purpose of prosecuting the person or imposing a sentence on — or enforcing a sentence imposed on — the person if
>
> (*a*) subject to a relevant extradition agreement, the offence in respect of which the extradition is requested is punishable by the extradition partner, by imprisoning or otherwise depriving the person of their liberty for a maximum term of two years or more, or by a more severe punishment; and
>
> (*b*) the conduct of the person, had it occurred in Canada, would have constituted an offence that is punishable in Canada,
>
> (i) in the case of a request based on a specific agreement, by imprisonment for a maximum term of five years or more, or by a more severe punishment, and
>
> (ii) in any other case, by imprisonment for a maximum term of two years or more, or by a more severe punishment, subject to a relevant extradition agreement.

That said, section 3 of the *Extradition Act* is subject to the relevant treaty, so that the threshold for extraditions to the United States, for example, is that the offence must be punishable by a minimum of one year's imprisonment.

126 *United States of America v Ferras; United States of America v Latty*, 2006 SCC 33 at para 21 [*Ferras*]. This aspect of *Ferras* has been interpreted restrictively by the senior appellate courts, but at the time of writing a more robust approach was being urged in an appeal of *France v Diab*, 2011 ONSC 337.

American citizens.[127] The extradition judge accepted that a *prima facie* case had been made, but refused to order extradition due to comments that had been made by an American judge and prosecutor. The American judge, in sentencing another person involved in the same scheme, had said that if those who were fighting their extradition were eventually found guilty, they would get "the absolute maximum jail sentence." More importantly, the prosecutor in charge of the case had said, in an interview broadcast on Canadian television, that anyone who insisted on an extradition hearing rather than voluntarily coming to face prosecution in the United States was "going to be the boyfriend of a very bad man" upon conviction. This threat of sexual violence as a way of inducing individuals to give up their legal rights was described by the Supreme Court of Canada as "shocking."[128] In all three cases, the Court concluded that the extradition proceedings had to be stayed, as both an abuse of process and a violation of the principles of fundamental justice.[129]

Those cases deal with extraordinary and unusual behaviour on the part of the requesting state. The *Burns* decision is therefore interesting because it deals with a reaction by Canada to a "usual" part of the law of another country — the death penalty.[130] In considering a request for extradition, the Supreme Court of Canada concluded that barring exceptional circumstances, a minister would be constitutionally bound to ask for and obtain an assurance that the death penalty will not be

---

127 See *United States of America v Cobb*, 2001 SCC 19; *United States of America v Tsioubris*, 2001 SCC 20; and *United States of America v Shulman*, 2001 SCC 21 [*Shulman*].

128 *Shulman*, *ibid* at para 41.

129 To similar effect, see the Ontario Court of Appeal decision in *United States of America v Khadr*, 2011 ONCA 358 [*Khadr 2011*], leave to appeal to SCC refused, [2011] SCCA No 316. The applicant (a Canadian) had been abducted by the Pakistani intelligence agency in exchange for half a million dollars paid by the American government, and was then held secretly in detention in Pakistan for fourteen months. He was beaten, was refused access to Canadian consular officials, was denied access to Pakistani courts, and was detained for months after any interrogations were over. This "shocking and unjustifiable" (*Khadr 2011* at para 57, citing *United States of America v Khadr*, 2010 ONSC 4338 at para 150) conduct warranted a stay of the extradition proceedings. See also *United States of America v Leonard*, 2012 ONCA 622, where the Court of Appeal held that the minister's decision to surrender the individuals sought breached both section 6 and 7 of the *Canadian Charter of Rights and Freedoms*, Part I of the *Constitution Act, 1982*, being Schedule B to the *Canada Act 1982* (UK), 1982, c 11 [*Charter*], due to the fact that their Aboriginal background would not be taken into account in the United States, though it would be in Canada.

130 *United States of America v Burns*, 2001 SCC 7 [*Burns*].

imposed as a condition of extradition. Such an obligation arises when the failure to do so would shock the conscience of the community, and "[a]n extradition that violates the principles of fundamental justice will *always* shock the conscience."[131] The Court concluded that the failure to seek assurances would violate the principles of fundamental justice based on a number of considerations. First, it observed that the death penalty had not in fact been used in Canada for forty years, which reflected "a fundamental Canadian principle about the appropriate limits of the criminal justice system."[132] In addition, it observed not only that there had been an international trend against the death penalty, but that "[t]here have been important initiatives within the international community denouncing the death penalty, with the government of Canada often in the forefront."[133] It therefore required the minister to seek and obtain assurances that the death penalty would not be used as a precondition to extradition.[134]

All of this points to the correctness of the Supreme Court's position articulated in *Zingre* more than thirty years ago: comity is important, and as a result, Canada is generally willing to accommodate extraterritorial action by other states.[135] Sometimes, however, the actions of other states can be "contrary to the public policy"[136] of Canada or inconsistent with values which are adopted by the international community generally. Our willingness to accept extraterritorial action by other states is proportional to the extent that those actions are based on shared values.[137]

---

131 *Ibid* at para 68 [emphasis in original].

132 *Ibid* at para 77.

133 *Ibid* at para 85.

134 To similar effect but in a somewhat different context, see *Suresh*, above note 113, holding that deporting a person to face a substantial risk of torture would generally violate section 7 of the *Charter*, above note 129. Isolating the relevant principle of fundamental justice involved taking "into account Canada's international obligations and values as expressed in '[t]he various sources of international human rights law — declarations, covenants, conventions, judicial and quasi-judicial decisions of international tribunals, [and] customary norms.'" *Suresh*, *ibid* at para 46, citing *Burns*, above note 130 at paras 79–81.

135 *Zingre*, above note 123.

136 *Ibid* at 401.

137 A similar point is made in a different context by the Supreme Court with its decision in *R v Hape*, 2007 SCC 26 at para 52:

> Comity means that when one state looks to another for help in criminal matters, it must respect the way in which the other state chooses to provide the assis-

We should expect to find, then, that extraterritorial action by other states becomes controversial when it is based on the pursuit of policy goals that are not widely shared, or at least are not shared by Canada.

For example, Canada passed the *Foreign Extraterritorial Measures Act* (*FEMA*) in 1985.[138] *FEMA* was passed in response to a number of American laws that were applied to activities in Canada by Canadians. These American acts included laws ordering disclosure of documents or issuing judgment for damages against companies that were operating in Canada in certain circumstances.[139] *FEMA* contains four responses to that extraterritorial action.

First, the Attorney General can prohibit the furnishing of documents ordered by foreign tribunals if it is deemed that Canadian sovereignty or commercial interests are likely to be infringed.[140] Second, the Attorney General can prohibit compliance in Canada with orders of foreign tribunals.[141] Third, a judge may order that a judgment issued by a foreign tribunal not be enforceable in Canada.[142] Finally, a Canadian against whom a foreign judgment has been executed by a person elsewhere can obtain a judgment in Canada against that person.[143]

Taken as a whole, these provisions limit the scope of some extraterritorial measures in Canada. The Minister of Justice at the time, John Crosbie, said this during the Hansard debates of the purpose of the bill:

> So what does the Bill do? It sets out a framework for Canadian governmental responses to foreign governmental measures or decisions by foreign courts which have unacceptable extraterritorial scope. Yes, we want foreign investment. Yes, we want a better relationship, and we have a better relationship with the United States of America as an example.

---

tance within its borders. That deference ends where clear violations of international law and fundamental human rights begin.

See, in this regard, the discussion of *Khadr 2008*, above note 30.

138 RSC 1985, c F-29 [*FEMA*].

139 In particular, these circumstances related to "restrictive business practices, export controls, securities (both in respect of corrupt practices and Arab boycott legislation), bankruptcy and insolvency, [and] taxation . . .": see William C Graham, "The Foreign Extraterritorial Measures Act" (1986) 11:4 Can Bus LJ 410 at 413 [Graham]. See also the discussion in H Scott Fairley, "Exceeding the Limits of Territorial Bounds: The Helms-Burton Act" (1996) 34 Can YB Int'l Law 161.

140 *FEMA*, above note 138, s 3.

141 *Ibid*, s 5.

142 *Ibid*, s 8.

143 *Ibid*, s 9.

> However, that does not mean to say that we are not going to defend our own vital national interests or our own Canadian sovereignty, and that is what the Bill does. The Bill gives us some muscle to do that. The Bill sets out the framework for us to respond to foreign government measures, or decisions by foreign courts, which we find to have unacceptable extraterritorial scope.[144]

FEMA was amended in 1996 to respond specifically to the American *Helms-Burton Act*, which penalized non-US businesses for dealing in property that had been expropriated from Americans in Cuba. Those amendments specifically hold that any judgment under the *Helms-Burton Act* "shall not be recognized or enforceable in any manner in Canada" and also permit the clawing back of any judgment ordered under *Helms-Burton*.[145]

What is noteworthy about this reaction is not just the departure from Canada's normal co-operative response to extraterritoriality, but the circumstances in which it arose. The US legislation to which *FEMA* was a response exerted an extraterritorial claim, but not in circumstances where there was prior international agreement, nor in circumstances where a properly domestic concern needed to be protected against action outside the territory of the state, nor even in circumstances where the domestic concern pursued policy goals that would be widely shared or widely seen by other states as legitimate ones to pursue. The *Helms-Burton Act* in particular attempted to impose the views of the United States with regard to Cuba on other states, even though the vast majority of other states do not share the idiosyncratic view of the United States in that regard.

D. CONCLUSION

We have argued that a guide to whether Canada should act extraterritorially depends on weighing the incentives and disincentives to do so in the given case. It will always be a very fact-dependent decision, and the major incentive in any given case will always be how important the government of the day regards the policy issue in question. As we have tried to explain at some length, however, that policy decision can be placed in a broader context and assessed with a view to the way in which such action will be perceived in the international community. Some struc-

144 Graham, above note 139 at 415.

145 Above note138, ss 7.1 and 8.1.

ture can be provided for how to make the assessment. For example, we have drawn the distinction between action that prohibits, controls, and facilitates. Extraterritorial action that merely facilitates Canadians in acting extraterritorially, as one example, is likely to be non-controversial with other states. As a result, the disincentives to acting in that way are much reduced, and even a relatively mild incentive might be sufficient to swing the balance in the direction of acting extraterritorially.

On the other hand, extraterritorial action that prohibits has a much greater potential to be controversial, though this will depend, of course, on the nature of the action. As we have seen in the discussion of incentives, there are circumstances in which nations act extraterritorially in Canada in ways that cause us no concern, while there are other circumstances in which Canada does not elect to co-operate with that action. In very large measure, the nature of Canada's response (and equally, the response other states might be expected to have to Canadian extraterritorial action) depends on the extent to which that action is seen as pursuing a legitimate domestic concern or a shared multilateral one. Prohibitory action to protect the integrity of the state through legislation to protect citizenship, to enforce immigration rules, to prevent the theft of official secrets, and so on — the sort of legislation every country is likely to create — is unlikely to be seen as controversial, even though it has an incidental extraterritorial application. Actions meant to prohibit, or even merely to control, when they are in pursuit of policy ends that are not widely shared, are far more likely to create backlash, and therefore there is a greater disincentive to act in that way. This does not mean such action cannot be justified, but it does mean that the incentive to do so must be that much more compelling if it is to outweigh the disincentives.

Further still, the weighing must take into account to whom the action will be applied. It is one thing to forbid Canadians from acting in a particular way while on foreign soil; it is quite another to purport to prohibit the world from doing so. Canada prohibits having sexual relations with minors everywhere in the world, but the prohibition applies only to Canadian citizens and permanent residents; despite being prohibitory, such legislation is less likely to threaten comity, and therefore does not require as strong an incentive as it might otherwise to outweigh the disincentives.[146] This will not be true of action that sets out

---

146 *Code*, above note 7, s 7(4.1). This exercise of extraterritorial jurisdiction is now in accordance with the international treaty, though in fact the Canadian legislation predated that treaty. Although the legislation does not threaten comity, its restriction

to govern the behaviour of everyone, Canadian or not. However, none of this is to say that such action cannot possibly be justified: our goal is merely to point out that the more that disincentives are added to one side of the scale, the greater the incentives on the other side must be for the decision to act extraterritorially to appear as the sensible one.

Consider, however, the "Turbot War" of 1995. The dispute was based on the fishing of "straddling stocks" by EU nations just outside of Canada's Exclusive Economic Zone (EEZ), the 200-nautical-mile zone that extends from Canada's coastline. Canada's EEZ was internationally recognized as Canadian territory for the purpose of certain resource ownership rights, but "straddling stocks" migrate between the high seas and EEZs. In 1995, the European Union set a quota on the Northwest Atlantic Fisheries Organization (NAFO) regulatory area that allowed Spanish and Portuguese vessels to fish straddling stocks. Canada considered these stocks to be part of its territorial fishery resources, and therefore, this fishing was contrary to Canadian regulations.[147] In particular, section 9 of the 1994 *Coastal Fisheries Protection Act* provided that a protection officer may, on reasonable grounds, seize a fishing vessel and any goods aboard it, provided that they were within the NAFO Regulatory Area, even if the location was outside of Canada's EEZ. In accordance with that provision, Canada seized the Spanish fishing trawler *Estai*, which was acting within the EU regulations, but was illegally fishing according to Canadian regulations.

This extraterritorial action had about as many disincentives on that side of the scale as there can be: it was legislation and executive action aimed at prohibition (or at least at controlling generally, though section 9 was a prohibition); it was not based on a shared international view; and it was action aimed not only at Canadians, but at the world. Canada faced much international scrutiny and a lawsuit in the International Court of Justice from Spain as a result of the actions. Nonetheless, the final result involved Canada succeeding in drawing a renegotiated agreement with the European Union over fishery resources in the NAFO Regulatory

to Canadian citizens and permanent residents has very likely not reduced enforceability concerns, though this is not necessarily because other states are unwilling to co-operate: see the discussion in the case study of child sex tourism in Chapter 7, Section E.

147 Hugh M Kindred & Phillip M Saunders, eds, *International Law: Chiefly as Interpreted and Applied in Canada*, 7th ed (Toronto: Emond Montgomery, 2006) at 985.

Area.[148] This is an example of aggressive, proactive measures by Canada to force political resolution through extraterritorial measures. It is, however, a rare example, and that is exactly as one would expect. To conclude as we began, the occasions when Canada *should* act extraterritorially are far narrower than those where it *can*. There are incentives and disincentives to be weighed, and to the extent that Canada acts to help promote a harmonious global governance regime, the side of the scale favouring extraterritorial action is more likely to prevail. Only particularly strong policy goals could provide the incentive to act extraterritorially in other circumstances.

---

148 And impelling the international community towards concluding the *United Nations Agreement for the Implementation of the Provisions of the United Nations Convention on the Law of the Sea of 10 December 1982 relating to the Conservation and Management of Straddling Fish Stocks and Highly Migratory Fish Stocks*, 4 December 1995, 34 ILM 1542.

CHAPTER 7

Case Studies of Extraterritorial Jurisdiction

In this chapter we use our evolving framework as a lens through which to conduct a series of case studies. These case studies touch on issues that are both old and new, yet all reflect the twin pressures of globalization and technological change. In these cases studies, we examine the extraterritorial application of human rights law, human rights claims in civil courts, data protection, terrorism, child sex tourism, Internet gambling and cybercrime, and virtual worlds.

A. EXTRATERRITORIAL APPLICATION OF HUMAN RIGHTS LAW

This case study will explore a particularly controversial topic within the scope of this book: the extraterritorial application of human rights law.[1]

1 There is a large literature on this topic, a sample of which is: Fons Coomans & Menno T Kamminga, eds, *Extraterritorial Application of Human Rights Treaties* (Antwerp: Intersentia, 2004); Mark Gibney & Sigrun Skogly, eds, *Universal Human Rights and Extraterritorial Obligations* (Philadelphia: University of Pennsylvania Press, 2010); Guy S Goodwin-Gill, "The Extra-Territorial Reach of Human Rights Obligations: A Brief Perspective on the Link to Jurisdiction" in Laurence Boisson de Chazournes & Marcelo Kohen, eds, *International Law and the Quest for its Implementation* (Leiden: Brill, 2010) 293; Ralph Wilde, "Triggering State Obligations Extraterritorially: The Spatial Test in Certain Human Rights Treaties" (2007) 40 Isr LR 503. One of the best recent treatments is Marko Milanovic, *Extraterritorial Application of Human Rights Treaties: Law, Principles and Policy* (Oxford: Oxford University Press, 2011) [Milanovic, *Extraterritorial Application*]. See also Robert J Currie & Hugh M Kindred, "Flux and

The dynamics of globalization discussed in Chapter 2 have obviously given rise to increasing extraterritorial activity of various sorts on the part of state officials. This is particularly the case with law enforcement officials, who are becoming more engaged in transnational co-operative activities, and the actions of military personnel involved in overseas conflicts. Yet along with this development has come uncertainty for both governments and individuals as to what controls exist — and can lawfully exist — on the exercise of their authority when it is desirable outside the state of origin.

There is a great deal to be said about this topic, as attested by the number of book-length treatments and other literature in existence. Given our focus on Canadian law and practice considered within the international context, this case study will bear down on two main arguments. First, Canadian caselaw on this topic — specifically, on the extraterritorial application of the *Charter*[2] — provides an effective demonstration of how the international law norms regarding extraterritorial jurisdiction have become "fragmented"[3] and how this fragmentation is both reflected by, and has contributed to, the difficulty of domestic judicial wrestling matches with the issue. The second and related argument will be that this particular application of extraterritorial jurisdiction has also led to a certain "cracking at the seams" of the Supreme Court of Canada's jurisprudence, both in cases dealing with international human rights law and those dealing with international law more generally.

Fragmentation in the International Law of State Jurisdiction: The Synecdochal Example of Canada's Domestic Court Conflicts over Accountability for International Human Rights Violations" in Ole Kristian Fauchald & André Nollkaemper, eds, *The Practice of International and National Courts and the (De-) Fragmentation of International Law* (Oxford: Hart, 2012) 217, from which portions of this case study are drawn.

2 *Canadian Charter of Rights and Freedoms*, Part I of the *Constitution Act, 1982*, being Schedule B to the *Canada Act 1982* (UK), 1982, c 11 [*Charter*].

3 The quotation marks are used in recognition of the fact that the issue of "fragmentation of international law" is one that has received a great deal of consideration in international law circles of late, not least by the International Law Commission (the work of which can be found online: International Law Commission http://legal.un.org/ilc/guide/1_9.htm). See Martti Koskenniemi & Päivi Leino, "Fragmentation of International Law? Postmodern Anxieties" (2002) 15:3 Leiden J Int'l L 553; Joost Pauwelyn, "Bridging Fragmentation and Unity: International Law as a Universe of Inter-Connected Islands" (2004) 25:4 Mich J Int'l L 903; Anne Charlotte Martineau, "The Rhetoric of Fragmentation: Fear and Faith in International Law" (2009) 22:1 Leiden J Int'l L 1.

1) The International Experience

Since customary international human rights law is an uncertain quantity, the discussion regarding the extraterritorial application of human rights norms has been based around the various human rights treaty regimes. As state activities became increasingly transnationalized, individuals who interacted with state officials began to seek remedies for state activities that occurred beyond the impugned state's borders — territorially based activities obviously attracting no controversy regarding jurisdiction. The starting point of the difficulty with the proposition that remedies might be available in such situations was that the human rights treaties are silent about their extraterritorial reach. The relevant provisions[4] describe the member states' obligations in terms of a state's "jurisdiction," as in article 2 of the *International Covenant on Civil and Political Rights* (*ICCPR*), which provides for applicability to persons "within [the state's] territory and subject to its jurisdiction." This kind of prescription has spawned various exercises in treaty interpretation from which may be discerned a clear trend towards extraterritoriality being permissible and even obligatory among states that have entered into treaty-based human rights obligations. Under the *ICCPR*, for example, the United Nations Human Rights Committee (HRC) decided in two 1981 complaints against Uruguay[5] that a state party could be held "accountable for violations of rights under the Covenant which its agents commit upon the territory of another State, whether with the acquiescence of the Government of that State or in opposition to it"[6] and that "it would be unconscionable to so interpret the responsibility under Article 2 of the Covenant as to permit a State party to perpetrate violations of the Covenant on the territory of another State, which violations it could not perpetrate on its own territory."[7] In the UN Human Rights Committee's General Comment 31 it affirmed this interpretation of article 2 and stated that it applied even when the individuals in question are not nation-

---

4 *Convention for the Protection of Human Rights and Fundamental Freedoms*, 4 November 1950, 213 UNTS 221, art 1 [*ECHR*]; *International Covenant on Civil and Political Rights*, 16 December 1966, 999 UNTS 171, Can TS 1976 No 47, art 2 [*ICCPR*]; *American Convention on Human Rights "Pact of San José, Costa Rica,"* 22 November 1969, 1144 UNTS 123, art 1.

5 *Lopez Burgos v Uruguay*, Comm No R/12/52, UN Doc Supp No 40 (A/36/40) at 176 (1981) [*Lopes Burgos*]; and *Celiberti de Casariego v Uruguay*, Comm No R/13/56, UN Doc Supp No 40 (A/36/40) at 185 (1981) [*Celiberti*].

6 *Lopez Burgos*, *ibid* at para 12.3; *Celiberti*, *ibid* at para 10.3.

7 *Ibid* to both cases.

als of the state party.[8] This was further confirmed by the International Court of Justice (ICJ) in the Palestinian wall case.[9] Similar findings have been made by the Inter-American Commission on Human Rights regarding the applicability of the Charter of the Organization of American States and the American Declaration of the Rights and Duties of Man.[10]

The European Court of Human Rights (ECtHR) has wrestled with the permissibility of extraterritorial application of the *European Convention on Human Rights* (*ECHR*) on a number of occasions since the early 1990s and has the most well-developed jurisprudence, though one marked by vacillation. Article 1 of the *ECHR* requires member states to secure the Convention protections "to everyone within their jurisdiction," and the Court has essentially taken two approaches to interpreting this phrase:

> [T]he *spatial model* of jurisdiction — a state possesses jurisdiction whenever it has *effective overall control of an area* . . . [and] the *personal model* of jurisdiction (or 'state agent authority') — a state has jurisdiction whenever it exercises *authority or control over an individual*.[11]

In the 2001 *Banković* case, the Grand Chamber of the Court took the spatial model approach, employing the international law of jurisdiction as interpretive principles to find that jurisdiction was territorially based and could only be extraterritorial in exceptional circumstances.[12] However, in a number of subsequent cases,[13] lower Chambers and the Grand

8 Office of the United Nations High Commissioner for Human Rights, *General Comment No 31 Nature of the General Legal Obligation Imposed on States Parties to the Covenant*, CCPR/C/21/Rev.1/Add.13, (2004) at para 10 [General Comment 31]. Put another way, the UN HRC interpreted "and" in the phrase "within its territory and subject to its jurisdiction" disjunctively so that a state party is responsible towards persons either in its territory or subject to its jurisdiction.

9 *Legal Consequences of the Construction of a Wall in the Occupied Palestinian Territories*, Advisory Opinion, [2004] ICJ Rep 136 at paras 107–13 [*Legal Consequences of the Construction of a Wall*].

10 See *Coard v United States* (1999), Inter-Am Ct HR No 109/99, Case 10.951, *Annual Report of the Inter-American Commission on Human Rights: 1999*; *Alejandre v Cuba* (1999), Inter-Am Ct HR No 86/99, Case 11.589.

11 Marko Milanovic, "*Al-Skeini* and *Al-Jedda* in Strasbourg" (2012) 23:1 EJIL 121 at 122 [emphasis in the original, footnotes omitted] [Milanovic, "*Al-Skeini* and *Al-Jedda*"].

12 *Banković v Belgium* [GC], No 52207/99, [2001] XII ECHR 333 [*Banković*], see paras 59 and 71.

13 *Issa v Turkey*, No 31821/96, (2004) 41 EHRR 27 (ECtHR) [*Issa*]; *Pad v Turkey*, No 60167/00 (28 June 2007) (ECtHR) [*Pad*]; *Solomou v Turkey*, No 36832/97 (24 June 2008) (ECtHR) [*Solomou*]; *Medvedyev v France* [GC], No 3394/03 (2010), 51 EHRR 39 (ECtHR).

Chamber sometimes took a more robust and personal model approach, finding that states can be held liable for violations by officials who are operating in a foreign state. Examples are: (1) when the state agents are in effective military control of the territory upon which the violation is committed, (2) if the individual is "under the authority or control" of the state agents,[14] and (3) even if the individual is simply killed by the state's forces outside the state's territory.[15]

The ECtHR's most recent treatment of the issue, in *Al-Skeini v United Kingdom*,[16] seemed to combine the two approaches. The case arose from the British occupation of Basra, Iraq, and involved six people who were killed (or allegedly were killed, in some cases) by British forces.[17] The families of the victims (or alleged victims) asked the UK government for a full, independent, and effective investigation, as required under article 2 of the *ECHR*, but alleged that article 2 had been breached because the investigation was ineffective. The Crown conceded the ineffectiveness of the investigation, but argued that the exercise of extraterritorial jurisdiction which the claimants' case required was unlawful. While the House of Lords (now the UK Supreme Court) ruled all but one claim to be impermissibly extraterritorial,[18] the Grand Chamber held that the United Kingdom was obliged to exercise extraterritorial jurisdiction over the acts of these soldiers. The Grand Chamber determined that the United Kingdom was exercising "some of the public powers normally to be exercised by a sovereign government" during its occupation; and thus its exercise of "authority and control over individuals" that arose from those public powers was sufficient to create a jurisdictional link.[19]

As Milanovic points out,[20] there are a number of unanswered questions stemming from *Al-Skeini* and it seems clear that *Banković* has not been completely overruled, in the sense that some kind of spatial connection is still required.[21] For present purposes, it is sufficient to note

14 *Issa, ibid* at para 71; *Solomou, ibid* at para 45.

15 *Pad*, above note 13 at paras 53–54.

16 [GC], No 55721/07, (2011) 53 EHRR 18 (ECtHR) [*Al-Skeini*].

17 Five were basically killed in firefights, while the sixth, Mousa, was taken to a British detention facility in Basra, where he was mistreated and then killed.

18 Mousa's was allowable on the basis that he was in a UK detention facility.

19 *Al-Skeini*, above note 16 at paras 149 &150.

20 Milanovic, "*Al-Skeini* and *Al-Jedda*," above note 11 at 131–33.

21 Even though this arguably contradicts the earlier findings in *Issa* and *Pad*, both above note 13.

that the Court is more sympathetic to the exercise of extraterritorial jurisdiction over human rights claims than it had been for the previous decade, though its approach is still not as expansive as that of either the HRC or the Inter-American Commission. More to the point, all of these decisions arise from courts or treaty bodies that are administering (in some sense) the application of specific treaty obligations, and thus only constitute a certain amount of state practice that is not decisive evidence of any overall norm. The broader international law regarding the exercise of extraterritorial jurisdiction over human rights claims is still in flux.

2) The Supreme Court of Canada's Wrestling Match

The issue of whether and how the *Charter* can be applied in an extraterritorial manner has bedevilled Canadian courts — most notably, the Supreme Court of Canada — since the mid-1990s.[22] The resolution to the issue depends in large part on international law, including the *ICCPR* to which Canada is a party and, as such, is obliged to give domestic effect to its provisions. The *Charter* does not expressly implement the *ICCPR*, but its provisions clearly draw upon the treaty and it is treated by the government and the courts as the principal means by which Canada's international human rights obligations are given effect.[23] Section 32 of the *Charter* provides that it applies to all Canadian government entities and their agents, but is silent as to whether it has extraterritorial reach.

All of the Supreme Court's jurisprudence on point, until recently, addressed the question of whether evidence gathered in a foreign state should be admitted in criminal prosecutions, or excluded on the basis that it violated certain human rights — either section 8 on privacy (search warrants) or section 10 (rights upon detention or arrest). While international law has been the major basis for each decision, none of the Supreme Court decisions have acknowledged (let alone dealt with) the developments in the international caselaw around article 2(1) of the *ICCPR* (or the European or Inter-American angles). Two early decisions refused to apply the *Charter* to foreign police and consequently would

---

22 This caselaw is reviewed in detail (current up to 2010, prior to *Khadr 2010*) in Robert J Currie, *International & Transnational Criminal Law* (Toronto: Irwin, 2010) at 509–37 [Currie, *Criminal Law*].

23 Mark Freeman & Gib van Ert, *International Human Rights Law* (Toronto, Irwin Law, 2004) at 188.

not give effect to *Charter* rights at trial to the extent that the violations directly implicated foreign police conduct.[24] The 1998 case of *R v Cook*[25] addressed whether the *Charter* could apply to the actions of Canadian police when they were in a foreign state — in that case, the interrogation of a suspect in New Orleans by Canadian officers who had been invited to do so by local police. The decision of the Supreme Court of Canada was divided, but most of the judges recognized and engaged with the international law issues involved. The majority opinion ultimately decided that the *Charter* could apply, in part because the nationality principle justified extending Canada's jurisdiction over the actions of its police officers, and because the conduct of the officers created no "objectionable extraterritorial effect," that is, interference with the foreign state's sovereignty.

In 2007, however, the Supreme Court abruptly reversed the *Cook* holding in the case of *R v Hape*,[26] a money laundering prosecution where Canadian police (in co-operation with local police) had searched premises — that were located in Turks & Caicos — belonging to the Canadian accused. At his trial in Canada, Hape sought to have the documents seized during the searches excluded on the basis that the searches did not comply with section 8 of the *Charter*, even though they complied with local law, citing *Cook* in support. However, the Supreme Court held that effect could not be given at trial in Canada to *Charter* rights vis-à-vis police activities in the foreign state.

The Court's starting point was twofold: first, Canada's laws should be interpreted in conformity with international law, unless the contrary was obvious;[27] and second, the distinction between prescriptive and enforcement jurisdiction should be maintained, in that Canada might be free to legislate extraterritorially but had to recognize the limits placed

---

24 *R v Harrer*, [1995] 3 SCR 562; *R v Terry*, [1996] 2 SCR 207. In both these and subsequent cases, the Court has ruled that evidence can nonetheless be excluded under sections 7 and 11(d) of the *Charter* if its admission would render the trial unfair, due to the manner in which it was gathered.

25 [1998] 2 SCR 597.

26 2007 SCC 26 [*Hape*]. Some of the best recent scholarship on this line of jurisprudence has been done by Professor John H Currie; see John H Currie, "*Khadr*'s Twist on *Hape*: Tortured Determinations of the Extraterritorial Reach of the Canadian *Charter*" (2008) 46 Can YB Int'l Law 307 [Currie, "Twist on *Hape*"]; John H Currie, "International Human Rights Law in the Supreme Court's *Charter* Jurisprudence: Commitment, Retrenchment *and* Retreat — In No Particular Order" (2010) 50:2 Sup Ct L Rev (2d) 423.

27 *Hape*, *ibid* at paras 34–39.

by international law on its ability to enforce its laws extraterritorially. The goal of this aspect of the *Charter* was essentially to prescribe rules for police conduct that would ensure respect for the accused person's *Charter* rights — in this case, the right to be free from unreasonable search and seizure. Making Canadian police comply with this Canadian law during their investigations would be essentially an act of enforcement jurisdiction. However, such an act of extraterritorial enforcement jurisdiction would be a violation of the *locus* state's sovereignty, without consent of that state being given.[28] In this instance, despite the fact that the investigation was a co-operative one, there was no evidence that Turks & Caicos had given permission for Canadian law to be applied. The local law must govern any government activities there, including law enforcement. Therefore any attempt by Canadian officials to act in accordance with the *Charter* would be an illegal exercise of enforcement jurisdiction, and *ipso facto* no *Charter* remedy could be given at trial.

It is important to bear in mind that the *Charter* is the only human rights law of domestic application that restrains the actions of Canadian state officials. The effect of the majority's decision outlined above is that Canadian police officers and other state officials are essentially immunized from the *Charter*'s application when they are acting abroad. But if only the foreign state's law applied, the Canadian officials might be subject to more lax human rights standards or even none at all, depending upon the foreign state in question. The Court implicitly recognized that this was an unpalatable result, and thus carved out an exception: the *Charter* could apply where complying with local law would cause Canadian officials to contravene Canada's international human rights law obligations.[29]

Next came the *Afghan Detainees* case,[30] where Justice MacTavish of the Federal Court of Canada presided over a motion by Amnesty International and other interveners to apply the *Charter* to the actions of Canadian soldiers in Afghanistan. This proceeding had been preceded by significant controversy generated over allegations that detainees handed over by Canadian forces were being tortured and otherwise

---

28 *Ibid* at paras 83–92 and 96.

29 *Ibid* at paras 96–101.

30 *Amnesty International Canada v Canada (Canadian Forces)*, 2008 FC 336 [*Afghan Detainees*], aff'd 2008 FCA 401, leave to appeal to SCC refused, [2009] SCCA No 63. The Federal Court of Appeal restricted its reasons to a review of whether the motions judge had made any errors of law, without any substantial discussion of *Hape* or *Khadr*. All subsequent references are to the motion decision.

abused by their Afghan captors. The applicants were seeking the possibility of human rights remedies for the detainees under the *Charter*, and it was clear from the outset that the case would involve an application of *Hape*. The applicants argued that the military context was distinguishable, on both law and facts, from the kind of police co-operation dealt with in *Hape* and called for a different result—in particular because it was more in line with the kinds of cases dealt with by the UN Human Rights Committee and the European Court of Human Rights where extraterritorial jurisdiction had been ruled lawful.

Justice MacTavish applied *Hape* to answer the question in the negative. She found on the facts that, while the government of Afghanistan had agreed to allow Canadian forces to engage in certain activities—even enforcement-type activities—on Afghan soil, it had not consented to the application of Canadian law, including the *Charter*, as would be required to make the *Charter* applicable.[31] Rather, Canada and Afghanistan had agreed that Afghan law and international law, including international human rights and international humanitarian law, would govern the activities of Canadian Forces personnel. Accordingly, the *Charter* could not be applicable on this basis, since to apply it would be to violate Afghan sovereignty.

She further dismissed an argument by the applicants that it was accepted under international law that states were entitled to apply extraterritorial human rights jurisdiction over the acts of their officials in situations where there was "effective military control of the person." In so doing, she made interesting use of the decision of the UK House of Lords in *Al-Skeini*[32]—on one hand, adopting the finding of various Law Lords that the more conservative position of the European Court of Human Rights on jurisdiction from *Banković*[33] was "better law" than the more recent finding in *Issa*,[34] and on the other hand, rejecting the Lords' conclusion that extending extraterritorial jurisdiction to a British prison facility in Iraq was an acceptably modest move. While acknowledging the trend towards positive findings on extraterritorial jurisdiction in the international human rights caselaw,[35] she ultimately ruled that

---

31 *Ibid* at para 170 (FC).

32 *Al-Skeini and others v Secretary of State for Defence*, [2007] UKHL 26.

33 Above note 12.

34 Above note 13.

35 And considering both General Comment 31, above note 8 and United Nations Committee Against Torture, *General Comment No 2: Implementation of article 2 by States Parties*, CAT/C/GC/2/CRP.1/Rev.4 (2007).

this position was too unsettled to merit a different application than that dictated by *Hape*.[36]

However, the Court's "human rights exception" from *Hape* came home to roost in two subsequent decisions that dealt with the detention of Canadian citizen Omar Khadr in the notorious Guantanamo Bay detention facility.[37] In 2003 and 2004, while Khadr was detained at Guantanamo (but before charges had been laid against him before the US Military Commission which would eventually convict him), Canadian Security Intelligence Service (CSIS) agents and Department of Foreign Affairs and International Trade (DFAIT) officials were at the facility with the permission of American authorities and interrogated him about various topics, including conduct that would eventually be the subject of the charges. The 2004 interview with DFAIT officials took place when those officials knew that Khadr had been subjected to the "frequent flyer program," an interrogation technique involving sleep deprivation in order to make the subject more amenable to talking.[38] The Canadian officials passed summaries of this information on to US authorities. Through other proceedings, Khadr's lawyers had received partial disclosure of these documents, but the copies were heavily redacted, and the Crown refused to disclose the unredacted documents. *Khadr 2008* arose from an application by Khadr's counsel to the Federal Court for a *Charter* remedy on the basis that Khadr's right to disclosure under section 7 of the *Charter* had been infringed by the refusal, which impaired his right to full answer and defence before the US court. The question was whether the *Charter* had such extraterritorial reach.

When the case reached the Supreme Court of Canada, the Court applied *Hape* and found that Khadr was entitled to disclosure. It emphasized that applying the *Charter* to the acts of Canadian officials abroad would normally amount to an impermissible extension of extraterritorial jurisdiction. This conclusion was, however, "based on international law principles against extraterritorial enforcement of domestic laws and the principle of comity which implies acceptance of foreign laws and procedures when Canadian officials are operating abroad."[39] The Court fastened on the "human rights exception" articulated by LeBel J for the

36 *Afghan Detainees*, above note 30 at paras 214 and 281.

37 *Canada (Justice) v Khadr*, 2008 SCC 28 [*Khadr 2008*]; and *Canada (Prime Minister) v Khadr*, 2010 SCC 3 [*Khadr 2010*].

38 *Khadr 2010*, *ibid* at para 5.

39 *Khadr 2008*, above note 37 at para 17.

majority in *Hape*, noting that despite a three-way split on the law in *Hape*, all judges had been united on the point that international law and comity would give way in any situation where Canadian officials were participating "in activities of a foreign state or its agents that are contrary to Canada's international obligations."[40] Both the conditions of Khadr's detention at Guantanamo and the trial that he faced there had already been ruled illegal by the US Supreme Court,[41] in that they violated both US law and the *Geneva Conventions*. Since Canada is a signatory to the *Geneva Conventions*, "[t]he *Charter* bound Canada to the extent that the conduct of Canadian officials involved it in a process that violated Canada's international obligations."[42] The Court was careful to rule that it was simply participation in the illegal process that entitled Khadr to a remedy under section 7, and it was not

> necessary to conclude that handing over the fruits of the interviews in this case to U.S. officials constituted a breach of Mr. Khadr's s. 7 rights. It suffices to note that at the time Canada handed over the fruits of the interviews to U.S. officials, it was bound by the *Charter*, because at that point it became a participant in a process that violated Canada's international obligations.[43]

Accordingly, since Khadr's right to liberty was engaged by Canada's participation in the foreign process, a remedy was necessary.

Khadr 2010 arose from an application by Khadr to declare that the government's refusal to request his repatriation from Guantanamo was a violation of his section 7 *Charter* rights. The Court made two findings relevant here. First, the question of the applicability of the *Charter* was essentially *res judicata* from *Khadr 2008* and the *Charter* applied under the *Hape* "human rights exception." Second, the extraterritorial aspect of the case meant that section 7 could not be applied in a conventional fashion to Khadr's interrogation, and the case required a finding of a new principle of fundamental justice under the criteria outlined in the Court's earlier decision of *R v DB*.[44] It concluded that the participation of Canadian officials in Khadr's detention violated principles of fundamental justice, which it summarized as follows:

---

40 *Ibid* at para 18.

41 In *Rasul v Bush*, 542 US 466 (2004) and *Hamdan v Rumsfeld*, 548 US 557 (2006).

42 *Khadr 2008*, above note 37 at para 26.

43 *Ibid* at para 27.

44 2008 SCC 25, cited in *Khadr 2010*, above note 37 at para 23.

> Interrogation of a youth, to elicit statements about the most serious criminal charges while detained in these conditions and without access to counsel, and while knowing that the fruits of the interrogations would be shared with the U.S. prosecutors, offends the most basic Canadian standards about the treatment of detained youth suspects.[45]

3) Analysis and Conclusions

In our view, the Supreme Court's wrestling match with the issue of exerting extraterritorial jurisdiction in human rights matters illustrates interesting sets of problems on both the international and domestic levels. Internationally, the predominantly customary international law of jurisdiction, and the treaty-based law of jurisdiction with respect to international human rights, coexist and interact in a state of, if not tension, then uneasiness, and certainly not unity. For many years, states have universally accepted that the activities of one state's national in a foreign state can give rise to the home state's right to exercise its public law powers, in the sense of a criminal prosecution based on the nationality principle or another acceptable ground of extraterritorial prescriptive jurisdiction. However, increasingly it is the activities of a state official in the foreign state that are being dealt with, activities which are overlain with the prohibition on extraterritorial enforcement jurisdiction. Human rights treaties oblige states to require their officials and agents to comply with human rights norms, and as noted above, a number of international courts and adjudicative bodies have extended that obligation extraterritorially.

However, as *Hape* shows, this perspective is at odds with the conservative approach national courts have traditionally taken to extraterritorial jurisdiction out of reciprocal respect for state sovereignty. As a result, the Canadian courts have become unsure about the scope of their jurisdiction. In Canada, the courts are particularly puzzled about the degree of jurisdictional deference they should accord to foreign sovereigns in the face of obligations to assert jurisdiction to protect international

---

45 *Khadr 2010*, *ibid* at para 25. It has been observed that this rule is "narrowly tailored to Khadr's specific case, but the principles of fundamental justice are supposed to be basic tenets that can guide us about the limitations of the legal system generally," and that "[t]his unclear formulation of the principles of fundamental justice . . . might have a serious effect on ongoing matters involving Canadian authorities abroad": Jonathan Shapiro, "*Khadr v. Canada (Prime Minister)*, Annotation (2010) 71 CR (6th) 204.

human rights and to remediate their violations. So when does foreign state sovereignty trump the permissive powers, or even the mandatory responsibilities, of domestic jurisdiction? These are big issues that national court systems cannot resolve individually. Their decisions do add to the corpus of state practice from which customary international law may, perhaps, grow. But such cumulative state practice as exists at present around these jurisdictional issues is too indefinite within particular domestic court systems, and too various between different national legal systems, to found customary international law norms.

In a sense, domestic courts should not be blamed for this disunity since they do not directly create international law by their individual decisions but only seek what it is in order to apply it. Most of international law is made, as well as administered, by the executive, that is, the government, of the state. However, the rules of jurisdiction are pre-eminently examples of international law that fall to the judicial organ of the state — the domestic courts — to apply in the course of their work. Consequently, their performance bears witness to the condition of this law. Moreover, in an era of increasing interjudicial dialogue between and among the courts of different states and international courts and interpretive bodies,[46] how one court makes its finding on the current state of international law can affect others. In the Canadian context, this was illustrated in *Afghan Detainees* by the Federal Court of Canada's use of the Law Lords' decision in *Al-Skeini*, discussed above. In this sense, then, national courts can be prime movers towards either unity or fragmentation of this body of international law, since the views expressed by national courts can affect the findings of other courts, and all of them contribute to a matrix of state practice that, as a result, may trend towards consistency or confusion.

This fragmentation is reflected by the Canadian caselaw discussed above. Canadian courts have been resisting treaty-based developments because they feel constrained by more traditional international jurisdictional principles. While *Afghan Detainees* contained laudatory first efforts at dealing with the international developments regarding extraterritorial jurisdiction under the *ICCPR* regime, Canada's highest court has yet to engage this jurisprudence on interpretation of the human

---

46 As noted in Chapter 2, there is a large and interesting literature on this trend. See Anne-Marie Slaughter, "Judicial Globalization" (2000) 40:4 Va J Int'l L 1103; Carl Baudenbacher, "Judicial Globalization: New Development or Old Wine in New Bottles?" (2003) 38:3 Tex Int'l LJ 505.

rights treaties. On the surface it appears that while some of the world is attempting to explore the parameters of how and when human rights obligations may apply extraterritorially, Canada has fallen back on the restraining principles of sovereignty as the dominant rule, without adequately factoring in the new and dynamic international human rights jurisdictional norms. The Supreme Court continues to use the broader contours of the international law of jurisdiction without inquiry into how these apply in the context of human rights. Put this way, it might be said simply that the Supreme Court is swimming against the tide. More significantly, recent Canadian caselaw as a whole is an example of state practice that reflects, even contributes, to fragmentation in the international law of jurisdiction — ironically, this is because Canadian courts, as in the *Afghan Detainees* case, view that law as being fragmented.

These cases also illustrate problems that extraterritorial jurisdiction can cause in terms of exposing weakness in a court's international law methodology, even in using such international legal norms that are relatively well-settled. The *Khadr* cases, in particular, demonstrate a certain amount of disarray, precisely because of the domestic-international law interface. The post-*Hape* cases generally have manifested confusion and doctrinal uncertainty, which the Supreme Court could only manage in both *Khadr* decisions by confining the scope of the matter so narrowly. However, the *Hape/Khadr* framework contains such profound methodological problems that there is little to go on for counsel and courts in determining how to apply the framework to different facts. At the centre is the idea that applying the *Charter* to Canadian officials in a Canadian proceeding somehow violates the sovereignty of the state in which the Canadian officials acted. This is the starting presumption in *Hape*, but it is difficult to see where the sovereignty violation happens. To be sure, and as the Court pointed out in *Hape*, Canadian officials cannot necessarily adhere to every letter of *Charter* standards when they go abroad because they are bound to follow the procedural law of the foreign state. However, there is nothing to stop Canadian courts from scrutinizing the extraterritorial actions of those officials under the *Charter*, though obviously the analytical framework must take account of the fact that they are operating in a foreign country.[47]

---

47 Recall that, in *Al-Skeini*, above note 16, the ECtHR opined that human rights are not indivisible — the way that a state tries to adhere to its human rights obligations abroad need not look the same as it would at home, due to the fact that they are acting in another state.

If there is no international law imperative here, then the next obvious question is whether the law *should* contain the *Hape* presumption as a starting point. As Professor John Currie commented:

> The profound asymmetry between the fact of extensive extraterritorial government activity and *Hape*'s principle of non-applicability of the *Charter* to such activity is both confounding and troubling. That Canadian officials should in fact be competent to act abroad and yet not be subject to any *Charter* constraints in doing so seems at best counter-intuitive and at worst unwise.[48]

Similarly, in *Afghan Detainees*, Justice MacTavish applied *Hape* but queried the wisdom of its central principle:

> It is also troubling that while Canada can prosecute members of its military after the fact for mistreating detainees under their control, a constitutional instrument whose primary purpose is, according to the Supreme Court, to limit the exercise of the authority of state actors so that breaches of the *Charter* are prevented, will not apply to prevent that mistreatment in the first place.[49]

To be perfectly fair to the Supreme Court, the "human rights exception" applied in the Omar Khadr decisions responds, at least implicitly, to these concerns. Yet here, too, there is doctrinal confusion,[50] which leads to uncertainty. Applying the *Charter* extraterritorially will violate the sovereignty of other states, so cannot be done; except where the actions of Canadian officials might violate international human rights law, at which point the *Charter* can be applied extraterritorially. The problem is that the Supreme Court has set up a state of opposition between the law of jurisdiction and state sovereignty, on the one hand, and international human rights law, on the other, without justifying its ultimate exercise in line-drawing. It is not clear why Canada's participation in a process

---

48 Currie, "Twist on *Hape*," above note 26 at 316.

49 Above note 30 at para 340.

50 Not least because the Court's creation of an exception for when the officials' activities would offend Canada's international human rights obligations is also troubling, because it draws a false dichotomy between the *Charter* (a domestic law implementing international human rights law) and the international human rights obligations themselves. Once the international law is implemented in Canadian law then for practical purposes the two bodies of law are integrated; it makes little sense to say that the *Charter* applies only where international human rights law is engaged. See Currie & Kindred, above note 1, for a more detailed treatment.

that violates some international law obligations, and thus mandates extraterritorial application of the *Charter*, trumps other international law obligations that prevent extraterritorial application of the *Charter*. As Professor John Currie points out, the Court simply did not engage with this question, "deepen[ing] the legal and logical morass currently governing, in the name of respect for Canada's international legal obligations, the extraterritorial applicability of the *Charter*."[51]

While, as noted above, there is a certain amount of fragmentation around this very question, it is not as if there is no international law relating to these questions upon which the Court could draw, framing it either as the law of Canada (which it is) or at least as giving guidance on how the domestic analytical framework should play out. This is another problem with Canadian international law methodology that is brought into sharp relief by the *Khadr* cases: lost opportunities to utilize and apply international law, and in such a way as to give much-needed direction to the state and to parties that may contest its activities. For example, the Court held in both Omar Khadr decisions that it is the fact of Canadian participation in the illegal Guantanamo regime that triggers *Charter* application, the interrogation and the sharing of information with American authorities providing the factual hooks. Yet since this is being analyzed under the "human rights exception," this must be an act of a state official that violates international human rights law — but what is the legal basis for saying that it is this kind or degree of co-operation that constitutes participation in the unlawful activity, and thus a violation? What threshold was crossed? How can Crown officials avoid crossing it again? The international law of state responsibility is the most obvious route to try to delineate the government's responsibilities here,[52] and since the bulk of that law is customary, it is automatically part of Canadian law and can be applied or used by Canadian judges.

It may be that the complex matrix of concurrent and perhaps conflicting international law norms involved in an examination of extraterritorial jurisdiction over human rights laws makes it unfair to harshly criticize any particular domestic court's attempt to wrestle the issue. Embarking on this inquiry, as this case study shows, sends any court charged with it out into a maelstrom that is unusually intense, even from an international law perspective. However, it may simply represent the extreme end of a spectrum, and a harbinger of future problems.

---

51 Currie, "Twist on *Hape*," above note 26 at 332.

52 Accord, *ibid*.

B. EXTRATERRITORIAL ACCOUNTABILITY FOR HUMAN RIGHTS ABUSES

1) Introduction

As the previous case study in Section A discloses, the *Charter* has proved to be a fertile ground for litigation about the extent of Canadian and international human rights standards applicable to RCMP officers and other Canadian government agents when engaged in investigative and enforcement activities abroad. By comparison, the occasions when private claims in Canadian courts for civil remedies have been brought against the foreign perpetrators of human rights abuses committed abroad have been infrequent and ineffective. This case study explores the extraterritorial jurisdictional reach and responsibility of Canadian courts in civil suits — tort actions — when challenged to provide remedies for foreign violations of international human rights laws.[53]

The typical circumstances of such actions involve a Canadian resident, the victim of grave abuse by international human rights standards in a foreign state, who wants to sue the perpetrator and/or the foreign state in Canada. Such a case presents problems of adjudicative jurisdiction over the foreign defendant and over the foreign events, as well as potential claims to immunity from jurisdiction by the foreign state and its officials. The publicly discussed cases of Houshan Bouzari,[54] Mahar Arar,[55] and Zahra Kazemi[56] are examples.[57]

Bouzari[58] illustrates the typical claim and response. Mr Bouzari was robbed, abducted, arbitrarily incarcerated, and brutally tortured in Iran by agents of its government. After his release on ransom, he was able to emigrate to Canada where he continued to suffer from his injuries as he

53 See Murray Hunt, *Using Human Rights Law in English Courts* (Oxford: Hart, 1997); Craig Scott, ed, *Torture as Tort: Comparative Perspectives on the Development of Transnational Human Rights Litigation* (Oxford: Hart, 2001); and Milanovic, *Extraterritorial Application*, above note 1.

54 *Bouzari v Iran* (2004), 71 OR (3d) 675 (CA), leave to appeal to SCC refused, 2004 SCCA No 410 [*Bouzari*].

55 *Arar v Syrian Arab Republic* (2005), 28 CR (6th) 187 (Ont SCJ) [*Arar*].

56 *Kazemi (Estate of) v Islamic Republic of Iran*, 2011 QCCS 196 [*Kazemi* Qc Sup Ct], rev'd in part 2012 QCCA 1449 [*Kazemi* Qc CA], leave to appeal to SCC granted (*sub nom Kazemi Estate v Islamic Replubic of Iran*), 2013 CanLII 11303 (SCC) [*Kazemi* SCC]. The appeal was argued 18 March 2014 but no judgment had been rendered at the time of publication.

57 *Jones v Ministry of Interior of the Kingdom of Saudi Arabia*, [2006] UKHL 26 [*Jones*], is the leading decision in United Kingdom.

58 Above note 54.

sued Iran for damages. Iran did not defend the action, but successfully pleaded foreign state immunity from suit. The Ontario Court of Appeal held, even though protection from torture is a peremptory rule of international customary law (*jus cogens*), a foreign state's right to immunity from a Canadian court's adjudicative jurisdiction was not displaced.

The ongoing case of *Kazemi (Estate of) v Iran*[59] concerned similar claims, but presented some different issues because of the involvement of multiple plaintiffs and defendants. Ms Kazemi was arrested while on a visit to Iran and was subsequently imprisoned, grossly abused, tortured, and killed. Her son, Stephen Hashemi, brought suit in Canada on behalf of Ms Kazemi's estate and on his own behalf. The estate's action against Iran was not significantly different from the *Bouzari* precedent, but Mr Hashemi's claim was for psychological trauma suffered within Canada and hence did not raise the problem of extraterritorial injury. He also instituted the action both for his mother's estate and for himself against three additional individual defendants, Ayatollah Ali Khamenei, the Supreme Leader of Iran; Saeed Mortazavi, the chief public prosecutor for Tehran; and Mohammad Bakhshi, the deputy chief of intelligence for Evin Prison in Tehran.

The suits by the two plaintiffs against the state of Iran were met by the same claim to state immunity as in the *Bouzari* case, but the addition of personal defendants raised a new issue for Canadian courts about the immunity of state officials. In the event, the Quebec Superior Court, following *Bouzari*, dismissed the action on behalf of Ms Kazemi's estate, both against the state on the grounds of Iran's immunity from Canadian jurisdiction for its extraterritorial conduct, and against the state's officials since they were acting on behalf of Iran. However, Mr Hashemi's suit against Iran did not face the same restraints. His action concerned injuries he received in Quebec even though the events giving rise to his injuries occurred outside of Canada. He claimed the benefit of an exception to the principle of state immunity for proceedings that relate to personal or bodily injury that occurs in Canada.[60] The Quebec Superior Court allowed his suit against both Iran and the three state agents to go forward, but the Quebec Court of Appeal reversed that decision. The case as a whole is now pending before the Supreme Court of Canada.[61]

---

59 *Kazemi* SCC, above note 56.

60 *State Immunity Act*, RSC 1985, c S-18, s 6 [*SIA*].

61 *Kazemi* SCC, above note 56.

Ordinarily, the victim of human rights violations would be expected to bring suit in the courts in the state where the abuse occurred, but frequently in such cases local access to remedies is not available. The reasons for failure revolve around the state's inadequate system of governance. It may be that the state itself has failed and has no working legal system of any sort; corruption is rife in the courts, which consequently lack judicial impartiality; the state and its officials have immunity, even impunity, by local law; or the courts are subject to government influence and the judges lack independence.

While abused individuals deserve reparation, indeed are legally entitled to remedies, they have generally been non-suited in Canadian courts for lack of adjudicative jurisdiction. The civil process of Canadian courts is designed to accommodate actions for private wrongs committed within the court's territorial reach. The concept of territorial jurisdiction has received an extended interpretation, as discussed in Chapter 4, Section D, so as to avoid interjurisdictional conflicts in actions that involve transnational elements. These situations are distinguishable from wholly extraterritorial incidents of foreign human rights claims against foreign abusers, which the courts typically decline to adjudicate either for supposed lack of jurisdiction, or on the grounds of the sovereign immunity of foreign states and their officials.[62]

However, among the common law principles and statutory provisions for determining the extent of the court's civil jurisdiction is an exceptional rule that allows for the assertion of extraterritorial jurisdiction in certain circumstances. The rule permits a Canadian court to take jurisdiction if it is the forum "of last resort" or "of necessity." The uniform *Court Jurisdiction and Proceedings Transfer Act* (*CJPTA*),[63] as enacted in British Columbia, Nova Scotia, and the Yukon,[64] specifically includes the concept as a separate ground of civil court jurisdiction by way of exception to the ordinary statutory requirement of "territorial competency." The *CJPTA* states:

---

62 For discussion, see text accompanying note 109, below in this chapter.

63 Prepared by the Uniform Law Conference of Canada (ULCC) and discussed in Chapter 4, Section D (adopted in 1994), online: ULCC/CHLC www.ulcc.ca/en/uniform-acts-en-gb-1/183-court-jurisdiction-and-proceedings-transfer-act/1092-court-jurisdiction-proceedings-transfer-act [*CJPTA*].

64 SBC 2003, c 28; SNS 2003 (2d Sess), c 2; and SY 2000, c 7 (not yet in force) [*Yukon CJPTA*], respectively. Saskatchewan has also enacted the *CJPTA* but its version does not include curial jurisdiction of necessity: SS 1997, c C-41.1.

> A court that . . . lacks territorial competence in a proceeding may hear the proceeding . . . if it considers that
> (a) there is no court outside [enacting province or territory] in which the plaintiff can commence the proceeding, or
> (b) the commencement of the proceeding in a court outside [enacting province or territory] cannot reasonably be required.[65]

According to the Ontario Court of Appeal, a parallel doctrine exists in the common law in the case of *Charron Estate v Village Resorts Ltd*:

> The forum of necessity doctrine recognizes that there will be exceptional cases where, despite the absence of a real and substantial connection [of the case with the forum], the need to ensure access to justice will justify the assumption of jurisdiction. . . . Where there is no other forum in which the plaintiff can reasonably seek relief, there is a residual discretion to assume jurisdiction. In my view, the overriding concern for access to justice that motivates the assumption of jurisdiction despite inadequate connection with the forum should be accommodated by explicit recognition of the forum of necessity exception . . . .[66]

However, the Supreme Court, on further appeal, declined to address the matter as it was not a live issue in the case.[67]

The scope of the court's jurisdiction as a forum of last resort under the *CJPTA* and the common law has yet to be thoroughly tested.[68] The jurisdiction is clearly discretionary, so the court's assent is necessary: the plaintiff cannot simply institute proceedings and compel the action to default judgment. So in what circumstances might a court be persuaded to assume jurisdiction? The indications in the *CJPTA* and at common law in *Charron Estate* are similar. To gain the court's assent to take jurisdiction under the *CJPTA*, the plaintiff must establish that there is no other available court or no court in which proceedings may reasonably be required. The Ontario Court of Appeal essentially wrapped these

---

65 *CJPTA*, above note 63, s 6.

66 2010 ONCA 84 at para 100 [*Charron Estate*]. See also paras 54 and 109.

67 *Club Resorts Ltd v Van Breda*, 2012 SCC 17 at paras 59, 82, 86, and 100 [*Club Resorts*].

68 Few cases have discussed it seriously and even fewer have applied it. Compare *Josephson (Litigation guardian of) v Balfour Recreation Commission*, 2010 BCSC 603; *Piscedda Mining Construction International Inc v Crew Gold Corp*, 2011 YKSC 79 [*Piscedda Mining*]; and Janet Walker, "Muscutt Misplaced: The Future of Forum of Necessity Jurisdiction in Canada" (2009) 48:1 Can Bus LJ 135.

two criteria together in the one test of whether there is no other court in which the plaintiff can reasonably seek relief.

As part of this requirement, the court, presumably, would expect compliance with the international law practice that the plaintiff must demonstrate she has tried, so far as reasonably possible, to exhaust opportunities for a local remedy.[69] But an extraterritorial wrong may also engage more than one foreign state in a transnational situation. Then the plaintiff must produce evidence that she cannot reasonably be expected to seek a remedy in the courts of any of the associated jurisdictions. A failure to persuade the court in respect of any one of those jurisdictions means the Canadian court cannot be said to be a forum of last resort, and an order staying the action may be expected.

However, in *Piscedda Mining*,[70] the court moderated this outcome in its order. The case involved a multi-jurisdictional contract dispute in which the jurisdiction of the Yukon court was contested on several grounds. One ground revolved around the concept of forum of last resort, which the court accepted as valid by reference to the Ontario Court of Appeal judgment in *Charron Estate*[71] and the *CJPTA* as enacted (but not in force) in the Yukon.[72] On the evidence and arguments put before it, the court was not convinced that no foreign court would hear the action and so it stayed the proceedings, but it also indicated a readiness to reconsider its position as the forum of last resort if all the possible foreign courts should subsequently decline jurisdiction.[73]

The provision in the *CJPTA* is said to track the language of an existing ground of jurisdiction of the courts of Quebec[74] pursuant to the *Civil Code of Quebec* which states:

> Even though a Québec authority has no jurisdiction to hear a dispute, it may hear it, if the dispute has a sufficient connection with Québec, where proceedings cannot possibly be instituted outside Québec or where the institution of such proceedings outside Québec cannot reasonably be required.[75]

---

69 *Ambatielos Claim (Greece v United Kingdom)* (1956), 12 RIAA 83, 23 ILR 306 (International Court of Justice); International Law Commission, *Draft Articles on Diplomatic Protection*, UNGAOR 59th Sess, Supp No 10, UN Doc A/59/10 (2004), arts 14–16.

70 Above note 68.

71 Quoted, above at note 66.

72 *Yukon CJPTA* above note 64, cited in *Charron Estate*, above note 66 at paras 42 and 59.

73 *Charron Estate*, *ibid* at paras 59–60.

74 See the ULCC's comments on the *CJPTA*, above note 63, regarding s 6.

75 Art 3136 CCQ.

The criteria for a court's assumption of jurisdiction in the last two clauses are certainly reflected in the *CJPTA* but a third condition paralleling the requirement that "the dispute has a sufficient connection with Quebec" is absent. Requiring a connection to the forum is definitely restrictive and is contrary to the spirit of jurisdiction in the last resort, as expressed by the Ontario Court of Appeal in *Charron Estate*, quoted above.[76] This restriction was a stumbling block to the jurisdiction of the Quebec courts in two cases in which forum of necessity was discussed,[77] but it would not impede the assertion of jurisdiction in the last resort by the courts in other provinces and territories of Canada.

Violent abuses of human rights committed extraterritorially are situations in which a Canadian court might very well be the last resort for a remedy. Since torture and other egregious human rights violations are typically perpetrated by state agents of repressive regimes that are unaccountable in their own courts, the claims of their victims would present a real test of the doctrine of forum of necessity or last resort. Moreover, a number of international legal provisions, which are in force for Canada, regulate the protection and remediation of such claims. While conventions to which Canada is a party enshrine state protection of individuals and personal remedies in the event of abuse, customary rules of international law binding on Canada establish state immunity from foreign domestic jurisdiction. In exploring the impacts of these international provisions in Canadian courts as fora of last resort, two grounds for the exercise of extraterritorial jurisdiction are presented here. The first is founded in Canada's obligations under international human rights laws, and the second rests on Canada's responsibilities under international criminal law. Afterwards, the limitations on the assertion of jurisdiction by the laws of state immunity will be taken up.

2) The Requirements of International Human Rights Law

Victims of human rights abuses are entitled to personal remedies under international human rights laws. The provision of protections and remedies is ordained in the International Bill of Rights,[78] in particular the

---

76 Above note 66.

77 *Lamborghini (Canada) Inc c Automobili Lamborghini SPA*, [1997] RJQ 58 (CA), and *Anvil Mining Ltd c Association canadienne contre l'impunité*, 2012 QCCA 117.

78 The International Bill of Rights is a colloquial name for the *Universal Declaration of Human Rights*, GA Res 217(III), UNGAOR, 3rd Sess, Supp No 13, UN Doc A/810, (1948) at 71, and the two subsequent treaties associated with it, namely the *International*

International Covenant on Civil and Political Rights (ICCPR),[79] and other human rights treaties such as the *Convention Against Torture* (CAT).[80] Canada is a party to both the latter treaties. Like any ordinary treaty, *ICCPR* and *CAT* create obligations interstate to protect human rights. Unlike other treaties, they also directly invoke the human rights of individuals, who thus acquire limited international legal personality and status. The forceful effect of the remedial provisions in these treaties will become evident as a result of first exploring the special character of the legal protections they grant.

a) Protection of Human Rights by International Law

The most fundamental protections for every individual are expressed in three articles of *ICCPR*:

> Art 6(1) — Every human being has the inherent right to life . . . .
>
> Art 7 — No one shall be subjected to torture or to cruel, inhuman and degrading treatment or punishment . . . .
>
> Art 8(1) — No one shall be held in slavery . . . .
>
> Art 8(2) — No one shall be held in servitude.

Protection from torture and other cruel treatment is also specifically reinforced by the separate CAT.[81]

The rights enumerated in *ICCPR* articles 6 to 8 have a number of important and distinctive features in international law. First, they are non-derogable. *ICCPR* article 4 allows states to restrict protected human rights in times of public emergency and upon strict conditions but it expressly forbids any derogation from the rights in articles 6, 7, and 8, paragraphs 1 and 2.[82] Thus, in addition to rendering these rights unretractable, *ICCPR* heavily implies they are among the most basic of rights in the panoply of human protections.

Covenant on Economic, Social and Cultural Rights, 16 December 1966, 993 UNTS 3, Can TS 1976 No 46, and the ICCPR, above note 4.

79 *Ibid.*

80 *Convention Against Torture and Other Cruel, Inhuman or Degrading Treatment or Punishment*, 10 December 1984, 1465 UNTS 85, Can TS 1987 No 36 [CAT].

81 *Ibid*, arts 1, 2, and 16.

82 Above note 4. Article 4 also forbids derogation from the rights expressed in arts 11, 15, 16, and 18.

The treaty-based implication of the importance of these particular human rights is endorsed by customary international law. A second singular feature attaching to them is that the obligations of protection are owed to the international community as a whole. Specifically, they operate among all signatory states for the benefit of all individuals. As the International Court of Justice declared in the *Barcelona Traction* case:[83]

> [33] When a State admits into its territory foreign investments or foreign nationals, whether natural or juristic persons, it is bound to extend to them the protection of the law and assumes obligations concerning the treatment to be afforded them. These obligations, however, are neither absolute nor unqualified. In particular, an essential distinction should be drawn between the obligations of a State towards the international community as a whole, and those arising vis-à-vis another State in the field of diplomatic protection. By their very nature the former are the concern of all States. In view of the importance of the rights involved, all States can be held to have a legal interest in their protection; they are obligations *erga omnes*.
>
> [34] Such obligations derive, for example, in contemporary international law, from the outlawing of acts of aggression, and of genocide, as also from the principles and rules concerning the basic rights of the human person, including protection from slavery and racial discrimination. Some of the corresponding rights of protection have entered into the body of general international law . . . others are conferred by international instruments of a universal or quasi-universal character.[84]

While the precise scope of the "rules concerning the basic rights of the human person" has not been determined, there can be little doubt that the protections for individuals from extreme abuse to the person as encompassed by the cited provisions of *ICCPR* and *CAT* are *erga omnes* obligations[85] under the Court's criteria. As *erga omnes* obligations, every state party owes duties towards every other state party for these protections of all individuals within their jurisdictional reach, regardless of

83 *Case Concerning The Barcelona Traction, Light and Power Company, Limited (Belgium v Spain) (Second Phase)*, [1970] ICJ Rep 3 [*Barcelona Traction*].

84 *Ibid* at paras 33 & 34.

85 More precisely, since not all states are yet parties to these treaties, the obligations are owed *erga omnes partes*.

the usual limitations on the espousal of claims to the national state of the victim.[86]

Lastly, customary international law also infuses these human rights with a peremptory character: they bear the force of *jus cogens*. As the *Vienna Convention on the Law of Treaties*[87] article 53 explains: "a peremptory norm of general international law is a norm accepted and recognised by the international community of States as a whole as a norm from which no derogation is permitted . . . ." Thus *jus cogens* (literally "compelling law") is a customary international law rule of public order in the international legal system. This legal concept has been judicially affirmed internationally by the International Court of Justice in *Nicaragua v United States*,[88] and in Canada by the Ontario Court of Appeal in *Bouzari*[89] and the Supreme Court of Canada in *Suresh v Canada (Minister of Citizenship and Immigration)*.[90]

Though the concept of *jus cogens* is well established, difficulty persists over its contents. Legal opinions differ over whether all or only some (and if some, which) human rights norms have attained *jus cogens* status. Yet the typically blurry edges of customary law rules hardly leave room for doubt that the rights that are central to human life and existence and are non-derogable *erga omnes* obligations, have the force of *jus cogens*.[91]

Further, since the Supreme Court has affirmed that customary international law is automatically adopted as part of Canadian law,[92] unless there is legislation that is clearly contradictory, these human rights of *jus cogens* status have compelling legal force in Canadian courts.[93]

---

86 See International Law Commission, *Draft Articles on the Responsibility of States for Internationally Wrongful Acts*, in *Report of the International Law Commission on the Work of its Fifty-third Session*, UNGAOR 56th Sess, Supp No 10, UN Doc A/56/10, (2001) art 48 [*ILC Wrongful Act Draft Articles*].

87 23 May 1969, 1155 UNTS 331 (1969), Can TS 1980 No 37.

88 *Military and Paramilitary Activities in and against Nicaragua (Nicaragua v United States of America)*, [1986] ICJ Rep 14 at para 190.

89 Above note 54.

90 2002 SCC 1 at paras 61–65 [*Suresh*].

91 Compare the judgments on this point in *Bouzari*, above note 54 and *Suresh*, *ibid*.

92 *Hape*, above note 26.

93 Subject to the discussion of state immunities, below at note 109ff.

b) Remedies for the Violation of International Human Rights

The duty to protect every individual's human rights falls on the state. The ways in which those international duties are to be performed are also stated affirmatively in *ICCPR*. Article 2 requires Canada:

> 1. . . . to respect and to ensure to all individuals within its territory and subject to its jurisdiction the rights recognised in the present Covenant, without distinction of any kind . . . .
>
> 3. . . .
>
> (a) [t]o ensure that any person whose rights or freedoms as herein recognized are violated shall have an effective remedy, notwithstanding that the violation has been committed by persons acting in an official capacity;
>
> (b) [t]o ensure that any person claiming such a remedy shall have his right thereto determined by competent judicial, administrative or legislative authorities . . . ;
>
> (c) [t]o ensure that the competent authorities shall enforce such remedies when granted.

Where the human rights violation constitutes torture, *CAT* reinforces the remedial system demanded by *ICCPR*. Canada is obliged under *CAT* to "take effective legislative, administrative, judicial or other measures to prevent acts of torture in any territory under its jurisdiction,"[94] which must include ensuring that victims have the right to complain, that competent authorities promptly and impartially investigate allegations of torture, and that the legal system affords the victim an enforceable right to fair and adequate compensation and rehabilitation.[95]

Noticeably, under *ICCPR*, the duty to protect human rights does not permit discrimination between nationals and others. Further, the duty is not limited to respect in the actions of Canada and its officials, but also requires Canadian authorities to ensure they are not violated by the activities of others.[96] Nor are these duties necessarily constrained territorially; as noted in the previous case study in Section A, the International Court of Justice, when faced with contending interpretations of the phrase "within its territory and subject to its jurisdiction," determined in effect that it operates disjunctively, and concluded that the *ICCPR* "is

---

94 Above note 80, art 2(1).

95 *Ibid*, arts 12–14 & 16.

96 Compare *Velásquez Rodríguez Case* (1988), Inter-Am Ct HR (Ser C) No 4.

applicable in respect of acts done by a state in the exercise of its jurisdiction outside its own territory."[97]

While this holding of the International Court of Justice about the scope of the duty to protect expressed in article 2, paragraph 1, of the *ICCPR* may be controversial, it is important to note that no such territorial limitation is mentioned regarding a state's obligations to remedy violations set out in paragraph 3. It explicitly states that Canada must "ensure" that an abused individual "shall have an effective remedy" that is "determined by competent judicial . . . authorities" and is "enforce[d] . . . when granted." Further, it foreshadows the potential claims to immunity from jurisdiction by perpetrators who are agents of the state and sets them aside by its express directions that the required remedies for victims must be available "notwithstanding that the violation has been committed by persons acting in an official capacity . . . ." In short, Canada has a treaty obligation to provide access to judicial remedies for the victims, national or foreign, of international human rights abuses.[98]

---

97 *Legal Consequences of the Construction of a Wall*, above note 9 at paras 107–11. The UN HRC in General Comment No 31 also advises that a state party's duties under art 2(1) apply "to anyone within the power or effective control of that State Party, even if not situated within the territory of the State Party" (above note 8 at 10). The same conclusion was reached by the Inter-American Commission on Human Rights with respect to the *American Declaration of the Rights and Duties of Man* in *Coard v United States*, above note 10. The controversy regarding these findings is explored in the previous case study in Section A, above in this chapter.

98 The assertion of extraterritorial jurisdiction over international human rights violations is open to other states parties to the same human rights conventions as Canada. The argument made here could rebound on Canada. Indeed it has in a fashion: in *Presbyterian Church of Sudan v Talisman Energy Inc*, 453 F Supp 2d 633 (SDNY 2006), aff'd 582 F3d 244 (2d Cir 2009), cert denied US Sup Ct October 4, 2010, the Canadian corporation, Talisman Energy, was sued in tort in the US court for the Southern District of New York on account of its alleged collaboration with the government of Sudan in the commission of egregious human rights abuses upon the Sudanese plaintiffs. The US court took jurisdiction under the *Alien Tort Claims Act* and made requests for international judicial assistance in the form of oral and documentary evidence, which were granted by the Ontario Superior Court (see *Presbyterian Church of Sudan v Rybiak*, 2005 CanLII 27013). The Canadian government was sufficiently concerned about this assertion of civil jurisdiction over the case that it filed a statement of interest in which, *inter alia*, it argued that the US court was violating traditional restraints on the exercise of extraterritorial jurisdiction. Yet the court proceeded with the case, ultimately granting summary judgment to Talisman Energy because the plaintiffs were unable to establish Talisman's purposeful complicity in the human rights abuses they suffered.

3) The Expectations of International Criminal Law

In addition to international human rights laws, a second basis for the extraterritorial exercise of civil jurisdiction by Canadian courts is provided by international criminal law. Canada already asserts criminal jurisdiction over a variety of illegal activities committed abroad, pursuant to obligations in the transnational criminal law "suppression conventions."[99] That is to say, Parliament has prescribed and the courts exercise jurisdiction over offenders for proscribed extraterritorial activities. In most instances, the extraterritorial reach of Canadian criminal jurisdiction fulfills the treaty obligations assumed by Canada. These treaties place obligations on state parties, such as Canada, by imbuing them with a quasi-universal jurisdiction over offenders or requiring them either to prosecute perpetrators or to extradite them to another state party for prosecution.[100]

There is a range of particularly serious offences that are criminalized under both treaty and customary international law, sometimes referred to as international crimes *stricto sensu*,[101] including genocide, crimes against humanity, war crimes, torture, slavery, and perhaps some forms of terrorism. These crimes have attracted the attention of the international community because they are so heinous. Their perpetrators are *hostis humani generis*—enemies of humankind—whose wrongdoings constitute both contemptible crimes under international law and, at the same time, gross violations of the basic human rights protected by international law.

The risk of extraterritorial jurisdiction being asserted against Canada only arises if Canada falls down on its obligations to provide access to remedies and redress for human rights abuses. Such a failure is not to be expected for human rights violations committed within Canada since territorial jurisdiction is assured. But cases in which a resident Canadian national is a party to the perpetration of human rights abuses abroad raise significant curial doubts about Canadian jurisdiction. The suit against Talisman Energy was just such a case. As the US court opined in rejecting the Canadian government's objection to the US exercise of extraterritorial jurisdiction, Canadian courts are unable to consider such actions for violations of international law. This point of view is what this case study seeks to dispel.

99 See Chapter 6, Sections A & B, and Robert J Currie & Steve Coughlan, "Extraterritorial Criminal Jurisdiction: Bigger Picture or Smaller Frame?" (2007) 11:2 Can Crim L Rev 141.

100 These treaties and the types of jurisdiction they authorize are discussed in Chapter 3, Section A(3).

101 See Currie, *Criminal Law*, above note 22, ch 3.

The treaties and customary norms that define the international offences and prescribe the jurisdictional authority of states parties to prosecute the perpetrators in national courts traditionally do not design remedies for the victims of these crimes. But civil law interests in violations of international standards of human conduct match criminal law concerns in the same wrongdoing. Prosecution of perpetrators mirrors remediation of victims.[102] The only difference in operation is that on the criminal side, Canadian legislation instructs the courts to take extraterritorial jurisdiction, but on the civil side, there is no directly comparable legislative authority. Yet, since these internationally prohibited acts constitute violent abuses of internationally protected human rights, victims of such crimes have a legitimate expectation of a remedy for their injuries.[103] This expectation is bolstered in international law by the *Rome Statute of the International Criminal Court*,[104] which directs the court to organize reparations for victims[105] and to establish a trust fund[106] for that purpose. The expectation is also supported in Canadian law by analogy to Canada's own victims of crime legislation[107] and an injured individual's freedom to sue for personal compensation from the criminal for acts within Canada that also constitute torts.

The personal expectations of the abused are also supported by the international interests of Canadians generally. Canada has a deep concern

---

102 As Breyer J of the US Supreme Court opined in *Sosa v Alvarez-Machain*, 542 US 692 at 762–63 (2004), "consensus as to universal criminal jurisdiction itself suggests that universal tort jurisdiction would be no more threatening . . . . That is because the criminal courts of many nations combine civil and criminal proceedings, allowing those injured by criminal conduct to be represented, and to recover damages, in the criminal proceeding itself." The ICJ also noted the civil claims of crime victims when it commented in *Jurisdictional Immunities of the State (Germany v Italy)*, [2012] ICJ Rep 99 at 145, online: International Court of Justice www.icj-cij.org/docket/files/143/16883.pdf [*Jurisdictional Immunities of the State*] that it "need not rule on whether . . . international law confers upon the individual victim of a violation of the law of armed conflict a directly enforceable right to claim compensation."

103 See *Declaration on Basic Principles of Justice for Victims of Crime and Abuse of Power*, UNGA 96th Plen Mtg, UN Doc A/Res/40/34 (1985) Annex, and *Basic Principles and Guidelines on the Right to a Remedy and Reparation for Victims of Gross Violations of International Human Rights Law and Serious Violations of International Humanitarian Law*, UNGA 60th Sess, UN Doc A/Res 60/147 (2005).

104 (1998) 2187 UNTS 53.

105 *Ibid*, art 75.

106 *Ibid*, art 79.

107 For example, *Compensation for Victims of Crime Act*, RSO 1990, c C.24; *Victims of Crime Act*, RSA 2000, c V-3.

for the maintenance of an orderly international society, in particular in upholding human rights worldwide. It is party to a large number of human rights conventions. It has an immediate involvement in cases of abuse of human rights abroad that concern victims of Canadian origin and refugees or stateless persons who come to Canada. Furthermore, Canada's promotion internationally of the principle of responsibility to protect populations at risk from genocide, war crimes, ethnic cleansing, and crimes against humanity[108] shows that it cares about violations of human rights everywhere.

In sum, since Canadian courts, consistently with international law, assert criminal jurisdiction over acts that involve the commission of egregious human rights abuses extraterritorially, it is open to them to assert parallel civil jurisdiction as well.

* * *

The exercise of jurisdiction as forum of last resort would provide the opportunity and legitimacy to exert civil jurisdiction extraterritorially in fulfillment of the expectations arising from Canada's obligations under both international human rights and international criminal laws. Even so, the occasions when this jurisdiction might be exercised are typically when the human rights violations are committed by agents of a foreign state. Then additional obstacles will be encountered in the form of a claim by the foreign state and its representatives to an international legal right to immunity from the jurisdiction of Canadian courts. The leading cases support this limitation of jurisdiction, but alternative approaches to the domestic interpretation and application of this international law are available. They are also founded in the abused victim's rights and correlative state's responsibilities under the human rights conventions—particularly the *ICCPR*—that bind Canada. But before discussion of them is engaged, it is necessary to appreciate the scope and interpretation of state immunity from jurisdiction as applied to date in Canada.

4) The Limitations of Foreign State Immunity from Jurisdiction

One of the oldest rules of customary international law attests to the immunity of one state from the law and jurisdiction of another. As

108 The principle was endorsed by the UN General Assembly at the World Summit of Heads of States and Governments in September 2005, *Resolution adopted by the General Assembly on 16 September 2005*, UNGA, 60th Sess, UN Doc A/RES/60/1 (2005) at paras 138–39.

sovereign equals, states may not subject each other to their national legal systems.[109] This principle was once observed almost absolutely, but it became somewhat restrictive during the last century when governments, in addition to their interstate diplomatic interactions, began to engage much more in commercial and other transactions with domestic legal persons, both individuals and corporations. In Canada the customary international law rules of restrictive immunity are now found in the *State Immunity Act* (*SIA*).[110] Under the *SIA*, the foreign state, its political subdivisions, its government and governmental agencies as well as its head of state and representative officials, are all declared completely immune from Canadian jurisdiction except as expressly stated.[111] Since the restrictions, in the form of exceptions to this immunity, may apply in different ways for the state and its organs when compared to how it is applied to its officers and other officials, they will be discussed separately.

a) Immunity of the Foreign State

Canadian courts may not assert jurisdiction against a foreign state unless its activities fall within a recognized exception to immunity. In cases involving egregious abuses of human rights, two grounds for exceptions to the immunity of the responsible foreign state are likely to be urged by complainants. One is an express exception to immunity within the *SIA* for torts committed in Canada, and the other is an assertion that peremptory norms, such as the human rights rules against torture and other grievous bodily harm, override state rights to immunity. For convenience, these two sets of arguments will be referred to as the "tort exception" and the "*jus cogens* rule against torture."

---

109 *The Schooner Exchange v M'Faddon*, 11 US (7 Cranch) 116 (1812); *The Parlement Belge* (1878), [1879–1880] 5 PD 197 (UKCA); *Dessaulles v Republic of Poland*, [1944] SCR 275 at 277; and *Jurisdictional Immunities of the State*, above note 102 at paras 56 & 57.

110 Above note 60. In March 2012 Parliament enacted the *Justice for Victims of Terrorism Act*, SC 2012, c 1, s 1. This Act is intended to amend the *SIA* by amplifying the exceptions to state immunity in respect of victims of terrorist acts imputable to a foreign government that has been designated by Canada as a supporter of terrorism. This amendment of the *SIA* seems to draw on the experience of the US *Torture Victim Protection Act of 1991*, 28 USC §1350 (1992) and will likely help only a limited number of victims of human rights abuse since violations occur in many more countries than designated terrorist states and in many more ways than by acts of terror.

111 *SIA*, *ibid*, ss 2 & 3.

The leading case in Canada is *Bouzari*,[112] decided by the Ontario Court of Appeal. Bouzari, it may be recalled, was abused and tortured in Iran and continued to suffer from those injuries after he reached Canada, but his suit against Iran was met by that state's claim to immunity from the jurisdiction of the Canadian court. In response, both the tort exception and the *jus cogens* rule against torture were presented to the court.

The tort exception found within section 6 of the *SIA* is obviously relevant to cases like *Bouzari* involving violent human rights abuses since it covers "any death or personal or bodily injury . . . that occurs in Canada." On a first reading of this provision, it might seem that victims of foreign human rights violations will not be prevented from suing the responsible foreign state if they continue to suffer injury from their abuse after returning or coming to Canada. However, the Ontario Court of Appeal in *Bouzari* ruled otherwise. In a brief passage, it affirmed the motion judge's ruling that section 6 "requires that the physical breach of personal integrity giving rise to the claim take place in Canada."[113]

Section 6 is capable of bearing a different reading: continuing injury within Canada from an initial act or course of abuse abroad is a plausible interpretation of the clause "occurs in Canada." Although there is no guidance in the *SIA* itself as to which interpretation is to be preferred, the international human rights law binding on Canada provides strong contextual support, as explained previously,[114] that would favour the alternative conclusion and would sustain the court's jurisdiction over the suit.

It could be argued that the Ontario Court of Appeal did not give sufficient weight to the international legal context of section 6 in rendering its determination that continuing injury within Canada does not meet the test of personal hurt required to invoke the exception. The court was properly apprised of the role of international law within the Canadian legal system, for later in its judgment it observed (about binding treaty provisions) that "Parliament is . . . presumed to legislate consistently with those obligations" and thus "so far as possible, courts should interpret domestic legislation consistently with [them]," yet "it is open to Canada to legislate contrary to them" even though to do so "would put Canada in breach."[115] But the Court of Appeal expressed these opinions in the context of the second argument around the *jus cogens* rule against

112 Above note 54.

113 *Ibid* at para 47.

114 See text accompanying note 78ff.

115 Above note 54 at paras 64 and 66.

torture.[116] It did not appear to give the attention these admonitions call for when considering the scope of application of the express exception for personal injury in section 6. Had it done so, it would have considered, as part of the context of interpretation of that section, the provisions of *CAT* and *ICCPR*, both of which oblige signatory states to ensure that victims of torture have access to effective and enforceable means of redress,[117] as discussed previously. In the uncertainty surrounding the language of section 6 of the *SIA* as to whether injury that continues but did not originate in Canada may be said to "occur in Canada," the Court of Appeal might have found that Canada's treaty obligations to ensure the provision of remedies to torture victims such as Bouzari would lead to an affirmative interpretation.

The *Kazemi* case, it may be recalled,[118] raised factual variations on the tort exception compared to *Bouzari*. Proceedings were begun against Iran on behalf of the late Ms Kazemi and Mr Hashemi, her son. The judgment followed the *Bouzari* precedent in respect of the claim by Ms Kazemi's estate: since she had suffered and died outside Canada, Iran was able to assert immunity. But her son's claim was for psychological trauma that he suffered as a consequence of his mother's mistreatment while he was resident in Canada, so his claim against Iran would appear to be within the tort exception to state immunity expressed in section 6 of the *SIA*. Indeed, the Quebec Superior Court allowed Mr Hashemi's suit against Iran to proceed to trial but, subsequently, the Quebec Court of Appeal dismissed it on the ground that the character of his injury—psychological trauma—did not satisfy the statutory requirement of "personal or bodily injury" as it did not breach his physical integrity. However, the Supreme Court of Canada has since granted leave to appeal the Quebec Court of Appeal's decision.[119]

The *jus cogens* rule against torture grounded the alternative attempt in *Bouzari*[120] to counter Iran's claim of immunity. The intervener who raised it invited the court to engraft a fresh exception onto the *SIA* on two grounds: (1) as a consequence of the duty expressed in *CAT* article

116 *Ibid* at para 60.

117 *CAT*, above note 80, art 14 and *ICCPR*, above note 4, art 2.

118 *Kazemi* Qc Sup Ct, above note 56.

119 *Kazemi* SCC, above note 56.

120 And in *Kazemi* Qc Sup Ct, above note 56, to no better effect, following *Bouzari*, above note 54.

14[121] that a state party, such as Canada, must ensure redress for a torture victim; and (2) pursuant to the peremptory norm of customary international law against torture.

Earlier in its judgment the Ontario Court of Appeal had observed about the *SIA*:

> Section 3(1) could not be clearer. To reiterate, it says:
>
> > 3. (1) *Except as provided by this Act*, a foreign state is immune from the jurisdiction of any court in Canada.[122]

At first reading, such explicit statutory language would appear to present formidable difficulty for arguments favouring new exceptions to foreign state immunity. The plain meaning of section 3 certainly seems to restrain the exercise of judicial authority, urged in the intervener's first line of argument, to add a separate exception to immunity through the process of interpreting the *SIA* in the context of Canada's international obligations. The Ontario Court of Appeal did not accept that *CAT* article 14 required it to do so, opining that it only imposes the duty on state parties of providing access to redress for torture committed within their own territory, not extraterritorially.[123] Though it did allow that *CAT* itself provides no answer to the question whether the scope of this remedial duty extends to victims of torture extraterritorially, it also accepted the finding of the motion judge regarding state practice around *CAT* that "no state interprets Article 14 to require it to take civil jurisdiction over a foreign state for acts committed outside the forum state."[124] Ultimately, the Court of Appeal approved the motion judge's conclusion, which was based on her adoption of the opinion of one of two opposing experts in international law, which was that *CAT* article 14 is limited to providing civil remedies for torture committed within the forum state.[125]

The appellant's second line of argument was to press the overriding authority of the peremptory norm against torture. Indeed, the court acknowledged and accepted the *jus cogens* status of the rule, but it sep-

---

121 Above note 80, referred to in *Bouzari*, above note 54 at para 72. A similar proposition under *ICCPR*, above note 4, art 14, was also presented in *Bouzari*, above note 54 at para 82.

122 *Ibid* at para 57 [emphasis in the original]. And see *ibid* at para 67.

123 *Ibid* at para 81. Justice of Appeal Goudge held likewise under *ICCPR*, above note 4, art 14, in *Bouzari*, above note 54 at para 82.

124 *Ibid* at para 78.

125 *Ibid* at paras 76–81.

arated the substance of the obligation from the process of remediation for its violation. The court found no fault with the motion judge's determination that:

> An examination of the decisions of national courts and international tribunals, as well as state legislation with respect to sovereign immunity, indicates that there is no principle of customary international law which provides an exception from state immunity where an act of torture has been committed outside the forum, even for acts contrary to *jus cogens*.[126]

The Ontario Court of Appeal's view of *CAT* has been criticized internationally by the Committee against Torture established under *CAT*[127] when reviewing the fourth and fifth periodic reports of Canada[128] in 2005. The Committee expressed concern about the "absence of effective measures to provide civil compensation to victims of torture in all cases" and recommended Canada "should review its position under article 14 of the Convention to ensure the provision of compensation through its civil jurisdiction to all victims of torture."[129] The Committee expressed further criticism of Canada upon considering its sixth periodic report in 2012. The Committee regretted that "Canada has not incorporated all provisions of the Convention into domestic law and that those provisions cannot be argued independently as the basis for a legal claim in courts other than through domestic legal instruments." It urged Canada to rectify this situation, in particular "to ensure that provisions of the Convention that give rise to extraterritorial jurisdiction can be directly applied before domestic courts." It also sought action by Canada to "ensure that all victims of torture are able to access remedy and obtain redress, wherever acts of torture occurred and regardless of the nationality of the perpetrator or victim" and specifically mentioned amendment of *SIA*.[130] In comparison, when the House of Lords faced a similar case to *Bouzari*, their lordships cited the Ontario Court of Appeal judgment with approval and remarked on the commentary of the Committee of *CAT* that "[w]hatever its value

---

126 *Ibid* at para 88, citing *Bouzari v Iran (Islamic Republic)*, 2002 CarswellOnt 1469 at para 63 (SCJ).

127 Above note 80, art 17.

128 Pursuant to *CAT*, *ibid*, art 19.

129 Committee against Torture, *Conclusions and Recommendations of the Committee against Torture: Canada*. UNHRC, 34th Sess, UN Doc CAT/C/CR/34/CAN (2005).

130 Committee against Torture, *Concluding Observations of the Committee against Torture: Canada*. UNHRC, 48th Sess, UN Doc CAT/C/CAN/CO/6 (2012).

in influencing the trend of international thinking, the legal authority of this recommendation is slight."[131]

The position taken by the court in *Bouzari* has attracted considerable judicial and legislative[132] (as well as scholarly) attention. While Canadian and British[133] (and other) national courts followed the approach of *Bouzari*, Italian and Greek courts[134] accepted the argument that the *jus cogens* rule against torture overreaches the violating state's claim to immunity from suit. The tension around this issue was made abundantly evident when Germany instituted a case against Italy in the International Court of Justice.

In *Jurisdictional Immunities of the State*,[135] Germany asserted that Italy had violated international law by failing to respect the jurisdictional immunity of Germany in actions brought by Italian and Greek nationals before Italian courts against Germany. The Italians claimed compensation for gross mistreatment by Nazi German authorities during the German occupation of much of Italy in 1943–1945. The Greeks sought enforcement in Italy of judgments rendered by Greek courts against Germany arising from the massacre of civilians by German forces in the Greek village of Distomo in 1944.

In its decision in February 2012, the International Court of Justice upheld Germany's right to immunity from the jurisdiction of the Italian courts both to adjudicate the Italian claims and to enforce the Greek

---

131 *Jones*, above note 57 at para 23.

132 For example, the private member's Bill C-483, *An Act to Amend the State Immunity Act (Genocide, Crimes against Humanity, War Crimes or Torture)*, 2d Sess, 40th Parl, 2009, reintroduced under the same number and title in 2010 (3d Sess, 40th Parl) but not enacted. See also the *Justice for Victims of Terrorism Act*, above note 110.

133 For example, *Arar*, above note 55; *Kazemi* Qc Sup Ct, above note 56; *Jones*, above note 57; and *Al-Adsani v United Kingdom* [GC], No 35763/97, [2001] XI ECHR 81, 29 EHRR CD99 (split decision 9:8), online: European Court of Human Rights www.echr.coe.int/hudoc.

134 For example, *Ferrini v Federal Republic of Germany*, Decn No 5044/2004 (2004), 128 ILR 658, 99 AJIL 242 (Italian Court of Cassation Plenary Session) and *Prefecture of Voiotia v Federal Republic of Germany*, Case No 137/1997 (1998), 92 AJIL 765 (Court of First Instance of Leivadia, Greece), aff'd Case No 11/2000 (2001), 129 ILR 513, 95 AJIL 198 (Hellenic Supreme Court), but overruled in a 6:5 split decision in *Federal Republic of Germany v Margellos*, Case No 6/2002 (2002), 129 ILR 525 (Greek Special Supreme Court) and discussed in Kerstin Bartsch & Björn Elberling, "*Jus Cogens* vs. State Immunity, Round Two: The Decision of the European Court of Human Rights in the *Kalogeropoulou et al. v. Greece and Germany* Decision" (2003) 4:5 German Law Journal 477.

135 Above note 102.

judgments. The judgment addressed both the tort exception to state immunity and the *jus cogens* status of rules of human rights and humanitarian law as a basis for overreaching state immunity.

Regarding the tort exception, the International Court of Justice concluded that "customary international law continues to require that a State be accorded immunity in proceedings for torts allegedly committed on the territory of another State by its armed forces and other organs of State in the course of conducting an armed conflict."[136] This conclusion is an authoritative statement of the customary international rule of state immunity in cases arising from situations of armed conflict, but it is not, and was not intended to be, a definitive declaration of the scope of the tort exception. Indeed, the International Court of Justice expressly did not address the question whether there is such an exception in customary international law.[137] The court's discrete holding is limited to foreign state torts committed by their armed forces in the course of armed conflict. The Canadian tort exception in section 6 of the *SIA* was mentioned by the International Court of Justice in the course of a wide review of state practice in the form of national legislation and court decisions only for the purpose of determining the customary law specifically related to the immunity of the state for the acts of its armed forces. The tort exception in the *SIA* remains a legitimate legislative enactment by Canada whatever may be its rightful interpretation and application.

The International Court of Justice also could not discern a customary international law exception to state immunity on account of the seriousness of the violation of human rights law or the law of armed conflict, even if it was a breach of a rule of *jus cogens*. Like the Ontario Court of Appeal in *Bouzari*, to which it had occasion to refer,[138] the International Court of Justice drew a distinction between substantive and procedural rules and between their effects. It stated:

> Assuming for this purpose that the rules [violated by Germany] . . . are rules of *jus cogens*, there is no conflict between those rules and the rules on State immunity. The two sets of rules address different matters. The rules of State immunity are procedural in character and are confined to determining whether or not the courts of one State may exercise jurisdiction in respect of another State. They do not bear upon the question

---

136 *Ibid* at para 78.

137 *Ibid* at para 65.

138 *Ibid* at para 96.

> whether or not the conduct in respect of which the proceedings are brought was lawful or unlawful.[139]

Thus, though no derogation from a *jus cogens* rule is permissible, the court concluded that "the rules which determine the scope and extent of jurisdiction and when that jurisdiction may be exercised do not derogate from those substantive rules which possess *jus cogens* status . . . ."[140]

The logic of this conclusion is unimpeachable so long as the prior distinction between the effects of substantive and procedural rules is sustainable. It is a recognized distinction in both Canadian and international law, but it is capable of being overreached by *jus cogens* rules against torture and other abuses of human rights if the international community gives them such scope and effect. The majority judgment of the International Court of Justice made a survey of the national practice of state immunity that showed this is not so at present. However, state practice is not static. As the Ontario Court of Appeal observed in *Bouzari*:

> Both under customary international law and international treaty there is today a balance struck between the condemnation of torture as an international crime against humanity and the principle that states must treat each other as equals not to be subjected to each other's jurisdiction. It would be inconsistent with this balance to provide a civil remedy against a foreign state for torture committed abroad. In the future, perhaps as the international human rights movement gathers greater force, this balance may change, either through the domestic legislation of states or by international treaty.[141]

This concluding comment of the Court of Appeal shows an appreciation of the unfortunate predicament of the victims of human rights abuse before domestic courts and an awareness of the possibilities of international treaties coming to their aid. But both the Ontario Court of Appeal and the International Court of Justice reached their decisions on the basis of the customary international law of state immunity with-

---

139 *Ibid* at para 93.

140 *Ibid* at para 95, where the ICJ also referred to its judgments in *Armed Activities on the Territory of the Congo (New Application: 2002) (Congo v Rwanda)*, [2006] ICJ Rep 6; and *Case Concerning the Arrest Warrant of 11 April 2000 (Congo v Belgium)*, [2002] ICJ Rep 3 [*Congo v Belgium*]. See also *Jurisdictional Immunities of the State*, above note 102 at para 100.

141 Above note 54 at para 95.

out regard for the available treaty law on state responsibility, such as the provisions of *ICCPR* outlined in this case study,[142] which might support a different conclusion.

b) Immunity of Foreign State Officials

The right of foreign state officers to any immunity is dependent on their official capacity as representatives or agents of the state. As already noted, a foreign state is granted immunity under customary international law out of respect for its sovereignty.[143] State officials are immune only as far as is necessary to maintain the sovereign immunity of the state for which they act. Individuals have no personal immunity: whether they are clothed with immunity from jurisdiction in another state depends on the extent to which they represent or exercise some element of the sovereignty of their state.[144] This functional approach is evident in the *SIA*. Section 2 defines a "foreign state" to include:

> (a) any sovereign or other head of the foreign state or of any political subdivision of the foreign state while acting as such in a public capacity,
>
> (b) any government of the foreign state or of any political subdivision of the foreign state, including any of its departments, and any agency of the foreign state . . . .

This provision sets both the class of individuals and the scope of their activities that attract immunity as embodiments of the state. First, the class of persons could be read as extending only to the head of state and the leaders of the government, and not to lower officials, like police and jailors who are generally the individuals who actually commit the human rights abuses. But in international practice, however lowly the official, his acts are still done on behalf of and in the name of the state, and therefore attract the immunity of the state.[145] This feature is captured in section 2 of the *SIA* by its reference to "government of the

---

142 Compare the individual dissenting judgments of judges Bennouna, Conçado Trindade, and Yusuf in *Jurisdictional Immunities of the State*, above note 102, for thoughtful reflections on the balancing of state immunity, human rights, and state responsibility in international law.

143 Above note 109.

144 *Congo v Belgium*, above note 140 at para 53.

145 *Twycross v Dreyfus* (1877), LR 5 Ch D 605 at 618–19 (UK); *Zoernsch v Waldock*, [1964] 1 WLR 675 at 692 (UKCA); *Jaffe v Miller* (1993), 13 OR (3d) 745 at 758–59 (CA); *Jones*, above note 57; *Kazemi* Qc Sup Ct, above note 56.

foreign state," as the exercise of governmental authority is inevitably carried out by individuals, be they at the apex of political power or at the base of operational activity. Thus all government officers represent the state in the fulfillment of their official functions. This proposition was confirmed in that part of the *Kazemi* case involving Stephen Hashemi's suit against named officers of the state of Iran.[146]

But belonging to the class of persons who are state officials is not sufficient by itself to attract immunity. The right to immunity is only available to state officials for acts done in their official capacity. This limitation is explicit in the *SIA* section 2(a) in respect of the head of a foreign state, and is implicit in section 2(b) with regard to state officials since they are the means by which the "government of the foreign state" is conducted. The limitation to official activities supposes there may be instances when a state employee commits unofficial or personal acts that do not attract the right to immunity from suit.[147] For example, arguments may be made that officials who commit torture and other acts of violence in breach of human rights do not have immunity from suit because their activities are illegal actions outside their job descriptions.

Such arguments have not succeeded in the cases to date because the alleged abuses have typically been perpetrated in prisons and other places of governmental detention by on-duty officials.[148] As the Quebec Superior Court in *Kazemi* summed up, "foreign functionaries, while carrying out their official duties may commit illegal acts but this does not mean that as soon as they do so, they are automatically considered as acting as private individuals as opposed to 'acting in public capacity.'"[149]

The House of Lords has similarly supported the immunity of foreign state officials but set forth the circumstances in more affirmative language: "International law does not require, as a condition of a state's entitlement to claim immunity for the conduct of its servant or agent, that the latter should have been acting in accordance with his instructions

---

146 *Kazemi* Qc Sup Ct, *ibid* at paras 105–14 and *Kazemi* Qc CA, above note 56 at paras 87–93.

147 As the court remarked in *Jones*, above note 57 at para 11: "In some borderline cases there could be doubt whether the conduct of an individual, although a servant or agent of the state, had a sufficient connection with the state to entitle it to claim immunity for his conduct."

148 See *Bouzari*, above note 54 at para 12; *Arar*, above note 55 at para 2; and *Jones*, above note 57 at para 12.

149 *Kazemi*, QC Sup Ct, above note 56 at para 151, confirmed by *Kazemi* Qc CA at paras 94–97.

or authority."[150] As a result, state officials who commit crimes against humanity may be prosecuted to conviction in any foreign country because they are subject to universal jurisdiction and have no personal immunity,[151] but they may not be sued in any foreign country by the victims of those crimes for the consequent violations of their human rights, so long as those officials are cloaked with their national state's right to immunity. The appropriate scope of the foreign state's right to immunity from jurisdiction therefore remains the key concern.

It is also still an open question, as no Canadian court has considered the kind of arguments based on *ICCPR* that were offered earlier in this case study. They might affect both the interpretation of the exception in section 6 and the scope of application of the *SIA* as a whole. Not only are the provisions in *ICCPR* article 2(3) about victims' redress most explicit but also, it is worth emphasizing, they specifically require that effective remedies be made available, "notwithstanding that the violation has been committed by persons acting in an official capacity" — that is, on behalf of the state. This is an obligatory treaty responsibility on Canada that Canadian courts are bound to take into account in interpreting legislation, although it was not addressed by the Ontario Court of Appeal in *Bouzari*.

Since the *SIA*, like any other Canadian statute, must be interpreted so far as possible consistently with Canada's international obligations,[152] a Canadian court is capable of finding a mandate for fulfilling the duties in *ICCPR* to provide remedial access for human rights victims against foreign states. In *Suresh v Canada (Minister of Citizenship and Immigration)*[153] the Supreme Court set a precedent for reference to the provisions of *ICCPR* and *CAT* as aids in the interpretation of a statute, namely the *Immigration Act* as it was then.[154] Their provisions were used to cut down the effect of seemingly plain language in that Act that would have allowed a refugee who was a security risk to Canada to be *refouled* (returned) even in the face of persecution and torture. The *ICCPR* might be employed similarly towards the *SIA*.

---

150 *Jones*, above note 57 at para 12. And see ILC *Wrongful Act Draft Articles*, above note 86, art 4.

151 See, for example, *R v Bow Street Metropolitan Stipendiary Magistrate, Ex parte Pinochet Ugarte (No 3)*, [2000] 1 AC 147 (HL).

152 As explained previously: see the quotations from *Bouzari*, in the text accompanying above note 115.

153 2002 SCC 1.

154 RSC 1985, c I-2.

First, as to the tort exception, a definitive interpretation of section 6 of the *SIA* has yet to be made. The Supreme Court has addressed section 6 in *Schreiber v Canada (AG)*[155] to the extent of determining it is "restricted to a class of claims arising out of a physical breach of personal integrity, consistent with the Quebec civil law term '*préjudice corporel*,'"[156] but it has not spoken on whether injury that continues to occur, as opposed to originates, within Canada is sufficient to activate the exception to immunity. The remedial provisions of the *ICCPR* would add weight to the victim's side of the argument over the appropriate interpretation of this aspect of the *SIA* section 6. Rejecting the plea of state immunity in circumstances where victims of abuse continue to suffer (rather than first incur) personal injury in Canada would fulfill the requirement in the *ICCPR* that effective remedies be provided regardless of whether the acts causing their injuries were committed by state officials. The claim of Mr Hashemi against Iran in the *Kazemi* case, currently *sub judice* by the Supreme Court, may be the occasion when the Court addresses both these issues around the interpretation and application of section 6 of the *SIA*.

Secondly, the directives of *ICCPR* provide strong support for a separate exception to state immunity in the event of violation of its fundamental human rights by a state party. Although the Ontario Court of Appeal in *Bouzari* took a literal view of the language of section 3 of the *SIA* that "[e]xcept as provided by this Act, a foreign state is immune from the jurisdiction of any court in Canada," these words may be read functionally as a limitation of the scope of operation of the Act and not as an exclusion of other rules and exceptions regarding state immunity. The Supreme Court has recognized this possibility without ruling on it. First, in *Re Canada Labour Code*, LaForest J spoke for the Court in writing:

> I view the Canadian *State Immunity Act* as a codification that is intended to clarify and continue the theory of restrictive immunity, rather than to alter its substance.[157]

More recently in *Kuwait Airways Corp v Iraq*, Lebel J expressed the view of the Supreme Court that:

---

155 2002 SCC 62 [*Schreiber*].

156 *Ibid* at para 80.

157 [1992] 2 SCR 50 at para 30.

> [T]he *SIA* . . . reflects a recognition that there are now exceptions to the principle of state immunity and in so doing reflects the evolution of that principle at the international level. But I need not determine here whether the *SIA* is exhaustive in this respect or whether the evolution of international law and of the common law has led to the development of new exceptions to the principles of immunity from jurisdiction . . . .[158]

Thus the Supreme Court is alert to the fact that the *SIA* is a statutory enactment of international legal norms. What these two quoted judgments do not say is that the legislation implements customary international law. Such legislation is very unusual and unnecessary since customary international law, as the Supreme Court confirmed in *R v Hape*,[159] is adopted into Canadian law without any need for transformation by legislation, such as binding treaty provisions regularly do. The important point here is that the *SIA*, when read in the context of its legislative history, is intended to reflect the then current principle of foreign state immunity as well as the restrictive exceptions to it, *under customary international law*.[160] It did not and does not speak to other exceptions to the principle of foreign state immunity by treaty, such as the *ICCPR*.

The remedial provisions of the *ICCPR* create an additional exception to the principles of state immunity from jurisdiction. As we have already indicated, there is no right of immunity for states parties to the *ICCPR*. As a result, there are competing sources of relevant rules governing foreign state immunity. There is the general principle of state immunity, subject to some restrictive exceptions, under customary international law, and there is a specific exclusion of state immunity for state violators of human rights under the *ICCPR*. Applying the usual judicial approach to interpreting international law found in parallel sources, sense and effect are given to both sources where possible. It is open to a court to find the rule in the *ICCPR*, being a later development than the well-recognized customary law principle of state immunity, that overreaches that

---

158 2010 SCC 40 at para 24. And see Francois Larocque, "La *Loi sur l'immunité des États* canadienne et la torture" (2010) 55:1 McGill LJ 81.

159 Above note 26 at paras 37–39.

160 As LeBel J wrote in *Schreiber*, above note 155 at para 1: "Originating from international customary law, the principle of sovereign immunity and the exceptions thereto are incorporated into domestic law by the enactment of the federal [*SIA*] . . . ." See also HL Molot & ML Jewett, "The *State Immunity Act* of Canada" (1982) 20 Can YB Int'l Law 79, and Hugh M Kindred & Phillip M Saunders, eds, *International Law: Chiefly as Interpreted and Applied in Canada*, 7th ed (Toronto: Emond Montgomery, 2006) at 291.

customary international law so far as necessary to respect the *ICCPR* provision. Or a court may note that the *ICCPR* rule is a binding engagement deliberately made by explicit agreement between states parties in full knowledge of their right to immunity under the customary international law and may therefore be taken to be intended to supersede the customary law principle.[161] Both interpretive methods lead to the same result: the specific rule in the treaty may take effect as an exception to the more general customary principle.

On turning back to the interpretation of the *SIA* with this construction of the international law on state immunity in mind, the fact that the *SIA* was enacted to give statutory effect in Canada to state immunity as *practised under customary international law* becomes abundantly significant. The *SIA* was not passed to exclude Canada's treaty obligations. To the contrary, it is supposed to be interpreted, if possible, so as not to confound them; indeed, it is expected to be construed to conform to them. This could be done by reading the *SIA* as applying the international law of foreign state immunity binding on Canada that includes the treaty exception decreed by the *ICCPR*. Subject to the pending judgment of the Supreme Court in the *Kazemi* case, this alternative interpretation of the *SIA* to the stance of the Ontario Court of Appeal in *Bouzari* is available to the victim of extraterritorial human rights abuse before a Canadian court that agrees to take jurisdiction as the forum of last resort.

5) Conclusion

In most civil actions involving extraterritorial features, the central issue is whether Canadian courts are empowered to assert territorial jurisdiction.[162] In human rights cases arising from violations suffered in a foreign state at the hands of foreign agents — that is, wholly extraterritorial claims — the crucial issue coming before the courts is whether they may be obliged to assert adjudicative jurisdiction. International treaties, particularly the *ICCPR*, demand the provision of effective remedies for the

---

161 See *Vienna Convention on the Law of Treaties*, above note 87, art 31(3)(c); *Case Concerning the Delimitation of the Continental Shelf between the United Kingdom and France* (1977), 18 RIAA 3 at paras 47–48; the "Danube Dam Case," *Case Concerning Gabčikovo-Nagymaros Project (Hungary v Slovakia)*, [1997] ICJ Rep 7 at paras 111–13; Martin Dixon, *Textbook on International Law*, 6th ed (Oxford: Oxford University Press, 2007) at 38–39; Kindred & Saunders, *ibid* at 108–9.

162 Compare with Chapter 4.

victims of human rights violations even in the face of foreign sovereign claims to immunity from jurisdiction. While the concept of forum of last resort provides a discretionary foundation in Canadian law for the court to assume jurisdiction in such cases, international legal obligations accepted by Canada may impel the court to exercise it.

C. TRANSNATIONAL DATA PROTECTION

Data protection offers an interesting case study for a number of reasons. In the first place, like gambling (discussed below in Section F of this chapter), there is as of yet no international consensus as to specific norms for data protection.[163] Some jurisdictions, such as the member states of the European Union, have put in place fairly stringent data protection norms, whereas others, like the United States, have thus far largely left data protection to voluntary self-regulation by the private sector.[164] Studying data protection also offers an interesting case study because it reveals how, as a consequence of both globalizing forces and technology, personal information flows readily and unstoppably across national borders. This happens in a number of ways. Consumers may share their personal information with organizations in other countries when they engage in activities such as e-commerce, online gaming, or social networking activities. Personal information may also cross borders when companies in one country outsource the processing of personal information to another. The rapid expansion of cloud computing can also result in a very broad range of personal information being hosted outside the country of residence of the data subject. Although there are also issues around the cross-border sharing of information between national governments, for the purposes of this case study, the focus will remain on private sector activities.

---

163 It is perhaps worth noting that there has been a growing level of discussion regarding the need for developing an international consensus on data protection norms.

164 This too may be changing. Until recently, the United States placed legislative limits on privacy-invasive activity by the private sector only with respect to children's online activities (see *Children's Online Privacy Protection Act*, 15 USC §§ 6501–6506 (2006)). More recently, the US federal government has proposed a consumers' data protection "bill of rights" in order to address growing concerns over digital privacy. See the White House, *Consumer Data Privacy in a Networked World: A Framework for Protecting Privacy and Promoting Innovation in the Global Digital Economy* (23 February 2012), online: www.whitehouse.gov/sites/default/files/email-files/privacy_white_paper.pdf.

Issues of territoriality and extraterritoriality arise in the data protection context in different ways. The following key issues will be considered here: (1) developing norms; (2) investigation and enforcement; (3) normative reach; and (4) setting limits.

1) Developing Norms

In the 1970s, growing concerns regarding data protection, particularly in Western nations, led to the development of a set of guidelines by the Organisation for Economic Co-operation and Development (OECD). The OECD *Guidelines Governing the Protection of Privacy and Transborder Flows of Personal Data*[165] identified eight principles that together established a basic standard for data protection that could be implemented in OECD member states. The guidelines came with no commitment to impose the principles, nor was there any direction as to how they should be given effect. In Canada, these guidelines were used in the development of the federal *Privacy Act*,[166] which governs the federal public sector in its handling of the personal information of Canadians. Provincial governments later developed similar public sector data protection statutes.

It was not until business-to-consumer e-commerce became a phenomenon that there was much impetus to extend data protection norms to the private sector. This was an area that was predominantly governed, if at all, by voluntary codes of conduct, although some specific regulations existed for particular sectors, such as credit reporting agencies and the financial sector.[167] The technological changes that allowed the digitization of information, its automated processing, and its rapid communication over the Internet, gave a dramatic new importance to information. The use of data mining to profile customers and to tailor promotional materials to their profiles similarly increased. Although these activities raised privacy concerns, it was not until consumers began to balk at engaging in the new realm of online commerce that

---

165 OECD, Directorate for Science, Technology and Industry, adopted 23 September 1980, online: OECD www.oecd.org/sti/ieconomy/oecdguidelinesontheprotectionofprivacyandtransborderflowsofpersonaldata.htm. Note that the OECD is currently engaged in a review of these guidelines and discussions regarding whether and how the guidelines should be adapted to the contemporary information technology context.

166 *Privacy Act*, RSC 1985, c P-21, as amended. This Act, of course, was limited in its application to the federal public sector.

167 For example, in the United States, see 12 USC §3401 (2006), and 15 USC §1681 (2006).

national governments sought to take action to address data protection in the private sector. In Canada, the goal of stimulating electronic commerce and the digital economy was a key factor in the enactment of the *Personal Information Protection and Electronic Documents Act* (PIPEDA).[168]

The desire to develop the digital economy was not the only motivating factor for the new Canadian legislation. In 1997, the European Union passed its *Data Protection Directive 95/46/EC*,[169] which established significant minimum standards for data protection and set a firm timeline for member states to implement the standards through legislation. A key element of the Directive was a provision that would prevent the personal data of Europeans from being sent to other countries for processing if the European Union did not find that those other countries had implemented data protection measures that offered an equivalent level of protection. Fearing that this provision might create a "major non-tariff trade barrier with Canada,"[170] the federal government was motivated to enact legislation that could offer comparable levels of protection.

The European approach did not amount to extraterritorial action, but it could be characterized as action that had extraterritorial effect. In essence, the *Data Protection Directive 95/46/EC* was a significant motivating factor in driving the adoption of data protection legislation in Canada. The need to provide a level of protection equivalent to that available under the *Data Protection Directive 95/46/EC* did more than

---

168 *Personal Information Protection and Electronic Documents Act*, SC 2000, c 5 [*PIPEDA*].

169 EC, *Directive 95/46/EC of the European Parliament and of the Council of 24 October 1995 on the Protection of Individuals with regard to the Processing of Personal Data and on the Free Movement of Such Data*, [1995] OJ, L 281/31, art 29(1) [*Data Protection Directive 95/46/EC*].

170 Canada, Task Force on Electronic Commerce, *The Protection of Personal Information: Building Canada's Information Economy and Society* (Ottawa: Industry Canada/Department of Justice, 1998) at 8. In an opinion issued by the Working Party on the Protection of Individuals with regard to the Processing of Personal Data established pursuant to *Data Protection Directive 95/46/EC*, above note 169, art 29(1), *PIPEDA* was assessed in order to determine whether it offered a level of protection that was adequate to permit transborder flow of personal information from European Union countries to Canada. Noting a number of concerns, including the long phase-in period for the legislation and the fact that the Act would apply only to personal information collected, used, and disclosed in the course of "commercial activity," the Working Party recommended that any adequacy finding reflect these limitations. EC, *2002/2/EC: Commission Decision of 20 December 2001 pursuant to Directive 95/46/EC of the European Parliament and of the Council on the Adequate Protection of Personal Data provided by the Canadian Personal Information Protection and Electronic Documents Act (Notified under Document Number C(2001) 4539)*, [2002] OJ, L 002/13.

motivate Canada to enact legislation — it was also influential in shaping the normative content of the new law.

As electronic and mobile commerce mature and expand, and as a vast array of services such as social networking are delivered across national boundaries, not only is the flow of personal information across borders increasing, it is changing in kind and character. For example, mobile devices and even web browsers now regularly communicate location information to online businesses, application developers, website operators, and so on. Internet browsing history is tracked and communicated, and such information is combined with huge amounts of other data to produce increasingly complex data profiles of individuals. The European Union continues to develop new normative instruments to address these advancing technologies.[171] By contrast, *PIPEDA* has yet to be substantially amended, and is no longer regarded as adequate to meet the data protection challenges raised by Big Data.[172] However, the direct normative influence of the European Union may be changing somewhat. The international community seems to be transitioning from unilateral action with extraterritorial effect to much greater dialogue and co-operation at the level of oversight and enforcement, and perhaps a push towards consensus on the development of new international norms.

A final phenomenon to note in relation to the development of privacy and data protection norms is the growing co-operation that has blossomed between data protection commissioners around the world, and the increase in international efforts to harmonize data protection norms. For example, data protection commissioners from countries around the

---

171 For example, see *Directive 2002/58/EC of the European Parliament and of the Council of 12 July 2002 Concerning the Processing of Personal Data and the Protection of Privacy in the Electronic Communications Sector (Directive on Privacy and Electronic Communications)*, [2002] OJ, L 201/37 [ePrivacy Directive 2002/58/EC]. The European Union is also planning to implement new data protection legislation; see "New Draft European Data Protection Regime to Apply Also to All US Companies Processing Data of European Residents" (2 February 2012), online: Law Patent Group www.mlawgroup.de/news/publications/detail.php?we_objectID=227.

172 A bill to reform *PIPEDA*, (Bill C-12, *An Act to amend the Personal Information Protection and Electronic Documents Act*, 1st Sess, 41st Parl, 2011) died on the order paper, and has not been reintroduced. The Privacy Commissioner of Canada has recently called upon the government to enact key reforms to enable her office to meet the challenges of Big Data; see: Office of the Privacy Commissioner of Canada, "The Case for Reforming the *Personal Information Protection and Electronic Documents Act*" (May 2013), online: OPC www.priv.gc.ca/parl/2013/pipeda_r_201305_e.pdf.

world have formed an informal Global Privacy Enforcement Network to facilitate co-operation in cross-border privacy enforcement.[173] There is also an Asia-Pacific Economic Cooperation (APEC) Privacy Enforcement Arrangement, which facilitates information-sharing with a view to aiding enforcement activities. Canada is involved in both initiatives.[174]

2) Investigation and Enforcement

It is frequently the case that a company based in another country engages in activities that involve the collection, use, or disclosure of the personal information of Canadians. Yet because the company is not based in Canada, issues may arise as to the ability of the Privacy Commissioner to exercise her powers under *PIPEDA*. Since personal data flows increasingly easily across national borders, this can raise interesting challenges for data protection, particularly where offshore companies engage in activities that raise data protection issues for Canadians, but are located in countries with lower data protection standards than Canada.

In 2005, the director of a public interest legal clinic based in Ottawa made a complaint against a US-based company. The complainant alleged that the American Internet company was collecting and disclosing the personal information of Canadians by offering to carry out a variety of searches for background information on individuals. The Office of the Privacy Commissioner (OPC) of Canada declined to investigate the matter. The Assistant Privacy Commissioner explained that the US-based company, Abika.com, refused to co-operate with the OPC. As a result, since it had no authority under *PIPEDA* to exercise its investigatory powers in another country, the OPC could not investigate the complaint. In particular, the Assistant Privacy Commissioner noted that "we lack jurisdiction to compel U.S. organizations to produce the evidence necessary for us to conduct the investigation."[175]

The complainant sought judicial review of the Commissioner's decision not to investigate. In *Lawson*,[176] Harrington J of the Federal Court

173 Online: Global Privacy Enforcement Network www.privacyenforcement.net. This network flows from the OECD's 2007 "Recommendation on Cross-Border Cooperation in the Enforcement of Laws Protecting Privacy," online: OECD www.oecd.org/internet/ieconomy/oecdrecommendationoncross-borderco-operationinthe enforcementoflawsprotectingprivacy.htm.

174 "International Initiatives," online: OPC www.priv.gc.ca/au-ans/ii_e.asp.

175 Cited in *Lawson v Accusearch, Inc (cob Abika.com)*, 2007 FC 125 at para 18 [*Lawson*].

176 *Ibid*.

ruled that the Commissioner had erred in failing to "distinguish her power to investigate from the effectiveness of her investigation."[177] He found that the complaint revealed a sufficient connection to Canada on the facts. The personal information relied upon by Abika to prepare its profiles had to have come from Canadian sources, but because Abika would not co-operate with the investigation, it was impossible to determine who those sources were. Nevertheless, it seemed clear that there had been a collection and disclosure of personal information with a sufficient connection to Canada. There was thus subject matter jurisdiction under the Act.

Justice Harrington acknowledged that an investigation of an uncooperative foreign company might prove fruitless. However, the particular scheme of *PIPEDA* required a complainant to complain to the Commissioner, and to receive the Commissioner's report of findings prior to being able to take the matter to Federal Court to seek a court order or monetary damages. The judge noted that it was possible for an individual to seek enforcement of a monetary award against a US-based company; US courts frequently give effect to such judgments. Thus a complainant who could show that her personal information was collected, used, or disclosed improperly by an offshore company might have some hope of recourse. However, the structure of the legislation made it impossible for a complainant to proceed to that stage without the Commissioner's report. Justice Harrington concluded that "*PIPEDA* gives the Privacy Commissioner jurisdiction to investigate complaints relating to the transborder flow of personal information"[178] so long as there is a real and substantial connection to Canada.

The OPC eventually carried out an investigation of the practices of Abika.com. Abika flatly denied that it collected, used, or disclosed the personal information of Canadians without their consent. Although the OPC could not exercise its statutory investigatory powers in the United States, it took advantage of the fact that the US Federal Trade Commission (FTC) had already carried out its own investigation of the practices of Abika. Upon the Commissioner's request, the FTC shared information from its investigation with the OPC. It also obtained documents that were part of the public record relating to the FTC's prosecution of Abika. The combination of shared information and public record docu-

---

177 *Ibid* at para 27. See Donna L Davis, "Tracking Cross-Border Data Flows: A Comment on *Lawson v. Accusearch Inc.*," Case Comment (2007) 6:2 CJLT 119.

178 *Lawson*, above note 175 at para 51.

ments permitted the Commissioner to conclude that Abika had, in fact, collected, used, and disclosed the personal information of Canadians without their consent. Although it made recommendations aimed at correcting Abika's improper practices, these were, of course, non-binding. The complainant did not proceed to Federal Court for an order in damages, the enforcement of which might have been sought in the United States.

The matter reveals some of the limitations of the OPC's jurisdiction to investigate complaints against foreign companies. Like every other arm of the Canadian government, the Commissioner could not investigate in the United States, as this would be an unlawful exercise of investigative jurisdiction. Without the evidence provided by the FTC and the public record flowing from the FTC's own proceedings against Abika, it would have been difficult for the Commissioner to obtain the evidence necessary to reach conclusions on the issues raised in the complaint. Without a co-operative respondent, resolving the matter through voluntary changes in practices is not possible, and while an action in Federal Court might eventually lead to an enforceable order in damages, the amounts awarded by the Federal Court have tended to be too small to make US enforcement a realistic option for a complainant.

The Commissioner has taken the *Lawson* decision to heart and is now clearly prepared to deal with complaints involving companies based outside of Canada. Indeed, the Commissioner's jurisdiction has been expressed in these terms:

> A statute may apply to persons, property or transactions physically located outside the enacting body's jurisdiction, where there is a sufficient link between the matter at issue and the jurisdiction of the enacting body. In such cases, the convergence of linking factors effectively brings the matter within the jurisdiction.[179]

Without explicitly naming it, then, the OPC is exerting jurisdiction based on the extended territoriality principle. That this is being done with regard to the powers exercised under a federal regulatory statute, and outside the criminal realm, underscores the Ontario Court of Appeal's recent remark that this principle, as embodied in the *Libman* test

---

179 *Law School Admission Council Investigation* (29 May 2008), *PIPEDA* Case Summary 2008-389 at para 41, online: OPC www.priv.gc.ca/cf-dc/2008/389_rep_080529_e.cfm [*PIPEDA LSAC* case].

of "real and substantial connection," is fast becoming part of the overall law regarding jurisdiction.[180]

In determining whether to take jurisdiction over a complaint, factors that will be considered by the Commissioner include:

> location in which the activity takes place; location to which profits flow; location of preparatory activities; residency of parties involved; location of contract; location of any potential related proceedings; jurisdiction where promotional efforts primarily targeted; location of content provider; location of host server; location of intermediaries; location of the end user.[181]

Thus, in a case involving the Law School Admissions Council, a US-based non-profit organization that administered law school aptitude tests in the United States and in Canada, the Commissioner found sufficient links to Canada. These included the fact that the organization accepted cheques and money orders in Canadian funds, and that it administered its tests to Canadians in Canada. The collection of the personal information at issue in the complaint — the thumbprints of those who wrote the tests — took place in Canada as well.[182]

In the report of findings in *Privacy Commissioner of Canada v SWIFT*,[183] the OPC found that a Belgian-based co-operative that served financial institutions worldwide was subject to *PIPEDA*. The Commissioner noted that the company "collects personal information from and discloses it to Canadian banks as part of a commercial activity; and charges a fee to the banks for providing this service."[184] She noted as well that fourteen of the organization's shareholders were Canadian and it had a director from a Canadian bank. She concluded that SWIFT had a "significant presence" in Canada,[185] given that it was the SWIFT network that was used for the vast majority of international funds transfers made by Canadian financial

---

180 *R v Stucky*, 2009 ONCA 151, leave to appeal to the SCC granted but later abandoned, [2009] SCCA No 186.

181 *PIPEDA LSAC* case, above note 179 at para 42.

182 *Ibid.*

183 *Privacy Commissioner of Canada v SWIFT*, Report of Findings (2 April 2007), online: OPC www.priv.gc.ca/cf-dc/2007/swift_rep_070402_e.asp; see also *Responsibility of Canadian Financial Institutions in SWIFT's Disclosure of Personal Information to US Authorities Considered* (archived); *PIPEDA* Case Summary #365, [2007] CPCSF No 1 [*PIPEDA SWIFT* case].

184 *Ibid* at para 41.

185 *Ibid.*

institutions. She noted as well that "[s]imply because an organization might operate in two or more jurisdictions will not alleviate it of its obligations to comply with Canadian law."[186] In another case, the OPC found that it had jurisdiction over an international airline company because the complainant was a Canadian resident, the company offered services within Canada (and had employees located at several Canadian airports), it had a Canadian version of its website in order to serve Canadian customers, it offered regular flights to and from Canada, and it needed to collect personal information from Canadian passengers in order to offer them services.[187]

In spite of the Commissioner's new willingness to pursue complaints against foreign-based companies, the *Abika* case highlights the limits of such investigations. It also demonstrates how interjurisdictional co-operation can be essential to deriving results from such actions. In cases where there is a co-operative respondent, some positive results may be possible. In the *PIPEDA LSAC* case, for example, the company agreed to change its practices. Further, as a result of the report of findings in a complaint made against Facebook, a California-based company voluntarily changed some of its privacy practices.[188] In both cases, the companies did substantial, open, and high-profile business in Canada. This likely increased their incentive to co-operate with the OPC and to seek to resolve any privacy compliance concerns.

3) Normative Reach

In the section above, we considered how the EU's *Data Protection Directive 95/46/EC* created a strong incentive for its trading partners not just to enact data protection legislation, but to meet certain basic standards in doing so. This is an example of a legislative body acting with extraterritorial effect. In this section, we consider a somewhat different issue: the *normative reach* of enacted provisions. Thus, instead of looking at a country or region's ability to push other countries to enact laws, we consider here how a country's enacted laws may have broad effects on

186 *Ibid* at para 54.

187 *Airline Must Ensure Policies Comply with Canadian Privacy Law* (15 April 2011), *PIPEDA* Case Summary 2011-002 at para 5, online: OPC www.priv.gc.ca/cf-dc/2011/2011_002_0415_e.asp.

188 This complaint and its outcomes are discussed in greater detail in Section C(3), below in this chapter.

behaviour both within and outside its jurisdictional boundaries. We offer two examples here. The first relates to the impact of EU norms on the operations of the Internet search giant Google. The second considers the impact of actions by Canada's Privacy Commissioner on the privacy practices of the social networking corporation Facebook.

The European Union has remained at the forefront of the development of data protection norms, and it is interesting to note the extent to which these norms shape the behaviour of countries located outside of the EU's borders simply by virtue of their need to operate seamlessly on the Internet across multiple jurisdictions. In 2007, concerns grew among EU data protection regulators that Google's retention of information about the search data relating to the users of its Internet search engine violated EU data protection norms. Relying on *Data Protection Directive 95/46/EC*, as well as the *ePrivacy Directive 2002/58/EC*, as providing the legal basis for its actions,[189] the Article 29 Working Party notified Google that its retention of user search data needed justification.[190] The Working Party was not satisfied with Google's position that it would make search data anonymous after a period of between eighteen and twenty-four months. Instead, it took the position that Google should destroy the data after six months had passed from its initial collection.[191] Google took the position that it was not subject to regulation by the European Union as the information is managed in the United States.[192] Nevertheless, Google eventually decided that it would make anonymous the Internet Protocol Addresses linked to searches after nine months had passed.[193] By 2010, the Working Party remained dissatisfied: in a press release, it stated "Google, Yahoo! and Microsoft['s] [. . .] methods of making users' search data anonymous still do not comply with the European Union's *Data Protection Directive 95/46/EC*."[194] Although Goo-

---

189 "Data Protection Watchdogs' Letter to Google Goes Public" (30 May 2007), online: Out-Law.com www.out-law.com/page-8099.

190 Majia Palmer, "EU Probes Google Grip on Data" (24 May 2007), online: FT.com www.ft.com/cms/s/2/dc89ec96-0a24-11dc-93ae-000b5df10621.html#axzz1iolHjqUC.

191 "Google Says EU Data Laws Do Not Catch Its Search Logs" (9 September 2008), online: Out-Law.com www.out-law.com/page-9411.

192 *Ibid.*

193 *Ibid.*

194 EC, Article 29 Data Protection Working Party, Press Release, "EU Data Protection Group Says Google, Microsoft and Yahoo! Do Not Comply with Data Protection Rules" (26 May 2010), online: EC http://ec.europa.eu/justice/policies/privacy/news/docs/pr_26_05_10_en.pdf at 1. Note that in late 2012, the Working Party filed a com-

gle may not have complied fully with the Working Party's wishes, the example illustrates how one regulator can attempt to impose changes that affect the global operations of a multinational company. This is a phenomenon most likely to occur with companies that offer Internet-based services at a global level.

Another example is found in the case of Facebook. On 30 May 2008, the Canadian Internet Policy and Public Interest Clinic (CIPPIC) filed a complaint with Canada's OPC against the social networking company Facebook Inc. The complaint maintained that a number of Facebook's practices were not compliant with *PIPEDA*. The complaint included allegations relating to Facebook's use of default privacy settings, the collection of certain types of personal information, the granting of access to personal information to providers of third-party applications, and to difficulties encountered in deactivating or deleting accounts. The greatest concern overall was with Facebook's compliance with its obligations under *PIPEDA* to give appropriate notice and to obtain its users' consent in an appropriate manner.

Although Facebook is a California-based company that operates worldwide and that boasts more than 845 million users,[195] it did not object to the Commissioner's jurisdiction, and it co-operated with the OPC's investigation. The OPC issued a detailed report in 2009,[196] which found that some, although not all, of the complainant's allegations were well-founded. Of the group of well-founded issues, Facebook took steps during the course of the investigation to rectify a number of these concerns. These were ruled "well-founded but resolved" by the OPC. A number of concerns were considered well-founded and not resolved by the time the investigation report was issued.[197] This included concerns

---

plaint against Google regarding its data retention practices. See Letter from Article 29 Data Protection Working Party to Mr. Page (16 October 2012), online: EC http://ec.europa.eu/justice/data-protection/article-29/documentation/other-document/files/2012/20121016_letter_to_google_en.pdf.

195 Emil Protalinski, "Facebook Has over 845 Million Users" (1 February 2012), online: ZDNet www.zdnet.com/blog/facebook/facebook-has-over-845-million-users/8332.

196 Elizabeth Denham, "Report of Findings into the Complaint Filed by the Canadian Internet Policy and Public Interest Clinic (CIPPIC) against Facebook Inc under the *Personal Information Protection and Electronic Documents Act*"(16 July 2009), *PIPEDA* Case Summary 2009-008, online: OCP www.priv.gc.ca/cf-dc/2009/2009_008_0716_e.cfm.

197 The OPC had issued a preliminary report of findings to both parties on 27 March 2009. This report was the subject of subsequent meetings between Facebook and the OPC, and did lead to some issues being resolved to the satisfaction of both parties.

raised about third-party applications, practices around account deactivation and deletion, dealing with accounts of deceased users, and practices regarding the personal information of non-users of Facebook. With respect to third-party applications, the Commissioner's report of findings determined that Facebook did not have adequate safeguards in place to prevent unauthorized access by application developers to the personal information of users, nor did it do enough to make sure that meaningful consent was obtained from individuals for the disclosure of their personal information to application developers.

After issuing its final report and identifying the unresolved and well-founded issues, the OPC gave Facebook thirty days to comply with the recommendations. It explicitly indicated that it would not rule out taking the matter to Federal Court if Facebook did not take satisfactory steps. It is not clear what remedy would have been sought in Federal Court, and whether it would have ultimately been enforceable against Facebook in California. The matter became moot after Facebook committed to resolving the outstanding privacy concerns within a one-year period. The OPC undertook to supervise Facebook's progress in implementing the recommendations. The agreement led to the conclusion that the complaint was resolved, and the investigation was concluded. On 22 September 2010, the OPC announced that it had reviewed the changes implemented by Facebook, and had found the issues to be resolved to its satisfaction.

The end result of this process was that a number of Facebook's privacy practices were altered by Facebook following a complaint brought under Canada's data protection legislation, and pursuant to an investigation by Canada's federal Privacy Commissioner. Yet the resolution of these complaints affected not only those Canadians who used Facebook's site; the changes applied across the board to all users regardless of geographic location.[198]

4) Setting Limits

A number of issues have arisen around the outsourcing of personal information for offshore processing or, as noted above, the use of cloud

198 "Canada Approves Facebook Changes" (22 September 2010), online: BBC News www.bbc.co.uk/news/technology-11392454. Troy McMullen, "Canada's Privacy Commissioner Probes Facebook over Users Private Information" (29 January 2010), online: ABC News http://abcnews.go.com/Technology/canada-investigates-facebook-privacy-settings/story?id=9691133#.T3sUuXLcitw.

computing facilities based in other countries. A particular concern in such contexts is the vulnerability of this personal information to access by law enforcement or other government officials in the country to which the data is outsourced. In general, complaints against Canadian companies under *PIPEDA* for outsourcing activities have not been considered well-founded. In the first place, the Privacy Commissioner has observed that "the *Act* cannot force Canadian companies to stop outsourcing to foreign-based service providers."[199] Once information has been outsourced, the position of the Privacy Commissioner is that *PIPEDA* "cannot prevent foreign authorities from lawfully accessing the personal information of Canadians held by organizations within their jurisdiction."[200] She has also noted that "[m]ulti-national organizations must comply with the laws of those jurisdictions in which they operate."[201] Even though *PIPEDA* requires organizations that outsource personal information to have in place a contract with the third-party processor that provides for adequate safeguards for the information, such a contract cannot be expected to override the laws of the third-party's country.[202] Further, the Assistant Privacy Commissioner has noted that data subjects faced comparable risks in Canada, as a number of Canadian laws permit access to personal information by law enforcement and national security authorities. However, an organization that outsources data for processing "should notify its customers that information may be available to the U.S. government or its agencies under a lawful order made in that country."[203]

In the *PIPEDA LSAC* case,[204] the Assistant Privacy Commissioner considered a complaint against an organization that outsourced its e-mail operations to a US-based company. The complainants were concerned

---

199 *PIPEDA SWIFT* case, above note 183 at para 40.

200 *Ibid.* See also *Bank's Notification to Customers Triggers* PATRIOT Act *Concerns* (19 October 2005), *PIPEDA* Case Summary 2005-313, online: OPC www.priv.gc.ca/cf-dc/2005/313_20051019_e.asp [*PIPEDA* Banking Group case]; *Outsourcing of canada.com E-mail Services to US-based Firm Raises Questions for Subscribers* (7 August 2008), *PIPEDA* Case Summary 2008-394, online: OPC www.priv.gc.ca/cf-dc/2008/394_20080807_e.asp [*PIPEDA* canada.com case].

201 *PIPEDA SWIFT* case, above note 183 at para 48.

202 *PIPEDA* Banking Group case, above note 200; *PIPEDA* canada.com case, above note 200.

203 *PIPEDA* Banking Group case, above note 200. See also *PIPEDA SWIFT* case, above note 183.

204 Above note 179.

that this would make their e-mails subject to access by US government authorities. The situation considered in this complaint is similar to what might arise in a cloud computing context.[205] The Assistant Commissioner simply applied the *PIPEDA* norms to the facts of the case. She found that customer consent to the outsourcing had been appropriately obtained, and clear notice was given that the information stored in the United States might be accessed by government authorities. She concluded that the contract between the Canadian and US-based company contained all of the necessary provisions regarding security and confidentiality of personal information.

Not all movement of data from Canada to the United States will occur in the context of outsourcing. In *DataTreasury Corp v Royal Bank of Canada*,[206] the personal information of Canadians was sent to the United States as part of a complex piece of litigation. In the course of proceedings, Prothonotary Aalto considered a motion to settle the terms of an order sought to protect confidential information relating to patented technology, as well as other confidential business information, which included personal information of clients. Only one paragraph of the order was in dispute between the parties. This paragraph contained a "Canada only" clause designed to prevent certain documents from being sent to the United States during the course of litigation between the parties. As DataTreasury was a US-based corporation, they argued that such a clause would unduly prejudice them, as their "central document database, its document management consultants, United States counsel, witnesses and experts"[207] were all based in the United States. On the other side of the issue was a group of Canadian banks (the Banking Group) which expressed concerns that the sending of certain documents to the United States would expose them to the application of the *USA PATRIOT Act*,[208] which would then raise difficulties for their compliance with *PIPEDA*. Other concerns raised included the potential harm to the security of the Canadian banking system and the absence of an implied undertaking rule in the United States.

205 See, for example OPC, "OPC Guidance Documents: Cloud Computing for Small and Medium-sized Enterprises: Privacy Responsibilities and Considerations" (14 June 2012), online: OPC www.priv.gc.ca/information/pub/gd_cc_201206_e.asp.

206 2008 FC 955 [*DataTreasury*].

207 *Ibid* at para 3.

208 Pub L No 107-56, 115 Stat 272 (2001) [*PATRIOT Act*]. Among other things, the *PATRIOT Act* gives the US government authority to demand information in the hands of private sector companies in the United States.

The Banking Group's *PIPEDA*-related objections were based on the possibility that some documents might be required to be sent to the United States during the discovery process, and that these documents might contain personal information about identifiable individuals. In order to send this material in a *PIPEDA*-compliant manner, the Banking Group argued, it would need to get consent from affected clients, a practice that would be costly, and that would raise public concerns that the banks were shipping personal information south of the Canadian border. The result, it was argued, would be an increase in complaints to the OPC, and harm to the goodwill of the companies in the Banking Group.

Prothonotary Aalto found that the Banking Group had legitimate concerns. He noted: "Once documents are sent beyond the borders of Canada to the United States they may be subject to production in ways not anticipated and which may be beyond the control of DataTreasury."[209] He described the "Canada only" clause as a "laudable attempt" to respond to concerns about disclosure of third-party personal information. However, he also noted that the "Canada only" clause, which would require judicial scrutiny of all contested information being sent south of the border, would, in complex litigation such as that at issue between the parties, lead to "endless motions and mire these proceedings in endless squabbling and interlocutory proceedings."[210]

Aalto observed that the *PIPEDA* Banking Group case[211] had found that complaints against CIBC for sending customer data to the United States for processing and storage were not well-founded. He also noted that other members of the Banking Group regularly sent customer data to the United States for processing. He found that the concerns of the Banking Group in this case were speculative, and not related to any particular documents containing personal information. Aalto also noted that DataTreasury had indicated that they were not interested in customer personal information for the purposes of this litigation, and that any such information could be redacted from documents sent to the United States. Finally, Aalto noted that section 7(3) of *PIPEDA* permitted an organization to disclose personal information without the knowledge or consent of the individual to whom it relates where it is:

---

209 *DataTreasury*, above note 206 at para 10.

210 *Ibid*.

211 Above note 200.

> . . . required to comply with a subpoena or warrant issued or an order made by a court, person or body with jurisdiction to compel production of information, or to comply with rules of court relating to the production of records . . . .[212]

In this case, he noted that the documents at issue were ones that would need to be produced to comply with the Federal Court rules relating to the production of documents in the course of litigation.

Aalto ultimately ruled against the inclusion of a "Canada only" clause. Instead, he ordered that any documents produced would be subject to a protective order, and that "personal information of customers of the Banking Group need not be produced and may be redacted."[213]

The *DataTreasury* case illustrates how domestic courts may set parameters for the flow of personal information across borders. Neither in this case, nor in the cases of cloud computing and outsourcing of data processing, does the law prohibit such data flows; rather, it imposes conditions on the organization that is acting as the data custodian in order to ensure that steps are taken to offer a level of protection to personal data that is comparable to what is required by Canadian law. Yet these protections cannot include imposing limits on the power of foreign states to access personal data in the possession or control of organizations operating within their own borders.

5) Conclusion

This case study has considered how data protection law in Canada has evolved in a context in which dramatic technological changes have resulted in the kinds of transborder flows of information for which the law is not ideally adapted. Canada's *PIPEDA* arose out of concerns over the extraterritorial impact of new data protection norms in the European Union. The statute itself applies to organizations engaged in commercial activity, and gives the OPC the power to investigate complaints brought by the general public regarding the data protection practices of such organizations. Increasingly, however, the flow of data across borders, and the ready engagement of Canadians in electronic commerce, social networking, and other transboundary activities, has presented challenges for the successful investigation of complaints and for the enforcement

---

212 Above note 206 at para 20.

213 *DataTreasury*, above note 206 at para 25.

of the legislative norms. The OPC has sought to minimize deficiencies in the legislation through co-operation with comparable agencies in other countries. It has also brought complaints against offshore companies. In a number of these cases, in spite of the lack of any clear avenues for enforcement, the OPC has been successful in reaching acceptable compromises with the targeted company. At the same time, the OPC has made it clear that it has no ability to protect the personal information of Canadians in the hands of foreign companies when it comes to foreign states' legislation that provides for access to this information.

D. INTERNATIONAL TERRORISM

In this chapter's first case study, we explored how a push towards exercises of extraterritorial jurisdiction—whether coming from states themselves or from supranational courts or other decision-making bodies—can have a corrosive or fragmenting effect upon international law norms. Sharp disagreements among international actors can produce conflicting findings among domestic courts when they are called upon to determine whether particular exercises of extraterritorial jurisdiction are lawful. Since court decisions are themselves part of the body of state practice, the fragmenting effect is amplified.

This brief case study will make the point that, in some situations, the opposite can occur: a push towards particular exercises of extraterritorial jurisdiction can cause a previously fragmented normative landscape to solidify, and result in (or at least move strongly towards) the crystallization of jurisdictional rules in customary international law. In particular, this case study will argue that the 9/11 terrorist attacks on the United States may have resulted in new, expansive, and permissive customary international law rules regarding the exercise of extraterritorial jurisdiction over acts of terrorism, or something very close thereto.

1) Setting the Scene: Anti-Terrorism Law before and after 9/11

Despite continued and sustained disagreement on an actual, working definition of the crime of "terrorism,"[214] international efforts to suppress

214 There is an enormous literature on this issue, in both law and criminology circles. For review of the relevant arguments, see George P Fletcher, "The Indefinable Concept of Terrorism" (2006) 4:5 Journal of International Criminal Justice 894, and other articles in the same issue; and see Reuven Young, "Defining Terrorism: The

this activity have been under way since early in the twentieth century.[215] Since the 1970s, there has been a reasonably constant and quite successful effort at concluding suppression conventions that target various specific acts of international terrorism. There are over a dozen of these treaties, most of which were sponsored or brokered by the United Nations,[216] and the more prominent ones will be familiar to many readers: the *Convention for the Suppression of Unlawful Seizure of Aircraft*,[217] the *International Convention against the Taking of Hostages*,[218] the *International Convention for the Suppression of Terrorist Bombings*,[219] the *International Convention for the Suppression of the Financing of Terrorism*,[220] and the *International Convention for the Suppression of Acts of Nuclear Terrorism*.[221]

As with all of the major crime suppression treaties,[222] each of these is designed to deal with crimes that have a transnational nature, and one of the major tools is the inclusion of broad grounds of extraterritorial jurisdiction. The goal is to oblige state parties to the treaties to accept or make greater use of extraterritorial jurisdiction than they might normally be comfortable with or would be available within their respective domestic laws. The relevant clauses in each treaty can be framed in mandatory or permissive terms, or some combination of both. For example, the *Terrorist Bombings Convention requires* states to exercise

---

Evolution of Terrorism as a Legal Concept in International Law and its Influence on Definitions in Domestic Legislation" (2006) 29:1 BC Int'l & Comp L Rev 23. An ad hoc committee established by the United Nations has been working on the issue (in the context of developing a comprehensive terrorism treaty) since 1996, and has recently produced a draft. The committee's work can be traced online: UN www.un.org/law/terrorism/index.html.

215 An early effort is the League of Nations' 1937 *Convention for the Prevention and Punishment of Terrorism*, 19 League of Nations OJ 23 (1938), which was ratified by only a small number of states.

216 See Andrea Gioia, "The UN Conventions on the Prevention and Suppression of International Terrorism" in Giuseppe Nesi, ed, *International Cooperation in Counter-terrorism* (Aldershot, UK: Ashgate, 2006) 3.

217 16 December 1970, 860 UNTS 105, Can TS 1972 No 23.

218 17 December 1979, 1316 UNTS 205, Can TS 1986 No 45.

219 15 December 1997, Can TS 2002 No 8, 37 ILM 249 (1997) [*Terrorist Bombings Convention*].

220 9 December 1999, Can TS 2002 No 9 [*Terrorist Financing Convention*].

221 GA Res 51/210, UNGA 59th Sess, UN Doc A/Res/59/290 (2005) [*Nuclear Terrorism Convention*].

222 For detailed consideration see Neil Boister, *An Introduction to Transnational Criminal Law* (Oxford: Oxford University Press, 2012) and Currie, *Criminal Law*, above note 22, ch 7.

jurisdiction over their flagged ships and registered aircraft (on a sort of "extended territoriality" theory) and over their nationals (the nationality principle), and *permits* the use of the passive personality and protective principles, the latter in both general and explicitly robust provisions targeting crimes against embassies or protected officials.[223] Note that the permissive clauses regarding the more controversial principles of extraterritoriality means that state parties to a treaty are not required to use them if they do not wish to — for example, if a particular ground of jurisdiction is incompatible with a state's legal order. However, by signing the treaty, such states have consented to and cannot protest situations where other state parties are using these principles of jurisdiction, at least regarding the particular crime which is the subject of the treaty.[224]

These grounds typically work hand-in-hand with two other mechanisms: (1) the requirement for a state with custody over an alleged perpetrator to prosecute that individual, even if the state has none of the usual links to the crime or the individual, often referred to as "conditional universal jurisdiction";[225] and (2) an "extradite or prosecute" (*aut dedare aut judicare*) obligation, which obliges states that have (or can obtain) custody over a person accused of the treaty crime to either prosecute or, if the state cannot or prefers not to prosecute,[226] then to extradite the individual to a state that is willing to do so. This kind of scheme makes for a potentially expansive jurisdictional scope, and is designed to prevent or obstruct perpetrators from finding safe haven and to "draw the jurisdictional net as tightly as possible around the offender."[227]

While each of these treaties deals with only a particular kind of terrorist crime, they were nonetheless quite heavily subscribed to even prior to the 9/11 terrorist attacks. In the wake of those attacks, however, the situation began to change quite dramatically, starting with an intense program of anti-terrorism work by the UN Security Council and the General As-

---

223 *Terrorist Bombings Convention*, above note 219, arts 6(2)(a)–(e).

224 Some treaties contain a clause permitting states to exercise any principle of jurisdiction consistent with their national laws, for example, art 6(5) of the *Terrorist Bombings Convention*, *ibid*, which has the potential to create a limited application for some very expansive uses of extraterritorial jurisdiction.

225 See Chapter 3, Section A(3)(a)(iii).

226 A state might "prefer not to" on the basis that another state would be a better location for the prosecution for any number of reasons, including the foreign state having a stronger jurisdictional claim.

227 Currie, *Criminal Law*, above note 22 at 309.

sembly.[228] The Security Council, at the urging of the United States, became convinced that the now ramped-up terrorist threat was best combated by way of terrorist financing laws. In *Resolution 1373*, the Council imposed upon all UN member states a regime very similar to, but potentially more expansive than, the substantive provisions of the *Terrorist Financing Convention* — essentially, the entire world. While the Council did not impose extraterritorial jurisdiction requirements explicitly, the language of *Resolution 1373* is replete with requirements that states "[d]eny safe haven" to terrorists and their supporters,[229] "[e]nsure that" terrorist supporters "[are] brought to justice,"[230] and "[a]fford one another the greatest measure of assistance in connection with criminal investigations or criminal proceedings relating to the financing or support of terrorist acts . . . ."[231] As well, states were called upon to become parties to "relevant international conventions and protocols," including the *Terrorist Financing Convention*.[232] Similarly, in its 2006 *United Nations Global Counter-Terrorism Strategy*,[233] the UN General Assembly urged all UN member states to become parties, and to implement, the anti-terrorism treaties.[234] All of these exhortations may well have had the desired effect, as all of the major anti-terrorism treaties are even better subscribed than they had been previously. For example, the *Convention for the Suppression of Unlawful Seizure of Aircraft* currently has 185 parties and the *Terrorist Bombings Convention* has 164 parties, while the *Terrorist Financing Convention* has 179 parties.[235]

What is even more interesting here is the pattern of exercising unilateral (non treaty-based) extraterritorial jurisdiction over terrorist crimes that emerged from the practice of a large number of states that considered themselves participants in the "Global War on Terror." Of these states, unsurprisingly, the United States had the least amount of work to do in formulating a robust regime of extraterritorial juris-

---

228 For a detailed account, see Kent Roach, *The 9/11 Effect: Comparative Counter-Terrorism* (New York: Cambridge University Press, 2011) ch 2 [Roach, *The 9/11 Effect*].

229 *Resolution 1373 (2001)*, SC Res, UNSC, 4385th Mtg, UN Doc S/RES/1373 (2001), Operative paragraph 2(c) [*Resolution 1373*].

230 *Ibid*, Operative paragraph 2(e).

231 *Ibid*, Operative paragraph 2(f).

232 *Ibid*, Operative paragraph 3(d).

233 GA Res 60/288, UNGA, 60th Sess, UN Doc A/RES/60/288 (2006).

234 *Ibid*, Annex at para 2(a).

235 Ratification status (including a timeline indicating dates of ratification by parties) available online: United Nations Office on Drugs and Crime www.unodc.org/tldb/universal_instruments_NEW.html.

diction over terrorism, given that it had already taken significant steps in this direction.[236] However, the US *PATRIOT Act*[237] and legislation that has followed it provides for extraterritorial jurisdiction over a number of criminal acts that are not covered by any of the terrorism suppression treaties. For example, section 808 of the Act extended extraterritorial jurisdiction over a large number of "ordinary" criminal offences committed as part of the "federal crime of terrorism," such as "homicides and other violence against United States nationals occurring outside of the United States."[238] Nor did the United States hesitate to extend both judicial jurisdiction (Guantanamo Bay)[239] and investigative jurisdiction (wiretaps upon persons outside the US)[240] extraterritorially.[241]

Of concern here is Canada's response, which was to enact a scheme that has been referred to elsewhere as "The 'New' Terrorism."[242] After the 9/11 terrorist attacks, the federal government introduced the omnibus *Anti-terrorism Act*,[243] which made amendments to a wide range of legislation, notably the *Criminal Code*,[244] the *Canada Evidence Act*,[245] the *Official Secrets Act* (which became the *Security of Information Act*[246]), the *United Nations Act*,[247] and the *Proceeds of Crime (Money Laundering) Act*

---

236 See Christopher Blakesley, *Terrorism and Anti-Terrorism: A Normative and Practical Assessment* (Ardsley, NY: Transnational Publishers, 2006) ch 4; Tyler Raimo, "Winning at the Expense of Law: The Ramifications of Expanding Counter-Terrorism Law Enforcement Jurisdiction Overseas" (1999) 14:5 Am U Int'l L Rev 1473. And see The White House, *Presidential Decision Directive/NSC 39: US Policy on Counterterrorism* PDD/NSC39 (21 June 1995): "We shall vigorously apply extraterritorial statutes to counter acts of terrorism and apprehend terrorists outside of the United States," online: Federation of American Scientists www.fas.org/irp/offdocs/pdd39.htm.

237 Above note 208.

238 *Ibid*, § 808, s 2.

239 Specifically, the *Military Commissions Act*, 10 USC 948a (2006).

240 Specifically, the *FISA Amendments Act of 2008*, Pub L No 110-261, 122 Stat 2477.

241 And see John T Parry, "Terrorism and the New Criminal Process" (2007) 15:3 Wm & Mary Bill Rts J 765.

242 Currie, *Criminal Law* above note 22 at 367, the ungrammatical label being intended to mean that Canada's new laws had introduced new terrorist crimes. The description here of the revamped anti-terrorism jurisdictional provisions is largely drawn from Currie, *ibid* at 367–69. It may be worth noting that in that book, the author expressed some doubt as to the proposition being made in this case study, but times have changed.

243 SC 2001, c 41.

244 RSC 1985, c C-46 [*Criminal Code*].

245 RSC 1985, c C-5.

246 RSC 1985, c O-5.

247 RSC 1985, c U-2.

(which became the *Proceeds of Crime (Money Laundering) and Terrorist Financing Act*[248]). This new anti-terrorism regime in Canada is best characterized as a combination of criminal law, investigative measures and powers, and other legislative mechanisms which are geared towards promoting national security. Most notable for our purpose here are the amendments to the *Criminal Code*, which provided for new offences and an expanded extraterritorial jurisdiction.

Section 83.01(1) provides the relevant definitions for the new Part II.1 of the *Criminal Code*, entitled "Terrorism," and central is the definition of "terrorist activity." Section (a) of that definition refers to the offences covered under the terrorism suppression conventions that Canada has ratified,[249] extraterritorial jurisdiction for which is provided under section 7. Section (b) then extends the definition of "terrorist activity" to include acts, whether inside or outside of Canada, intentionally causing serious threats to life or safety, substantial property damage, and serious interference with essential services, when those acts are meant to intimidate the public or a government and are committed for a political, religious or ideological cause.[250] The rest of Part II.1 includes a number of other, specific terrorism offences, including provision, use, or possession of property for terrorist purposes (ss 83.03–.04); participation in the activity of a terrorist group (s 83.18); facilitating terrorist activity (s 83.19); committing an indictable offence for the benefit of or in association with a terrorist group (s 83.2); instructing to carry out an activity for a terrorist group (s 83.21); instructing to carry out a terrorist activity (s 83.22); and harbouring or concealing terrorists (s 83.23).

In terms of extraterritorial jurisdiction, the amended section 7(3.74) of the *Criminal Code* extends jurisdiction not over "terrorist activity" but over "terrorism offences" committed outside Canada, on the bases of nationality, stateless resident, or permanent residency (the latter only if found in Canada after the offence). "Terrorism offence" is defined in section 2 of the *Criminal Code*: it includes "terrorist activity," but also includes all of the specific offences in Part II.1 of the *Criminal Code* and indictable offences committed for the benefit of a terrorist group. However, section

248 SC 2000, c 17.

249 Including, by way of a recent amendment (in the *Nuclear Terrorism Act*, SC 2013, c 13), the *Nuclear Terrorism Convention*, above note 221, which Canada has signed but not yet ratified.

250 The latter motive requirement was recently upheld as being constitutional, rejecting constitutional challenges that had found some traction in the lower courts; see *R v Khawaja*, 2012 SCC 69.

7(3.74) specifically excludes from this extension of jurisdiction offences under section 83.02 (financing of terrorism) and those listed in section 83.01(1)(a); that is, it excludes the terrorist activity explicitly covered by treaties and implemented by other *Criminal Code* provisions.

Section 7(3.75) gives Canada jurisdiction over "terrorist activity committed outside Canada," on the bases of passive personality and protective authority, as well as when the act was intended to compel the government of Canada or a province. The section is limited to conduct that is an indictable offence and is a "terrorist activity" as defined in section 83.01(1)(b); that is, it too deals with terrorism offences *other than* those specifically covered by a treaty.

While this is a complex jurisdictional formula, the net result is this: a set of treaty-based terrorist offences for which extraterritorial jurisdiction is provided in strict accordance with the provisions of the treaties themselves; and on the other hand, a set of Canadian-designed "terrorism offences" for which extraterritorial jurisdiction is also asserted without any specific international law basis. The latter is completely out of keeping with Canada's usual practice[251] of asserting extraterritorial jurisdiction only in accordance with treaty obligations to do so, or in accordance with applicable customary international law principles. To be sure, the drafting reflects consideration of the international law implications of these assertions of jurisdiction. The "new terrorism" jurisdiction is, generally speaking, extended over offences that have some connection to Canada — to wit, there is no assertion of custodial universal jurisdiction since there would be no *aut dedare aut judicare* obligation to back it. Accordingly, jurisdiction over extraterritorial "terrorist activity," for example, is limited to attacks on Canadian nationals or other interests.

That said, what does characterize Canada's new regime is that a large number of crimes are brought within the rubric of "terrorist activity" or "terrorist offence," and a much expanded jurisdictional "net" for alleged terrorists. However, this development is not just a reflection of American practice, but can be observed in the post-9/11 laws of a number of states, including Australia,[252] India,[253] New Zealand,[254] the Phil-

251 Discussed in Chapter 6.

252 *Criminal Code Amendment (Terrorism) Act 2003* (Cth); *Security Legislation Amendment (Terrorism Act) 2002* (Cth); *Anti-Terrorism Act (No 2) 2005* (Cth).

253 *Prevention of Terrorism Act, 2002*; *Unlawful Activities (Prevention) Amendment Ordinance, 2004*.

254 *Terrorism Suppression Act 2002* (NZ) 2002/34, as amended.

ippines,[255] Russia,[256] and the United Kingdom.[257] A close look at each of these national law regimes shows approaches very similar to Canada's, in that extraterritorial jurisdiction is extended over a range of crimes far beyond anything provided for in the terrorism suppression conventions.

2) Implications

Detailed research would doubtless reveal various differences among states in terms of approach and how much restraint or lack thereof is shown in particular national laws.[258] However, even on this lighter review of current developments, we are struck by three features: first, that there has been a significant increase in the amount and types of extraterritorial jurisdiction exerted over terrorist crimes and criminals in the years since the 9/11 terrorist attacks; second, that the vast majority of this jurisdictional extension was done unilaterally, or at most, by loose agreement that was not formalized via treaty; and third, that there does not appear to have been any significant amount of protest by states to the more robust use of extraterritorial jurisdiction by other states. Indeed, the primary dialogue in counter-terrorism circles has been on topics like rationalizing the distinction between intelligence and evidence,[259] and whether human rights are being sufficiently protected in the rush to ramp up anti-terrorism measures.[260] In terms of extending legislative jurisdiction over terrorism crimes, at least, states seem to be using the same playbook or else sitting quietly on the sidelines. While more exhaustive investigation of state practice would have to be undertaken to confirm this, there appears to be a strong case that there is a

---

255 *Human Security Act of 2007*.

256 *Federal Law on Counteraction against Terrorism*, No 35-FZ of 6 March 2006. See Seth T Bridge, "Russia's New Counteracting Terrorism Law: The Legal Implications of Pursuing Terrorists beyond the Borders of the Russian Federation" (2009) 3:1 Colum J E Eur L 1.

257 *Anti-Terrorism, Crime and Security Act 2001* (UK), c 24; *Terrorism Act 2006* (UK), c 11; *Counter-Terrorism Act 2008* (UK), c 28. See Roach, *The 9/11 Effect*, above note 228, ch 5.

258 The interested reader might refer to Victor V Ramraj et al, eds, *Global Anti-Terrorism Law and Policy*, 2d ed (Cambridge: Cambridge University Press, 2012).

259 See Commission of Inquiry into the Investigation of the Bombing of Air India Flight 182, *Research Studies: The Unique Challenges of Terrorism Prosecutions: Towards a Workable Relation between Intelligence and Evidence* by Kent Roach, vol 4 (Ottawa: Government of Canada, 2010).

260 See, generally, Roza Pati, *Due Process and International Terrorism: An International Legal Analysis* (Leiden: Martinus Nijhoff, 2009).

permissive customary international law norm allowing broad extraterritorial legislative jurisdiction over terrorist crimes in a variety of circumstances. That this developed in the face of a lack of any generally agreed upon definition of terrorism is even more remarkable.

As a concluding thought, this development might be more ominous than it appears, particularly on the enforcement jurisdiction side of the ledger. Consider, most drastically, two targeted extraterritorial assassinations of prominent terrorists made by the US government over the last few years:[261] Osama bin Laden, famously killed in Pakistan by a US Navy tactical team; and Anwar al-Awlaki, killed in Yemen by a drone strike.[262] Both actions appear to violate the ban on the extraterritorial exercise of enforcement jurisdiction, as there is no official indication[263] that either Pakistan or Yemen authorized the US incursions into their respective territories. However, international reaction to both extrajudicial killings was not all negative; indeed, the bin Laden assassination was lauded by foreign ministers the world over as a salutary development. Of course, the difficulty with failure by states to protest violations of customary norms (like this one, the bar on extraterritorial enforcement jurisdiction) is that the failure to protest — or, as here, the public ratification of the act by state officials with authority to speak for the state on the international level — will tend to water down the strength of the norm. Should Russia, for example, use a drone to assassinate a "dangerous" terrorist on the territory of Georgia, it is possible that there might be protest from other states, particularly given the troubled history between the Russia and Georgia.[264] While this might be something of an oversimplification, "the Americans did it to bin Laden, and none of you complained" would be a difficult argument to meet.[265]

---

261 To say nothing of the now well-publicized use of drones by the US government to assassinate security targets in a number of states.

262 Neil MacDonald, "US Jeopardizes Justice with al-Awlaki Execution from the Sky" *CBC News* (4 October 2011), online: cbc.ca www.cbc.ca/news/world/story/2011/10/03/f-rfa-macdonald.html.

263 There has been a suggestion, officially denied by Pakistan, that advance permission was given for the bin Laden incursion by an earlier Pakistani government. See "Musharraf Denies U.S. bin Laden Deal Report" *CBC News* (10 May 2011), online: cbc.ca www.cbc.ca/news/world/story/2011/05/10/bin-laden-us-pakistan.html.

264 Specifically, given the Russo-Georgian War of 2008.

265 For an interesting exploration of the even murkier world of extraterritorial intelligence gathering (aka "spying") by states, see Craig Forcese, "Spies without Borders: International Law and Intelligence Collection" (2011–2012) 5 Journal of National Security Law & Policy 179.

E. CHILD SEX TOURISM

Interesting points arise out of examining the international response to child sex tourism and the extraterritorial application of law. First, it is an illustration of an area in which there is a widespread international consensus that the problem extends beyond the borders of any one country, and therefore that a co-ordinated international effort is required. Second, there is widespread consensus that that co-ordinated effort properly involves extraterritorial action by states with regard to their own nationals and residents. Third, although there is consensus that action is necessary, the different approaches taken by states demonstrate that there is more than one way to tackle the problem.

Perhaps the most interesting point that the problem of child sex tourism demonstrates is that extraterritorial legislation is not necessarily the answer, even if the problem is one that extends beyond the borders of any single country. It is apparent from the various approaches taken, the relative lack of success of any of them, and the calls for change, that the difficulties in some cases are not simply formal ones of jurisdiction. In some measure, a decision only to legislate territorially is based on practical considerations about conducting an effective prosecution. The experience of various countries with regard to child sex tourism shows that having jurisdiction to prosecute offences that occur halfway around the world does nothing to resolve those practical problems. Focusing on solutions that can actually be implemented is likely to be more effective, and in practical terms that might well mean *not* looking extraterritorially after all.

1) The Problem

The problem with child sex tourism is self-describing. Although there are different views around the world as to the appropriate age of consent to sexual activity, there is a near-universal view that it is wrong and should be illegal to engage in sexual acts with children. Countries might disagree over whether a sixteen-year-old, for example, falls into the category of "child," but no one seriously questions that those who are ten or twelve or younger qualify as children. Whatever one's view about prostitution generally, there is no real debate among policy-makers that obtaining the services of a child for the purpose of prostitution should be illegal.

As a matter of fact, however, economic conditions in many countries force some children into prostitution; in turn, people who desire to obtain the sexual services of children travel to those countries. The phenomenon reflects the economic disparity in the world. The locations where child prostitutes can be found — the destination countries — are poorer ones, and include the Philippines, Thailand, Cambodia, Sri Lanka, Vietnam, India, and Fiji, as well as countries in Africa and Central and South America.[266] The source countries for the customers are wealthier nations, including Canada, the United States, Great Britain, Australia, and Japan. Estimates of the number of child prostitutes worldwide range as high as 3 million.[267]

For several reasons, the problem genuinely is an international one. One reason is that, as noted, that the victims come from one group of countries while the offenders come from another group. More than that, however, the problem engages conflict of law issues: in some cases the age of consent is lower in destination countries than in the source country, and so the behaviour of the customer will have been illegal in his home country but legal where it occurred — thus leading to the "tourism." This tourism is formalized, with some tour agencies catering (through thinly veiled advertisements) to the particular market involved.[268] The existence of a wealthy tourist market for prostitutes drives up the price, which institutionalizes the international nature of the situ-

266 Daniel Edelson, "The Prosecution of Persons Who Sexually Exploit Children in Countries Other Than Their Own: A Model for Amending Existing Legislation," Note (2001) 25:2 Fordham Int'l LJ 483 at 485; Naomi L Svensson, "Extraterritorial Accountability: An Assessment of the Effectiveness of Child Sex Tourism Laws," Notes & Comment (2006) 28 Loy LA Int'l & Comp L Rev 641 at 643.

267 Edelson, *ibid* at n 39.

268 Heather C Giordanella, "Status of 2423(b): Prosecuting United States Nationals for Sexually Exploiting Children in Foreign Countries" (1998) 12 Temp Int'l & Comp LJ 133 at nn 20 and 22; Jonathan Todres, "Prosecuting Sex Tour Operators in U.S. Courts in an Effort to Reduce the Sexual Exploitation of Children Globally" (1999–2000) 9:1 BU Pub Int'l LJ 1 at 4; Svensson, above note 266. In 1996, there were over twenty-five companies in the United States that offered sex tour packages to developing countries using "thinly-veiled promises of facilitated sexual encounters with local girls" such as "fresh young ladies" and "beautiful, unspoiled girls." (Sara K Andrews, "U.S. Domestic Prosecution of the American International Sex Tourist: Efforts to Protect Children from Sexual Exploitation" (2004) 94:2 J Crim L & Criminology 415 at 425, n 70.) Sex tour operators are typically situated in wealthy, industrialized countries, and the number of such operators is increasing steadily. (Kalen Fredette, "International Legislative Efforts to Combat Child Sex Tourism: Evaluating the *Council of Europe Convention on Commercial Child Sexual Exploitation*" (2009) 32:1 BC Int'l & Comp L Rev 1 at 6.)

ation.[269] Further, the attraction to travelling to engage in child sex prostitution is not simply that it might be legal in the destination country: even if it is illegal, in many destination countries prosecutions are rare and enforcement is inconsistent to non-existent.[270] Even if a customer is charged, the economic conditions which make the destination country a location for prostitution are also likely to make bribing police officers or other officials as a way of avoiding prosecution a viable option.[271] Finally, if this situation changes in some particular destination country, the result is simply that tourists will switch destinations rather than the problem disappearing.[272] It has been recognized for some time that the problem is not one that can be solved by any country acting alone. In

---

269 Benjamin Perrin, "Our Child Sex Offender Laws Should Cross Borders" *The Lawyers Weekly* (11 April 2008) 1, online: Liu Institute for Global Issue www.ligi.ubc.ca/?p2=/modules/liu/publications/view.jsp&id=2092; Vickie F Li, "Child Sex Tourism to Thailand: The Role of the United States as a Consumer Country" (1995) 4:2 Pac Rim L & Pol'y J 505 at 509; Andrews, *ibid* at 419. "Although foreign demand for commercial sex in developing countries is significantly outweighed by local demand, the presence of international customers and the financial resources that accompany them are significant factors in the perpetuation of the sex industry worldwide." (*Ibid* to Andrews.)

270 Andrews, *ibid* at 426. With the police protecting the child sex industry for monetary compensation, arrests and subsequent prosecution are elusive. In India, where prostitution is illegal, there are "carefully maintained arrangements between the police and the *gharwali*, who manage the brothels," and weekly police bribes are so commonplace that they are termed *hafta*, which is Hindi for "week." (Mary Catherine Hendrix, "Enforcing the U.S. *Trafficking Victims Protection Act* in Emerging Markets: The Challenge of Affecting Change in India and China," Note (2010) 43:1 Cornell Int'l LJ 173 at nn 166 & 167, citing Susan Dewey, *Hollow Bodies: Institutional Responses to Sex Trafficking in Armenia, Bosnia, and India* (Sterling, VA: Kumarian Press, 2008) at 133 and 131, respectively.)

271 Perrin, above note 269 at 1: "In the past, foreign sex tourists received lenient treatment and were often only fined and deported." (Li, above note 269 at 514, citing Cameron W Barr, "Thais Target World Trade in Child Sex, But Police Enforcers Get Little Support from Government" *Christian Science Monitor* (17 April 1995).) In 1992, the newly elected Thai prime minister announced his commitment to combat child prostitution. "Today, affluent foreign offenders may escape prosecution by bribing Thai officials and then fleeing the country while on bail. Meanwhile, the Thai police have been known to guard brothels, as well as traffic or procure children for prostitution . . . . Worse yet, Thai police are often customers themselves, but they are rarely investigated or prosecuted." (*Ibid to Li* [footnotes omitted].)

272 Catherine Beaulieu, "Extraterritorial Laws: Why They Are Not Really Working and How They Can Be Strengthened" *ECPAT International Compendium of Articles* (September 2008) at n 43, online: ECPAT http://resources.ecpat.net/worldcongressIII/PDF/Journals/EXTRATERRITORIAL_LAWS.pdf.

particular, the argument has for some time been put forward that any effective solution must rest as much with the source countries as with the destination countries, which seems to require extraterritorial legislation.

2) The International Response

In fact, there has been international co-operation on the issue for some time. In 1989 the United Nations *Convention on the Rights of the Child* (*UNCRC*) was put forward: articles 34 and 35 of that Convention require signatories to take measures to prevent the sexual exploitation or abuse of children, and to prevent their abduction, sale, or trafficking.[273] The *UNCRC* defines a child as anyone under the age of eighteen years, unless a different age is established in domestic legislation (article 1).[274] The Committee has asked that signatories set the age at eighteen, but that is neither required nor enforced, and this is problematic for prosecution. For example, in countries where prostitution is illegal and a child is defined as anyone under the age of fourteen, a sixteen-year-old child sex worker may be treated as an offender. Additionally, when a nation has a double criminality requirement (discussed in the section on the United Kingdom below), different age limits for the definition of a child in two states can bar the prosecution of an offender.[275]

The *UNCRC* has been signed by every member of the United Nations other than Somalia and the United States. Article 3 of the *UNCRC* requires that signatories criminalize the offering, obtaining, procuring, and providing of a child for child prostitution. In addition, article 2 extends prostitution to include the provision of sexual services in exchange for any form of consideration, be it money, goods, or necessities.[276] However, the *UNCRC* contains no particular measures for dealing with the problem.[277] Although child sex tourism is not directly addressed by the *UNCRC*, child prostitution, child pornography, and the sale of children

---

273 *Convention on the Rights of the Child*, GA Res 44/25, UNGA 61st Plen Mtg, UN Doc A/RES/44/25 (1989), online: UN www.un.org/documents/ga/res/44/a44r025.htm [*UNCRC*].

274 *Ibid*.

275 Svensson, above note 266 at 656.

276 United Nations Children's Fund, Innocenti Research Centre, *Handbook on the Optional Protocol on the Sale of Children, Child Prostitution and Child Pornography* (Florence: UNICEF, 2009), online: UNICEF www.unicef-irc.org/publications/pdf/optional_protocol_eng.pdf at 11 [UNICEF].

277 Svensson, above note 266 at 646.

are often part and parcel of that activity. The Committee on the Rights of the Child recommends combative efforts such as promoting responsible tourism and working with travel operators and NGOs.[278]

Subsequently, in 1996, delegates from 122 countries held a meeting in Stockholm and produced an "Agenda for Action," a non-binding resolution calling on states to create extraterritorial legislative measures to prevent the sexual exploitation of children. Some countries, Canada and Australia among them for example, did act to make their laws apply extraterritorially, prior to having any obligation to do so under a convention.[279]

Later still, in 2000, the United Nations sponsored the creation of the Optional Protocol on the Rights of the Child on the Sale of Children, Child Prostitution and Child Pornography (*OPSC*). This protocol (ratified by 137 states)[280] requires signatories to enforce their legislation regarding child sexual exploitation extraterritorially and allows jurisdiction where the victim is a national of that party state.[281] The implementation of this optional protocol is also overseen by the Committee on the Rights of the Child. Paragraph 3 delineates that signatories must adopt legislation that requires courts to exercise jurisdiction to prosecute where they do not extradite a national of their country for involvement in the sale of children, child prostitution, or child pornography.

---

278 UNICEF, above note 276 at 12.

279 In Australia, the *Crimes (Child Sex Tourism) Amendment Act 1994* (Cth) [*Australian Child Sex Tourism Act*] preceded that conference. Australia has been on the leading edge in this area. Along with France, it proposed in the early 1990s the Draft *Optional Protocol to the United Nations Convention on the Rights of the Child Concerning the Elimination of Sexual Exploitation and Trafficking of Children*, which would have defined sexual exploitation of children as a crime against humanity and would have required prosecution on the basis of universal jurisdiction, i.e., a state could punish anyone, whether that offender was a national or resident of that state or not. (Giordanella, above note 268 at nn 56–65, citing Margaret A Healy, "Prosecuting Child Sex Tourists at Home: Do Laws in Sweden, Australia, and the United States Safeguard the Rights of Children as Mandated by International Law? (1995) 18:5 Fordham Int'l LJ 1852 at 1879.)

280 "New Push to Protect Children" (27 May 2010), online: United Nations Human Rights, Office of the High Commissioner for Human Rights www.ohchr.org/EN/NewsEvents/Pages/Newpushtoprotectchildren.aspx.

281 *Optional Protocol to the Convention on the Rights of the Child on the Sale of Children, Child Prostitution and Child Pornography*, 25 May 2000, 2171 UNTS 227, arts 3–4 (entered into force 18 January 2002), online: Office of the United Nations High Commissioner for Human Rights http://treaties.un.org/doc/publication/UNTS/Volume%20 2171/v2171.pdf [*OPSC*].

Table 7.1. **Jurisdictional requirements for commercial sexual exploitation of children (CSEC) crimes under the OPSC**

Summary of the Basic Forms of Jurisdiction in the Context of CSEC Crimes	
Type of Jurisdiction	*OPSC Requirements*
Territorial If a crime is committed in country A, this country is the primary "jurisdiction holder," with the authority to arrest and prosecute.	States must exercise territorial jurisdiction. If states have constitutional difficulty in extraditing, they must prosecute.
Extraterritorial • If the victim is a national of country A • If the suspect is a national of country A • If the national interests of country A are threatened • If country A applies the principle of universal jurisdiction	States may choose to exercise jurisdiction based on any of these principles.

Source: Beaulieu, above note 272 at 7.

3) The Domestic Responses

a) Canada

Canada's response to child sex tourism is found in section 7(4.1) of the *Criminal Code*, which provides that any Canadian citizen or permanent resident who commits a sexual offence against a child while outside Canada will be deemed to have committed the act while in Canada. In other words, the Canadian response simply ignores the extraterritorial aspect of the offence and treats it like any other piece of criminal behaviour. There is a requirement for consent of the Attorney General to any such prosecution, but this requirement is not unique to that section.[282]

When extraterritorial jurisdiction over child sexual offences was initially legislated in Canada in 1997, there was also a requirement for a request from the destination country before a prosecution could be

282 Some other instances of extraterritorial jurisdiction have a similar requirement: see, for example, s 7(2.33) of the *Criminal Code*, above note 244, dealing with consent to prosecution of offences on the International Space Station or s 7(7), requiring consent where the person being prosecuted for an extraterritorial offence (for example, on an aircraft) is not a Canadian citizen. In addition, there is a requirement for the Attorney General's consent to the prosecution of a few offences even if committed in Canada: see, for example, s 174(3), requiring consent of the Attorney General for a prosecution for public nudity.

carried out. One can see the argument in favour of such a requirement, in that a successful prosecution would depend on the co-operation of the destination country, and a prerequisite for consent would mean that any concerns about comity were satisfied. However, that requirement was criticized as undermining the effectiveness of the provision,[283] and it has since been repealed.

It has been observed that Canada's approach to child sex tourism prosecutions is essentially a passive and reactive one. This passive approach to enforcement, it is argued, undermines any deterrent effect the prohibition might otherwise have.[284] From 1993 until 2007, only one Canadian of the 146 charged with child sex offences abroad was convicted.[285] In 2008, the number of convictions increased to three, when two Canadian aid workers in Haiti were convicted.[286]

It is also generally felt that prosecution of these offences is hampered by the obvious difficulties of proof where all the evidence is located in another country. The first prosecution under the provisions occurred only because videotapes disclosing the sexual abuse of children were discovered while the accused was already being investigated

---

283 Edelson, above note 266 at 517.

284 Perrin, above note 269 at 2, has argued that "because Canada's approach to enforcing its extraterritorial child sex offender law has been passive, it is likely not deterring child sex offenders from travelling overseas to seek out victims."

285 "Child-Sex Tourism Law Not Enforced: A Canadian Passport Is Essentially a 'Get out of Jail Free Card' for People Having Sex with Children Overseas, a B.C. Law Professor Says" *Vancouver Sun* (3 April 2008), online: CanWest MediaWorks Publications www.canada.com/story_print.html?id=e89e954f-2aba-46f6-8685-30d10876631a&sponsor.

286 With two Quebec men, Armand Huard and Denis Rochefort, having been convicted in 2008 of sexual assault involving minors in Haitian orphanages, the number of Canadian convictions related to sexual offences against children extraterritorially now totals three. (Marianne White, "Canadian Aid Worker Guilty of Assaulting Haitian Boys" *Ottawa Citizen.com* (17 November 2008), online: canada.com www2.canada.com/ottawacitizen/news/story.html?id=ba814e0a-8f11-408d-b5c0-1b6af28ed000.) One might observe that these most recent cases do not strictly fall into the child sex "tourism" category.

for other offences,[287] and without those tapes it is unlikely the prosecution would have succeeded.[288]

b) Australia

The *Australian Child Sex Tourism Act* is legislation dealing specifically with the issue of child sex tourism, as opposed to simply extending the reach of existing legislation extraterritorially. The Act makes it illegal for an Australian citizen or resident to engage in sexual activity with a person under the age of sixteen anywhere in the world. In addition, it makes it illegal to induce, benefit from, or encourage sexual acts between an Australian and a person under sixteen.[289]

The extraterritorial nature of the offence was also addressed to a certain extent with the *Crime (Child Sex Tourism) Amendment Act 1994*, which permits testimony to be given in a trial by video-link if certain

---

287 Perrin, above note 269 at 2. This is also true of the more recent prosecution of Kenneth Klassen, who pleaded guilty to several charges after video evidence was discovered on DVDs in his mail ("'Sex tourist' Kenneth Klassen Sentenced to 11 Years" *The Globe and Mail* (23 August 2012), online: The Globe and Mail www.theglobeandmail.com/news/british-columbia/sex-tourist-kenneth-klassen-sentenced-to-11-years/article1654820.

288 "G8 Experience in the Implementation of Extraterritorial Jurisdiction for Sex Crimes against Children" (18 April 2007), online: Tourism Online Resource Center www.linkbc.ca/torc/downs1/Extraterritorial%20Jurisdiction.pdf. Note that a guilty plea can render video testimony unnecessary, as was the case at the trial of one of the Canadian aid workers in Haiti, Armand Huard. However, sex tourism cases typically require victim testimony. Cases involving film or photographic documentation of sex acts with children abroad are unlike sex tourism cases in that prosecutions can proceed without the victim. (*Ibid.*) There is, however, no history of this occurring in Canada since the Donald Bakker case involving such circumstances resulted in a conviction largely due to the eventual identification of the location and victims in the footage (Svensson, above note 266). Australia does have a history of convicting without the identification of the victim. In the *Pearce* case, a confession was obtained to support a conviction, but in the *Lee* case a conviction was founded on photographs that showed only Lee's fingers, the prints from which forensic scientists were able to match to Lee (*ibid* at 660–61). A key obstacle for conviction is the difficulty associated with gathering evidence from a crime committed outside the country. Part IV of Svensson's article contains a discussion of some of these evidentiary obstacles (*ibid* at n 56).

289 Svensson, *ibid* at n 79, notes that this is a lower age than that of eighteen in the *UNCRC*, meaning that children aged sixteen and seventeen are not protected by Australian legislation though the *UNCRC* suggests they should be.

conditions are met.[290] This provision is not exclusive to the child sex tourism context, but is potentially applicable there.[291]

Further, the *Child Sex Tourism Act* is aimed specifically at sex tour operators to facilitate their prosecution, making it an offence to act with the intent of benefitting from or encouraging conduct that would constitute a violation of the prohibition against child sex tourism.[292]

c) United Kingdom

The approach taken in the United Kingdom falls somewhere between that in Canada and Australia, though it has unique elements as well. Like Canada, the United Kingdom has simply legislated that existing sexual offences against children constitute an offence in the United Kingdom even if they were committed outside its territory.[293] Unlike Canada, the United Kingdom imposes a requirement that the behaviour must also have been an offence in the country in which it occurred. It has been argued that this "double criminality" requirement simply has the effect of causing sex tourists from the United Kingdom to engage in forum shopping, whereby they choose destination countries where child prostitution has not been outlawed.[294] Some nations have eliminated their double criminality requirements, such as Sweden and Denmark in 2005 and 2006 respectively, due to the obstacle they posed to prosecuting offenders.[295] Like Australia, however, the United Kingdom has taken steps to establish liaisons with some destination countries, providing support and training to them.[296]

d) Japan

Japan's legislative response is interesting because it demonstrates the possibility of enforcing sexual offences extraterritorially in an entirely different manner from domestic sexual offence laws.

---

290 Above note 279.

291 Edelson, above note 266 at 508–9; Andrews, above note 268 at n 187; Svensson, above note 266 at n 125.

292 Svensson, *ibid* at n 108. In this regard, see also New Zealand's *Crimes Act 1961* (NZ), 1961/43, 1 RS 635, which makes it an offence to make travel arrangements for, or to print or publish information intended to, promote child sex tours, and Svensson, above note 266 at nn 108–9.

293 *Sex Offenders Act 1997* (UK), c 51, ss 7 & 8.

294 Svensson, above note 266 at 650.

295 Beaulieu, above note 272 at 12–13.

296 *Ibid* at n 50.

Article 3 of the Japanese *Penal Code* applies as a matter of course to Japanese nationals wherever they are, and so the provisions dealing with sexual offences against children apply extraterritorially.[297] In that sense, the Japanese law could already be used to prosecute those involved in hiring child prostitutes in destination countries. Japan is thought to be one of the major source countries for child sex tourists,[298] and so this would be an important part of a co-ordinated solution.

However, Japan's domestic law on sexual assault is not designed well enough to address the problem. The crime of rape can only be committed against a female victim, for example, and the age of consent in Japan is thirteen. In addition, the law creates a prerequisite of a complaint by the victim of the offence within six months if a prosecution is to succeed.[299] The first two requirements limit the usefulness of Japanese law with regard to child sex tourism, while the third makes worse the already significant practical difficulties in conducting a prosecution.[300]

In 1999, however, Japan passed special legislation with regard to child pornography and child prostitution entitled the *Act on Punishment of Activities Relating to Child Prostitution and Child Pornography and the Protection of Children*. This more specific law defines a child as anyone under the age of eighteen, and draws no distinction based on sex. In addition, this law does not require that a complaint be laid by the victim within six months. Finally, these offences are specifically made subject to prosecution on an extraterritorial basis, as article 10 of this Act specifically outlines that the crimes related to child sex tourism are governed by article 3 of the *Penal Code*.[301] The practical difficulties presented by the ordinary law around sexual offences are largely overcome by this special legislation. However, Japan has been criticized (as have many other countries) for not taking steps to effectively enforce the law.[302]

Noteworthy is article 5 of the Japanese *Penal Code*, which states that additional punishment in Japan is not precluded by a judgment being

---

297 Japanese *Penal Code*, Act No 45 of 1907 [*Penal Code*]; Edelson, above note 266 at n 191.

298 Svensson, above note 266 at n 68.

299 Edelson, above note 266 at 519ff.

300 Beaulieu, above note 272 at 11–12, notes that requirements for a victim's consent to prosecution provide an opportunity for the offender to "buy off" the victim and his/her family.

301 *Act on Punishment of Activities Relating to Child Prostitution and Child Pornography, and the Protection of Children*, Act No 52 of 1999, online: Japanese Law Translation www.japaneselawtranslation.go.jp/law/detail/?id=100&vm=04&re=02.

302 Svensson, above note 266 at n 70.

rendered in another jurisdiction. It is therefore possible that a Japanese national could be punished in two jurisdictions, although article 5 also stipulates that any portion of the punishment served abroad must be considered in mitigating punishment in Japan.[303]

e) United States

The United States has taken, in two steps, a somewhat different approach to dealing with child sex tourism. The first step was the *Child Sexual Abuse Prevention Act* of 1994.[304] The United States already had the *Mann Act*, which made it an offence to cross state lines with the intention of engaging in illegal sexual activity; the *Child Sexual Abuse Prevention Act* was an extension of that Act. It made it an offence for a US citizen or permanent resident to travel outside the country with the intention of engaging in behaviour that would constitute a sexual offence against a child if it occurred in the United States.

Note that this is not (as in Canada or Australia) an extension of the law itself extraterritorially — it is an "intention-based" offence committed territorially.

It has been observed that this approach avoids many of the evidentiary difficulties of extraterritorial legislation, because there is no need to prove that any sexual act occurred. The only requirement under the legislation was to prove that sex tourism was a significant — but not necessarily the only — purpose of travel.[305]

Subsequently, in 2003, the United States amended this law with the *Prosecutorial Remedies and Other Tools to end the Exploitation of Children Today (PROTECT) Act of* 2003 (*PROTECT Act*). That Act did a number of things, such as increase the penalties and include a "two strikes" mandatory life sentence provision. For purposes of the discussion here, there were two noteworthy changes. First, the *PROTECT Act* added provisions that criminalized assisting in or organizing sex tours.[306] This aspect of the Act therefore also focuses on behaviour that occurred in the United States, rather than behaviour that occurred extraterritorially. Second, the *PROTECT Act* expanded the scope of the Act to include some behaviour that did occur outside the country; under the new legislation, travel

303 *Penal Code*, above note 297.

304 18 USC § 2423(b) (1994).

305 See the discussion in Edelson, above note 266 at n 265.

306 Andrews, above note 268 at n 262; *PROTECT Act*, Pub L 108-21, 117 Stat 650 at 105(d) (2003) [*PROTECT Act*].

with the intention to engage in illicit sexual conduct with a minor remains an offence, but culpability could also be proven by showing that the accused actually engaged in sexual conduct with a minor extraterritorially, or attempted or conspired to violate the Act.[307] It enhances and works in tandem with section 2423 of the *United States Criminal Code*, particularly section (c), which criminalizes the individual who "travels in foreign commerce . . . and engages in any illicit sexual conduct."[308] The applicability of section 2423(c) in cases where the alleged conduct is not a commercial sex act has been left undetermined.[309]

This approach has been generally seen as successful. It was noted in 2008 that:

> With such strong laws in place and efficient enforcement, in recent years the US has achieved impressive results in arresting child sex offenders, with approximately 55 child sex tourism indictments/complaints and approximately 36 convictions in 2006.[310]

Unlike Australia, the United States does not have specific legislation to allow for the video testimony of victims abroad. It is possible, in fact, that such legislation would conflict with the Sixth Amendment of the US Constitution guaranteeing defendants the right to confront their accusers.[311]

4) Conclusion

As noted in the introduction, several useful things flow from this discussion. The first is to note that, despite the widespread consensus among virtually all countries that something needs to be done about child sex tourism — indeed, despite the agreement as to what means should be taken — there is still a surprisingly wide range of legislative responses in different countries. One commentator has summarized the differences among several countries on points such as age of consent, whether double criminality is required, and so on:

307 *Ibid*, §§ 105 (c) and (e).

308 18 USC § 2423(c) (2013).

309 Amy Messigian, "Love's Labour's Lost: Michael Lewis Clark's Constitutional Challenge of 18 U.S.C. 2423(C)," Note (2006) 43:3 Am Crim L Rev 1241 at n 12.

310 Beaulieu, above note 272 at 8.

311 Svensson, above note 266 at n 127.

Table 7.2. Comparison of extraterritorial legislation in various nations

	Age of Protection?	*Requires Double Criminality?*	*Maximum Sentence (Years)*	*Application to Nationals and Residents?*	*Offence to Travel with Intent*	*Provision to Prosecute Child Sex Tour Operators?*	*Requirement of Previous Denunciation?*	*Number of Convictions*	*Overall Effectiveness*
Australia	16	N	12 or 17*	Y	N	Y	N	11	B
Canada	18	N	5	N	N	N	N	1	B
Japan	18	N	U	N	N	Y	N	0	C-
New Zealand	16	N	14	Y	N	Y	Y	U	B-
UK	16	Y	U	Y	N	N	N	5	B-
US	18	N	30	Y	Y	Y	N	12	A-

*= depends on the nature of the sexual act; U = unknown; (shading) = needs improvement

Source: Svensson, above note 266 at 654.

There is, however, one fairly common feature of almost all attempts to act extraterritorially with respect to child sex tourism, which is that those efforts have been criticized as ineffective.[312] Japan specifically enacted legislation aimed at child sex tourism, but it is rarely prosecuted: as of 2008 there had been four charges laid and no convictions. Canada has had a law on the books for nearly fifteen years and has only three convictions. New Zealand and Spain have no convictions, Italy has only two, and France has only six.[313]

Australia and the United States, on the other hand, have higher figures: twenty and thirty-six convictions, respectively.[314] In both of those countries, the legislation does not simply target behaviour that has occurred overseas; Australia and the United States also prosecute the domestic actions of child sex tourism agencies, and the United States

312 See, for example, *ibid* at 642: "In its current form, most ET [extraterritorial] legislation is insufficient, facing many evidentiary and procedural obstacles that hinder its effectiveness . . . operat[ing] as an empty shell, failing to protect countless, vulnerable children all over the world."

313 Beaulieu, above note 272 at charts 10–11.

314 *Ibid* at charts 9 and 11.

prosecutes travelling with the intent to commit the offence. These approaches avoid dependency on gathering evidence overseas.

Recall the difficulties that led to the call for source countries to participate in the solution in the first place:

> A major obstacle to effective enforcement of anti-prostitution laws is corruption among police officers and public officials. In Cambodia, for example, Dr. Kek Galabru, president of Licadho, a human rights group, asserts that public officials profit greatly from protection of the child sex trade and are themselves frequent patrons of brothels where children are sold. This serves to discourage enforcement by police. In addition, in some host countries, the police are willing to accept protection fees from brothel owners or bribes from customers. In certain countries, allowing the sexual exploitation of women and children to take place is regarded as a necessary component of maintaining local order. Additionally, many developing countries simply do not have adequate resources to invest in proper training and law enforcement.[315]

These are practical difficulties with the enforcement of a law against child prostitution that have little, if anything, to do with the question of where the trial of an offender will occur. If police cannot or will not investigate in destination countries, the simple fact that source countries have extraterritorial jurisdiction to prosecute is not by itself helpful.

All of this suggests that even if a problem is transnational or extraterritorial, this does not necessarily lead to the conclusion that extraterritorial jurisdiction is the solution. Informal methods (such as the liaison offices set up by Australia and the United Kingdom) can be undertaken without the need for extraterritorial legislation. Formal methods (such as prosecuting sex tour operators or tourists who intend to travel abroad for the purpose of child sex tourism) can focus on the behaviour that occurs domestically and can be prosecuted based simply on territorial jurisdiction.

Beaulieu, for example, has recommended that all states should review their legislation with regard to child sex tourism to ensure that its elements include:

> (1) engaging in sexual conduct with a child abroad, including non-commercial and commercial illicit sexual conduct with a child under 18; (2) travelling with the intent of engaging in sexual activities with a child

315 Andrews, above note 268 at 426–27 [footnotes omitted].

> abroad; (3) advertising or promoting child sex tours; (4) making travel arrangements for a person for the purpose of engaging in sexual activity with a child at the destination; and (5) transporting a person for the above purpose — the liability of tour operators should extend to local partners on the ground in order to ensure that the former's liability does not end once the clients have reached their destination.[316]

It is worth noting that only the first of these five responses depends on an extraterritorial approach. Even when extraterritorial legislation is sensibly on the table as an option, it might not be the most effective solution.

F. INTERNET GAMBLING

Internet gambling raises interesting issues of extraterritorial regulation. Before the rise of the Internet, the two questions, "is it legal to gamble here" and "is it legal for our citizens/residents to gamble" were treated for most purposes as the same question. It was always possible for people to leave their own jurisdiction and visit a place where gambling was legal, but that raised no unusual extraterritorial issues.

Gambling, however, is an interaction which is quite readily carried on over the Internet. It requires no physical exchange of goods, and the activities involved (betting on sporting events in other countries, participating in a lottery conducted online, playing casino games such as virtual slot machines, or playing poker online against live opponents) are easily conducted with the use of a computer. Accordingly, the Internet makes it possible for residents of one country to gamble on servers located in a different country where gambling is legal, without leaving their own home, thus, the behaviour and the location of the behaviour have become, in a sense, unlinked. Where at one point enforcing the rule "gambling is not permitted here" and enforcing the rule "our citizens/residents are not permitted to gamble" was the same thing, now those two rules require different enforcement mechanisms.

This situation would not necessarily lead to difficulties if there were consensus about the underlying issue. If gambling were to be perceived in the same way that terrorism, piracy, and child pornography are regarded, co-ordinated international efforts to solve the "problem" could be undertaken. Unlike those phenomena, however, the attitudes towards gambling in general, and Internet gambling in particular, vary widely

316 Beaulieu, above note 272 at 16.

from jurisdiction to jurisdiction. In 2003, the global online gross gambling revenue (the difference between the total amount received and wagered on games, and the amount paid out to winning bettors) was US$4.1 billion.[317] By 2005, it was US$12 billion, and by 2010 it had grown to nearly US$30 billion.[318] As online gambling is such a thriving and growing market, it is not surprising that there are many different approaches to its regulation.

Some states see gambling as potentially socially harmful and prohibit it for that reason; some see it as acceptable and a potential source of revenue; some states see gambling as both socially harmful and a potential source of revenue, and attempt to legalize it in a way which minimizes the threat while maximizing the profit. Even states that consider gambling acceptable are concerned enough to regulate it so that it is carried out fairly; those concerns are magnified when it comes to Internet gambling, where the possible methods of running an unfair game are so much broader.

It is also worth noting that the attitude towards gambling varies depending on the nature of the activity in question. States tend to be more comfortable allowing horse races or lotteries, for example, than they are about allowing casino games, slot machines, or poker. This attitude tends to transfer over to online gambling.

In this case study, therefore, we shall pursue the issue of Internet gambling with a view to demonstrating how the lack of international consensus creates a real bar to extraterritorial action. In particular, we shall: (1) briefly review the variety of approaches taken in different countries; (2) discuss the approach taken in Canada; and (3) look at the complaint by Antigua against the United States before the World Trade Organization (WTO) to show how extraterritorial action in the absence of consensus can lead to disputes rather than effective governance of Internet gambling.

There are other issues concerning Internet gambling that could arise, but we will not be pursuing them in any detail. For example, all

---

317 Gregory Manter, "The Pending Determination of the Legality of Internet Gambling in the United States" (2003) Duke L & Tech Rev 0016 at paras 1390–391, online: www.law.duke.edu/journals/dltr/articles/2003/dltr0016.html.

318 Pedro Raventós & Sandro Zolezzi, "Sportsbooks and Politicians: Place Your Bet!" (2011) 64:3 Journal of Business Research 299 at 300; "Real-Money Gambling Emerges as Massive Global Revenue Opportunity for Games Developers According to New Report by H2 Gambling Capital and Odobo" (28 March 2013), online: H2 Gambling Capital www.h2gc.com/article/h2-interactive-gambling-report-commisioned-by-odobo.

jurisdictions that legalize gambling in some form have regulations governing it, such as rules around the age of participants, measures to help protect problem gamblers, and measures to ensure the honesty of the games. The moment the gambling is transferred from a physical environment to a virtual one, enforcing these regulations becomes much more difficult. Further, the fact that the gambling is conducted through the use of computers and servers raises practical considerations. These range from the possibility of denial of service attacks against providers[319] to the use of non-legal methods of law enforcement, such as seizing domain names[320] or persuading services that transfer money over the Internet not to do so for certain businesses.[321] Finally, even without

---

319 In 2006, British and Irish online casinos and betting shops were blackmailed for over £2 million by a gang that used denial of service attacks, threatening that the sites would be attacked and left unusable for customers. (Fiona Raisbeck, "Russian Internet Blackmailers Jailed" *SC Magazine UK* (6 October 2006), online: Scmagazineuk.com www.scmagazineuk.com/russian-internet-blackmailers-jailed/article/106968.) A man in Germany was convicted in 2011 for extorting money from online sports-betting sites during the month before the 2010 football World Cup in South Africa, threatening those sites with denial of service attacks. (Graham Cluley, "World Cup DDoS Blackmailer Sentenced to Jail" *Naked Security* (16 June 2011), online: nakedsecurity.sophos.com http://nakedsecurity.sophos.com/2011/06/16/world-cup-ddos-blackmailer-sentenced-to-jail.)

320 In 2008, Kentucky tried to seize the Internet domains of 141 online gambling sites in *Commonwealth of Kentucky v 141 Internet Domain Names* (Cir Ct Franklin 2008), alleging that domain names fall under the umbrella of illegal "gambling devices" under Kentucky law. The court ruled that the sites could keep their domains so long as software to deny access to Kentucky users was installed, but the Kentucky Court of Appeals subsequently blocked enforcement of this order, ruling that domain names are not "gambling devices" (*Interactive Media Entertainment and Gaming Ass'n, Inc v Wingate*, 2009 WL 142995 (Ct App Ky Jan 20, 2009)). The Kentucky Supreme Court later reversed the Kentucky Court of Appeals decision, with the result that the domain-name seizures were legal, but the reversal was based only on a question of standing: *Commonwealth of Kentucky v Interactive Media Entertainment & Gaming Association, Inc* (Ky Sup Ct 2010). Ultimately, in 2013, Kentucky obtained a settlement against the group of domain names after it joined a federal action led by the United States attorneys for both the Southern District of New York and the District of Maryland of $6.2 million: "Kentucky Gets $6 Million in Online Gambling Settlement" *Business First* (19 June 2013), online: American City Business Journals www.bizjournals.com/louisville/news/2013/06/19/kentucky-gets-6-million-in-online.html.

321 In 2002, before relevant legislation was passed, the New York Attorney General, Eliot Spitzer, compelled Citibank to agree to block payments to offshore gambling sites via their Visa and MasterCard credit cards, subpoenaing PayPal for records of transactions with offshore gambling sites and ultimately inducing PayPal to stop sanctioning such payments. See David O Stewart, "An Analysis of Internet Gambling

acting extraterritorially, there is scope for disagreement as to where a transaction conducted over the Internet occurred.[322]

1) The Variety of Approaches

It has been argued that the majority of approaches to Internet gambling fall into one of four categories:[323]

1) Laissez-faire: Businesses pay money for a licence and locate a gambling server in the host country. Countries falling into this category (such as Antigua, Gibraltar, or Panama) allow online gambling to operate from within the country and allow anyone, within or outside the country, to take part;[324]
2) Online gambling restricted to residents: An extension of the normal rules around gambling to cover Internet gambling as well. Countries falling into this category might simply allow online lotteries or betting on sporting events (such as Canada or Austria) or might also allow online slot machines and casino games (such as Finland);[325]
3) Online gambling restricted to foreign players: Businesses are licensed to operate from a host country, but residents of that host country are not permitted to gamble (such as Australia or Papua New Guinea);[326] and
4) Outright prohibition: Businesses cannot operate gambling sites from within the country, and citizens and residents of the country

---

and its Policy Implications" *10th Anniversary White Paper Series* (2006), online: American Gaming Association www.americangaming.org/industry-resources/research/white-papers.

322 Although this conflict of laws point will not be considered in detail, it will arise in looking at the approaches taken by some countries.

323 Robin Kelley, Peter Todosichuk, & Jason J Azmier, "Gambling@Home: Internet Gambling in Canada" *Gambling in Canada Research Report No. 15* (Calgary: Canada West Foundation, 2001) at 12–14, online: University of Calgary http://dspace.ucalgary.ca/bitstream/1880/48403/1/gambling@home.pdf.

324 Robert T Wood & Robert J Williams, "Internet Gambling: Prevalence, Patterns, Problems, and Policy Options" Final Report Prepared for the Ontario Problem Gambling Research Centre (5 January 2009) at 10, online: www.nsgamingfoundation.org/uploads/Internet%20Gambling%20Wood%20and%20Williams%20Final%20Report%20FINAL.pdf.

325 *Ibid* at 11–12.

326 *Ibid* at 10.

cannot gamble online with businesses located elsewhere (such as the United States, Russia, and Saudi Arabia).[327]

Looking at the specifics of a few countries will reveal the variety of ways Internet gambling has been dealt with.

a) Australia

Australia has federal legislation — the *Interactive Gambling Act* — which permits individual states to create their own rules around online lotteries, sports betting, or casino games. However, although Australian states can issue licences allowing online gambling generally, Australians themselves are not necessarily permitted to participate. Australians can participate in online lotteries and sports betting, but are not allowed to gamble at the online casinos licensed under Australian law.[328] In other words, online casino gambling is legal in Australia, but not for Australians. However, other countries can also apply to Australia to have their citizens prohibited from gambling in Australian-based online casinos.[329]

b) Finland

Like many countries, Finland allows some forms of online gambling domestically, such as lotteries, but does not allow for online casinos.[330] However, the Finnish Supreme Court has concluded that online gambling occurs at the location where the server is located, and not where the player is located.[331] As a result, although online casinos are not legal in Finland, Finns can gamble at online casinos if those casinos are located elsewhere.[332] The same is true in New Zealand, where although

327 *Ibid.*

328 *Interactive Gambling Act 2001* (Cth), ss 3(a) and 15 [*Interactive Gambling Act*].

329 Wood & Williams, above note 324 at 14; Kelley et al, above note 323 at 13; Valerie Jepson, "Internet Gambling and the Canadian Conundrum" (2000) 6 Appeal 6 at 10–11; *Interactive Gambling Act*, above note 328, ss 3(aa) and 9A. Essentially, "providing gambling sites to Australian residents [is] an offence, but it's perfectly legal to play poker or casino games online — from any country — as long as the operators don't advertise in Australia." ("Online Gambling Rules and Laws around the World" (11 August 2010), online: Gambling Blog: Gamesnomy http://gamesnomy.blogspot.com/2010/08/online-gambling-rules-and-laws-around.html.)

330 Wood & Williams, above note 324 at 10. Other countries acting in this way include Sweden, Germany, Hong Kong, Liechtenstein, and New Zealand.

331 Rob van der Gaast & Franka Pals, "Novamedia European Gaming & Lottery Files Finland" (v 25022003) *Novamedia* (2010), online: Gaming & Lottery Files www.gamingandlotteryfiles.com/novamediafile.php?file=Finland.htm.

332 Kelley et al, above note 323 at 13.

online casinos are not legal, New Zealanders are not prohibited from gambling with offshore online casinos.[333]

c) France

France can be seen as taking exactly the opposite approach to Finland. Finns are allowed to gamble at online casinos if the casino is *not* located in the country; the French are allowed to gamble at online casinos only if the casino *is* located in the country.[334] France's legislation permits online casinos and permits French citizens to gamble at them, but it prevents foreign operators from establishing online casinos in France or from accepting bets from French citizens.[335] The rationale for this approach is to maintain a government-based monopoly over online gaming.[336] However, France started issuing licences to foreign operators in 2010 following the passing of a bill that legalized and regulated online poker, sports betting, and horse racing. This eliminated the duopoly of the two state-run organizations that previously regulated and ran all online gambling in France.[337]

d) United Kingdom

The *Gambling Act (2005)* permits all forms of online (or remote) gambling, including lotteries and online casinos, and requires all site operators within the United Kingdom to obtain a remote operating licence issued by the Gambling Commission.[338] Foreign jurisdictions that are deemed to have regulation standards equivalent to those in the United Kingdom are placed on a so-called white list, and site operators located and registered in such jurisdictions do not require a remote operating

---

333 Wood & Williams, above note 324 at 14. The *Gambling Act 2003* (NZ), 2003/51, s 9(2) prohibits all remote interactive (Internet) gambling, but s 4(1) excludes "gambling by a person in New Zealand conducted by a gambling operator located outside New Zealand" from the definition of "remote interactive gambling."

334 Wood & Williams, above note 324 at 20.

335 *Ibid* at 13, which says that the law is aimed at foreign operators, who cannot be located in France and cannot accept bets from French citizens. The prohibition is not directed at citizens.

336 Kelley et al, above note 323 at 13; Wood & Williams, above note 324 at 13.

337 Wood & Williams, *ibid* at 23; Brett Collson, "France Ends Internet Gambling Monopoly" (11 April 2010), online: Poker News Daily.com www.pokernewsdaily.com/france-ends-internet-gambling-monopoly-9642; "France Revolutionizes the Online Gambling Market" (6 October 2010), online: Poker-on-line.com http://poker-on-line.com/news/1006/france-revolutionizes-online-gambling-market-1188.html.

338 *Gambling Act 2005* (UK), c 11, ss 33(1), 33(2), and 67(1).

licence to operate and advertise within the United Kingdom.[339] Prior to the passage of that Act, some forms of online gambling, including casino games, could not lawfully be located in the United Kingdom, but UK citizens could gamble online elsewhere. As a result, citizens of the United Kingdom can now gamble online either in the United Kingdom or elsewhere[340] In addition, citizens of other countries can gamble at UK-based online casinos.[341] The *Gambling Act* created the UK Gambling Commission for the licensing and regulation of gambling within the United Kingdom. Between 2008 and 2011, the United Kingdom grew as an online gambling jurisdiction from hosting ninety-two sites to hosting 118 sites.[342]

e) United States

In the United States, criminal law is governed at the state level, and so there is a wide variety of responses to gambling and Internet gambling. There are nonetheless some federal aspects to it, and the general position is that Internet gambling is against the law in the United States in every sense: online casinos cannot operate from there and American citizens are not permitted to gamble online, whether the server is located in the United States or elsewhere.[343] The federal *Wire Act* made it an offence to offer or take bets over telephone lines "or through other wire devices."[344] That statute has been used to successfully prosecute non-US based companies and providers of online gambling.[345]

---

339 "Internet Gambling in the UK" (2010), online: Care www.care.org.uk/advocacy/gambling/internet-gambling-in-the-uk.

340 "UK Considers Banning Foreign Gambling Websites" (25 January 2011), online: Casino People www.casinopeople.com/news/uk-considers-banning-foreign-gambling-websites.html.

341 Wood & Williams, above note 324 at 24.

342 *Ibid* at 17; "Online Gaming Jurisdictions" (2011), online: Online Casino City http://online.casinocity.com/jurisdictions/.

343 John D Andrle, "A Winning Hand: A Proposal for an International Regulatory Schema with Respect to the Growing Online Gambling Dilemma in the United States," Note (2004) 37:5 Vand J Transnat'l L 1389 at 1394.

344 *Ibid* at 1396; Jenna F Karadbil, "Casinos of the Next Millenium: A Look into the Proposed Ban on Internet Gambling," Note (2000) 17:2 Ariz J Int'l & Comp L 413 at 426–27.

345 Wood & Williams, above note 324 at 10; Kelly B Kramer, "The Jay Cohen Affair: Lessons in the Legality of Internet Betting" (2001) 5:6 Gaming Law Review 551. *United States v Cohen*, 260 F3d 68 (2d Cir 2001) resulted in the prosecution under the *Wire Act* of an American citizen abroad who provided online gambling services to US cus-

More recently, the *Unlawful Internet Gambling Enforcement Act 2006* (*UIGEA*) was enacted, which makes it illegal for financial transaction providers to transfer funds to any online gambling site, or for online gambling providers to accept bets from US citizens.[346] Presumably as a response, approximately 50 percent of all Internet gambling sites began to refuse to accept bets from US residents.[347]

---

tomers. (Yevgeniya Roysen, "Taking Chances: The United States' Policy on Internet Gambling and its International Implications," Notes & Recent Developments (2009) 26:3 Cardozo Arts & Ent LJ 873.)

346 31 USC § 5361–5366 (2006). Also, a Congressional Research Service report says this:

> In November 2008, the Treasury Department and the Board of Governors of the Federal Reserve System issued a final rule implementing the provisions of the 2006 Unlawful Internet Gambling Enforcement Act (UIGEA), P.L. 109-347, Title VIII.254. The statute prohibits gambling businesses from accepting checks, credit cards, electronic transfers and similar forms of payment in connection with illegal Internet gambling, while exempting intrastate and intratribal Internet gambling operations that include age and location verification requirements imposed as a matter of law.

Jeanne J Grimmett, "WTO Dispute Settlement: Status of U.S. Compliance in Pending Cases" (23 April 2012) at 99, online: Congressional Research Service www.fas.org/sgp/crs/misc/RL32014.pdf. The *UIGEA* relies on federal and state laws to delineate which gambling activities are unlawful. (Testimony of Louise L Roseman, Director, Division of Reserve Bank Operations and Payment Systems before the United States House Subcommittee on Domestic and International Monetary Policy, Trade, and Technology of the Committee on Financial Services: Hearings on Internet Gambling, 110th Cong, 2d Sess (2008), online US Government Printing Office www.gpo.gov/fdsys/pkg/CHRG-110hhrg42714/pdf/CHRG-110hhrg42714.pdf.) The rule became effective on 19 January 2009, with the original compliance date of 1 December 2009 extended to 1 June 2010. In addition, various bills were introduced in the 111th Congress to permit Internet gambling under a federal licensing program, such as the bill to amend title 31 of the United States Code, "to provide for the licensing by the Secretary of the Treasury of Internet poker and other games that are predominantly of skill, to provide for consumer protections on the Internet, to enforce the tax code, and for other purposes." (US, Bill S 1597, *Internet Poker and Game of Skill Regulation, Consumer Protection, and Enforcement Act of 2009*, 111th Cong, 2009.) Also introduced was US, Bill HR 2267, *Internet Gambling Regulation, Consumer Protection, and Enforcement Act*, 111th Cong, 2009, a bill to amend title 31 of the United States Code "to provide for the licensing of Internet gambling activities by the Secretary of the Treasury, to provide for consumer protections on the Internet, to enforce the tax code, and for other purposes" and US, Bill HR 4976, *Internet Gambling Regulation and Tax Enforcement Act of 2010*, 111th Cong, 2010, to "amend the Internal Revenue Code of 1986 to regulate and tax Internet gambling."

347 Wood & Williams, above note 324 at 20 according to "Online Gaming Jurisdictions," above note 342; Bradley Vallerius, "Gambling Sites Will Change Software to Stay in U.S. Market" (20 October 2006), online: Casino City Times http://bradleyvallerius.

These examples illustrate some of the options with regard to online casino gambling. To recap colloquially:

- Australia: Others can gamble here, but we can't.
- Finland: We can't gamble here, but we can gamble elsewhere.
- France: We can't gamble elsewhere, but we can gamble here.
- United Kingdom: We can gamble here or elsewhere, and others can gamble here.
- United States: We can't gamble here or elsewhere, and others can't gamble here.

f) The Canadian Approach

Canada's approach to gambling avoids any extraterritorial effect. However, that is in a sense only incidental to the point that Canadian law aims at preventing extra*provincial* effect. No Canadian laws deal specifically with online gambling and so that issue falls to be settled by the ordinary rules applicable to gambling generally.[348] The *Criminal Code* does not refer to Internet gambling at all, except that section 207 includes in the definition of lottery schemes those operated via computer. Some provinces have used this section in support of offering some online gambling.[349]

The starting premise of Canadian criminal law is that gambling is illegal. As the Prince Edward Island Court of Appeal has noted: "Parliament does not happily abide gaming activities of any sort in Canada. The little it tolerates, it does so grudgingly."[350] Accordingly, the *Criminal Code* makes it an offence to keep "a common gaming house."[351] Similarly, recording bets, selling a pool, placing bets on behalf of another person, running a lottery, and operating a game of chance are all illegal.[352]

---

casinocitytimes.com/article/gambling-sites-will-change-software-to-stay-in-u-s-market-30608.

348 Jepson, above note 329 at n 2. "The leading case on the extra-provincial conduct of lotteries is *Reference re: Earth Future Lottery*. . . ." (*British Columbia v Haptom*, 2008 BCPC 126 at para 17.)

349 Justin Rex & David J Jackson, "The Options for Internet Gambling in Canada" (2007) 1:3 Association for Canadian Studies in the United States: Occasional Papers on Public Policy Series, online: ACSUS www.acsus.org/public/pdfs/OP_v1n3.pdf.

350 *Reference Re: Earth Future Lottery*, 2002 PESCAD 8 at para 7 [*Earth Future*].

351 *Criminal Code*, above note 244, s 201.

352 *Ibid*, ss 202, 203, and 206.

These rules, however, are subject to exceptions. Some betting on horse racing, for example, is permitted.[353] Most relevant to the discussion here is section 207 of the *Criminal Code*, which creates an exception for lottery schemes that are licensed by a province.[354] In particular, section 207(1)(a) provides that:

> Notwithstanding any of the provisions of this Part relating to gaming and betting, it is lawful
>
> (*a*) for the government of a province, either alone or in conjunction with the government of another province, to conduct and manage a lottery scheme in that province, or in that and the other province, in accordance with any law enacted by the legislature of that province.

The meaning of this provision was considered by the Prince Edward Island Supreme Court Appellate Division in the *Earth Future* case.[355] The province of Prince Edward Island licensed a non-profit charitable corporation to conduct the Earth Future Lottery, which would be located in the province. The plan was to sell tickets worldwide, by telephone or over the Internet. The question that arose, and that was sent on a reference to the Court of Appeal, was whether this scheme would satisfy the requirement in section 207(1)(a) that what was licensed was "a lottery in that province." If it were not, then of course the proposed lottery would violate the general prohibition on gambling in the *Criminal Code*. The Court of Appeal held that the exception in section 207(1)(b) did not apply, and therefore the lottery scheme could not be implemented.

All of the infrastructure for the lottery, the court noted, would be located in Prince Edward Island. However, the intention was to sell tickets worldwide. Accordingly, advertising would be taking place outside the province, and many ticket purchases would take place both where the seller was and where the buyer was. The fact that according to the condi-

---

353 *Ibid*, s 204.

354 The definition of "lottery scheme" in s 207(4) of the *Criminal Code*, *ibid*, includes games operated through a computer, video device, or slot machine, as well as dice games. It is on that basis that provincially run casinos can be licensed. See also Colin S Campbell, Timothy F Harnagel, & Garry J Smith, "The Legalization of Gambling in Canada," Prepared for the Law Commission of Canada "*What is a Crime?*" (6 July 2005), online: Government of Canada Publications http://publications.gc.ca/collections/collection_2008/lcc-cdc/JL2-64-2005E.pdf.

355 *Earth Future*, above note 350. Note that this case was appealed to the Supreme Court of Canada and was dismissed "substantially for the reasons of the Chief Justice of Prince Edward Island." (*Reference re Earth Future Lottery*, 2003 SCC 10 at para 1.)

tions of sale the ticket purchase was deemed to occur in Prince Edward Island was relevant to civil contract law, the court held, but was not "determinative of where the *actus reus* of a criminal offence occurs."[356] In sum, it held: "conducting a lottery 'from' Prince Edward Island is not the same as conducting it 'in' Prince Edward Island."[357]

Given this interpretation, operating an Internet gambling site from Canada on an extraterritorial basis is not possible under the current state of Canadian law. In this regard, one might note as well section 197(4) of the *Criminal Code*, which provides that a place can be a common gaming house notwithstanding that "another part of the game is played elsewhere." That conclusion is further supported by the prosecution in the *Starnet* case.

Starnet was a corporation incorporated in Delaware and operating through wholly owned subsidiaries. Most of these were located in Antigua, where online gambling is legal, and Starnet had an online gambling licence. Starnet also had a subsidiary located in Vancouver, which hosted a number of computer servers. Canadian customers wishing to gamble through Starnet could download software from the BC servers, and then would access those BC servers before being redirected to offshore servers. Based on these facts and a few other aspects of the corporate structure, Starnet was charged under the *Criminal Code*.[358]

Ultimately a plea bargain was reached and Starnet pled guilty to a charge under section 202(1)(b) of the *Criminal Code* of keeping a device for gambling or betting. Starnet then relocated the Vancouver servers outside the country, avoiding future criminal liability. It has also been argued that simply ensuring that Canadians could not access the Vancouver servers might also have been sufficient to avoid violating the *Criminal Code*.[359]

It appears that Canadian law should also be taken to forbid most gambling by Canadians in other locations, at least if it is done from Canada. Section 206(1) of the *Criminal Code* makes it illegal to operate lotteries or games of chance. Section 206(4) then makes it illegal to buy a ticket or lot in one of those games, and section 206(7) specifies that

356 Above note 350 at para 14.

357 *Ibid* at para 10.

358 C Ian Kyer & Danielle Hough, "Is Internet Gaming Legal in Canada: A Look at Starnet" (2002) 1:1 CJLT, online: CJLT http://cjlt.dal.ca/vol1_no1/articles/01_01_KyeHou_gaming_fset.html.

359 *Ibid* at Conclusion.

foreign lotteries are included in the provision. The most likely interpretation is that the purchase of tickets in foreign lotteries is therefore also illegal in Canada, though the matter is not beyond argument. In any case, even that interpretation leaves a faint ambiguity over whether participating in foreign-based games of chance is forbidden. No prosecutions that would cast light on this issue seem to have occurred.[360]

A further issue relevant to Internet gambling, as evidenced in the *Earth Future* case, is that gambling is generally illegal with a few exceptions, such as lotteries. However, section 207(4) imposes limits on what can qualify as a "lottery scheme": specifically, although some games that might otherwise be illegal can qualify as a lottery, this is not the case if the game is "operated on or through a computer." Obviously that acts to limit online gambling even more than most gambling in Canada.

Although that generally describes the approach in Canada to online gambling, the discussion would be incomplete without mention of one further (and surprising) fact: in 2008, the location of more online gambling sites than any other place in the world, and one of the largest online gambling locations by volume of transactions, was the Kahnawake Mohawk Reserve in Quebec.[361] Since then, however, other locations have grown considerably while the number of sites hosted in Kahnawake has decreased by over 100.[362]

Online gambling is no less illegal on the Kahnawake Reserve, or any other reserve, than elsewhere in Canada.[363] However, for political reasons governments can find it awkward to prosecute First Nations for this activity, and so tend to turn a blind eye. The Kahnawake reserve has been hosting online gambling sites since 1999, and received a major boost when the United States introduced its *Unlawful Internet Gambling Enforcement Act*. Many online gambling operations moved to Kahnawake in the wake of that legislation, "in the belief that the U.S.

360 Kelley et al, above note 323 at 4.

361 Wood & Williams, above note 324 at 8, table 1.

362 "Online Gaming Jurisdictions," above note 342.

363 See *R v Pamajewon*, [1996] 2 SCR 821 [*Pamajewon*]. Strictly the *Pamajewon* decision only determined that the Shawanaga First Nation and the Eagle Lake First Nation did not have the Aboriginal right to conduct gambling activities on their reserves. Claims for the existence of an Aboriginal right must be determined on a First Nation-by-First Nation basis, but the approach taken in *Pamajewon* makes it very unlikely any other claim could succeed.

would be less likely to prosecute individuals from this jurisdiction."[364] To date they have been correct in this prediction.[365]

2) International Conflict: The WTO Dispute

As noted above, there is a wide range of responses to Internet gambling, ranging from complete prohibition to complete permission. This leads, not surprisingly, to some inconsistencies. The United States, for example, has historically taken one of the strictest approaches to Internet gambling—not only forbidding its citizens from taking part, but also purporting to criminalize the behaviour of organizations in other countries that accept bets from US citizens. Despite this, most sources agree that US citizens make up a very sizeable portion of the consumers of Internet gambling services worldwide,[366] though subsequent to the passing of the *Internet Gambling Prohibition Act* in 2006, the proportion of US citizens in global online gambling declined significantly. In 2010, less than 15 percent of the US$30 billion global online gambling revenue was from the United States.[367]

---

364 Wood & Williams, above note 324 at 22.

365 There seem to be no prosecutions with respect to Kahnawake, but in 2008 a BC-based site that processed bets from US residents with offshore providers was able to agree to pay the US justice department US$9.1 million to escape prosecution. (David Baines, "U.S. Cracks Down on Unlicensed Online Gambling, But Canada Prefers Just to Look the Other Way" *The Vancouver Sun* (28 May 2011), online: canada.com www2.canada.com/vancouversun/columnists/story.html?id=23767865-6e37-47b0-b279-25131e84178b&p=2.) In June of 2010, the Kahnawake Gaming Commission and the Antigua and Barbuda Financial Services Regulatory Commission signed a memorandum of understanding (MOU), under which an operator with a primary licence in either jurisdiction can apply for interjurisdictional authorization in the other jurisdiction, allowing for hosting in both jurisdictions. The MOU stipulates that the regulatory body, which issues primary licences, will regulate and supervise operators in both jurisdictions. (Kahnawake Gaming Commission, Press Release "Remote Gaming Regulators in Kahnawake and Antigua Agree to Create Inter-Jurisdictional Authorization Regime" (17 June 2010), online: Kahnawake Gaming Commission www.gamingcommission.ca/news/pr06172010a.pdf.)

366 Andrle, above note 343 at 61, estimates 65 percent. In 2005, the United States accounted for about US$6 billion of online gambling revenue, which represented about half of the global revenue. (Gerd Alexander, "The U.S. on Tilt: Why the Unlawful Internet Gambling Enforcement Act is a Bad Bet" (2008) Duke L & Tech Rev 0006 at n 3.)

367 Frank Fahrenkopf, "Now is the Time" *Global Gaming Business* (6 June 2011), online: GGB Magazine http://ggbmagazine.com/issue/vol-10-no-6-june-2011/article/now-is-the-time.

Antigua, on the other hand, is a nation that allows Internet gambling, and indeed revenue from the many Internet gambling licences issued there made up 10 percent of the gross domestic product of the country in 1999.[368] In 2003, Antigua brought a complaint to the WTO under the *General Agreement on Trade in Services* (GATS), alleging that the United States was in violation of its obligations. In particular, they noted that the United States had various pieces of legislation that prohibited cross-border gambling, and therefore denied Antigua (by way of the Internet) access to the US gambling market. In particular, the claim was based on the fact that interstate betting on horse races was possible within the United States but not outside it. The history of the claim in detail is not important, but Antigua argued that this was a matter of recreational services, and that equal treatment of other GATS partners was necessary. The United States argued that a public morals exception permitted them to act as they did. The WTO ruled partially in Antigua's favour, finding the United States not to be in compliance.[369]

An interesting fact to note from an extraterritorial perspective is that this successful ruling was not on its own of much assistance to Antigua. It meant that Antigua — the smallest member of the WTO — was entitled to take retaliatory measures against the United States if they did not comply. The United States subsequently enacted the *UIGEA* (discussed above), but as this took measures to make it illegal for financial transaction providers to transfer funds to any online gambling site, or for online gambling providers to accept bets from US citizens, it was not found to be compliant with the WTO ruling.

In addition, in May 2007 the United States formally withdrew from its commitments with regard to gaming under *GATS*.[370] As a condition of withdrawal, the United States entered into compensation agreements with several WTO members. The agreement with Antigua gave it the right to request authorization from the WTO Dispute Settlement Body (DSB) not to make payments to the United States under the *Agreement on Trade-Related Intellectual Property Rights* (*TRIPS*) in the amount of $21 million annually.[371] Antigua has not requested that the DSB authorize this right, however, and since 2009 has instead been negotiating with

---

368 James D Thayer, "The Trade of Cross-Border Gambling and Betting: The WTO Dispute Between Antigua and the United States" (2004) Duke L & Tech Rev 0013 at n 21.

369 Grimmett, above note 346.

370 *Ibid* at 15.

371 *Ibid* at 48, n 248.

the United States to reach "a mutually agreeable resolution."[372] Until the compensation agreement with Antigua is formalized, the United States cannot formally withdraw from its *GATS* commitments.[373]

As a practical matter, Antigua might not have the ability to bring sufficient economic pressure to cause the United States to act in a different manner. However, in 2009, the European Union, which has much greater economic influence, initiated an investigation under the European Union Trade Barriers Regulation due to concerns that US online gambling regulations are inconsistent with US *GATS* obligations. Although the report detailing the investigation found that WTO action would be justified, it did not recommend such action and suggested instead negotiating with the United States.[374] Perhaps the conclusion to draw is that in some matters that engage extraterritorial issues, politics outweighs law.

3) Conclusion

As noted at the start of this case study, attitudes towards gambling vary dramatically from state to state. This situation caused no particular problem when gamblers had very little ability to gamble anywhere other than the place in which they were physically located. In that reality, each state could set the rules for gambling in its own territory. Once Internet gambling became a reality, however, gamblers could in principle engage in the activity anywhere in the world. That created the incentive for states to legislate extraterritorially, either to govern the interaction of individuals outside that state with gaming providers inside it, or to govern the interaction of individual inside that state with gaming providers outside it.

As a result, more than one state might try to set rules governing the very same transaction. This would not necessarily cause problems if the rules did not conflict: because of the differing attitudes towards gambling, however, it is very likely that they will. As a result, Internet gambling offers a very clear object lesson in the dangers inherent in the exercise of extraterritorial jurisdiction. In the absence of international consensus, attempts to regulate Internet gambling extraterritorially are,

---

372 *Ibid* at 49, n 250.

373 *Ibid* at Summary. As of January 2014 negotiations between the two nations had still not reached an agreement.

374 *Ibid* at 49.

rather than leading to the state of order the law tries to achieve, likely to lead to disorder, international trade disputes, and retaliatory measures.

G. VIRTUAL WORLDS

In the early days of the Internet there was a view that it was a separate place, that one travelled to "cyberspace." Further, it was seen by some as ungovernable, as a kind of Wild West. There was the idea not only that there were practical difficulties in exerting jurisdiction over cyberspace, but that governments had no legitimate claim to try to do so.[375]

For the most part, none of these views holds much currency any more. That, in general, governments can regulate the Internet in many ways is pretty well-established, and the view that they ought not to is held only by a diminishing group. For the most part, regulation of the Internet has become incorporated into questions of where contracts are formed, whose law applies in the case of conflicts, whether there is a real and substantial connection between the activity on the Internet and a country, the terms and conditions in an end-user licence agreement (EULA), and so on. There is not always consistency among countries as to how to resolve these issues,[376] but they are not generally seen as unresolvable.[377]

Further, the notion of the Internet as some separate location has largely faded. As Kerr points out:

---

375 The most widely cited such claim is John Perry Barlow, "A Declaration of the Independence of Cyberspace" (8 February 1996), online: Electronic Frontier Foundation https://projects.eff.org/~barlow/Declaration-Final.html.

> Governments of the Industrial World, you weary giants of flesh and steel, I come from Cyberspace, the new home of Mind. On behalf of the future, I ask you of the past to leave us alone. You are not welcome among us. You have no sovereignty where we gather . . . .
>
> Governments derive their just powers from the consent of the governed. You have neither solicited nor received ours. We did not invite you. You do not know us, nor do you know our world. Cyberspace does not lie within your borders. Do not think that you can build it, as though it were a public construction project. You cannot. It is an act of nature and it grows itself through our collective actions.

376 In the previous case study in Section F, above in this chapter, for example, it is noted that courts in countries can take different views as to "where" gambling on the Internet takes place: where the bettor is or where the server is located, for instance.

377 On this point, see Jack L Goldsmith & Tim Wu, *Who Controls the Internet? Illusions of a Borderless World* (Oxford: Oxford University Press, 2006).

> In the last decade, the virtual metaphor of cyberspace has seemed increasingly outdated. Today the internet is everywhere. It is integrated into the physical world through wireless networks, BlackBerries, and cell phones. Most internet users no longer think of spending time in "cyberspace." Instead, the internet comes to them. Connectivity is the norm, and most users experience using the internet as a connection to services rather than entrance into cyberspace.[378]

The arguable exception to both these developments, however, is the phenomenon of "virtual worlds." In roughly the past decade a number of virtual worlds have appeared and now attract millions of subscribers worldwide.[379] They are the one aspect of the online experience that still is perceived by many as a separate place, and with some justification. In this case study we will consider the particular issue of the application—or non-application—of real world law to virtual worlds. Should ordinary rules about territorial and extraterritorial jurisdiction be applied to "take apart" virtual worlds and ignore their unique features, or should special rules, which amount to extraterritorial claims, be applied?

This is a subject that has attracted a great deal of attention.[380] One might think of this question as similar to sections 7(2.3) to 7(2.34) of the

---

378 Orin S Kerr, "Criminal Law in Virtual Worlds: Law in a Networked World" (2008) U Chicago Legal F 415; Jonathon W Penney, "Understanding the New Virtualist Paradigm" (2009) 12:8 Journal of Internet Law 3.

379 In 2006, global subscriber estimates were 9.4 million. (Viktor Mayer-Schönberger & John Crowley, "Napster's Second Life?: The Regulatory Challenges of Virtual Worlds" (2006) 100:4 Nw UL Rev 1775 at 1781.) In 2007, it was estimated that there would be 50–60 million subscribers worldwide. (Wagner James Au, "Virtual World Population: 50 Million by 2011" (20 May 2007), online: Gigaom http://gigaom.com/2007/05/20/virtual-world-population-50-million-by-2011.) Reportedly more people in South Korea participate in virtual worlds than watch television, and there are an estimated 17 million accounts worldwide with just one South Korean "environment" by the name of Lineage II, though a determination of the number of subscribers can be more telling than the number of accounts. At its peak in 2004, Lineage I had an estimated 4 million subscribers. (Joshua AT Fairfield, "Virtual Property" (2005) 85:4 BUL Rev 1047 at nn 65–66.)

380 Kerr, above note 378; David G Post, "Governing Cyberspace: Law" (2008) 24:4 Santa Clara Computer & High Tech LJ 883; Stephen J Davidson, "An Immersive Perspective on the Second Life Virtual World" (2008) 25:3 Computer & Internet Lawyer 1; Susan W Brenner & Leo L Clarke, "Distributed Security: A New Model of Law Enforcement," *Social Science Research Network Working Paper Series* (14 November 2005); Ethan Katsh, "Bringing Online Dispute Resolution to Virtual Worlds: Creating Processes Through Code" (2004–2005) 49:1 NYL Sch L Rev 271; David G Post & David R Johnson, "The Great Debate: Law in the Virtual World" (2006) 11:2 First Monday,

Criminal Code, which anticipate questions of criminal jurisdiction for offences committed in outer space: the demands on that area of law are not yet noticeable, but we can see a future in which they could be.

1) Virtual Worlds Defined

A virtual world is an immersive environment in which a person controls a character (referred to as an "avatar") as he moves about. Many of these virtual worlds are essentially online versions of tabletop games: *Dungeons & Dragons* played through a computer rather than through miniature models and twenty-sided dice. In these virtual worlds such as *EverQuest*, *World of Warcraft*, *Lineage*, and others there are particular goals. These can be quite specific (go on a quest to a particular cave to slay the dragon that lives there) or more open-ended ("level up"—that is, gain enough experience that one's character is "promoted" to a higher level and according to the coding of the game is more capable in certain ways). Other virtual worlds have no such explicit goals. Worlds like *Second Life* or *There*[381] exist primarily as means of social interaction, with no particular goals directed by the world itself and no equivalent to "levelling." It might be possible to play games in those worlds,[382] but they are simply social activities, not the purpose of the world.

---

online: First Monday http://firstmonday.org/htbin/cgiwrap/bin/ojs/index.php/fm/article/view/1311/1231. Criminal theft is not necessarily limited to tangible property. A Texas appellate court held computer program codes to be property because they are writings that possess an ascertainable value. Under such a definition of property, virtual goods should be considered property, as they too are of ascertainable value and are made up of computer code (Andrea Vanina Arias, "Life, Liberty, and the Pursuit of Swords and Armor: Regulating the Theft of Virtual Goods" (2008) 57:5 Emory LJ 1301 at 1313, nn 100 and 103.) Post & Johnson, above in this footnote; Penney, above note 378; James Grimmelmann, "Virtual Worlds as Comparative Law" (2004–2005) 49:1 NYL Sch L Rev 147 at 170–71, nn 98–101.

381 There.com existed from 2003 until 2010, but shut down at that point, citing the economic recession: Michael Wilson, "There.com closed on March 9th, 2010 . . . but has re-opened in 2012," online: there.com www.there.com/info/announcement.

382 There included paintball, for example, and *Second Life* did allow casino games for a period of time, and still contains many other games such as fighting, puzzle, and board games ("Goals of Second Life," online: Second Life Wiki http://wiki.secondlife.com/wiki/Goals_of_Second_Life), as well as paintball ("CP Sponsors Paintball Field in Virtual World" (February 2007), online: World and Regional Paintball Information Guide www.warpig.com/paintball/articles/news/cpvirtual).

Even the virtual worlds which have goals, however, involve a much richer social environment than might be immediately obvious. It is, of course, possible to do well in such games by being good at fighting, by being hard to kill, or by having skill at healing; in addition, however, there are successful strategies which rely on blacksmithing, mining, cooking, baking, tanning leather, prospecting for jewels, sewing, and so on. In most worlds, items can be bought and sold (between players or between players and the world), the world has its own currency, and a real economy exists.[383] Those features encourage a variety of interactions. In addition, even in the game-like virtual worlds, many of the quests cannot be accomplished by a single character[384] in isolation. It is possible to form casual alliances to undertake particular quests, but in addition, players tend to form into "guilds," which are permanent associations among members.[385]

Various features justify the use of the word "world" to refer to these environments.[386] They are experienced visually and have a distinct

---

383 See Edward Castronova, "Virtual Worlds: A First-Hand Account of Market and Society on the Cyberian Frontier," *CESifo Working Paper No. 618* (December 2001), online: Social Science Research Network http://ssrn.com/abstract=294828. Castronova studied "Norrath," the world in the game *EverQuest*. *EverQuest*'s currency could be bought and sold on eBay, which meant in effect that there was an exchange rate allowing calculations about the virtual world in real world dollars (Norrath's currency traded at a slightly higher rate than the yen or the lira). Castronova calculated that (in 2001) the hourly wage was US$3.42 and that the GNP of Norrath placed it between Russia and Bulgaria.

384 It is necessary to think of "characters" rather than "people," because it is generally possible in a virtual world to be something other than a human being: an elf, dwarf, gnome, ogre, and so on. This phenomenon is not limited to game-like virtual worlds.

385 "Every major game has some variant on the guild concept. *EverQuest* has guilds and raid parties, *Asheron's Call* has allegiance hierarchies, *Star Wars Galaxies* has player associations, and many games have more complex systems. Across these disparate games, guilds almost always have several important features in common: the games make some explicit provision for their existence, the powers granted to them by the games are very weak, and yet they are somehow key to the social energy of a virtual world." (Grimmelmann, above note 380 at 170–71 [footnotes omitted].) Guilds can be understood as groups that help to reduce transaction costs and help the players in them complete tasks co-operatively (*ibid* at 171–72).

386 Virtual worlds in their current form are an evolution of previous versions, and will no doubt evolve further. For descriptions of the historical development of virtual worlds over the last twenty years from the first purely text-based MUD (multi-user domain) to MMORPGs (massively multi-player online role-playing games) to their current forms, see Richard A Bartle, "Virtual Worldliness: What the Imaginary Asks of the Real" (2004–2005) 49:1 NYL Sch L Rev 19 at part I, online New York Law

physical geography through which one moves, encountering objects and other characters. In broad terms, they appear to obey the laws of physics: one can pick up and put down solid objects, be kept outside by locked doors, walk up hills, sit down or stand up, ride in vehicles, and so on.[387] Generally speaking, movement and vision is unrestricted — one can choose to move in any cardinal direction as well as up or down, and one can change the direction of one's gaze essentially largely without limits, just as in real life (or "RL" as it is sometimes referred to). For the most part, interactions take place with the avatars of other players, rather than with programmed aspects of the game (though some worlds do have non-player characters (NPCs,) who have scripted responses and provide information about quests and so on). In some virtual worlds, the majority of the content in the world has been created by other users, not by the world's programmers (*Second Life* is the best example of this).[388] Virtual world communication was originally text-based, in that conversations took place in writing, though voice communication is increasingly common.

The feature that most distinguishes a virtual world from a computer game is that a virtual world is continuous and persistent. If one pauses or stops playing a puzzle or adventure-based computer game, then the program saves its status and is picked up from that point whenever it is next played. A virtual world, however, always exists: if it is left for a

---

School http://a.nyls.edu/user_files/1/3/4/17/49/v49n1p19-44.pdf; Sarah E Galbraith, "Second Life Strife: A Proposal for Resolution of In-World Fashion Disputes" (2008) Brown College Intellectual Property & Technology Forum at 32; F Gregory Lastowka & Dan Hunter, "The Laws of the Virtual Worlds" (2004) 92:1 Cal L Rev 1 at 39.

387 The ordinary laws of physics might not apply in all situations, and so one might be able to fly, teleport, have telescopic vision, or walk through some solid objects, for example.

388 Most virtual environments, including *Second Life*, allow for enduring user-created content, but *World of Warcraft* does not. (Brian Partridge, "'The Play's the Thing': *World of Warcraft* and Legal Philosophy" (2010) 3:2 Phoenix Law Review 769 at n 31.) Games like *The Sims* and *Second Life*, which have social interaction as their central concern, encourage users to "create their own content, economies, and entertainment," instead of fulfilling a quest or playing a game. (Miriam A Cherry, "Working for (Virtually) Minimum Wage: Applying the *Fair Labor Standards Act* in Cyberspace" (2009) 60:5 Ala L Rev 1077 at 1085, n 52.) Second Life uniquely gives users the ability to create anything they desire. Users retain the rights to their creations and thus have the ability to sell and profit from any of their creations. (Elkia Manglona, "An Avatar's Parody: Considering a First Amendment Right to Parody Real World Trademarks in a Three-Dimensional Virtual World" (2009) 19:1 Alb LJ Sci & Tech 183 at nn 19 and 22.)

month, then a month's time has passed in the virtual world, and all the other inhabitants will have continued to interact with one another. This depends, of course, on other players being there, but that is realistically a non-issue. In 2006, roughly 10 million players worldwide were registered in a variety of virtual worlds,[389] and many of those players spend a lot of time there.[390] By 2008, *World of Warcraft* alone had more than 11 million players.[391] According to a study done by KZero, a British analytics company that focuses on virtual worlds, in the third quarter of 2010, the number of virtual world players exceeded 1 billion globally, with about half of those players being under the age of fifteen.[392]

2) Virtual Worlds and the Need for Law

There are many ways in which legal issues could arise in connection with virtual worlds, but a good number of them are not unique to these worlds. Real world crimes such as money-laundering can be committed through the use of virtual worlds, since it is possible to put money into the virtual economy and to take it out again; claims of breach of copyright can occur;[393] trademarks can be improperly used in a virtual world;[394] contractual

---

389 Schönberger & Crowley, above note 379 at 1787.

390 Castronova, above note 383 at 20–21, conducted a survey (non-random, he acknowledges) of *EverQuest* users and found that nearly a third of the adults in the world spent more time in Norrath in a typical week than they did working for pay. He also reports that:

> About 40 percent indicate that if a sufficient wage (self-defined) were available in Norrath, they would quit their economic activity on Earth (work or school, as the case may be) and devote their labor hours to the Norrathian economy. (*Ibid* at 22.)

Yee found that players spent a median of 21.9 hours per week in game-like virtual worlds: Nick Yee, "The Daedalus Project: the Psychology of MMORPGS" (9 March 2009), online: The Daedalus Project http://nickyee.com/daedalus/archives/000758.php.

391 Partridge, above note 388 at n 9.

392 Audrey Watters, "Number of Virtual World Users Breaks 1 Billion, Roughly Half under Age 15" (1 October 2010), online: Read, Write, Web www.readwriteweb.com/archives/number_of_virtual_world_users_breaks_the_1_billion.php.

393 See Davidson, above note 380 at 8, for discussion of a copyright claim brought by one *Second Life* user against another *Second Life* user who was said to have copied his software that simulates erotic acts. Davidson quotes the plaintiff's lawyer to the effect that although the context was titillating and unusual, fundamentally it was only about copyright in software and graphics, which were not novel subject areas.

394 *Ibid* at 9.

disputes between users and service providers can arise;[395] aspects of a real-world stalking can occur in a virtual world.

Some crimes could "cross over," having a relationship both to the game and the real world. In a Dutch case, for example, two fourteen-year-old boys were convicted of theft when they forced a thirteen-year-old boy to give them two items in the game *Runescape*.[396] The theft in that case was of virtual items, but the threats made and physical force applied to accomplish the threat occurred in the real world. It is nonetheless significant that the court was willing to recognize the virtual items as property, analogizing the offence to theft of electricity.[397]

Some legal disputes could be much more closely tied to the virtual world, however. Items are bought and sold within worlds, thereby forming contracts. Items are sometimes declared in-world to be subject to copyright, though various in-world permissions are given.[398] Items can be stolen, sometimes through mechanisms permitted in the world and sometimes in others ways. Interestingly, some of the ways of obtaining items that are permitted by the programming in a virtual world might be *perceived* as theft by inhabitants of that world. For example, an avatar who is the first to pick up an item will become its owner. Players engaged in a quest together might have agreed in advance upon how the spoils will be divided, but as a practical matter, that agreement does not prevent another player from picking up the item instead. This practice is referred to in some worlds as "ninja-ing" or "loot ninja-ing," and is decidedly socially unacceptable:

---

395 Steven J Horowitz, "*Bragg v. Linden*'s Second Life: A Primer in Virtual World Justice" (2008) 34:1 Ohio NUL Rev 223. See Horowitz's discussion of *Bragg v Linden*, a lawsuit that was filed, but settled out of court. In virtual world settings, consumers are very much at the mercy of service providers. Although users can litigate some problems that may arise with service providers, well-written EULAs can greatly reduce chances of success (Jennifer Gong, "Defining and Addressing Virtual Property in International Treaties" (2011) 17 BUJ Sci & Tech L 101 at 136–37.)

396 "Dutch Court Rules Virtual Theft Is Real" (22 October 2008), online: Radio Netherlands Worldwide www.rnw.nl/english/article/dutch-court-rules-virtual-theft-real.

397 See similarly Castronova, above note 383, who observes at n 20:

> The reader who doubts the real economic value of items created in the Norrath economy, and hence the utility concerns of the people who spend time there, is invited to go to Norrath, steal something, and observe reactions.

398 Davidson, above note 380 at 6. Some of these issues are subject to technological considerations as well as legal ones. In *Second Life*, for example, anyone creating an item can decide whether that item is capable of being copied, modified, or transferred to another person.

> Loot ninjas are, understandably, not well liked by other players. Often, a ninja will get a bad reputation on a realm which eventually prevents them from being invited to participate in any high level instances . . . . Many guilds also have rules stating that ninjas/pirates should be kicked from the guild on their first offense.[399]

A similar practice is "kill-stealing." In some worlds where experience points are gained in fighting monsters, those points are awarded to the player(s) dealing the killing blow, whether she did the majority of damage or not. This creates the possibility of one player stepping in at the last minute to gain the benefit of work done by others: again, something seen as socially unacceptable.[400]

It might not be immediately intuitive that ninja-ing or kill-stealing are practices that should attract the attention of the law, whether private or public—and perhaps they should not. But fundamentally, kill-stealing is no different from a question that has long been seen as a legitimate one for the law: "At what point does one acquire a protectable interest in a wild animal one is hunting?" The question is addressed differently within the various virtual worlds.[401]

Further, items from these worlds and the avatars themselves (especially high-level ones) can be bought and sold in real world dollars, and so there is a measurable loss of the sort with which the law normally concerns itself. These amounts are not small: in 2003 alone, eBay saw trades totalling US$9 million in virtual goods for virtual worlds, and total trade in virtual goods is variously estimated as between US$200 million and US$2 billion annually.[402] In 2008, the sale of virtual curren-

399 See the *World of Warcraft* wiki: "A loot ninja, AKA ninja looter or simply ninja, is a player who takes loot to which he or she is not entitled. The act is referred to as ninja looting or ninjaing." WoWWiki, "Loot Ninja," online: Wikia www.wowwiki.com/Loot_ninja.

400 See, for example, Zam *EverQuest*, "Geno Kanan's Guide to Dealing with Kill Stealers," online: Zam Network http://everquest.allakhazam.com/editorial/082099_Geno_kill_Stealing.htm.

401 Grimmelmann, above note 380 at 155–56. The author points out that *EverQuest*, for example, awards the experience of killing a monster to the players who inflicted the most damage on the monster, whereas *Asheron's Call* divides this experience up in proportion to the amount of damage done by each player involved in the kill.

402 Arias, above note 380 at 3–4. In addition, it is worth noting the extraterritorial economic effects of virtual worlds. See the discussion in Lastowka & Hunter, above note 386 at 39, regarding Blacksnow Interactive, which hired unskilled labourers in Mexico to play "Dark Age of Camelot" and create virtual items, which they then sold. Similarly, "gold farming" is common in *World of Warcraft*, and there are com-

cy and goods for real currency was estimated to be a US$200 million to over US$1 billion-dollar industry annually.[403] In 2008, *Second Life* saw their players spend over US$1 million daily on virtual products.[404]

Even more subtle issues arise around avatars in virtual worlds. A player might *own* a hover bike or castle or spaceship in a virtual world, but that player *is* his or her avatar; as has been stated, "people rarely think of their avatar as something completely distinct from themselves ."[405] Players perceive the things that happen to their avatars as happening to them — not literally, of course, since they will not be affected physically by what happens, but effects can be quite real in non-physical ways. A person whose avatar is harassed in-world (or "griefed") might easily feel as much frustration as a person harassed in real life, and feel equally unable to visit her favourite places. Or what of a person who is falsely accused of ninja-looting? His reputation (or more accurately, his avatar's

---

panies in China that hire workers to play the game to produce virtual gold which can be sold to other players in more prosperous countries. An estimated 80 percent of all gold farmers reside in China, employing what is thought to be about 100,000 full-time gold farmers. (Danny Vincent, "China Used Prisoners in Lucrative Internet Gaming Network: Labour Camp Detainees Endure Hard Labour by Day, Online 'Gold Farming' by Night" *The Guardian* (25 May 2011), online: Guardian News and Media Limited www.theguardian.com/world/2011/may/25/china-prisoners-internet-gaming-scam.) However, this sector has spread throughout Asia and is projected to continue to do so as virtual world subscription grows. (Richard Heeks, "Current Analysis and Future Research Agenda on 'Gold Farming': Real-World Production in Developing Countries for the Virtual Economies of Online Games," *Development Informatics Working Paper Series No. 32* (2008), online: University of Manchester, Institute for Development Policy and Management www.sed.manchester.ac.uk/idpm/research/publications/wp/di/documents/di_wp32.pdf.) Wages of $1 to $4 hourly could be earned farming gold in virtual worlds and selling it on eBay. (Edward Castronova, *Exodus to the Virtual World: How Online Fun Is Changing Reality* (New York: Palgrave MacMillan, 2007) ch 1.) In fact, a Chinese national recently shared his tale of being forced by prison bosses to gold-farm in virtual worlds during his incarceration at the Jixi labour camp in China. Although he saw no profit from this labour, he heard prison bosses say that they could earn the equivalent of £470–£570 per day from 300 prisoners working twelve-hour shifts. (Vincent, above in this footnote.) However, in 2009, the Chinese government banned the trading of virtual currency for real-world goods or services. (Thomas Claburn, "China Limits Use of Virtual Currency" (29 June 2009), online: InformationWeek www.informationweek.com/news/internet/ebusiness/218101859.)

403 Heeks, above note 402 at 10.

404 Brendan Burns, "Do Virtual World Activities Give Rise to Real Canadian Tax Liabilities?" (2010) 10 Asper Review of International Business and Trade Law 163 at 170.

405 Lastowka & Hunter, above note 386 at 65.

reputation) might suffer, he might be ejected from his guild, and others might refuse to allow him to join quests. Any of these things might have a direct impact on a person's ability to enjoy life in a virtual world, a privilege for which they will likely be paying a monthly subscription fee. One can say "move to a different virtual world," but this could involve giving up the accrued benefits of many hours devoted to levelling an avatar, or involve abandoning the circle of friends one has grown close to.

Even granting that such claims might be plausible, one question that arises is how to classify them. Does one actually have property rights in the items in a virtual world as though they are tangible assets, or does one simply have a licence to play the game?[406] Can an avatar be libelled, or is the claim for some type of interference with economic relations? Is it a claim against the programmers for permitting particular types of behaviour?

Beyond even that, however, is the question that we must turn to next. Presuming that there are legal claims to be made, and that the nature of those claims could be settled, what mechanism would be best for settling them? Do virtual worlds require special legal rules or regimes?

3) Do Virtual Worlds Require a Special Approach?

The answer to this question might depend in part on the kind of activity involved. Money laundering conducted through a virtual world can very likely be dealt with through the application of ordinary rules of domestic law and, where needed, extraterritorial jurisdiction. Many disputes might simply reduce to contractual ones, and the law is quite capable of dealing with contracts that were entered into by parties in different jurisdictions. Similarly, Davidson observes that virtual worlds are

> merely the Internet experienced in a different way. It does not require much thought to realize that the use, policing, and enforcement of trademarks in a metaverse such as Second Life are not much different than in the real world of the World Wide Web.[407]

---

406 Horowitz, above note 395 at 235. At 234–35, Horowitz points out that Linden Labs, the developers of *Second Life*, have an interest in acknowledging that users own the land they purchase, rather than, for example, merely having a licence to use dedicated server space which is represented in the virtual world as land. *Second Life*'s marketing strategy depends on subscribers believing that they own virtual land, and their primary revenue stream would be otherwise threatened.

407 Davidson, above note 380 at 9.

Although it has not become a major issue, some real-world courts have been called upon to settle disputes relating to virtual worlds. Among other instances, a suit was filed in California when Linden Labs seized the virtual real property of one of its subscribers,[408] and reportedly a Chinese court has ordered the return, in-world, of a piece of virtual property.[409]

However, not everyone agrees that no special rules are needed regarding cyberspace generally. Post refers to the two camps as "cyberspace exceptionalists" (into which he places himself) and "cyberspace unexceptionalists" (into which he acknowledges the majority of people who have considered jurisdictional issues fall).[410] He argues that virtual worlds create unusual and special considerations that cannot appropriately be dealt with simply by applying domestic law and the ordinary rules about extraterritoriality. He offers the example of someone creating a bank in *Second Life*: an in-world bank that accepts deposits, makes investments, and pays interest on money invested, all of which can be exchanged into real-world dollars. What law, he asks, governs that bank, and what happens in the case of conflicts:

> . . . what if, say, Korean banking or securities law prohibits any and all investment pools of this kind, while French banking or securities law allows them but only if they register with the relevant government authorities, and Russian law requires them to place a percentage of their funds into an insurance account, and U.S. law requires that once the fund reaches a certain dollar threshold the managers of the fund must make particular kinds of information available to the public about the compensation of the fund's managers, and . . .?[411]

On the unexceptionalist view, Post argues, interactions in a virtual world are in principle governed by *all* those laws: in practical terms, the people running or using the bank run the risk of becoming subject to enforcement of any of those laws if they or their assets are at some point in one of those countries. Post refers to this situation as "jurisdictional whack-a-mole," arguing that it will not work:

---

408 See discussion of this case, which was settled out of court, in Horowitz, above note 395 at 229.

409 See the discussion of this case and others in Nick Abrahams, "Media Laws for Virtual Worlds" (2007) 30 UNSWLJ 295 at heading "Case Law." See also Lastowka & Hunter, above note 386 at 71, discussing the "Giran Castle dispute" in South Korea.

410 Post, above note 380 at 889–94.

411 *Ibid* at 908–9; Schönberger & Crowley, above note 379.

> . . . by which I mean not just that some law professors (like me) think that it is theoretically unhinged, but that it won't do the things that law does when it *does* work, namely help people enter into complicated transactions involving lots of other people and with important things at stake, secure (to a degree) in their expectations of how others will behave and secure (to a degree) that they will be treated fairly in the event of a problem.[412]

Post argues that virtual worlds like *Second Life* contain enormous potential for the trade of goods or services that can be handled electronically, but that this potential will remain unrealized unless there is a legal system that can answer questions about an individual's rights and interests "without the need to consult the legal codes of every country in the world simultaneously."[413]

If the unexceptionalist position is preferable, there is no need (from an extraterritorial application of law perspective) for a separate discussion of virtual worlds. If there is something to be said for the exceptionalist view, however, then reasons to discuss the extraterritorial application of law—or more properly, reasons not to apply law extraterritorially—do arise.

4) How Should Virtual Worlds Be Regulated?

Virtual worlds seem to be a phenomenon in which the notion that "code is law" is directly applicable. The physical reality of virtual worlds exist only as code, and the laws of physics that do or do not apply are governed by that code, and so problems seem peculiarly amenable to simply being programmed out of existence. As has been pointed out, some types of behaviour can be effectively removed from virtual worlds simply by programming them away—if teleporting causes problems, teleporting can cease to exist.

Further, virtual worlds are well positioned to deal not only with particular types of behaviours, but with particular individuals. It has been pointed out that virtual worlds are run by administrators, and that "[g]ame administrators do not merely act like governments in virtual worlds: they act like gods."[414] In addition, troublesome users can simply

---

412 Post, above note 380 at 910 [emphasis in the original].

413 *Ibid* at 911.

414 Kerr, above note 378 at 425.

be banned from a game. A contract can be cancelled and the person's ability to sign into a game can be removed:

> Expulsion as an enforcement mechanism is effective because participants in virtual worlds incur significant social and financial costs when they are forced to leave. They not only have to leave behind a network of friends and their accumulation of social and other capital, but also are forced to abandon the persistent narrative that they have constructed around their avatar. There are additional financial costs: the required use of credit cards for payment of the virtual world's monthly fees ensures that individual participants are linked to specific credit cards (and thus, by approximation, people), making it difficult for individuals to re-register for a virtual world from which they have been banished. While it is not impossible to sign up again with a different credit card, it would still be a costly choice, as one would still have lost everything connected with the previous avatar.[415]

In the end, the world administrators have the ability not just to ban users, but to shut down the world entirely, to "pull the plug."[416] Virtual worlds involve a level of administrative control no government could ever aspire to. Even apart from administrative control, the fact that worlds are virtual can give rise to technological solutions that do not exist in real life.[417]

For that matter, there are other ways in which purely technological solutions can be implemented in virtual worlds. One problem in some games (from the perspective of the virtual world) is the extra-world market in game items — the fact, as noted above, that property and avatars in the game can be sold, and potentially sold outside of the game. It is argued, for example, that it is important to the integrity of a game that anyone playing a level 60 character actually has the level of skill and experience in the game necessary to have achieved that level.[418] In fact, though, since it is possible to buy an avatar that has already been levelled by someone else, there is no such guarantee. Similarly, items that are meant to be rare in a game and only to be obtainable by meet-

---

415 Schönberger & Crowley, above note 379 at 1793 [footnotes omitted].

416 Lastowka & Hunter, above note 386 at 56.

417 Schönberger & Crowley, above note 379 at 1800, talk about a dispute in *Second Life* where one inhabitant had ruined his neighbour's view by erecting a giant model of a toilet in what otherwise would have appeared to be a pastoral setting. The dispute was resolved when a third neighbour programmed a barrier that rendered the toilet invisible from one direction.

418 Bartle, above note 386.

ing particular in-world requirements might instead be bought online. As a result, *EverQuest* had at one point negotiated an agreement with eBay in which it would refuse to accept auctions related to the *EverQuest* world.[419] This technological solution is similar to that pursued by some jurisdictions with regard to online gambling; for example, in persuading Paypal not to engage in such transactions.[420]

However, there are limits to the extent to which solutions to virtual world problems can be hardwired away. The *EverQuest*/eBay arrangement, for example, did not actually solve the black market problem: it made it harder for people to engage in such trade, but it did not eliminate either the supply or the demand. Ultimately *EverQuest* itself was forced to change tactics. Rather than fight the sale of items, it created its own online auction house and took a portion of the proceeds.[421] This does not eliminate hardwired solutions (creating an auction house permits online "reputation" or dispute settlement mechanisms, such as those that exist in eBay, for example) but it does show that hardwiring will often not be enough.

What about kill-stealing, for example? The problem there was that the person who dealt the mortal blow gained all the benefits, no matter who did the majority of the work. That seems like a problem that could be easily hardwired away by having the world's programming award the benefits proportionally instead (in fact, that is the way some worlds are programmed). Interestingly, however, kill-stealing is *still* seen as socially unacceptable even in those worlds.[422]

The point to recognize is that these worlds, whether games or simply places for social interaction, are more than just the things the programming permits. They are genuine communities, with social norms, expectations, unwritten (or written) codes of behaviour, and shared expectations about how a player will behave that are not amenable to hardwired solutions.

To some extent, the solutions might only be limited by current technology. One could have a rule against swearing in public and impose a filter that blocks all use of particular words in public text-based chat,

---

419 Arias, above note 380 at 48.

420 See the previous case study in Section F, above in this chapter.

421 Schönberger & Crowley, above note 379 at 1800. In its first three months of operation, the site had trade in virtual objects amounting to more than US$540,000, of which 10 percent was paid in commissions to Sony, the owners of *EverQuest*.

422 Grimmelmann, above note 380 at 156.

and that type of rule might be reasonably successful.[423] The same is not true of a rule about making threats to other inhabitants — the software is not sophisticated enough to read all natural language and determine whether something seemingly innocuous is in context a threat, and vice versa.[424] It seems likely that the software will never be sophisticated enough to deal with issues of this sort, but perhaps it will develop that ability.

Even if we grant that hardwiring might improve, and that more solutions could be instituted in that way, there remains the difficulty that the social environment of a virtual world will always be more than just its coding. As Bartle points out, coding is at best the equivalent of the written rules of a game. No written rules of the board game *Clue* forbid a person from offering another player a bribe in order to be allowed to see their cards; nonetheless, we all know you "can't" do that.[425] Similarly for virtual worlds, no matter what parameters are set by the programming, there will still be things that, by the culture of the world, one cannot do. The social norms are never entirely written, and so hardwiring cannot be a complete solution.

What alternative is there, then, if social norms can trump hardwiring? In a broad sense, the solution then becomes "leave it to the game," but that can mean more than one thing. On one view, it means "leave it to the developers":

> Because software code can only limit and not eliminate conflict, virtual world providers must apply more old-fashioned governance mechanisms to deal with conflicts that cannot be constrained through modifications to the underlying code: codifying social norms into written rules and providing effective enforcement of these rules.[426]

On this view, virtual worlds:

---

423 Though only reasonably so. Bartle points out that AOL's filters originally blocked any reference to the English town of Scunthorpe because of the vulgarity contained in it. He asks "Do you ban all reference to its name . . . or do you allow reference to it in the full knowledge that people will then start using it as a profanity?" (Bartle, above note 386 at n 17.)

424 Schönberger & Crowley, above note 379 at 1791–92.

425 Bartle, above note 386 at 24.

426 Schönberger & Crowley, above note 379 at 1792.

> are like huge "virtual malls" in which the owners retain significant rights. Rulemaking is done by the virtual world provider, with no guarantee of democratic participation or assurance of transparency.[427]

On this approach, the "governance" of the world is divorced from its inhabitants, as rules are enforced by the administrators. Bartle points to this as his mechanism for enforcing a "no swearing" rule in *MUD*, the first virtual world: he created the command "FOD" ("finger of death"), which only he was able to use, and he disintegrated any character who swore.[428]

That solution does not entirely address the issue of social norms, however. The ways in which inhabitants actually interact are not necessarily the ways in which the rules created by the developers say they should, and it is difficult in such situations to say that the inhabitants are necessarily wrong. In the virtual world "City of Heroes," for example, players create avatars which have superpowers and who are either heroes or villains. The rules of the world designated a particular area as one where combat could take place, but by the common practice of all players but one, it grew to be a location where no combat occurred and where heroes and villains could visit and interact "out of character." One avatar, a hero named Twixt, ignored this custom and regularly captured villains there. Though he was acting in accordance with the written rules, he was violating custom, and rapidly became known as the most hated player in the world.[429]

A further alternative favoured by some is to harness those social norms in the way one generally does in any other society: through decision making,[430] or law making by the society itself. Some argue that

---

427 *Ibid* at 1794 [footnotes omitted].

428 Bartle, above note 386 at 27. Bartle acknowledges that this would likely not be a practical solution in a larger world.

429 Ramon Antonio Vargas, "'City of Heroes' Character 'Twixt' Becomes Game's Most Hated Outcast Courtesy of Loyola Professor" *The Times-Picayune* (31 July 2009), online: Nola Media Group www.nola.com/news/index.ssf/2009/07/loyola_university_professor_be.html. Twixt was an avatar of David Myers, a professor at Loyola University's School of Mass Communication. He claimed to have been acting in this way as a sociological experiment. (David Myers, "Play and Punishment: The Sad and Curious Case of Twixt" (Paper delivered at the [Player] Conference Proceedings, The Centre for Computer Games Research, IT University of Copenhagen, Denmark, 2008 [unpublished].) One might be forgiven for thinking that the point he was purporting to prove did not need much proof.

430 Katsh, above note 380, argues that alternative dispute resolution is particularly suited to virtual worlds through, for example, online dispute resolution.

virtual worlds could become, within some limits, self-governing communities. This is the option Post prefers, referring back to his concept of "jurisdictional whack-a-mole" and the question of how a bank that exists solely in *Second Life* should be regulated:

> asking those who spend their time in Second Life for the answers to those questions . . . seems a *lot* more reasonable to me than asking the people of Malaysia how Malaysian law answers those same questions.[431]

This option does not have to mean that virtual worlds are recognized as somehow equivalent to other states. Post and Johnson argue elsewhere:

> Sovereigns should allow their citizens who wish to travel to online spaces and, while there, to be governed by the rules applicable there, provided that those rules don't allow the online spaces to become havens for actions causing substantial harm to outsiders. Just as governments now defer to private ordering by organizations of all kinds that primarily "govern their own affairs," they will be persuaded to defer to congruent online regimes — because this will allow the resources of local governments to be devoted to the real world problems only they can solve.[432]

One might question whether this suggests too much of a "hands-off" proposal. Private organizations are subject to the dictates of human rights legislation, for example. One would need a pretty strong justification to conclude that the private social activity of a virtual world is immune to such control in a way that other private social activity is not.

Further, one might question the extent to which this is a realistic or workable proposal. An early virtual world, *LambdaMOO*, saw the "wizards," who had run the game as benevolent dictators, abdicate control, publicly announcing that users must now decide on dispute settlement mechanisms for themselves; in effect, they tried to turn the game into a democracy. The experiment was not a success, in that only the wizards actually had effective power to enforce decisions; ultimately, the wizards were forced to reassert control.[433]

There might also be mid-range solutions, especially if the goal is not to declare virtual worlds sovereign over everything, but simply to create

---

431 Post, above note 380 at 912 [emphasis in original].

432 Post & Johnson, above note 380.

433 See the discussions in Schönberger & Crowley, above note 379 at 1795–796; Lastowka & Hunter, above note 386 at 57.

a workable system of rule making. *Second Life*, for example, grants copyright to its users in any content that they create in-world. It has been pointed out that this aspect of the agreement between the programmers and the inhabitants attaches limits to the otherwise absolute power of programmers. There can be potential for incorporating some aspects of "bottom up" control into an otherwise "top down" model.[434]

In the end, this is not a matter over which any real conclusion can be reached at present. Perhaps virtual worlds never will attract the kind of numbers or type of activity that would lead to any need to worry about the extraterritorial application of law at all, whether special rules are needed or not. If they do, however, it might be equally premature to reach the conclusion that no special rules could possibly be needed. As Post argues, it might be too soon to conclude that "we've somehow finished designing legal institutions, and are stuck, forevermore, with the ones we happen[ed] to have come up with by 1995."[435]

H. CONCLUSION: IMPLICATIONS OF THE SEVEN CASE STUDIES FOR EXTRATERRITORIAL ACTION

In concluding this chapter of seven independent case studies, it will be instructive to consider how they expose the vagaries and push the boundaries of extraterritorial jurisdiction. Taken together, they present a clearer picture of the urge to exercise extraterritorial jurisdiction under the pressures of globalization and technological change, but they provide less certainty in answer to inquiries about when and how extraterritorial action is legitimate.

---

434 See the discussion in Schönberger & Crowley, *ibid*, generally, and in particular at 1800:

> The virtual world *A Tale in the Desert* established a method for avatars to develop laws in a democratic fashion, so long as the enforcement of those laws could be made using software code. It also has a policy of not protecting players from these laws. Punishments have included limiting the geographic movements of an avatar as well as permanent banishment from the world. [Footnotes omitted]

See also Lastowka & Hunter, *ibid* at 72, arguing:

> Nor can the wizards who create and maintain the worlds simply assert that they can do as they wish. The issues are more complex than that, and the users and community will need to have a say in the formation of the laws of virtual worlds.

435 Post, above note 380 at 913.

In considering what lessons may be learned from each case study, we will include a review of the rationale for the legal action that was, should have been, or might be taken in light of the four broad justifications for exercising extraterritorial jurisdiction that we divined by our analysis in Chapter 6. They posit that extraterritorial action is justifiable if it:

1) Has a strong connection to Canada;
2) Concerns an aspect of the public face of Canada;
3) Is needed to avoid lawless territory; or
4) Is required by an international convention.

Turning to the first two case studies on human rights,[436] it is clear that extraterritorial action in both of them may be justified on the basis of multilateral treaties — chiefly the *ICCPR* — which Canada, as a state party, is obliged to implement. Given such a sure foundation for action, it is wondrous that the extraterritorial protection of human rights has not been more deliberately exerted. A closer look at Canada's experience, whether over compliance with human rights laws (Section A, above in this chapter) or accountability for human rights abuses (Section B, above in this chapter), discloses very significant tensions, if not contradictions, in both the international and the domestic principles of jurisdiction. As we pointed out in the first case study,[437] the exercise of jurisdiction to protect human rights mandated by treaty fits uneasily in the context of the predominantly customary international law of jurisdiction. In addition, Canadian courts are unsure how to balance the obligation to assert jurisdiction to protect international human rights and to remediate their violations against the right of foreign states to respect for their sovereignty. The tensions in international law over contending principles of jurisdiction have confused the Canadian courts' determination of the degree of deference owed to foreign states.

But divisions in the applicable law should not be overemphasized. Canadian courts, as part of their regular adjudicative functions, are used to sorting out apparently conflicting sources of law. It seems, rather, that Canada's methodology in respect of international treaties is challenged by the specific jurisdictional obligations of the human rights conventions.

---

436 See Sections A and B, above in this chapter, for case studies on extraterritorial compliance with human rights law and extraterritorial accountability for human rights abuses, respectively.

437 Section A(3), above in this chapter.

An additional concern of the civil courts—indeed, a prerequisite to issues involved in the extraterritorial upholding of international human rights laws—is whether they may entertain an action involving wholly extraterritorial activities at all. Comity would suggest a Canadian court should defer adjudication to the courts of the state where the activities occurred. But, as discussed in the second case study in Section B, above in this chapter, sometimes no suit can be instituted, or, if begun, will not progress with due process. In such a situation, Canadian courts and legislatures have begun to assert jurisdiction to hear the case as the court of last resort. The practice of this form of extraterritorial jurisdiction is new and so limited that the courts have not expressed a definite foundation for it, other than applying the authority granted by provincial statute.

Upon reflection, perhaps the jurisdiction of a court of last resort may be justified on the third of the grounds listed above—that is, because extraterritorial action is necessary to avoid lawless territory. This justification is ordinarily operative, we have suggested, where the activity in question is outside the territory of *any* state, such as in space or on Antarctica, not within a *foreign* state. Yet the reason for asserting jurisdiction to adjudicate as a last resort is precisely because no system of curial justice with due process exists or operates within that foreign state. So perhaps the situations are parallel, and the avoidance of lawless territory within a failed or malfunctioning state will become acceptable as an extended yet justifiable basis for taking jurisdiction.

A feature that distinguishes the first two case studies from the rest is that Canada, having chosen to sign and ratify the human rights conventions, has become obliged to assert the jurisdictional authority the conventions set forth in order to ensure protection of the personal rights they affirm. The remaining case studies, by contrast, present situations in which extraterritorial action is by choice, not by obligation. Canada's social, economic, or cultural policy, once determined, will require action—maybe even extraterritorial action—but in that case, Canada will also need to demonstrate permissive authority for it.

The investigation of transnational data protection in the third case study bears out the last observation. Data flows unstoppably across state borders, yet there is no international consensus, let alone a treaty, to regulate it, or in particular, to control invasions of the right to privacy of personal information. While the European Union has adopted a stringent controlling directive, the United States has largely left the matter to voluntary self-regulation by the industry.

In the absence of international agreement, unilateral regulation has been decreed and applied by some states. The European Union is the prime example. Its directive only applies to member states, but its effects are nonetheless extraterritorial in impact. Canada enacted the *PIPEDA*[438] to shore up its international trade in goods and services. The Act was passed partly to reassure Canadian consumers that the privacy of their personal information disclosed in the course of their individual transactions would be protected (the micro level), but also, under pressure of the extraterritorial influence of the EU law, in order to avoid the interruption of commerce with EU states that are bound to apply the standards of the EU directive to international transactions (the macro level). This type of interstate reach and reaction may slowly foster a degree of collective regulatory unanimity, but is not a real substitute for international agreement. In practise, the rapid increases in the kinds and volumes of transnational data flows are impelling greater multilateral co-operation, if not yet a convention.

PIPEDA, though partly responsive to the extraterritorial impact of the EU *Data Protection Directive 95/46/EC*, also asserts its own extraterritorial authority. This jurisdictional reach may be justifiable out of strong concern for the protection of Canadians in Canada — that is, the first ground of justification previously listed. But, as we have frequently observed, while the passage of regulatory legislation is straightforward, its extraterritorial execution is much less so. After a false start, the Privacy Commissioner appointed under *PIPEDA* acknowledged that the Act grants jurisdiction, if not imposes a statutory duty, to investigate complaints against data holders outside Canada where there is a sufficient link to Canada. This is an expression of extended territorial jurisdiction, not extraterritorial jurisdiction, which may reflect a recognition of the uncertain scope of legislative jurisdiction or its practical application. Of interest here is the lengthy list of connecting factors stated by the Privacy Commissioner as relevant to the determination of a sufficient link to Canada. Its extensive nature suggests that the Privacy Commissioner is prepared to take a very extended perspective of extended territorial jurisdiction.

Actual investigation with a view to enforcing this jurisdiction still proves difficult. The Privacy Commissioner has found great difficulty in discovering evidence about the conduct of foreign data holders out-

---

438 Above note 168.

side Canada unless they co-operate, information is available on public record in the foreign state, or foreign state authorities are willing to assist. Co-operation by data holders, even the largest and most influential multinational ones like Google and Facebook, does occur. The authority of the regulatory office within a market that is important to a data holder may exert regulatory influence, rather than formal enforcement, over its conduct. For example, in response to investigation by the Canadian Privacy Commissioner, Facebook agreed to modify its privacy practices worldwide.

When like-minded states are prepared to co-operate over transnational complaints, investigation may readily move forward. When states are not like minded but have different policies and different laws, the application of the diverse regimes may not only defeat any attempts to assert jurisdiction, but also cause its own administrative and commercial problems. Multinational data holders are bound to comply with local law in all the states in which they operate. Where regulatory regimes differ, this requirement can lead to conflicts of responsibility for commercial corporations and knotty problems over jurisdictional limits for national regulators and domestic courts to resolve, as displayed by our discussion of the *DataTreasury*.[439]

The fourth case study in Section D, above in this chapter, demonstrates an interesting justification for extraterritorial jurisdiction that parallels the rationale we have suggested of action required by an international convention. There is no general international treaty to control terrorism, but there is plenty of unilateral activity to do so. Since the 9/11 terrorist attacks on the United States, many states have enacted criminal offences and unilaterally extended their criminal jurisdiction against international terrorists. The noteworthy feature of this activity is the absence of significant protests against its extraterritorial reach by most other states. The combination of unilateral assertions of extraterritorial jurisdiction against terrorism without concomitant objections between many states suggests the inchoate development of a customary practice, as compared to a treaty provision, recognizing that this particular extraterritorial activity is justified.

While the assertion of extraterritorial (legislative) jurisdiction against terrorism may be acceptable internationally to states, that does not mean extraterritorial authority automatically extends to all inves-

---

439 See Section C(4), above in this chapter.

tigation and enforcement of this conceded power. During the investigation of a terrorist act, there needs to be protection given to human rights — the rights of the victims, of the public generally, and also of the suspected terrorists. There exists the risk that the incompletely formed customary principle has provided cover for some states to trample onto, if not over, these rights — witness the wide involvement in extraordinary rendition that has taken place since the 9/11 terrorist attacks. Enforcement against terrorists is also nearly impossible when they are fugitives in a state that, far from co-operating, grants them "refuge." Yet attempts to destroy such terrorists *in situ* — for example, with targeted drones or SWAT teams — violates the international human rights standards of due process owed to them as well as the international law of state sovereignty, for which there appears to be no extraterritorial justification.

A similar limitation on extraterritorial enforcement is highlighted by international experience with national laws prohibiting child sex tourism, discussed in the fifth case study in Section E, above in this chapter. Canadian legislation proscribing child sex tourism was passed in advance of an international consensus to outlaw such conduct, but any doubt about this exercise of legislative jurisdiction for an extraterritorial objective has since been removed by the conclusion of an international convention containing clear authority. Yet under that authority, states have taken a great variety of actions that have mostly proved ineffective to stop such tourism. The main problems are practical obstacles to gathering evidence in foreign "tourist" centres, such as expense, complexity, and inadequate co-operation from local authorities. In short, a multilateral agreement is not necessarily a panacea for the extraterritorial control of conduct: its implementation may present very significant difficulties logistically.

Interestingly, Australia and the United States have fashioned legislation that avoids the difficulties of extraterritorial investigation and enforcement while still targeting the extraterritorial misbehaviour. Both states exert their criminal law powers against the activities of child sex tourist agencies operating within their territories, and the United States also takes aim at individuals for travelling with intent to engage in child sex tourism. Not only are these legislative techniques far more effective in practice, they also demonstrate that it is always better to implement national policy through the universally accepted principle of territorial jurisdiction than to overreach comity and risk a reaction from other states that an extraterritorial approach is likely to incur.

Internet gambling, the sixth case study in Section F, above in this chapter, illustrates, with even more clarity than the third case study on transnational data protection, the hopelessness of trying to regulate an activity extraterritorially in the absence of an international consensus between states. In the case of Internet gambling, the disarray among states is not just over how to regulate it, but even about whether to control it at all. There is no international treaty requiring implementation as there now is against child sex tourism, and there is no apparent trend in unilateral state practice towards incipient customary international recognition of jurisdiction similar to the experience around international terrorism. Thus, while a state might assert that regulating Internet gambling is justifiable on account of its intimate effect on its residents and the public mores of its society — in reliance on the first two grounds for legitimating extraterritorial action listed at the beginning of this concluding commentary — it has little hope at present of exerting generally applicable controls.

Indeed, to the contrary, attempts to regulate Internet gambling extraterritorially have been the subject not just of diplomatic objection from other states, but also the basis of international trade disputes and interstate "litigation" before the WTO. Yet Internet gambling is an activity that is pre-eminently national and transnational all at once — it is instantaneously both "here and there" — so it cannot be effectively regulated by one state without both territorial and extraterritorial action and the co-operation of other states.

It is of particular significance that the problems of extraterritorial regulation of Internet gambling do not only exist at the investigative and enforcement stages, as they do with state action against child sex tourism. The trade disputes just referred to have arisen over prior extraterritorial action; namely, the enactment of prohibitive legislation that has extraterritorial reach. This criminal legislation targets individuals, not states, but it does so without regard to their location or nationality. Yet in the diverse range of opinions and policies about Internet gambling, some states are surely agreed that it should be controlled or even banned. This prospect invites investigation whether it would be worthwhile trying to exert controls with the co-operation of similarly minded states in a series of bilateral, and likely reciprocal, agreements (a policy question) and, if so, whether the legislative jurisdiction to proscribe Internet gambling can be moulded effectively to target only individuals who have substantial connections with those particular foreign states (a legal question).

While it is hopeless to expect success in asserting extraterritorial jurisdiction in the absence of sufficient international support (as demonstrated by the experience around Internet gambling), it is evidently premature even to attempt to regulate other worlds — that is, virtual worlds. This is the conclusion of the seventh case study in Section G (above in this chapter) on the subject. Yet at least a watching brief will have to be held over the development of virtual worlds, for the in-world lives of avatars have impacts on the real-world lives of humans, both avatar owners and others, that may be harmful. While programming changes may eliminate some harms, and self-government systems of inhabitants may be able to police in-world activities, there likely will be concerns by some states about negative real-world impacts on their state inhabitants. Some states may wish to control these impacts with extraterritorial action, thereby forcing them to justify these negative implications as having a strong national impact, concerning the public face of the state, and avoiding lawless territory — in other words, all grounds of identified justification except treaty implementation.

In final summation, it may be said these case studies amply illustrate the justifications for extraterritorial action that we have elicited and discussed in Chapter 6 but they also display a prevalent disorder in the principles and practice of extraterritorial jurisdiction. The challenge remains — even grows — for both the international law and the domestic practice to catch up with the burgeoning globalization of life and the generally diminishing significance of state sovereignty, state territory, and state authority.

CHAPTER 8

A Prospective Framework for Extraterritorial Action

A. THE GOALS OF AN ANALYTIC FRAMEWORK

The exploration throughout this book of the conceptual foundations and Canadian practice of extraterritorial jurisdiction leads, in this final chapter, to our projection of a framework for future extraterritorial action. The experience recounted here calls for the promotion of a measured, restrained, and judicious approach to any consideration of extending Canada's claim to jurisdiction. A major question must always be not merely how to act extraterritorially, but whether to do so at all. The template that follows is an attempt to give guidance in answering both of those questions.

However, as we have repeatedly stated, no analytical framework can offer guidance on the wisdom of acting extraterritorially in a given case — that is a decision for policy-makers, based on their views of the desirable social policy for Canada. What follows, therefore, is an analytical tool that aims to set out the various considerations to take into account in deciding whether extraterritorial action is a practical and viable approach to whatever issue is perceived as a social problem. This tool does not attempt to say what such problems their solutions might be.

Further, as emphasized above, no single answer can be offered to the question of when and whether Canada should act extraterritorially. What we present, therefore, is a set of general legal and policy objectives that are particular to the exercise of extraterritorial jurisdiction and that will underpin decision making, followed by a series of questions aimed at deciding whether extraterritorial action is advisable in any given situation, in the sense that it is a practical response to the issue. As part of that analysis, the question of what sort of extraterritorial action might be appropriate will be incorporated. Further, within each question we will point to a number of considerations that will help guide the analysis.

This framework is meant to guide decision making by policy-makers; that is, of the three branches relevant to any discussion of extraterritorial action—legislative/prescriptive, executive/enforcement, and judicial/adjudicative—this framework primarily is directed at the first. The extent to which action by the first will create the need for the involvement of the latter two should be, however, a relevant consideration.

We will propose a series of questions that ought to be asked by policy-makers when deciding whether to act extraterritorially. We present them in the form of sequential steps towards a decision. Within this series of questions, we suggest there are three important variables to be taken into account. We do not suggest these three variables account for every consideration; but they often function to provide a good general guide to whether the contemplated action will be problematic, and if so, to what extent.

The first variable is the intrusiveness of the action proposed by Canada on the international stage. In that context, it is important to consider the gradation from extraterritorial impact without true extraterritorial action, to extraterritorial action undertaken in concert with one or more other states, to unilateral extraterritorial action. Obviously, the further one goes along that scale, the greater the intrusiveness, and so the stronger the justification needed.

The second variable is the nature of the extraterritorial action. As we discussed at length in Chapter 6, extraterritorial action can have a variety of goals: broadly, to prohibit, to control, or to facilitate activities. Generally speaking, a greater justification is required to prohibit an activity than to facilitate it.

The final variable to consider is the subject of the proposed extraterritorial legislation: to whom will it apply? We have noted that some legislation affects public actors while some affects private actors. On occasion, public actors may act privately. In the case of private actors, it will be worth considering exactly who might be affected by the legislation. Is the legislation intended to apply only to those present in Canada at a specific moment; to those with assets in Canada even if they are not personally present; to Canadian citizens or permanent residents, no matter where they might be; or to anyone in the world? This variable could also be relevant to how easy or difficult it might be to justify extraterritorial legislation. Further, the nature of the parties concerned might affect the issue of enforcement. This is clearly true in the case of action intended to prohibit, where the assistance of other states might be necessary (for example, through extradition). However, it is also worth recognizing that in the case of disputes that might arise in the context of attempts to control, the identity of the particular parties involved might affect the range of adjudicative options available: mediation, arbitration, or some other private dispute settlement mechanism might be the forum of choice rather than the courts, for example.

These three variables — particularly the last — can be seen in action in various ways through the case studies in the previous chapter. Many states have attempted to control only the behaviour of their own nationals, either by forbidding behaviour or by regulating it — consider the US approach to child sex tourism, discussed in the case study in Chapter 7, Section E, which only forbids US citizens or permanent residents from travelling outside the country with that intention, or the EU *Data Protection Directive* discussed in the case study in Chapter 7, Section C, which prevents states that are members of the European Union from sending data about its citizens to states without satisfactory data protection legislation. What these approaches have in common is that they are both relatively unintrusive, at least explicitly, in the legitimate spheres of other states and the behaviour of nationals; these approaches have also been relatively successful methods of achieving their goals.

In contrast, as our case study on extraterritorial accountability for human rights abuses (Chapter 7, Section B) points out, very little has been accomplished in that area. This should not be enormously surprising, we suggest, given that efforts in that regard combine intrusive options with all three variables: although a foundation for such efforts can be found in international law, it pushes at the limits of that justification by involving significant intrusion into the sphere of another state; it involves at least regulatory, if not prohibitory, action; and it purports to directly affect actors in other states by granting a remedy against them.

In addition to those three variables, the desirability of any proposed extraterritorial action ought to be assessed against the appropriate general policy objectives. Specifically, Canada should support the exercise of extraterritorial jurisdiction in a manner that encourages the maintenance of an international society that is ordered, fair, just, and peaceable, rather than chaotic and conflicted. This leads to several final considerations before presenting the framework itself.

First, Canada should legislate with regard to extraterritorial conduct only when Canada has a *bona fide* and substantive interest in that conduct. Second, international conventions should be implemented and executed in good faith. This principle is particularly important in regard to human rights treaties in connection with jurisdiction over the person. Third, Canada should uphold the international rule of law by extending its jurisdiction in a manner that inhibits lawless territories.

Beyond these principles, to promote an ordered international society, two particular considerations should be kept in mind:

1) All exercises of extraterritorial jurisdiction should, to the greatest extent possible, be consistent with the larger interests of interstate comity, and should apply the principles of non-intervention, accommodation, mutuality, and proportionality.
2) Extraterritorial legislation that requires the co-operation of other states for effective enforcement should not, in general, be created without some reasonable expectation that such co-operation will be obtained.

The above issues are integrated within the analytical framework presented below.

B. THE ANALYTIC FRAMEWORK

Question 1: Can the desired goals be accomplished, or largely so, based on a real and substantial connection to Canada, and therefore without any need to rely on genuinely extraterritorial measures?

Comments: The first question must always be whether extraterritorial action is actually required at all. This observation is not necessarily just a note of caution, but also an observation that much can be done that will be recognized by Canadian courts and others as based on the "extended territorial" principle — that is, via a real and substantial connection to Canada.[1] Anything that meets this criterion can be considered to be territorial, not extraterritorial, action. As explored in detail in Chap-

1 Consider, for example, the actions of the Privacy Commissioner of Canada with regard to Facebook or to Accusearch, both discussed in Chapter 7, Section C.

ter 4, this point is not always clearly recognized, and so is worth incorporating into any analysis.

Where legislation can be based on a real and substantial connection to Canada, the principle of comity will likely not be violated. Even in the case of extraterritorial action aimed at prohibition — the type most intrusive on the international sphere — it is unlikely that any problem would arise.[2] Further, to the extent that the co-operation of other states is required to enforce such prohibitions, it is reasonably likely that it would be found. As the transnational data protection case study in Chapter 7, Section C, illustrated, taking jurisdiction on this basis and then seeking assistance can be fruitful.

Question 2: If extraterritorial measures are necessary, is multilateral action possible?

Comments: As noted before, the greatest area of expansion by Canada in the exercise of extraterritorial jurisdiction has been in order to comply with its obligations under bilateral and multilateral treaties, protocols, conventions, or agreements with another state.[3] By any standard, multilateral action is to be preferred, where it is feasible, to unilateral action.[4] Legislation that is enacted to put Canada's international commitments into being will not offend the principle of comity, since other states will have consented. Problems of enforcement will also disappear or be reduced, since it will be reasonable, in these circumstances, to anticipate the assistance of other states — indeed, under many of these treaties, assistance is obligatory. As in Question 1, this would be true even in

2 One might recall in this context Canada's approach to child sex tourism, discussed in the case study in Chapter 7, Section F. That approach is to treat the offence as though it occurred in Canada if the offender is Canadian — that is, it essentially ignores the fact that another state is involved, but it only attempts to govern the behaviour of those individuals Canada can legitimately govern. Canada's legislation was enacted before the existence of any treaty permitting such extraterritorial action, and was even amended to remove the requirement for the consent to prosecution of the other state. Nonetheless, the international reaction was not outrage over an unjustified intrusion; rather, this was one of the impetuses to reaching a treaty. Of course, this is due in part to the underlying subject matter and the near-universal view that child prostitution is unacceptable, but it seems also likely to have been influenced by the fact that the Canadian offenders leave from and return to Canada, and thus there is a connection to Canada.

3 See the discussion in Chapter 6, Section B(1)(d).

4 See, for example, the discussion in Chapter 7, sections A and D.

the most intrusive case of actions aimed at prohibiting behaviour, but would also be true of any attempts to control or facilitate it.

In fact, multilateral action is, at present, frequently possible because so much of Canada's extraterritorial legislation is meant to enforce international obligations. Looking to the future, policy-makers ought to continue that trend. In many cases, that will mean initiating negotiations for a bilateral or multilateral agreement on a particular matter, rather than beginning with domestic action. This point will be especially true where a prohibition (such as legislation aimed at child sex tourism[5]), or an attempt to control (such as the *Antarctic Environmental Protection Act*[6]) is concerned.

Note that a multilateral response need not depend on the formalities of a treaty—it could simply arise by an individual request from another state.[7] Additionally, as the case study on international terrorism in Chapter 7, Section D, illustrated, it is possible to move in concert with a general trend in state practice towards particular extensions of extraterritorial jurisdiction without necessarily needing a formal agreement to do so. In a fast-changing legal environment, such as that which existed in the immediate aftermath of the 9/11 terrorist attacks, it might be possible to extend jurisdiction with little risk of adverse reaction if it can be accurately determined that large numbers of other (at least other like-minded) states are acting similarly.

In some cases, multilateral action might not be possible. If that is because international consensus cannot be reached, then it is time to move to the next consideration. However, it is worth observing that in some cases of action aimed at facilitating an activity, multilateral action might not be feasible simply because the subject matter of the legislation is of no genuine interest to other states. If Canada decides to grant compensation or benefits based on actions taken overseas (as with, for example, the *Government Employees Compensation Act*[8]), then no other state is likely to have much concern with whether Canada does so or not. Granting such benefits is unlikely to affect the principle of comity, and

5 As noted in Chapter 7, Section E.

6 SC 2003, c 20.

7 In this regard, note the *Canadian Transportation Accident Investigation and Safety Board Act*, SC 1989, c 3, s 3(1)(c)(i), which makes the Act apply to an occurrence anywhere if:

> (i) Canada is requested to investigate the aviation occurrence by an appropriate authority . . .

8 RSC 1985, c G-5, s 3(2).

will not generally depend on the co-operation of other states; accordingly, neither of those two considerations weigh against such action. The same is true of purely facilitative legislation permitting entities to operate extraterritorially, particularly when the legislation requires the entity to act in accordance with the laws of the other jurisdiction (as it generally does).[9]

Question 3: If unilateral action is necessary, will the proposed measures be effective? Will they be enforceable with the co-operation of other states (because they are recognized under jurisdictional principles at international law as legitimate steps for Canada to take)?

Comments: Assuming that the desired goals actually require extraterritorial action, the first practical question to be asked is whether such action on Canada's part will actually achieve the purpose of the legislation. Canada's goal ought not to be merely to assert jurisdiction symbolically over actions occurring outside Canada's territory. If extraterritorial action is worthwhile, it is because such action can have practical consequences.[10]

In this context, whether extraterritorial action is likely to have any practical effect will vary depending on whether the action is aimed at prohibiting, controlling, or facilitating behaviour. Unilateral prohibitions aimed at conduct outside Canada's borders will potentially infringe on the principle of comity, which should give pause. However, the more it is true that the action is grounded in recognized international law principles, the greater the likelihood that other states will view the legislation as legitimate. Laws aimed at border control or citizenship offences, for example, would likely be seen as uncontroversial due to the protective principle and therefore are unlikely to offend comity. By the

---

9 Recall from Chapter 6 that many statutes contain a provision very similar to that in the *Bank Act*, SC 1991, c 46, s 15(4):

> Subject to this Act, a bank has the capacity to carry on its business, conduct its affairs and exercise its powers in any jurisdiction outside Canada and in the manner that the laws of that jurisdiction permit.

10 One might contrast here the subject matters of two of the case studies in Chapter 7, sections D and F. In the former, we argue that states have moved towards an international consensus, and therefore widespread co-operation can be expected among nations. In contrast, attitudes towards gambling differ significantly from state to state, and so there is very little guarantee that a state trying to act extraterritorially could rely on the co-operation of others regarding this issue.

same token, the less that any law infringes comity, the more likely it is that there would be international co-operation in enforcement.

Much the same is true of attempts at controlling behaviour extraterritorially. Many attempts to control by imposing licensing fees or other conditions on activities in other states would be likely to offend comity and would be unlikely to receive assistance in enforcement. However, if the exercise of control concerns an otherwise lawless territory (such as the *Antarctic Environmental Protection Act*[11] or the *Remote Sensing Space Systems Act*[12]), the comity concern, at least, is assuaged to a degree. Further, legislation such as the *Quarantine Act*,[13] which isolates sources of disease before they enter Canada, would also be recognized at international law as justified under the protective principle.

Attempts to facilitate action extraterritorially, on the other hand (and as noted above), are far less likely to require the assistance of other states to make them effective. In that event, it is much easier to justify acting unilaterally in a facilitative way. Even then, however, it is worth paying attention to the principle of comity. It is typical, for example, for legislation empowering entities to operate in another jurisdiction to be explicit that the entity must comply with the laws of that other jurisdiction.[14]

Of course, even controlling and prohibiting actions can be implemented in ways that minimize the extent to which there is any infringement of comity. The *Non-smokers' Health Act*, for example, extends the obligation to provide a non-smoking work environment to transportation running between Canada and other states "to the extent that compliance with this Act within the territory of another jurisdiction does not result in the contravention of the laws of that jurisdiction."[15] The *Remote Sensing Space Systems Act* allows a person to plead *autrefois acquit*, *autrefois convict*, or pardon to an offence charged under the Act if it has already been dealt with in another jurisdiction.[16]

---

11 Above note 6.

12 SC 2005, c 45.

13 SC 2005, c 20.

14 See the statutes mentioned in footnotes 89–97 of Chapter 6.

15 *Non-smokers' Health Act*, RSC 1985, c 15 (4th Supp), s 2(2). That is, it will be observed, not the same as saying that the laws of the other jurisdiction will apply, as in the *Bank Act*, above note 9, and other examples. To say the laws of the other jurisdiction apply would be to allow smoking if no law of the other jurisdiction forbade it. Under the *Non-smokers' Health Act*, smoking would not be permitted unless some law of the other jurisdiction specifically said that it was allowed.

16 Above note 12, s 39(3).

Question 4: If the proposed unilateral measures are not recognized at international law as legitimate steps for Canada to take, is this an instance where it is worthwhile to act in the absence of international consensus? In particular, is the issue of enough significance that it is worth suffering whatever negative consequences might flow from such unilateral action? Further, is there a realistic prospect that the measures will achieve their ends without the initial support of other nations?

Comments: If the answer to our previous question is "no," then it would be surprising if it were still seen as worthwhile for extraterritorial measures to be introduced. However, that it would be surprising is not to say that it is unimaginable. Once again, in part, this question depends on whether the action is aimed at prohibiting, at controlling, or at facilitating, the latter being the occasion where unilateral action is the most likely.

There could be rare instances where, due to the importance of the issue at stake and the lack of other options, Canada might decide to attempt to prohibit or to control the actions of others in a way that is inconsistent with the accepted international view. Our framework can offer no guidance regarding *when* policy-makers should see an issue as being of such unusually pressing importance so as to justify unilateral action; only that this step should not be taken except when that decision has been made. Even then, or perhaps especially then, it is particularly relevant to consider the effectiveness of such action; by definition, Canada could expect little, if any, assistance from other states in enforcing the law. This might be satisfactory if the goal of the legislation was to lead "international public opinion," or if it were sufficient to enforce the law only when Canada could already exert effective control over the person.

A successful example of unilateral extension of jurisdiction by Canada was the enactment in 1970 of the *Arctic Waters Pollution Prevention Act* and regulations, by which jurisdiction for certain specific purposes was asserted over a 100-nautical-mile wide margin of coastal seas in the Arctic region—far broader than the internationally accepted twelve-nautical-miles wide territorial sea of a state.[17] Canada justified this extension of its jurisdiction on the grounds of pollution protection of a uniquely fragile environment of ice-infested seas. The legislative claim was met with considerable strong objections from significant and powerful states concerned about access to the Arctic, which could have

17 RSC 1985, c A-12 and CRC 1978, ch 353–56.

overwhelmed Canada's attempts to enforce its regulations against foreign shipping beyond its recognized twelve-nautical-mile limits. However, Canada coupled this initiative with a carefully planned strategy of multilateral negotiations, both informally with a number of states that were thought to be like-minded, and formally through the UN International Law of the Sea Conference that began soon thereafter. Eventually, Canada won general acceptance of its legislated goals, if not its unilateral method, through the multilateral conclusion of a provision for the protection of ice-covered areas in the *United Nations Convention on the Law of the Sea*, signed in 1982.[18] This instance of extraterritorial jurisdiction shows that a combination of approaches towards implementing a desired policy may be less risky in terms of foreign states' reactions and more likely to have a successful outcome. The strategy of dual actions — of pre-emptive unilateral legislation accompanied by engagement in multilateral negotiation — was significant in, indeed probably critical to, achieving the fulfillment of Canada's Arctic policy at the time.[19]

On the other hand, as we observed above, action aimed at facilitating extraterritorial activities is far less likely to offend comity even if it is not in accordance with international norms, and is far less likely to depend on international co-operation for implementation. It could be easier, then, to justify laws falling into this category.

It is worth noting, in this context, that the extent to which any type of legislation is likely to violate the principle of comity, and the extent to which it will be enforceable, can be dealt with to some degree by limiting to whom the legislation applies. Legislation applying only to Can-

18 (10 December 1982), 1833 UNTS 396, art 234.

19 See also the incident over the *Estai*, a fishing vessel that was part of the Spanish fleet which, in Canada's view, was overfishing the Northwest Atlantic banks. The vessel was seized by Canadian fisheries officers in accordance with Canadian fisheries regulations, even though it was outside the 200-nautical-mile fishery zone allowed to a coastal state by international law. The arrest raised raucous objections from Spain and the European Union generally, but the issue of overfishing that sparked the incident was ultimately resolved more or less successfully through the multilateral negotiation of the United Nations *Agreement for the Implementation of the Provisions of the United Nations Convention on the Law of the Sea of 10 December 1982 relating to the Conservation and Management of Straddling Fish Stocks and Highly Migratory Fish Stocks* (4 December 1995), 2167 UNTS 3, in which Canada took a leading part. See the discussion of this incident in Hugh M Kindred & Phillip M Saunders, *International Law Chiefly as Interpreted and Applied in Canada*, 7th ed (Toronto: Emond Montgomery, 2006) at 984–95.

adian citizens and permanent residents, for example, would be seen to be in accordance with the nationality principle. Accordingly, such laws would have a greater likelihood of being enforceable with the assistance of other states. Legislation that applies to anyone who is later present in Canada will not necessarily be recognized as in accordance with international principles of jurisdiction, and could offend comity, depending upon exactly who is in fact prosecuted. However, as a practical matter, Canada might be able to enforce such a law without the assistance of other states. That is, at a minimum, the person subject to the law would be in the effective control of Canada, though the relevant evidence might not be.

Note as well that enforceability need not depend on the physical presence of the person who is subject to the legislation. In the case of facilitating action, of course, "enforceability" is the wrong word, since at best it will only be a benefit that is conveyed. In the case of prohibitions or control, there may be other effective methods, particularly where the object of the legislation is a corporation rather than an individual. The *Foreign Publishers Advertising Services Act*, for example, is explicitly aimed extraterritorially at non-Canadian corporations, and fines can be imposed for violation of its terms.[20] However, the Act also provides that any such fine can be registered as a civil judgment and enforced in that way. Given that the potential offenders under this Act would be foreign corporations with assets in Canada, the legislation is likely enforceable even though it is extraterritorial.

Question 5: If the proposed unilateral measures are recognized at international law as legitimate steps for Canada to take, are they also measures that are consistent with the traditional Canadian approach to extraterritoriality? If they are not, can a departure from that tradition be justified because of the seriousness of the problem to be addressed (or because of other factors)?

Comments: Even if a proposed exertion of extraterritorial jurisdiction might be recognized at international law, it does not follow that the

---

20 SC 1999, c 23, s 3 provides:

> 3. (1) No foreign publisher shall supply advertising services directed at the Canadian market to a Canadian advertiser or a person acting on their behalf.

See also section 15 of the Act, which provides that:

> 15. (1) In a proceeding for a contravention of section 3, a foreign publisher who commits an act outside Canada that, if committed in Canada, would be an offence under that section is deemed to commit that act in Canada.

action is consistent with Canada's tradition in acting extraterritorially. We have frequently noted throughout this book that the question of when Canada *should* act extraterritorially is quite distinct from the question of when it *can* do so. To date, Canada has shown considerable restraint. As noted, Canada has very infrequently relied on (for example) the nationality principle, though such a claim is more frequently used by other states and is unequivocally recognized at international law. Canada has very few extraterritorial laws founded on the protective principle, and has only in extremely limited circumstances unilaterally asserted universal jurisdiction.[21]

In practice, Canada has tended to act extraterritorially almost exclusively in the context of multilateral international agreements. Nothing has occurred that should change that general tendency. Again, however, that is not to say that a departure from this approach could never be justified, merely that it would *need* to be justified. The exact nature of that justification cannot really be defined or limited, other than to note that it would require particularly compelling circumstances to rationalize a departure from Canada's traditional "comfort zone." This will be especially true in the case of prohibitions, and to a somewhat lesser extent, of attempts at controlling behaviour beyond Canadian borders.

An increasingly relevant query in those contexts will be whether, in appropriate circumstances, Canada should defer to an international forum that is or could become seized of the issue. For example, the United Nations Commission on International Trade Law (UNCITRAL) is currently at work on designing an online dispute resolution model that could be used internationally.[22] The goal is to put mechanisms in place to allow for adjudication of small-scale commercial disputes between vendors and customers, thereby avoiding the vagaries of dealing with

21 Note, for example, the discussion in Chapter 7, Section D. The great bulk of Canada's extraterritorial anti-terrorism laws are grounded in treaty. Unusually, Canada has gone beyond that and has also asserted extraterritorial jurisdiction over other "terrorism offences" without a specific international law basis. Even in that exceptional situation, however, Canada has claimed only to be able to prosecute its own nationals, stateless residents, or permanent residents who are found in Canada after the offence. That is, even in taking the step of extraterritorial action beyond the treaties, the protective and passive personality principles are relied on, but universal jurisdiction is not.

22 The working group documents can be found on the UNCITRAL website, online: www.uncitral.org/uncitral/commission/working_groups/3Online_Dispute_Resolution.html.

various national court systems while taking into account the fact that for most transactions, it is too expensive to do so. To the extent such an effort would require Canada to restrict the extraterritorial reach of courts under conflicts of law doctrines, it might nonetheless be an overall positive step as a matter of policy.

Question 6: If unilateral extraterritorial action is, in the circumstances, an approach Canada both can and should take, what is the proper method of acting extraterritorially? Is the goal enforcement of Canadian standards outside Canadian territory, which might be accomplished through mandatory legislation where the combination of legislative and judicial mechanisms make enforcement likely? Alternatively, might executive action to enlist foreign assistance in enforcing Canadian penal or regulatory laws be a better approach?

Comments: Presuming that it has been determined that the problem to be addressed falls into circumstances where Canada both can and should act extraterritorially, the next question becomes the method by which Canada should act. The answer to this inquiry will be shaped by the target of the action; that is, whether Canada is seeking to extraterritorially affect the behaviour of individuals, corporations, or other states.

Obviously it is possible to act through legislation. The most straightforward manner in which this can be accomplished is by way of prohibitory legislation: for the legislature to pass laws that are then left to the courts to enforce. However, other approaches, which need not depend on a purely prohibitory approach, are also available. For example, the Legislature may put legislation in place that provides for a directing role for the Crown to pursue extraterritorial objectives by executive action or before the courts or otherwise. Alternatively, the executive may put in place (with or without the participation of the Legislature) self-regulatory guidelines or economic incentives.[23] However, as we have noted above, these will not always be the most effective or most appropriate methods.

In some cases, purely executive action might be a more appropriate approach. There can, for example, be problems to which economic sanctions are the appropriate response, although that might be a confrontational approach. In other circumstances, as noted in the extraterritorial

23 See, for example, the discussion of statutes such as the *Official Languages Act*, RSC 1985, c 31 (4th Supp), s 22(b), or the *Health of Animals Act*, SC 1990, c 21, s 21 in Chapter 6, Section D(2).

compliance with human rights law case study in Chapter 7, Section A, agencies such as the RCMP can negotiate on an ad hoc basis with foreign states for the ability to conduct investigations in their territories. Further, some situations will best be addressed through trying to negotiate a Memorandum of Understanding or other arrangement with another state or states. This will be a less confrontational approach, since unilateral action is least likely to be desired when the potential solutions seem to involve prohibition and exercising control. However, the major potential drawback to negotiation is the risk that Canada's voice in a multilateral context might be drowned out by those of more powerful nations, with the result that executive action involving negotiation will not achieve the desired outcome.

Question 7: Does a cost-benefit analysis of the potential international impacts of this extraterritorial action indicate that it is the preferable route for Canada to take? In particular, do the potential responses by other states (if any) represent more in the way of "costs" than Canada is willing to bear in order to fulfil its extraterritorial objective?

Comments: Finally, even if based on all the considerations above it appears that the circumstances are such that extraterritorial action by Canada seems appropriate, any final decision should wait on inquiring what the consequences might be of the action. If the action is taken in accordance with a multilateral agreement, few concerns should arise in this regard. However, states normally do not unilaterally act extraterritorially because of concerns about comity: if Canada chooses on some occasion to unilaterally act extraterritorially, it is important to consider whether other states might take measures in response to Canada's decision, and what might be their nature and consequences. Possibly, any perceived gains to Canada from the extraterritorial action would be more than outweighed by the potential negative consequences.

Once again, relevant factors to consider here include the type of action contemplated — to prohibit, to control, or to facilitate — and the objects of the action. As has already been observed, prohibitions unilaterally aimed by Canada at non-Canadians are likely to be the most controversial. If the legislation can be restricted to Canadian citizens or permanent residents, its impact on foreign states will be reduced, though not eliminated. Such a limitation might or might not be a possibility, depending on the nature of the problem being addressed. Canadian legislation prohibiting bribery of foreign officials can be limited in its application to Canadians. However, if Canadian legislation aimed at preventing foreign publishers from advertising tobacco in ways directed at Canada were limited to Canadians, it would defeat the purpose of the legislation. Similarly, if data protection laws did not have some application to companies that are based outside of Canada, yet are connected to Canada through their operations, the effect of the protection offered by these laws would be substantially diminished in our increasingly globalized society.

By the same token, merely facilitative laws, as we have observed above, cause little affront to foreign states even if they do have an extraterritorial component. For instance, the payment of compensation or a pension by Canada to someone due to that individual's work in another state would, in most cases, be of little or no concern to that state.

Even if there are no direct retaliatory impacts, or, more subtly, no impacts from diminished relations with other states, a further issue to be considered is the attitude that Canada would adopt towards other states asserting a similar extraterritorial claim — in particular, whether such claims would unacceptably infringe on Canada's territorial jurisdiction. In assessing any extraterritorial approach, particularly mandatory laws, Canada should consider the potential for reciprocal application. From a purely national perspective, gains might be perceived from asserting an extraterritorial claim; however, if that same claim were made by other states impinging on Canadian sovereignty, once again the result might be a net loss for Canadian interests. In such circumstances, extraterritorial action would be ill advised. Also, as discussed in the international terrorism case study in Chapter 7, Section D, Canada should explicitly recognize that assertions of extraterritorial jurisdiction may contribute to a body of state practice that could develop into a new rule of customary international law, and should consider whether such a rule would be both in its own interests and beneficial to the international community as a whole.

C. CONCLUSION: EXTENDING EXTRATERRITORIAL JURISDICTION IN TUNE WITH GLOBALIZATION

As we have attempted to make clear throughout this book, Canada and the world face increasing globalization and other pressures, which carry with them the impetus towards greater exercises of extraterritorial jurisdiction, and also the accompanying hazards. To be sure, the route thus travelled is safe; Canada could easily continue to conservatively exercise extraterritorial jurisdiction in situations where doing so respects international comity, and to promote multilateral solutions for problems that might bring it into conflict with other states. By various means that have been proposed throughout this book and that are highlighted in this chapter, these tools can also be refined to suit particular problems. The hard questions are whether, when, and how to do more than that.

To some extent, our exploration of extraterritorial jurisdiction ends where it began. This particular legal tool was originally designed to deal with criminal law matters and, while there is no doubt of its importance in other settings, transnational crime continues to occupy a large part of the agenda for the future use of extraterritorial jurisdiction.[24] To combat the continuing evolution of transnational crime, Canada can expand its use of techniques that are legal, if not traditional (for example, making greater use of the nationality principle), while continuing to push for greater elasticity of jurisdictional principles as between states. In the short term, the courts can continue to develop the "real and substantial connection" test, making more nuanced and context-specific attempts than they have thus far to locate the point at which connectedness and interstate comity may collide.

The courts, however, have the resources to continue this jurisdictional "tweaking" only so far. In the longer term, these efforts can be supported by the executive, which is better equipped to develop actual policy responses to the pressures and changes stemming generally from globalization and Internet communication. The executive can negotiate international agreements that either dispense with the need for extraterritorial jurisdiction or compel states to exercise it. The Legislature can then implement these agreements, prescribing the exercise of extraterritorial jurisdiction clearly and in a manner that directly reflects the specifics of the particular subject matter. Indeed, as has been shown here, this kind of synergy between the branches of government in formulating extraterritoriality has served Canada reasonably well thus far.

---

24 Indeed, as this manuscript was being written, it was reported that Canadian police, with the help and co-operation of the FBI, had arrested two foreign nationals allegedly involved in a plot to derail a train running between Canada and the United States, with the alleged assistance of al-Qaeda elements in Iran, "Alleged 'al-Qaeda-supported' Plot against Via Train Thwarted" *CBC News* (22 April 2013), online: cbc.ca www.cbc.ca/news/politics/story/2013/04/22/pol-terror-plot-ontario-quebec-arrests.html.

However, there is more that can be done. The major lesson from extraterritorial criminal jurisdiction is that Canada has not acted unilaterally except in circumstances where there was a clear international consensus supporting its ability to do so. Thus, most exercises of extraterritorial jurisdiction are deliberately multilateral, and those that are not are supportable by general international consensus as to when it is legitimate to claim such jurisdiction.

That is not universally true, however. It is open to Canada to act extraterritorially in advance of consensus having formed; in effect, to attempt to lead international opinion by example. We noted earlier[25] how Canada's exertion of jurisdiction over Arctic waters was later approved by other countries. Similarly, as noted in the child sex tourism case study in Chapter 7, Section E, Canada's extraterritorial jurisdiction provisions, though now perfectly in line with international treaties, actually preceded the signing of those treaties. Perhaps the terrorism provisions not yet consequent on international treaties[26] will eventually lead to the existence of such treaties—one more building block towards a consensus that expansive use of extraterritorial jurisdiction is a necessary tool.

That said, this is an option that should be used sparingly and cautiously. Canada, though not the smallest boat on the lake, frequently sails with larger ones: the odds of it being caught in someone else's wake are far greater than Canada changing the course of others.

It is not impossible for Canadian action to have an international impact. Consider, for example, the investigation by the Privacy Commissioner of Canada into Facebook's privacy policy (discussed in Chapter 5), which had the effect of changing Facebook's practices on a global scale. That is not to say, however, that one should always confidently expect such a result. Canada could, for example, try to unilaterally impose its views on copyright on the international community. However, doing so would carry the risk of legitimizing the notion of one state unilaterally imposing its standards on another, helping free the dominant players to do the same. The dominance of US intellectual property interests makes it far more likely that the end result would be US copyright law being imposed on Canada, rather than Canada's authority being extended. Recall that Canada's domestic data protection legislation, as we have

---

25 In the discussion of Question 4 in Section B, above in this chapter.

26 See the discussion in Chapter 7, Section D.

noted in the case study on that subject in Chapter 7, Section C, was largely prompted by the economic influence of the European Union, which left Canada little practical alternative but to comply — the United States, being a larger market, did not create the same kind of legislation as Canada, but has not lost access to European markets.

Even allowing that exceptional circumstances might exist where Canada could and should act unilaterally in the absence of international consensus, it must choose the occasions sparingly. While the edifice of territoriality is being slowly dismantled by globalization, the changes impel Canada to be both defensive and proactive in equal measures as it seeks to protect and to promote its own interests in the changing global order.

Bibliography

Legislation

CANADIAN LEGISLATION

An Act Respecting the Buffalo and Fort Erie Public Bridge Company, SC 1934, c 63
Antarctic Environmental Protection Act, SC 2003, c 20
Anti-terrorism Act, SC 2001, c 41
Arbitration Act, 1991, SO 1991, c 17
Arctic Waters Pollution Prevention Act, RSC 1985, c A-12
Asia-Pacific Foundation of Canada Act, RSC 1985, c A-13

Bank Act, SC 1991, c 46
Blue Water Bridge Authority Act, SC 1964-65, c 6
Business Concerns Records Act, RSQ c D-12
Business Records Protection Act, RSO 1990, c B.19

Campobello-Lubec Bridge Act, SC 1958, c 23
Canada Business Corporations Act, RSC 1985, c C-44
Canada Cooperatives Act, SC 1998, c 1
Canada Elections Act, SC 2000, c 9
Canada Evidence Act, RSC 1985, c C-5
Canada Shipping Act, RSC 1985, c S-9
Canadian Charter of Rights and Freedoms, Part I of the *Constitution Act, 1982*, being Schedule B to the *Canada Act 1982* (UK), 1982, c 11
Canadian Forces Members and Veterans Re-establishment and Compensation Act, SC 2005, c 21
Canadian Human Rights Act, RSC 1985, c H-6

Canadian Transportation Accident Investigation and Safety Board Act, SC 1989, c 3
Charter of the French Language, RSQ c C-11
Chemical Weapons Convention Implementation Act, SC 1995, c 25
Citizenship Act, RSC 1985, c C-29
Civil Code of Québec, RSQ c C-1991
Civil International Space Station Agreement Implementation Act, SC 1999, c 35
Coastal Fisheries Protection Act, RSC 1985, c C-33
Compensation for Victims of Crime Act, RSO 1990, c C.24
Competition Act, RSC 1985, c C-34
Cooperative Credit Associations Act, SC 1991, c 48
Corruption of Foreign Public Officials Act, SC 1998, c 34
Court Jurisdiction and Proceedings Transfer Act, SBC 2003, c 28
Court Jurisdiction and Proceedings Transfer Act, SNS 2003 (2d Sess), c 2
Court Jurisdiction and Proceedings Transfer Act, SS 1997, c C-41.1
Court Jurisdiction and Proceedings Transfer Act, SY 2000, c 7 (not yet in force)
Crimes Against Humanity and War Crimes Act, SC 2000, c 24
Criminal Code, RSC 1985, c C-46

Extradition Act, SC 1999, c 18

Federal Courts Act, RSC 1985, c F-7
Federal Real Property and Federal Immovables Act, SC 1991, c 50
Fisheries Act, RSC 1985, c F-14
Foreign Enlistment Act, RSC 1985, c F-28
Foreign Extraterritorial Measures Act, RSC 1985, c F-29
Foreign Missions and International Organizations Act, SC 1991, c 41
Foreign Publishers Advertising Services Act, SC 1999, c 23

Government Employees Compensation Act, RSC 1985, c G-5

Health of Animals Act, SC 1990, c 21

Immigration and Refugee Protection Act, SC 2001, c 27
Income Tax Act, RSC 1985, c 1 (5th Supp)
Insurance Companies Act, SC 1991, c 47
Integrated Cross-Border Law Enforcement Operations Act, SC 2012, c 19
Interpretation Act, RSC 1985, c I-21

Marine Liability Act, SC 2001, c 6
Merchant Seamen Compensation Act, RSC 1985, c M-6
Migratory Birds Convention Act, 1994, SC 1994, c 22
Museums Act, SC 1990, c 3
Mutual Legal Assistance in Criminal Matters Act, RSC 1985, c 30 (4th Supp)

National Defence Act, RSC 1985, c N-5
National Housing Act, RSC 1985, c N-11
Non-smokers' Health Act, RSC 1985, c 15 (4th Supp)
North American Free Trade Agreement Implementation Act, SC 1993, c 44
Nuclear Terrorism Act, SC 2013, c 13

Oceans Act, SC 1996, c 31
Official Languages Act, RSC 1985, c 31 (4th Supp)

Personal Information Protection and Electronic Documents Act, SC 2000, c 5
Plant Breeders' Rights Act, SC 1990, c 20
Preclearance Act, SC 1999, c 20
Privacy Act, RSC 1985, c P-21
Proceeds of Crime (Money Laundering) and Terrorist Financing Act, SC 2000, c 17

Quarantine Act, SC 2005, c 20

Remote Sensing Space Systems Act, SC 2005, c 45
Royal Canadian Mounted Police Superannuation Act, RSC 1985, c R-11

Safe Streets and Communities Act, SC 2012, c 1
Security of Information Act, RSC 1985, c O-5
Special Economic Measures Act, SC 1992, c 17
State Immunity Act, RSC 1985, c S-18

Telecommunications Act, SC 1993, c 38
Tobacco Act, SC 1997, c 13
Trade-marks Act, RSC 1985, c T-13
Trust and Loan Companies Act, SC 1991, c 45

United Nations Act, RSC 1985, c U-2
United Nations Foreign Arbitral Awards Convention Act, RSC 1985, c 16 (2nd Supp)

Victims of Crime Act, RSA 2000, c V-3
Visiting Forces Act, RSC 1985, c V-2

CANADIAN BILLS

Bill C-12, *An Act to amend the Personal Information Protection and Electronic Documents Act*, 1st Sess, 41st Parl, 2011
Bill C-483, *An Act to Amend the State Immunity Act (Genocide, Crimes against Humanity, War Crimes or Torture)*, 2nd Sess, 40th Parl, 2009

CANADIAN REGULATIONS

Coastal Fisheries Protection Regulations, CRC, c 413

Confederation Bridge Area Provincial (PEI) Laws Application Regulations, SOR/97-375

Radio Regulations, 1986, SOR/86-982
Regulations Establishing a List of Entities, SOR/2002-284
Regulations Implementing the United Nations Resolution on Eritrea, SOR/2010-84

Television Broadcasting Regulations, 1987, SOR/87-49

FOREIGN LEGISLATION AND BILLS

12 USC §3401 (2006)
15 USC §1681 (2006)
18 USC § 2423(c) (2013)

Act on Punishment of Activities Relating to Child Prostitution and Child Pornography, and the Protection of Children, Act No 52 of 1999 [Japan], online: Japanese Law Translation www.japaneselawtranslation.go.jp/law/detail/?id=100&vm=04&re=02
Anti-Terrorism Acts (No. 2) 2005 (Cth)
Anti-terrorism, Crime and Security Act 2001 (UK), c 24
Australian Citizenship Act 2007 (Cth)

Child Sexual Abuse Prevention Act, 18 USC § 2423(b) (1994)
Children's Online Privacy Protection Act, 15 USC §§ 6501–6506 (2006)
Computer Fraud and Abuse Act of 1986, 18 USC §1001 (1986)
Counter-Terrorism Act 2008 (UK), c 28
Crimes (Child Sex Tourism) Amendment Act 1994 (Cth)
Crimes Act 1961 (NZ), 1961/43, 1 RS 635
Criminal Code Amendment (Terrorism) Act 2003 (Cth)

EC, *Commission Directive 2002/58/EC of the European Parliament and of the Council of 12 July 2002 concerning the processing of personal data and the protection of privacy in the electronic communications sector (Directive on privacy and electronic communications)*, [2002] OJ, L 201/37
EC, *Commission Directive 2006/24/EC of the European Parliament and of the Council of 15 March 2006 on the retention of data generated or processed in connection with the provision of publicly available electronic communications services or of public communications networks and amending Directive 2002/58/EC*, [2006] OJ, L 105/54
EC, *Commission Directive 95/46/EC of the European Parliament and of the Council of 24 October 1995 on the protection of individuals with regard to the processing of personal data and on the free movement of such data*, [1995] OJ, L 281/31

Federal Law on Counteraction against Terrorism, No 35-FZ of 6 March 2006 [Russian Federation]

FISA Amendments Act of 2008, Pub L No 110-261, 122 Stat 2477

Gambling Act 2003 (NZ), 2003/51
Gambling Act 2005 (UK), c 19

Human Security Act of 2007 [Philippines]

Interactive Gambling Act 2001 (Cth)

Military Commissions Act of 2006, 10 USC 948a (2006)

Official Secrets Act 1972 (Malaysia)
Official Secrets Act 1989 (UK), c 6

Penal Code, Act No 45 of 1907 [Japan]
Prevention of Terrorism Act, 2002 [India]
PROTECT Act of 2003, Pub L 108-21, 117 Stat 650 (2003)

Representation of the People Act 1983 (UK), c 2

Security Legislation Amendment (Terrorism) Act 2002 (Cth)
Sex Offenders Act 1997 (UK), c 51

Terrorism Act 2006 (UK), c 11
Terrorism Suppression Act 2002 (NZ) 2002/34, as amended
Torture Victim Protection Act of 1991, 28 USC §1350 (1992)

Unlawful Activities (Prevention) Amendment Ordinance, 2004 [India]
Unlawful Internet Gambling Enforcement Act 2006, 31 USC § 5361–5366 (2006)
US, Bill HR 2267, *Internet Gambling Regulation, Consumer Protection, and Enforcement Act*, 111th Cong, 2009, a bill to amend title 31 of the United States Code "to provide for the licensing of Internet gambling activities by the Secretary of the Treasury, to provide for consumer protections on the Internet, to enforce the tax code, and for other purposes"
US, Bill HR 4976, *Internet Gambling Regulation and Tax Enforcement Act of 2010*, 111th Cong, 2010 to "amend the Internal Revenue Code of 1986 to regulate and tax Internet gambling"
US, Bill S 1597, *Internet Poker and Game of Skill Regulation, Consumer Protection, and Enforcement Act of 2009*, 111th Cong, 2009
USA PATRIOT Act, Pub L 107-56, 115 Stat 272 (2001)

Treaties

Agreement between the Government of Canada and the Government of the United States Concerning the Operation of Commercial Remote Sensing Satellite Systems, 16 June 2000, Can TS 2000 No 14

Agreement between the Government of Canada and the Government of the United States Regarding the Application of Their Competition and Deceptive Marketing Practices Laws, 3 August 1995, Can TS 1995 No 15, 35 ILM 311 (1996)

Agreement for the Implementation of the Provisions of the United Nations Convention on the Law of the Sea of 10 December 1982 relating to the Conservation and Management of Straddling Fish Stocks and Highly Migratory Fish Stocks, 4 August 1995, 2167 UNTS 3, 34 ILM 1542

Agreement on Air Transport Preclearance between the Government of Canada and the Government of the United States, 18 January 2001, Can TS 2003 No 7

American Convention on Human Rights "Pact of San José, Costa Rica," 22 November 1969, 1144 UNTS 123

Asia-Pacific Trade Agreement, 2 November 2005 (previously known as the *First Agreement on Trade Negotiations among Developing Member Countries of the Economic and Social Commission for Asia and the Pacific (Bangkok Agreement)*, 31 July 1975)

Berne Convention for the Protection of Literary and Artistic Works, 9 September 1886, 828 UNTS 221

Central European Free Trade Agreement (CEFTA) 2006, 19 December 2006

Convention against Torture and Other Cruel, Inhuman or Degrading Treatment or Punishment, 10 December 1984, 1465 UNTS 85, Can TS 1987 No 36

Convention against Transnational Organized Crime, 15 November 2000, 2225 UNTS 209, TIAS No 13127

Convention between the Government of Canada and the Government of the French Republic for the Avoidance of Double Taxation and the Prevention of Fiscal Evasion with respect to Taxes on Income and on Capital, 2 May 1975, Can TS 1976 No 30

Convention between the Government of Canada and the Government of the United Kingdom for the Avoidance of Double Taxation and the Prevention of Fiscal Evasion with respect to Taxes on Income and Capital Gains, 8 September 1978, Can TS 1980 No 25

Convention between the Government of Canada and the Government of the United Kingdom providing for the Reciprocal Recognition and Enforcement of Judgments in Civil and Commercial Matters, 24 April 1984, Can TS 1987 No 29, UKTS 1988 No 74

Convention for the Prevention and Punishment of Terrorism, 16 November 1937, 19 League of Nations OJ 23 (1938)

Convention for the Protection of Human Rights and Fundamental Freedoms, 4 November 1950, 213 UNTS 221

Convention for the Suppression of Unlawful Seizure of Aircraft, 16 December 1970, 860 UNTS 105, Can TS 1972 No 23

Convention on Biological Diversity, 11 June 1992, Can TS 1993 No 24, 31 ILM 822 (1992)

Convention on Civil Aspects of International Child Abduction, 25 October 1980, Can TS 1983 No 35

Convention on Combating Bribery of Foreign Public Officials in International Business Transactions, 17 December 1997, Can TS 1999 No 23

Convention on Cybercrime, 23 November 2001, ETS No 185, 41 ILM 282 (2001)

Convention on International Civil Aviation, 7 December 1944, 15 UNTS 295, Can TS 1944 No 36

Convention on International Trade in Endangered Species of Wild Fauna and Flora, 2 July 1974, 993 UNTS 243, Can TS 1975 No 32

Convention on Protection of Children and Co-operation in Respect of Intercountry Adoption, 29 May 1993, Can TS 1997 No 12

Convention on the International Regulations for Preventing Collisions at Sea, 1972, 20 October 1972, Can TS 1977 No 45

Convention on the Nationality of Married Women, 20 February 1957, 309 UNTS 65, Can TS 1960 No 2

Convention on the Recognition and Enforcement of Foreign Arbitral Awards, 10 June 1958, Can TS 1986 No 43

Convention on the Rights of the Child, GA Res 44/25, UNGA 61st Plen Mtg, UN Doc A/RES/44/25, (1989)

Convention on the Service Abroad of Judicial and Extrajudicial Documents in Civil or Commercial Matters, 15 November 1965, Can TS 1989 No 2

Convention on the Taking of Evidence Abroad in Civil or Commercial Matters 18 March 1970, 847 UNTS 231

Exchange of Notes Constituting an Agreement between the Government of Canada and the Government of the United States to Facilitate Co-operation between Military Services of the Two Countries, 19 August 1994, Can TS 1994 No 34, with reference to *Agreement between the Parties to the North Atlantic Treaty regarding the Status of their Forces*, 19 June 1951, Can TS 1953 No 13

Final Act Embodying the Results of the Uruguay Round of Multinational Trade Agreements, 15 April 1994, 1867 UNTS 3 (December 1993 text) and 33 ILM 1143 (1994) (April 1994 text)

Framework Agreement on Integrated Cross-Border Maritime Law Enforcement Operations between the Government of Canada and the Government of the United States, Can TS 2012 No 25

General Agreement on Tariffs and Trade 1994, 15 April 1994, 1867 UNTS 187; 33 ILM 1153 (1994)

Hague Convention on the Service Abroad of Judicial and Extrajudicial Documents in Civil or Commercial Matters, 15 November 1965, TIAS No 6638, 20 UST 361

International Convention against the Taking of Hostages, 17 December 1979, 1316 UNTS 205, Can TS 1986 No 45

International Convention for the Suppression of Acts of Nuclear Terrorism, GA Res 51/210, UNGA 59th Sess, UN Doc A/Res/59/290 (2005)

International Convention for the Suppression of Terrorist Bombings, 15 December 1997, 2149 UNTS 256, 37 ILM 249 (1998)

International Convention for the Suppression of the Financing of Terrorism, 9 December 1999, Can TS 2002 No 9

International Covenant on Civil and Political Rights, 16 December 1966, 999 UNTS 171, Can TS 1976 No 47

International Covenant on Economic, Social and Cultural Rights, 16 December 1966, 993 UNTS 3, Can TS 1976 No 46

North American Free Trade Agreement, Can TS 1994 No 2, 32 ILM 289 and 605 (1993)

Optional Protocol to the Convention on the Rights of the Child on the Sale of Children, Child Prostitution and Child Pornography, 25 May 2000, 2171 UNTS 227

Paris Convention for the Protection of Industrial Property, 20 March 1883, 828 UNTS 305 revised at Stockholm 14 July 1967, amended on 28 September 1979

Rome Statute of the International Criminal Court, UN Doc A/CONF. 183/9, 37 ILM 999 (1998)

Treaty between the Government of Canada and the Government of the United States of America on Mutual Legal Assistance in Criminal Matters, 18 March 1985, Can TS 1990 No 19

Treaty between the United Kingdom and the United States of America relating to Boundary Waters and Questions Arising along the Boundary between Canada and the United States, 11 January 1909, UKTS 1910 No 23

United Nations Agreement for the Implementation of the Provisions of the United Nations Convention on the Law of the Sea of 10 December 1982 relating to the Conservation and Management of Straddling Fish Stocks and Highly Migratory Fish Stocks, 4 December 1995, 34 ILM 1542 (1995)

United Nations Convention on Contracts for the International Sale of Goods, 11 April 1980, 1489 UNTS 3, Can TS 1992 No 2

United Nations Convention on the Law of the Sea, 10 December 1982, 1833 UNTS 3

Vienna Convention on Diplomatic Relations, 18 April 1961, 500 UNTS 95, 1966 Can TS No 29

Vienna Convention on the Law of Treaties, 23 May 1969, 1155 UNTS 331, Can TS 1980 No 37

WIPO Copyright Treaty, 20 December 1996, 36 ILM 65 (1997)
WIPO Performances and Phonograms Treaty, 20 December 1996, 36 ILM 76

United Nations Documents (Other than Treaties)

Basic Principles and Guidelines on the Right to a Remedy and Reparation for Victims of Gross Violations of International Human Rights Law and Serious Violations of International Humanitarian Law, UNGA 60th Sess, UN Doc A/Res 60/147 (2005)

Committee against Torture, *Conclusions and Recommendations of the Committee against Torture: Canada*, UNHRC, 34th Sess, UN Doc CAT/C/CR/34/CAN (2005)

Declaration on Basic Principles of Justice for Victims of Crime and Abuse of Power, UNGA 96th Plen Mtg, UN Doc A/Res/40/34 (1985) Annex

International Law Commission, *Draft Articles on Diplomatic Protection*, UNGAOR 59th Sess, Supp No 10, UN Doc A/59/10 (2004)
———, *Draft Articles on the Responsibility of States for Internationally Wrongful Acts*, in *Report of the International Law Commission on the Work of its Fifty-third Session*, UNGAOR 56th Sess, Supp No 10, UN Doc A/56/10 (2001)

Office of the United Nations High Commissioner for Human Rights, *General Comment No 31 Nature of the General Legal Obligation Imposed on States Parties to the Covenant*, CCPR/C/21/Rev.1/Add.13 (2004)

Resolution 1373 (2001), SC Res, UNSC, 4385th Mtg, UN Doc S/RES/1373 (2001)
Resolution adopted by the General Assembly on 16 September 2005, UNGA, 60th Sess, UN Doc A/RES/60/1 (2005)

United Nations Committee against Torture, *General Comment No. 2: Implementation of Article 2 by States Parties*, CAT/C/GC/2/CRP.1/Rev.4 (2007)
United Nations Global Counter-Terrorism Strategy, GA Res 60/288, UNGA, 60th Sess, UN Doc A/RES/60/288 (2006)
Universal Declaration of Human Rights, GA Res 217(III), UNGAOR, 3rd Sess, Supp No 13, UN Doc A/810 (1948)

Secondary Materials

ARTICLES

Abrahams, Nick. "Media Laws for Virtual Worlds" (2007) 30:1 UNSWLJ 295
Akehurst, Michael. "Jurisdiction in International Law" (1972–73) 46 Brit YB Int'l L 145
Alexander, Gerd. "The U.S. on Tilt: Why the Unlawful Internet Gambling Enforcement Act is a Bad Bet" (2008) Duke L & Tech Rev 0006

Andrews, Sara K. "U.S. Domestic Prosecution of the American International Sex Tourist: Efforts to Protect Children from Sexual Exploitation" (2004) 94:2 J Crim L & Criminology 415

Andrle, John D. "A Winning Hand: A Proposal for an International Regulatory Schema with Respect to the Growing Online Gambling Dilemma in the United States," Note (2004) 37:5 Vand J Transnat'l L 1389

Archibugi, Daniele, & Jonathan Michie. "The Globalization of Technology: A New Taxonomy" (1995) 19(1) Cambridge Journal of Economics 121

Arias, Andrea Vanina. "Life, Liberty, and the Pursuit of Swords and Armor: Regulating the Theft of Virtual Goods" (2008) 57:5 Emory LJ 1301

Bartle, Richard A. "Virtual Worldliness: What the Imaginary Asks of the Real" (2004–2005) 49:1 NYL Sch L Rev 19

Bartsch, Kerstin, & Björn Elberling. "*Jus Cogens* vs. State Immunity, Round Two: The Decision of the European Court of Human Rights in the *Kalogeropoulou et al. v. Greece and Germany* Decision" (2003) 4:5 German Law Journal 477

Baudenbacher, Carl. "Judicial Globalization: New Development or Old Wine in New Bottles?" (2003) 38:3 Tex Int'l LJ 505

Beaulieu, Catherine. "Extraterritorial Laws: Why They Are Not Really Working and How They Can Be Strengthened" *ECPAT International Compendium of Articles* (September 2008)

Bexell, Magdalena, Jonas Tallberg, & Anders Uhlin. "Democracy in Global Governance: The Promises and Pitfalls of Transnational Actors" (2010) 16:1 Global Governance 81

"BGH, 12. 12. 2000 - 1 StR 184/00: Verbreitung der Auschwitz-Lüge im Internet" (2001) 8 Neue Juristiche Wochenschrift 624

Bigos, Oren. "Jurisdiction Over Cross-Border Wrongs on the Internet" (2005) 54:3 ICLQ 585

Blackmore, Joshua. "The Jurisdictional Problem of Extraterritorial Conspiracy" (2006) 17:1 Criminal LF 71

Blakesley, Christopher L. "Extraterritorial Jurisdiction" in M Cherif Bassiouni, ed, *International Criminal Law*, 3d ed (Leiden: Martinus Nijhoff Publishers, 2008) vol 2 at 33

Branson, Douglas M. "The Social Responsibility of Large Multinational Corporations" (2002) 16:1 Transnat'l Law 121

Brenner, Susan W, & Leo L Clarke. "Distributed Security: A New Model of Law Enforcement," *Social Science Research Network Working Paper Series* (14 November 2005)

Bridge, Seth T. "Russia's New Counteracting Terrorism Law: The Legal Implications of Pursuing Terrorists beyond the Borders of the Russian Federation" (2009) 3:1 Colum J E Eur L 1

Brookson-Morris, Kate. "Conflicts of Criminal Jurisdiction" (2007) 56:3 ICLQ 659

Brown, Chris. "Reimagining International Society and Global Community" in David Held & Anthony McGrew, eds, *Globalization Theory: Approaches and Controversies* (Cambridge, UK: Polity Press, 2007) 171

Burns, Brendan. "Do Virtual World Activities Give Rise to Real Canadian Tax Liabilities?" (2010) 10 Asper Review of International Business and Trade Law 163

Buxbaum, Hannah L. "Transnational Regulatory Litigation" (2006) 46 Va J Int'l L 251

Castronova, Edward. "Virtual Worlds: A First-Hand Account of Market and Society on the Cyberian Frontier," *CESifo Working Paper No. 618* (December 2001), online: Social Science Research Network http://ssrn.com/abstract=294828

Cherry, Miriam A. "Working for (Virtually) Minimum Wage: Applying the Fair Labor Standards Act in Cyberspace" (2009) 60:5 Ala L Rev 1077

Coughlan, Stephen et al. "Global Reach, Local Grasp: Constructing Extraterritorial Jurisdiction in the Age of Globalization" (2007) 6:1 CJLT 29

Currie, John H. "International Human Rights Law in the Supreme Court's *Charter* Jurisprudence: Commitment, Retrenchment *and* Retreat — In No Particular Order" (2010) 50:2 Sup Ct L Rev (2d) 423

———. "*Khadr*'s Twist on *Hape*: Tortured Determinations of the Extraterritorial Reach of the Canadian *Charter*" (2008) 46 Can YB Int'l Law 307

Currie, Robert J. "A Tale of Two Brothers: The Impact of the *Khadr* Cases on Canadian Anti-Terrorism Law" in C Forcese & F Crépeau, eds, *Terrorism, Law and Democracy: Ten Years After 9/11* (Montreal: Canadian Institute for the Administration of Justice, 2012)

———. "*Charter* without Borders? The Supreme Court of Canada, Transnational Crime and Constitutional Rights and Freedoms" (2004) 27 Dal LJ 235

———. "*Libman* at 25; or, Canada and Qualified Territoriality: Do We Understand Jurisdiction Yet?" in Chi Carmody, ed, *Is Our House in Order? Canada's Implementation of International Law* (Montreal/Kingston: McGill-Queen's University Press, 2010)

Currie, Robert J, & Hugh M Kindred. "Flux and Fragmentation in the International Law of State Jurisdiction: The Synecdochal Example of Canada's Domestic Court Conflicts over Accountability for International Human Rights Violations" in Ole Kristian Fauchald & André Nollkaemper, eds, *The Practice of International and National Courts and the (De-) Fragmentation of International Law* (Oxford: Hart, 2012) 217

Currie, Robert J, & Steve Coughlan. "Extraterritorial Criminal Jurisdiction: Bigger Picture or Smaller Frame?" (2007) 11:2 Can Crim L Rev 141

Davidson, Stephen J. "An Immersive Perspective on the Second Life Virtual World" (2008) 25:3 Computer & Internet Lawyer 1

Davis, Donna L. "Tracking Cross-Border Data Flows: A Comment on *Lawson v. Accusearch Inc.*," Case Comment (2007) 6:2 CJLT 119

DelBianco, Steve, & Braden Cox. "ICANN Internet Governance: Is it Working?" (2008) 21 Pacific McGeorge Global Business & Development Law Journal 27

de Mestral, Armand, & Evan Fox-Decent. "Rethinking the Relationship between International and Domestic Law" (2008) 53:4 McGill LJ 573

Edelson, Daniel. "The Prosecution of Persons Who Sexually Exploit Children in Countries Other than their Own: A Model for Amending Existing Legislation," Note (2001) 25:2 Fordham Int'l LJ 483

Edwards, Lilian. "Privacy and Data Protection Online: The Laws Don't Work?" in Lilian Edwards & Charlotte Waelde, eds, *Law and the Internet*, 3d ed (Portland: Hart, 2009)

El Fadl, Khaled Abou. "Striking a Balance: Islamic Legal Discourses on Muslim Minorities" in Yvonne Yazbeck Haddad & John L. Esposito, eds, *Muslims on the Americanization Path?* (New York: Oxford University Press, 2000) 47

Fairfield, Joshua AT. "Virtual Property" (2005) 85:4 BUL Rev 1047

Fairley, H Scott. "Exceeding the Limits of Territorial Bounds: *The Helms-Burton Act*" (1996) 34 Can YB Int'l Law 161

Farrow, Trevor CW. "Negotiation, Mediation, Globalization Protests and Police: Right Processes; Wrong System, Issues, Parties and Time" (2002–2003) 28 Queen's LJ 665

Fletcher, George P. "The Indefinable Concept of Terrorism" (2006) 4:5 Journal of International Criminal Justice 894

Forcese, Craig. "Spies without Borders: International Law and Intelligence Collection" (2011–2012) 5 Journal of National Security Law & Policy 179

Fredette, Kalen. "International Legislative Efforts to Combat Child Sex Tourism: Evaluating the Council of Europe *Convention on Commercial Child Sexual Exploitation*" (2009) 32:1 BC Int'l & Comp L Rev 1

Froomkin, A Michael. "ICANN's 'Uniform Dispute Resolution Policy' — Causes and (Partial) Cures" (2002) 67:3 Brook L Rev 608

Galbraith, Sarah E. "Second Life Strife: A Proposal for Resolution of In-World Fashion Disputes" (2008) Brown College Intellectual Property & Technology Forum

Geist, Michael. "Fair.com?: An Examination of the Allegations of Systemic Unfairness in the ICANN UDRP" (August 2001), online: uOttawa http://aix1.uottawa.ca/~geist/geistudrp.pdf

———. "Fundamentally Fair.Com? An Update on Bias Allegations and the ICANN UDRP," online: uOttawa http://aix1.uottawa.ca/~geist/fairupdate.pdf

Gillies, Lorna. "Addressing the "Cyberspace Fallacy": Targeting the Jurisdiction of an Electronic Consumer Contract" (2008) 16:3 Int'l JL & IT 242

Gioia, Andrea. "The UN Conventions on the Prevention and Suppression of International Terrorism" in Giuseppe Nesi, ed, *International Cooperation in Counter-terrorism* (Aldershot, UK: Ashgate, 2006) 1

Giordanella, Heather C. "Status of 2423(b): Prosecuting United States Nationals for Sexually Exploiting Children in Foreign Countries" (1998) 12 Temp Int'l & Comp LJ 133

Gong, Jennifer. "Defining and Addressing Virtual Property in International Treaties" (2011) 17 BUJ Sci & Tech L 101

Goodwin-Gill, Guy S. "The Extra-Territorial Reach of Human Rights Obligations: A Brief Perspective on the Link to Jurisdiction" in Laurence Boisson de Chazournes & Marcelo Kohen, eds, *International Law and the Quest for its Implementation* (Leiden: Brill, 2010) 293

Graham, William C. "The *Foreign Extraterritorial Measures Act*" (1986) 11:4 Can Bus LJ 410

Griffin, Ken, Mark McMurtrey, & LeaAnn Smith. "To Tax or Not to Tax? Foreign and Domestic Taxation of the Internet" (2008) 12:1 Proceedings of the Academy of Legal, Ethical and Regulatory Issues 1

Grimmelmann, James. "Virtual Worlds as Comparative Law" (2004–2005) 49:1 NYL Sch L Rev 147

Heeks, Richard. "Current Analysis and Future Research Agenda on 'Gold Farming': Real-World Production in Developing Countries for the Virtual Economies of Online Games," *Development Informatics Working Paper Series No.* 32 (2008), online: University of Manchester, Institute for Development Policy and Management www.sed.manchester.ac.uk/idpm/research/publications/wp/di/documents/di_wp32.pdf

Held, David. "Reframing Global Governance: Apocalypse Soon or Reform!" in David Held & Anthony McGrew, eds, *Globalization Theory: Approaches and Controversies* (Cambridge, UK: Polity Press, 2007)

Held, David, & Anthony McGrew. "Globalization at Risk?" in David Held & Anthony McGrew, eds, *Globalization Theory: Approaches and Controversies* (Cambridge, UK: Polity Press, 2007)

Helfer, Laurence R. "Whither the UDRP: Autonomous, Americanized or Cosmopolitan?" (2004) 12:2 Cardozo J Int'l & Comp L 493

Hendrix, Mary Catherine. "Enforcing the U.S. *Trafficking Victims Protection Act* in Emerging Markets: The Challenge of Affecting Change in India and China," Note, (2010) 43:1 Cornell Int'l LJ 173

Hill, Jonathan. "The Exercise of Jurisdiction in Private International Law" in Patrick Capps, Malcolm Evans, & Stratos Konstadinidis, eds, *Asserting Jurisdiction: International and European Legal Perspectives* (Oxford: Hart, 2003) 39

Hörnle, Julia. "The Jurisdictional Challenge of the Internet" in Lilian Edwards & Charlotte Waelde, eds, *Law and the Internet*, 3d ed (Portland: Hart, 2009)

Horowitz, Steven J. "*Bragg v. Linden*'s Second Life: A Primer in Virtual World Justice" (2008) 34:1 Ohio NUL Rev 223

Jepson, Valerie. "Internet Gambling and the Canadian Conundrum" (2000) 6 Appeal 6

Johnson, David R, & David Post. "Law and Borders: The Rise of Law in Cyberspace" (1996) 48 Stan L Rev 1367

Karadbil, Jenna F. "Casinos of the Next Millenium: A Look into the Proposed Ban on Internet Gambling," Note (2000) 17:2 Ariz J Int'l & Comp L 413

Katsh, Ethan. "Bringing Online Dispute Resolution to Virtual Worlds: Creating Processes through Code" (2004–2005) 49:1 NYL Sch L Rev 271

Kelley, Robin, Peter Todosichuk, & Jason J Azmier. "Gambling@Home: Internet Gambling in Canada," *Gambling in Canada Research Report No. 15* (Calgary: Canada West Foundation, 2001)

Kerr, Orin S. "Criminal Law in Virtual Worlds: Law in a Networked World" (2008) U Chicago Legal F 415

Keyser, Mike. "The Council of Europe *Convention on Cybercrime*" (2003) 12:2 J Transnat'l L & Pol'y 287

Khader, Naser, & Flemming Rose. "Reflections on the Danish Cartoon Controversy" (2007) 14:4 Middle East Quarterly 59

King, Kevin F. "Geolocation and Federalism on the Internet: Cutting Internet Gambling's Gordian Knot" (2010) 11 Colum Sci & Tech L Rev 41

Koskenniemi, Martti & Päivi Leino. "Fragmentation of International Law? Postmodern Anxieties" (2002) 15:3 Leiden J Int'l L 553

Kramer, Kelly B. "The Jay Cohen Affair: Lessons in the Legality of Internet Betting" (2001) 5:6 Gaming Law Review 551

Kuner, Christopher. "Data Protection Law and International Jurisdiction on the Internet (Part 1)" (2010) 18 Int'l JL & IT 176

Kur, Annette. "UDRP: A Study by the Max-Planck-Institute for Foreign and International Patent, Copyright and Competition Law" (Munich: Max-Planck-Institute, 2002)

Kyer, C Ian, & Danielle Hough. "Is Internet Gaming Legal in Canada: A Look at Starnet" (2002) 1:1 CJLT

Larocque, Francois. "La *Loi sur l'immunité des États* canadienne et la torture" (2010) 55:1 McGill LJ 81

Lastowka, F Gregory, & Dan Hunter. "The Laws of the Virtual Worlds" (2004) 92:1 Cal L Rev 1

Lavers, Troy. "Jurisdictional Issues in Extraterritorial Criminal Law" in Christopher PM Waters, ed, *British and Canadian Perspectives on International Law* (Leiden: Brill, 2006) 87

Leblanc, Jeff. "The Pursuit of Virtual Life, Liberty and Happiness and its Economic and Legal Recognition in the Real World" (2008) 9 Fla Coastal L Rev 255

Li, Vickie F. "Child Sex Tourism to Thailand: The Role of the United States as a Consumer Country" (1995) 4:2 Pac Rim L & Pol'y J 505

Lockridge, Lee Ann W. "Intellectual Property in Outer Space: International Law, National Jurisdiction, and Exclusive Rights in Geospatial Data and Databases" (2006) 32:2 J Space L 319

Lowe, Vaughan, & Christopher Staker. "Jurisdiction" in Malcolm D Evans, ed, *International Law*, 3d ed (Oxford: Oxford University Press, 2010)

Macklem, Patrick. "Corporate Accountability under International Law: The Misguided Quest for Universal Jurisdiction" (2005) 7:4 International Law Forum du droit international 281

Manglona, Elkia. "An Avatar's Parody: Considering a First Amendment Right to Parody Real World Trademarks in a Three-Dimensional Virtual World" (2009) 19:1 Alb LJ Sci & Tech 183

Mann, FA. "The Doctrine of Jurisdiction in International Law" (1964-I) 111 Rec des Cours 1

Martin, Charles H. "The Electronic Contracts Convention, the CISG, and New Sources of E-Commerce Law" (2008) 16:2 Tul J of Int'l & Comp L 467

Martineau, Anne Charlotte. "The Rhetoric of Fragmentation: Fear and Faith in International Law" (2009) 22:1 Leiden J Int'l L 1

Mayer-Schönberger, Viktor, & John Crowley, "Napster's Second Life?: The Regulatory Challenges of Virtual Worlds" (2006) 100:4 Nw UL Rev 1775

McBurney, Joseph J. "To Regulate or to Prohibit: An Analysis of the Internet Gambling Industry and the Need for a Decision on the Industry's Future in the United States" (2005–2006) 21 Conn J Int'l L 337

McCorquodale, Robert & Penelope Simons. "Responsibility Beyond Borders: State Responsibility for Extraterritorial Violations by Corporations of International Human Rights Law" (2007) 70:4 Mod L Rev 598

Messigian, Amy. "Love's Labour's Lost: Michael Lewis Clark's Constitutional Challenge of 18 U.S.C. 2423(C)," Note (2006) 43:3 Am Crim L Rev 1241

Milanovic, Marko. "Al-Skeini and Al-Jedda in Strasbourg" (2012) 23:1 European Journal of International Law 121

Mizuno, Sakura. "When Free Speech and the Internet Collide: Yahoo! — Nazi — Paraphernalia Case" (2001) 10 Currents 56

Molot, HL, & ML Jewett. "The *State Immunity Act* of Canada" (1982) 20 Can YB Int'l Law 79

Mueller, Milton. "Rough Justice: An Analysis of ICANN's Uniform Dispute Resolution Policy," V2.1, online: The Centre for Convergence and Emerging Networking Technologies http://dcc.syr.edu/PDF/roughjustice.pdf

Murphy Jr, Ewell E. "The Lessons of Seattle: Learning from the Failed Third WTO Ministerial Conference" (2000) 13:2 Transnat'l Law 273

Newman, Elizabeth. "EC Regulation of Audio-visual Content on the Internet" in Lilian Edwards & Charlotte Waelde, eds, *Law and the Internet*, 3d ed (Portland: Hart, 2009) 159

Parry, John T. "Terrorism and the New Criminal Process" (2007) 15:3 Wm & Mary Bill Rts J 765

Partridge, Brian. "'The Play's the Thing': *World of Warcraft* and Legal Philosophy" (2010) 3:2 Phoenix Law Review 769

Paust, Jordan. "International Law Before the Supreme Court: A Mixed Record of Recognition" (2005) 45 Santa Clara L Rev 829

Pauwelyn, Joost. "Bridging Fragmentation and Unity: International Law as a Universe of Inter-Connected Islands" (2004) 25:4 Mich J Int'l L 903

Penney, Jonathon W. "Understanding the New Virtualist Paradigm" (2009) 12:8 Journal of Internet Law 3

Pickett, Andrew M. "Much Yahoo! About Nothing: The Ninth Circuit, Jurisprudential Schizophrenia, and The Road Not Taken in *Yahoo! v. La Ligue Contre le Racisme et l'Antisémitisme*" (2006) 8 Tulane Journal of Technology and Intellectual Property 231

Port, Kenneth L. "Trademark Monopolies in the Blue Nowhere" (2002) 28:3 Wm Mitchell L Rev 1091

Post, David G. "Governing Cyberspace: Law" (2008) 24:4 Santa Clara Computer & High Tech LJ 883

Post, David G, & David R Johnson. "The Great Debate: Law in the Virtual World" (2006) 11:2 First Monday, online: First Monday http://firstmonday.org/htbin/cgiwrap/bin/ojs/index.php/fm/article/view/1311/1231

Qiu, Jack Linchuan. "Virtual Censorship in China: Keeping the Gate between the Cyberspaces" (1999–2000) 4 Int'l J Comm L & Pol'y 1

Raimo, Tyler. "Winning at the Expense of Law: The Ramifications of Expanding Counter-Terrorism Law Enforcement Jurisdiction Overseas" (1999) 14:5 Am U Int'l L Rev 1473

Raventós, Pedro, & Sandro Zolezzi. "Sportsbooks and Politicians: Place Your Bet!" (2011) 64:3 Journal of Business Research 299

Razzano, Robert T. "Error 404 Jurisdiction Not Found: The Ninth Circuit Frustrates the Efforts of Yahoo! Inc. to Declare a Speech-Restrictive Foreign Judgment Unenforceable" (2004–2005) 73 U Cin L Rev 1743

Reidenberg, Joel R. "Lex Informatica: The Formulation of Information Policy Rules Through Technology" (1998) 76 Tex L Rev 553

Rex, Justin, & David J Jackson. "The Options for Internet Gambling in Canada" (2007) 1:3 Association for Canadian Studies in the United States: Occasional Papers on Public Policy Series, online: ACSUS www.acsus.org/public/pdfs/OP_v1n3.pdf

Rogge, Malcolm J. "Towards Transnational Corporate Accountability in the Global Economy: Challenging the Doctrine of *Forum Non Conveniens* in *In Re: Union Carbide, Alfaro, Sequihua, and Aguinda*" (2001) 36:2 Tex Int'l LJ 299

Roysen, Yevgeniya. "Taking Chances: The United States' Policy on Internet Gambling and Its International Implications," Notes & Recent Developments (2009) 26:3 Cardozo Arts & Ent LJ 873

Ryngaert, Cedric. "Territorial Jurisdiction over Cross-frontier Offences: Revisiting a Classic Problem of International Criminal Law" (2009) 9:1 Int'l Crim L Rev 187

Sadat, Leila N. "Extraordinary Rendition, Torture and Other Nightmares from the War on Terror" (2007) 75 Geo Wash L Rev 1200

Sassen, Saskia. "The Places and Spaces of the Global: An Expanded Analytic Terrain" in David Held & Anthony McGrew, eds, *Globalization Theory: Approaches and Controversies* (Cambridge, UK: Polity Press, 2007) 79

Scassa, Teresa, & Robert J Currie. "New First Principles? Assessing the Internet's Challenges to Jurisdiction" (2011) 42:4 Geo J Int'l L 1017

Scheffel, Evan. "*Yahoo, Inc. v. La Ligue Contra Le Racisme et L'Antisemitism*: Court Refuses to Enforce French Order Attempting to Regulate Speech Occurring Simultaneously in the U.S. and in France" (2003) 19:2 Santa Clara Computer & High Tech LJ 549

Schultz, Thomas. "Carving up the Internet: Jurisdiction, Legal Orders, and the Private/Public International Law Interface" (2008) 19:4 EJIL 799

Shapiro, Jonathan. "*Khadr v. Canada (Prime Minister)*," Annotation (2010) 71 CR (6th) 204

Shinsato, Alison Lindsay. "Increasing the Accountability of Transnational Corporations for Environmental Harms: The Petroleum Industry in Nigeria" (2005–2006) 4:1 Northwestern Journal of International Human Rights 186

Sjolander, Claire Turenne. "The Rhetoric of Globalization: What's in a Wor(l)d" (1995–1996) 51:4 Int'l J 603

Slane, Andrea. "Tales, Techs and Territories: Private International Law, Globalization, and the Legal Construction of Borderlessness on the Internet" (2008) 71:3 Law & Contemp Probs 129

Slaughter, Anne-Marie. "Judicial Globalization" (2000) 40:4 Va J Int'l L 1103

Sokol, Daniel D. "International Antitrust Institutions" in Andrew T Guzman, ed, *Cooperation, Comity and Competition Policy* (Oxford: Oxford University Press, 2011) 186

Stewart, David O. "An Analysis of Internet Gambling and its Policy Implications," *10th Anniversary White Paper Series* (2006), online: American Gaming Association www.americangaming.org/industry-resources/research/white-papers

Svensson, Naomi L. "Extraterritorial Accountability: An Assessment of the Effectiveness of Child Sex Tourism Laws," Notes & Comment (2006) 28 Loy LA Int'l & Comp L Rev 641

Taubman, Antony. "International Governance and the Internet" in Lilian Edwards & Charlotte Waelde, eds, *Law and the Internet*, 3d ed (Portland: Hart, 2009)

Thayer, James D. "The Trade of Cross-Border Gambling and Betting: The WTO Dispute between Antigua and the United States" (2004) Duke L & Tech Rev 0013

Todres, Jonathan. "Prosecuting Sex Tour Operators in U.S. Courts in an Effort to Reduce the Sexual Exploitation of Children Globally" (1999–2000) 9:1 BU Pub Int'l LJ 1

Travis, Hannibal. "Building Universal Digital Libraries: An Agenda for Copyright Reform" (2005–2006) 33 Pepp L Rev 761

Twining, William. "Diffusion and Globalization Discourse" (2006) 47:2 Harv Int'l LJ 507

van der Gaast, Rob, & Franka Pals. "Novamedia European Gaming & Lottery Files Finland" (v 25022003) *Novamedia* (2010), online: Gaming & Lottery Files www.gamingandlotteryfiles.com/novamediafile.php?file=Finland.htm

Walker, Janet. "*Muscutt* Misplaced: The Future of Forum of Necessity Jurisdiction in Canada" (2009) 48:1 Can Bus LJ 135

Wells, Belinda, & Michael Burnett. "When Cultures Collide: An Australian Citizen's Power to Demand the Death Penalty under Islamic Law" (2000) 22 Sydney L Rev 5

Wilde, Ralph. "Triggering State Obligations Extraterritorially: The Spatial Test in Certain Human Rights Treaties" (2007) 40 Isr LR 503

Young, Reuven. "Defining Terrorism: The Evolution of Terrorism as a Legal Concept in International Law and its Influence on Definitions in Domestic Legislation" (2006) 29:1 BC Int'l & Comp L Rev 23

Zittrain, Jonathan, & Benjamin Edelman. "Documentation of Internet Filtering in Saudi Arabia" Berkman Center for Internet and Society (12 September 2002), online: Berkman Centre for Internet and Society http://cyber.law.harvard.edu/filtering/saudiarabia

BOOKS

American Law Institute. *Restatement of the Law Third: The Foreign Relations of the United States* (St. Paul, MN: American Law Institute Publishers, 1987)

Amnesty International. *State of Denial: Europe's Role in Rendition and Secret Detention* (London: Amnesty International, International Secretariat, 2008)

Aneesh, A. *Virtual Migration: The Programming of Globalization* (Durham: Duke University Press, 2006)

Bantekas, Ilias. *International Criminal Law*, 4th ed (Oxford: Hart, 2010)

Benkler, Yochai. *The Wealth of Networks: How Social Production Transforms Markets and Freedom* (New Haven, CT: Yale University Press, 2006)

Black, Vaughan, Stephen GA Pitel, & Michael Sobkin. *Statutory Jurisdiction: An Analysis of the* Court Jurisdiction and Proceedings Transfer Act (Toronto: Carswell, 2012)

Blakesley, Christopher. *Terrorism and Anti-Terrorism: A Normative and Practical Assessment* (Ardsley, NY: Transnational Publishers, 2006)

Boas, Gideon. *Public International Law: Contemporary Principles and Perspectives* (Cheltenham, UK: Edward Elgar, 2012)

Boister, Neil. *An Introduction to Transnational Criminal Law* (Oxford: Oxford University Press, 2012)

Botting, Gary. *Extradition between Canada and the United States* (Ardsley, NY: Transnational Publishers, 2005)

Brownlie, Ian. *Principles of Public International Law*, 7th ed (Oxford: Oxford University Press, 2008)

Cassese, Antonio. *International Law*, 2d ed (Oxford: Oxford University Press, 2005)

Castronova, Edward. *Exodus to the Virtual World: How Online Fun Is Changing Reality* (New York: Palgrave MacMillan, 2007)

Clarkson, Stephen, & Stepan Wood. *A Perilous Imbalance: The Globalization of Canadian Law and Governance* (Vancouver: UBC Press, 2010)

Coomans, Fons, & Menno T Kamminga, eds. *Extraterritorial Application of Human Rights Treaties* (Antwerp: Intersentia, 2004)

Côté, Pierre-André, Stéphane Beaulac, & Mathieu Devinat. *The Interpretation of Legislation in Canada*, 4th ed (Toronto: Carswell, 2011)

Currie, Robert J. *International & Transnational Criminal Law* (Toronto: Irwin Law, 2010).

Dixon, Martin. *Textbook on International Law*, 6th ed (Oxford: Oxford University Press, 2007).

Dugard, John. *International Law: A South African Perspective*, 2d ed (Cape Town: Juta, 2000)

Freeman, Mark, & Gib van Ert. *International Human Rights Law* (Toronto: Irwin Law, 2004)

Gibney, Mark, & Sigrun Skogly, eds. *Universal Human Rights and Extraterritorial Obligations* (Philadelphia: University of Pennsylvania Press, 2010)

Goldsmith, Jack L, & Tim Wu. *Who Controls the Internet? Illusions of a Borderless World* (Oxford: Oxford University Press, 2006)

Higgins, Rosalyn. *Problems and Process: International Law and How We Use It* (Oxford: Clarendon Press, 1994)

Hirst, Michael. *Jurisdiction and the Ambit of Criminal Law* (Oxford: Oxford University Press, 2003)

Hudec, Robert E. *Enforcing International Trade Law: The Evolution of the Modern GATT Legal System* (Salem, NH: Butterworths, 1993)

Hunt, Murray. *Using Human Rights Law in English Courts* (Oxford: Hart, 1997)

Kindred, Hugh M, & Phillip M Saunders, eds. *International Law: Chiefly as Interpreted and Applied in Canada*, 7th ed (Toronto: Emond Montgomery, 2006)

Kohl, Uta. *Jurisdiction and the Internet: A Study of Regulatory Competence over Online Activity* (Cambridge, UK: Cambridge University Press, 2007)

Koops, Bert-Jaap, & Susan Brenner. *Cybercrime and Jurisdiction: A Global Survey* (The Hague: TMC Asser Press, 2006)

Larocque, François. *Civil Actions for Uncivilized Acts: The Adjudicative Jurisdiction of Common Law Courts in Transnational Human Rights Litigation* (Toronto: Irwin Law, 2010)

Lessig, Lawrence. *Code and Other Laws of Cyberspace* (New York: Basic Books, 1999)

———. *The Future of Ideas: The Fate of the Commons in a Connected World* (New York: Vintage Books, 2002)

Malik, Kenin. *From Fatwa to Jihad: The Rushdie Affair and Its Aftermath* (Brooklyn: Melville House, 2010)

Milanovic, Marko. *Extraterritorial Application of Human Rights Treaties: Law, Principles and Policy* (Oxford: Oxford University Press, 2011)

Mills, Alex. *The Confluence of Public and Private International Law* (Cambridge, UK: Cambridge University Press, 2009)

McLeod, Kembrew. *Freedom of Expression: Overzealous Copyright Bozos and Other Enemies of Creativity* (New York: Doubleday, 2005)

Mueller, Milton. *Networks and States: The Global Politics of Internet Governance* (Cambridge, MA: MIT Press, 2010)

Narula, Rajneesh. *Globalization and Technology: Interdependence, Innovation Systems and Industrial Policy* (Cambridge, UK: Polity Press, 2003)

Pati, Roza. *Due Process and International Terrorism: An International Legal Analysis* (Leiden: Martinus Nijhoff, 2009)

Pitel, Stephen GA, & Nicholas S Rafferty. *Conflict of Laws* (Toronto: Irwin Law, 2010)

Ramraj, Victor V et al, eds. *Global Anti-Terrorism Law and Policy*, 2d ed (Cambridge: Cambridge University Press, 2012)

Rattle, Robert. *Computing our Way to Paradise?: The Role of Internet and Communications Technologies in Sustainable Consumption and Globalization* (Lanham, MD: Altamira Press, 2010)

Roach, Kent. *The 9/11 Effect: Comparative Counter-Terrorism* (New York: Cambridge University Press, 2011)

Ryngaert, Cedric. *Jurisdiction in International Law* (Oxford: Oxford University Press, 2008)

Sassen, Saskia. *Territory, Authority, Rights: From Medieval to Global Assemblages*, rev ed (Princeton: Princeton University Press, 2006)

Scassa, Teresa, & Michael Deturbide. *Electronic Commerce and Internet Law in Canada*, 2d ed (Toronto: CCH Canadian, 2012)

Scott, Craig, ed. *Torture as Tort: Comparative Perspectives on the Development of Transnational Human Rights Litigation* (Oxford: Hart, 2001)

Shaw, Malcolm N. *International Law*, 6th ed (Cambridge, UK: Cambridge University Press, 2008)

Simma, Bruno, & Andreas Müller. "Exercise and Limits of Jurisdiction" in James Crawford & Martti Koskenniemi, eds. *The Cambridge Companion to International Law* (Cambridge UK: Cambridge University Press, 2012)

Sullivan, Ruth, & Elmer A Driedger. *Sullivan and Driedger on the Construction of Statutes*, 4th ed (Markham, ON: LexisNexis Canada, 2002)

Sunstein, Cass. *Infotopia: How Many Minds Produce Knowledge* (New York: Oxford University Press, 2006)

Tomlinson, John. *Globalization and Culture* (Chicago: University of Chicago Press, 1999)

United Nations Children's Fund, Innocenti Research Centre. *Handbook on the Optional Protocol on the Sale of Children, Child Prostitution and Child Pornography* (Florence: UNICEF, 2009)

van Ert, Gibran. *Using International Law in Canadian Courts*, 2d ed (Toronto: Irwin Law, 2008)

Williams, Sharon A, & Armand LC de Mestral. *An Introduction to International Law: Chiefly as Interpreted and Applied in Canada*, 2d ed (Toronto: Butterworths, 1987)

Wu, Tim. *The Master Switch: The Rise and Fall of Information Empires* (New York: Alfred A Knopf, 2010)

Zittrain, Jonathan. *The Future of the Internet and How to Stop It* (New Haven, CT: Yale University Press, 2008)

NEWS SOURCES

Au, Wagner James. "Virtual World Population: 50 Million by 2011" (20 May 2007), online: Gigaom http://gigaom.com/2007/05/20/virtual-world-population-50-million-by-2011

Baines, David. "U.S. Cracks Down on Unlicensed Online Gambling, but Canada Prefers Just to Look the Other Way" *The Vancouver Sun* (28 May 2011), online: canada.com www2.canada.com/vancouversun/columnists/story.html?id=23767865-6e37-47b0-b279-25131e84178b&p=2

Beaumont, Claudine. "G20: Protesters Use Twitter, Facebook and Social Media Tools to Organise Demonstrations" *The Telegraph* (1 April 2009), online: The Telegraph www.telegraph.co.uk/finance/g20-summit/5090003/G20-summit-Protesters-use-Twitter-Facebook-and-social-media-tools-to-organise-demonstrations.html

Claburn, Thomas. "China Limits Use of Virtual Currency" (29 June 2009), online: InformationWeek www.informationweek.com/news/internet/ebusiness/218101859

Cluley, Graham. "World Cup DDoS Blackmailer Sentenced to Jail" *Naked Security* (16 June 2011), online: nakedsecurity.sophos.com http://nakedsecurity.sophos.com/2011/06/16/world-cup-ddos-blackmailer-sentenced-to-jail

Collson, Brett. "France Ends Internet Gambling Monopoly" *Poker News Daily* (11 April 2010), online: Poker News Daily.com www.pokernewsdaily.com/france-ends-internet-gambling-monopoly-9642

Dehghan, Saeed Kamali. "Iran Tightens Online Censorship to Counter US 'Shadow Internet'" *The Guardian* (13 July 2011), online: The Guardian www.guardian.co.uk/world/2011/jul/13/iran-tightens-online-censorship

Dutch Data Protection Authority. News Release, "Canadian and Dutch Data Privacy Guardians Release Findings from Investigation of Popular Mobile App" (28 January 2013), online: Dutch Data Protection Authority www.dutchdpa.nl/Pages/en_pb_20130128-whatsapp.aspx

Efrati, Amir, & Loretta Chao. "Google Softens Tone on China" *Wall Street Journal Online* (12 January 2012), online: The Wall Street Journal http://online.wsj.com/article/SB10001424052970203436904577155003097277514.html

EverQuest, Zam. "Geno Kanan's Guide to Dealing with Kill Stealers," online: Zam Network http://everquest.allakhazam.com/editorial/082099_Geno_kill_Stealing.htm

Fahrenkopf, Frank. "Now is the Time" *Global Gaming Business* (6 June 2011), online: GGB Magazine http://ggbmagazine.com/issue/vol-10-no-6-june-2011/article/now-is-the-time

Hilder, Paul. "How a Crowd Came to the Aid of Bullied Bus Monitor Karen Klein" *The Guardian* (25 June 2012), online: The Guardian www.guardian.co.uk/commentisfree/2012/jun/25/karen-klein-bus-monitor-bullied-online-campaign

Huang, Carol. "Facebook and Twitter Key to Arab Spring Uprisings: Report" *The National* (6 June 2011), online: The National www.thenational.ae/news/uae-news/facebook-and-twitter-key-to-arab-spring-uprisings-report

Humphreys, Adrian. "'A Spectacle of Hypocrisy and Farce': North Korea, Iran Attack Canada's Human Rights Record at UN Forum" *The National Post* (26 April 2013), online: National Post http://news.nationalpost.com/2013/04/26/north-korea-iran-attack-canadas-human-rights-record-at-un-forum

Kahnawake Gaming Commission. Press Release, "Remote Gaming Regulators in Kahnawake and Antigua Agree to Create Inter-Jurisdictional Authorization Regime" (17 June 2010), online: Kahnawake Gaming Commission www.gamingcommission.ca/news/pr06172010a.pdf

Konrad, Alex. "Tools of Victory: The Tech That Helped Turkish Protesters Save Taksim Square" *Forbes* (7 March 2013), online: Forbes www.forbes.com/sites/alexkonrad/2013/07/03/the-tech-that-helped-turkish-protesters

MacDonald, Chantelle. "U.S. Breaking Law in *Virgo* Case, Says International Law Expert" *The Lawyer's Weekly* (24 January 2003)

MacDonald, Neil. "US Jeopardizes Justice with al-Awlaki Execution from the Sky" CBC News (4 October 2011), online: CBC News www.cbc.ca/news/world/analysis-u-s-jeopardizes-justice-with-al-awlaki-execution-from-sky-1.1100716

McGregor, Janyce. "Same-Sex Divorce Options Explored by Harper Government" *CBC News* (12 January 2012), online: CBC News www.cbc.ca/news/canada/toronto/story/2012/01/12/pol-harper-same-sex-marriage.html?cmp=rss

McMullen, Troy. "Canada's Privacy Commissioner Probes Facebook over Users Private Information" (29 January 2010), online: ABC News http://abcnews.go.com/Technology/canada-investigates-facebook-privacy-settings/story?id=9691133#.T3sUuXLcitw

New Zealand, E-Government. "New Zealand Government Open Access and Licensing (NZGOAL) Framework," online: New Zealand Government http://ict.govt.nz/guidance-and-resources/information-and-data/nzgoal

Nicol, John, & Dave Seglins. "L.A. Cocaine Bust Threatens Canada-U.S. Police Relations" (12 February 2013), online: CBC News www.cbc.ca/news/canada/story/2013/02/11/canada-us-police-relations.html

O'Toole, Megan. "Rob Ford Crack-Cocaine Video Crowd-Funding Campaigns Spring Up to Purchase Alleged Tape" *The National Post* (17 May 2013), online: National Post http://news.nationalpost.com/2013/05/17/several-crowd-funding-campaigns-spring-up-to-purchase-video-allegedly-showing-rob-ford-smoking-crack-pipe

Office of the Privacy Commissioner of Canada. "The Case for Reforming the *Personal Information Protection and Electronic Documents Act*" (May 2013), online: OPC www.priv.gc.ca/parl/2013/pipeda_r_201305_e.pdf

———. News Release, "WhatsApp's Violation of Privacy Law Partly Resolved after Investigation by Data Protection Authorities: Canadian and Dutch Data Privacy Guardians Release Findings from Investigation of Popular Mobile App" (28 January 2013), online: Office of the Privacy Commissioner of Canada www.priv.gc.ca/media/nr-c/2013/nr-c_130128_e.asp

Office québécois de la langue française. "Information and Communication Technologies in French," online: www.oqlf.gouv.qc.ca/ressources/bibliotheque/depliants/20100212_depliant6fva.pdf

Palmer, Majia. "EU Probes Google Grip on Data" (24 May 2007), online: FT.com www.ft.com/cms/s/2/dc89ec96-0a24-11dc-93ae-000b5df10621.html#axzz1ioIHjqUC

Perrin, Benjamin. "Our Child Sex Offender Laws Should Cross Borders" *The Lawyers Weekly* (11 April 2008) 1

Protalinski, Emil. "Facebook Has Over 845 million Users" (1 February 2012), online: ZDNet www.zdnet.com/blog/facebook/facebook-has-over-845-million-users/8332

Raisbeck, Fiona. "Russian Internet Blackmailers Jailed" *SC Magazine UK* (6 October 2006), online: SC Magazine UK www.scmagazineuk.com/russian-internet-blackmailers-jailed/article/106968

Sedra, Mark. "Revolution 2.0: Democracy Promotion in the Age of Social Media" *The Globe and Mail* (2 February 2011), online: The Globe and Mail www.theglobeandmail.com/commentary/revolution-20-democracy-promotion-in-the-age-of-social-media/article564610

Tanner, Lindsay. "Declaration of Open Government" (16 July 2010), online: Australian Government Department of Finance www.finance.gov.au/e-government/strategy-and-governance/gov2/declaration-of-open-government.html

Vallerius, Bradley. "Gambling Sites Will Change Software to Stay in U.S. Market" (20 October 2006), online: Casino City Times http://bradleyvallerius.casinocitytimes.com/article/gambling-sites-will-change-software-to-stay-in-u-s-market-30608

Vargas, Ramon Antonio. "'City of Heroes' Character 'Twixt' Becomes Game's Most Hated Outcast Courtesy of Loyola Professor" *The Times-Picayune* (31 July 2009), online: Nola Media Group www.nola.com/news/index.ssf/2009/07/loyola_university_professor_be.html

Vincent, Danny. "China Used Prisoners in Lucrative Internet Gaming Network: Labour Camp Detainees Endure Hard Labour by Day, Online 'Gold Farming' by Night" *The Guardian* (25 May 2011), online: Guardian News and Media Limited www.theguardian.com/world/2011/may/25/china-prisoners-internet-gaming-scam

Vincent, James. "G8 Open Data Charter Will 'Increase Transparency' and 'Fuel Innovation'" *The Independent* (19 June 2013), online: The Independent www.independent.co.uk/life-style/gadgets-and-tech/g8-open-data-charter-will-increase-transparency-and-fuel-innovation-8665696.html

Watters, Audrey. "Number of Virtual World Users Breaks 1 Billion, Roughly Half under Age 15" (1 October 2010), online: Read, Write, Web www.readwriteweb.com/archives/number_of_virtual_world_users_breaks_the_1_billion.php

White, Marianne. "Canadian Aid Worker Guilty of Assaulting Haitian Boys" *Ottawa Citizen.com* (17 November 2008), online: canada.com www2.canada.com/ottawacitizen/news/story.html?id=ba814e0a-8f11-408d-b5c0-1b6af28ed000

Wilson, Michael. "There.com Closed on March 9th, 2010 . . . but Has Reopened in 2012," online: there.com www.there.com/info/announcement

Yee, Nick. "The Daedalus Project: the Psychology of MMORPGS" (21 February 2004), online: The Daedalus Project http://nickyee.com/daedalus/archives/000758.php

Zongker, Brett. "Hurricane Sandy Relief Gets Boost from Crowdfunding Efforts" *The Huffington Post* (22 December 2012), online: Huff Post Impact Canada www.huffingtonpost.com/2012/12/28/crowdfunding-sandy-relief_n_2376704.html

NEWS SOURCES WITHOUT AUTHOR

"ACTA Copyright Treaty in Doubt as EU Suspends Ratification" *Canadian Press* reprinted in Huffington Post (22 February 2012), online: huffingtonpost.ca www.huffingtonpost.ca/2012/02/22/acta-copyright-treaty-eu-suspends-ratification_n_1293198.html

"Blackberry Server in China? India Wants a Monitoring Unit Too" *The Times of India* (29 July 2010), online: The Times of India http://articles.timesofindia.indiatimes.com/2010-07-29/india/28316801_1_security-agencies-blackberry-server-security-concerns

"Canada's Action Plan on Open Government," online: data.gc.ca www.data.gc.ca/eng/canadas-action-plan-open-government

"Canada Approves Facebook Changes" (22 September 2010), online: BBC News www.bbc.co.uk/news/technology-11392454

"Child-Sex Tourism Law Not Enforced: A Canadian Passport Is Essentially a 'Get out of Jail Free Card' for People Having Sex with Children Overseas, a B.C. Law Professor Says" *Vancouver Sun* (3 April 2008), online: CanWest MediaWorks Publications www.canada.com/story_print.html?id=e89e954f-2aba-46f6-8685-30d10876631a&sponsor

"CP Sponsors Paintball Field in Virtual World" (February 2007), online: World and Regional Paintball Information Guide www.warpig.com/paintball/articles/news/cpvirtual

"CRTC Asks the Canadian Broadcast Standards Council to Review Decision to Ban Dire Straits Song" (21 January 2011), online: CRTC www.crtc.gc.ca/eng/com100/2011/r110121.htm

"Data Protection Watchdogs' Letter to Google Goes Public" (30 May 2007), online: Out-Law.com www.out-law.com/page-8099

"Dutch Court Rules Virtual Theft Is Real" (22 October 2008), online: Radio Netherlands Worldwide www.rnw.nl/english/article/dutch-court-rules-virtual-theft-real

"France Revolutionizes the Online Gambling Market" (6 October 2010), online: Poker-on-line.com http://poker-on-line.com/news/1006/france-revolutionizes-online-gambling-market-1188.html

"G8 Experience in the Implementation of Extraterritorial Jurisdiction for Sex Crimes against Children" (18 April 2007), online: Tourism Online Resource Center www.linkbc.ca/torc/downs1/Extraterritorial%20Jurisdiction.pdf

"Goals of Second Life," online: Second Life Wiki http://wiki.secondlife.com/wiki/Goals_of_Second_Life

"Google Says EU Data Laws Do Not Catch Its Search Logs" (9 September 2008), online: Out-Law.com www.out-law.com/page-9411

"Internet Gambling in the UK" (2010), online: Care www.care.org.uk/advocacy/gambling/internet-gambling-in-the-uk

"Iran Adamant over Rushdie Fatwa" *BBC News* (12 February 2005), online: BBC News news.bbc.co.uk/2/hi/4260599.stm

"Musharraf Denies U.S. bin Laden Deal Report" *CBC News* (10 May 2011), online: cbc.ca www.cbc.ca/news/world/story/2011/05/10/bin-laden-us-pakistan.html

"New Draft European Data Protection Regime to Apply Also to All US Companies Processing Data of European Residents" (2 February 2012), online: Law Patent Group www.mlawgroup.de/news/publications/detail.php?we_objectID=227

"New Push to Protect Children" (27 May 2010), online: United Nations Human Rights: Office of the High Commissioner for Human Rights www.ohchr.org/EN/NewsEvents/Pages/Newpushtoprotectchildren.aspx

"Online Gambling Rules and Laws around the World" (11 August 2010), online: Gambling Blog Gamesnomy http://gamesnomy.blogspot.com/2010/08/online-gambling-rules-and-laws-around.html

"Privacy Commissioner Completes Facebook Review" (22 September 2010), online: Office of the Privacy Commissioner of Canada www.priv.gc.ca/media/nr-c/2010/nr-c_100922_e.cfm

"Real-Money Gambling Emerges as Massive Global Revenue Opportunity for Games Developers According to New Report by H2 Gambling Capital and Odobo" (28 March 2013), online: H2 Gambling Capital www.h2gc.com/article/h2-interactive-gambling-report-commisioned-by-odobo

"'Sex Tourist' Kenneth Klassen Sentenced to 11 Years" *The Globe and Mail* (23 August 2012), online: The Globe and Mail www.theglobeandmail.com/news/british-columbia/sex-tourist-kenneth-klassen-sentenced-to-11-years/article1389746
"Social Media, Cellphone Video Fuel Arab Protests" *The Independent* (27 February 2011), online: The Independent www.independent.co.uk/life-style/gadgets-and-tech/social-media-cellphone-video-fuel-arab-protests-2227088.html
"UK Considers Banning Foreign Gambling Websites" (25 January 2011), online: Casino People www.casinopeople.com/news/uk-considers-banning-foreign-gambling-websites.html
"UK Government Licensing Framework," online: National Archives www.nationalarchives.gov.uk/information-management/uk-gov-licensing-framework.htm
"US and UK Refuse to Sign UN's Communications Treaty" *BBC News* (14 December 2012), online: BBC News www.bbc.co.uk/news/technology-20717774

Other Materials

Aboriginal Affairs and Northern Development Canada. *Memorandum of Understanding between the Department of Indian and Northern Affairs Canada and the Department of the Interior of the United States of America concerning Indigenous and Northern Issues* (15 September 2010), online: www.aadnc-aandc.gc.ca/eng/1100100014184
Acharya, Lalita. Bill C-25, *An Act Governing the Operation of Remote Sensing Space Systems* (20 December 2004), online: Parliament of Canada www.parl.gc.ca/About/Parliament/LegislativeSummaries/bills_ls.asp?Language=E&ls=C25&Mode=1&Parl=38&Ses=1&source=library_prb#4end
Article 29 Data Protection Working Party. Letter to Mr. Page (16 October 2012), online: European Commission http://ec.europa.eu/justice/data-protection/article-29/documentation/other-document/files/2012/20121016_letter_to_google_en.pdf
———. Press Release, "EU Data Protection Group Says Google, Microsoft and Yahoo! Do Not Comply with Data Protection Rules"(26 May 2010): online: EC http://ec.europa.eu/justice/policies/privacy/news/docs/pr_26_05_10_en.pdf
Barlow, John Perry. "A Declaration of the Independence of Cyberspace" (8 February 1996), online: Electronic Frontier Foundation https://projects.eff.org/~barlow/Declaration-Final.html

Campbell, Colin S, Timothy F Harnagel, & Garry J Smith. "The Legalization of Gambling in Canada," Prepared for the Law Commission of Canada "*What is a Crime?*" (6 July 2005), online: Government of Canada Publications http://publications.gc.ca/collections/collection_2008/lcc-cdc/JL2-64-2005E.pdf

Canada, Task Force on Electronic Commerce. *The Protection of Personal Information: Building Canada's Information Economy and Society* (Ottawa: Industry Canada, 1998)

Canadian Internet Policy and Public Interest Clinic (CIPPIC). Letter to Privacy Commissioner of Canada (30 May 2008), online: CIPPIC www.cippic.ca/uploads/CIPPICFacebookComplaint_29May08.pdf

———. Letter to Facebook (28 May 2010), online: CIPPIC www.cippic.ca/uploads/LT_Facebook-Re_Privacy_Response-FINAL-05282010.pdf

Canadian Radio-television and Telecommunications Commission. *Broadcasting Regulatory Policy* CRTC 2009-329 (4 June 2009), online: CRTC www.crtc.gc.ca/eng/archive/2009/2009-329.htm

Commission of Inquiry into the Actions of Canadian Officials in Relation to Maher Arar, *Report of the Events Relating to Maher Arar: Analysis and Recommendations* (Ottawa: Public Works and Government Services Canada, 2006), online: Security Intelligence Review Committee www.sirc-csars.gc.ca/pdfs/cm_arar_rec-eng.pdf

Commission of Inquiry into the Investigation of the Bombing of Air India Flight 182, *Research Studies: The Unique Challenges of Terrorism Prosecutions: Towards a Workable Relation between Intelligence and Evidence* by Kent Roach, vol 4 (Ottawa: Government of Canada, 2010)

Denham, Elizabeth. "Report of Findings into the Complaint Filed by the Canadian Internet Policy and Public Interest Clinic (CIPPIC) against Facebook Inc. under the *Personal Information Protection and Electronic Documents Act*" (16 July 2009), *PIPEDA* Case Summary 2009-008, online: Office of the Privacy Commissioner of Canada www.priv.gc.ca/cf-dc/2009/2009_008_0716_e.pdf

European Commission. *2002/2/EC: Commission Decision of 20 December 2001 pursuant to Directive 95/46/EC of the European Parliament and of the Council on the adequate protection of personal data provided by the Canadian Personal Information Protection and Electronic Documents Act (notified under document number C(2001) 4539)* [2002] OJ, L 002/13

———. *Trade in Seal Products* (11 March 2011), online: European Commission http://ec.europa.eu/environment/biodiversity/animal_welfare/seals/seal_hunting.htm

———. *The implementation of Commission Decision 520/2000/EC on the adequate protection of personal data provided by the Safe Harbour privacy Principles and related Frequently Asked Questions issued by the US Department of Commerce*, SEC (2004) 1323 final (20 October 2004)

Grimmett, Jeanne J. "WTO Dispute Settlement: Status of U.S. Compliance in Pending Cases" (23 April 2012), online: Congressional Research Service www.fas.org/sgp/crs/misc/RL32014.pdf

International Bar Association. *Report of the Task Force on Extraterritorial Jurisdiction* (London: International Bar Association, 2008)

Law Commission of Canada. *Crossing Borders: Law in a Globalized World — Discussion Paper* (Ottawa: Law Commission of Canada, 2006)

Moon, Richard. *Report to the Canadian Human Rights Commission Concerning Section 13 of the Canadian Human Rights Act and the Regulation of Hate Speech on the Internet* (Ottawa: Canadian Human Rights Commission, 2008)

Myers, David. "Play and Punishment: The Sad and Curious Case of Twixt" (Paper delivered at the [Player] Conference Proceedings, The Centre for Computer Games Research, IT University of Copenhagen, Denmark, 2008) [unpublished]

OECD, Directorate for Science, Technology and Industry. *Guidelines Governing the Protection of Privacy and Transborder Flows of Personal Data* (adopted 23 September 1980), online: OECD www.oecd.org/sti/ieconomy/oecd guidelinesontheprotectionofprivacyandtransborderflowsofpersonaldata.htm

Office of the Privacy Commissioner. Letter to CIPPIC (25 August 2009), online: Office of the Privacy Commissioner of Canada www.priv.gc.ca/media/nr-c/2009/let_090827_e.cfm

———. *OPC Guidance Documents: Cloud Computing for Small and Medium-sized Enterprises: Privacy Responsibilities and Considerations* (14 June 2012), online: OPC www.priv.gc.ca/information/pub/gd_cc_201206_e.asp

"Online Gaming Jurisdictions" (2011), online: Online Casino City http://online.casinocity.com/jurisdictions

Ram, Chris. "The Globalization of Crime as a Jurisdictional Challenge" (Paper delivered at the 2011 Annual Conference of the Canadian Council on International Law, Ottawa) [copy on file with authors]

Roseman, Louise L, Director, Division of Reserve Bank Operations and Payment Systems. Testimony before the United States House Subcommittee on Domestic and International Monetary Policy, Trade, and Technology of the Committee on Financial Services Hearings on Internet Gambling, 110th Cong, 2d Sess (2008), online: US Government Printing Office www.gpo.gov/fdsys/pkg/CHRG-110hhrg42714/pdf/CHRG-110hhrg42714.pdf

Transport Canada. *Memorandum of Understanding on the Lease of Aircraft Between Direction Générale de l'Aviation Civile (France) and Aviation Group, Department of Transport (Canada)* (18 March 1991), online: www.tc.gc.ca/eng/civilaviation/standards/int-memoranda-france-3684.htm

Uniform Law Conference of Canada. *Court Jurisdiction and Proceedings Transfer Act* (adopted in 1994), online: ULCC/CHLC www.ulcc.ca/en/uniform-acts-en-gb-1/183-court-jurisdiction-and-proceedings-transfer-act/1092-court-jurisdiction-proceedings-transfer-act

United Nations Office on Drugs and Crime. "Universal Instruments against Terrorism: Status of Ratifications," online: www.unodc.org/tldb/universal_instruments_NEW.html

White House, The. *Consumer Data Privacy in a Networked World: A Framework for Protecting Privacy and Promoting Innovation in the Global Digital Economy* (23 February 2012), online: www.whitehouse.gov/sites/default/files/email-files/privacy_white_paper.pdf

———. Presidential Decision Directive/NSC 39: US Policy on Counterterrorism PDD/NSC39 (21 June 1995), online: Federation of American Scientists www.fas.org/irp/offdocs/pdd39.htm

Wikia. "Definition of Loot Ninja," online: www.wowwiki.com/Loot_ninja

WIPO. *The Recognition of Rights and the Use of Names in the Internet Domain Name System: Report of the Second WIPO Internet Domain Name Process* (3 September 2001), online: WIPO www.wipo.int/amc/en/processes/process2/report/html/report.html

Wood, Robert T, & Robert J Williams. *Internet Gambling: Prevalence, Patterns, Problems, and Policy Options*, Final Report prepared for the Ontario Problem Gambling Research Centre (5 January 2009), online: www.nsgaming-foundation.org/uploads/Internet%20Gambling%20Wood%20and%20Williams%20Final%20Report%20FINAL.pdf

WTO. "Regional Trade Agreements Information System (RTA-IS)," online: http://rtais.wto.org/UI/PublicAllRTAList.aspx

WEBSITES

Foreign Affairs and International Trade Canada, Office of the Extractive Sector Corporate Social Responsibility (CSR) Counsellor www.international.gc.ca/csr_counsellor-conseiller_rse/index.aspx

Global Privacy Enforcement Network www.privacyenforcement.net

ICANN www.icann.org/en/dndr/udrp/approved-providers.htm
IGF www.intgovforum.org/cms/aboutigf

Table of Cases

CANADIAN JURISPRUDENCE

DECISIONS OF THE OFFICE OF THE PRIVACY COMMISSIONER

FOREIGN JURISPRUDENCE

Index

About the Authors

Steve Coughlan is a professor at the Schulich School of Law, Dalhousie University, in Halifax, Nova Scotia, where he is also the associate director of the Law & Technology Institute. He has been the recipient of the Association of Atlantic Universities Distinguished Teacher Award, as well as other teaching awards at the University and Faculty of Law level. He is the author of *Criminal Procedure* (Irwin Law, 2008 and 2012); the *Canadian Law Dictionary* (Barrons, 7th ed, 2013); and a co-author of many other books, including *Learning Canadian Criminal Law* (Carswell, 2006, 2009, 2012), *Detention and Arrest* (Irwin Law, 2010), and the *Annual Review of Criminal Law* (Carswell, 2004–2013). He is actively involved in judicial education and continuing legal education programs, and is a co-author of the National Judicial Institute's *Criminal Law Essentials e-Letter*, as well as a co-editor of the *Criminal Reports*, the *Canadian Journal of Law and Technology*, and the Canadian IT Law Association (IT.Can) Newsletter on law and technology issues.

Robert J. Currie is an associate professor and the director of the Law & Technology Institute at the Schulich School of Law, Dalhousie University. His teaching areas include international criminal law, criminal law, evidence, procedure, advocacy, and law and technology. He has won or been nominated for several teaching awards, and is active in doing continuing legal education for both legal practitioners and the judiciary. He is the author (with Joseph Rikhof) of *International & Transnational Criminal Law*, 2d ed (Irwin Law, 2013), and the co-editor of the *Handbook on Transnational Criminal Law* (Routledge, 2014) and the eighth edition of *International Law: Chiefly as Interpreted and Applied in Canada* (Emond Montgomery, 2014). Professor Currie is vice-president and a commissioner of the Law Reform Commission of Nova Scotia, and sits on the boards of the Canadian Council on International Law and the Canadian IT Law Association.

Hugh M. Kindred is professor emeritus at the Schulich School of Law, Dalhousie University, where he continues to research, write, and teach in the fields of international and maritime law. He is a co-author and general editor of multiple editions of *International Law: Chiefly as Interpreted and Applied in Canada* (Emond Montgomery) and is currently readying the eighth edition for publication in 2014. He is also the author with Edgar Gold and Aldo Chircop of *Maritime Law* (Irwin Law, 2003), which was co-winner of the 2005 Walter Owen Book Prize for the best legal text published in Canada in English. He is now engaged in developing the second edition for publication in 2015. Professor Kindred holds law degrees from Bristol, London, and Illinois universities and is a member of the bars of Nova Scotia and England. In 2003, he was honoured by the Canadian Association of Law Teachers with its Award of Academic Excellence.

Teresa Scassa is the Canada Research Chair in Information Law at the University of Ottawa, where she is also a professor at the Faculty of Law. She is a founder and former editor of the *Canadian Journal of Law and Technology*; author of *Canadian Trademark Law* (LexisNexis, 2010); co-author of *Electronic Commerce and Internet Law in Canada*, (CCH Canadian Ltd, 2012), which was the winner of the 2013 Walter Owen Book Prize; and co-author of *Canadian Intellectual Property Law: Cases, Notes and Materials* (Emond Montgomery, 2013). She is also a co-editor of the recently published *Intellectual Property for the 21st Century: Interdisciplinary Approaches* (Irwin Law, 2014). She is a member of the External Advisory Committee of the Office of the Privacy Commissioner of Canada, and of the Canadian Government Advisory Committee on Open Government. She has written widely in the areas of intellectual property law, law and technology, and privacy.

Kolibri 360 GmbH
Ferdinand-Jühlke-Straße 7
99095 Erfurt, Deutschland
produktsicherheit@kolibri360.de